Scale 1: 500,000
or 8 miles to 1 inch
(5km to 1cm)

Reprinted October 2011
13th edition October 2011

Cartography:
All cartography in this atlas edited, designed and produced by the Mapping Services Department of AA Publishing (A04830).

This atlas contains Ordnance Survey data © Crown copyright and database right 2011 and Royal Mail data © Royal Mail copyright and database right.

 Land & Property Services. This is based upon Crown Copyright and is reproduced with the permission of the Land & Property Services under delegated authority from the Controller of Her Majesty's Stationery Office, © Crown Copyright and database rights 2011. Licence No 100,363. Permit No. 110065.

 © Ordnance Survey Ireland/ Government of Ireland Copyright Permit No. MP000611.

Publisher's notes:
Published by AA Publishing (a trading name of AA Media Limited, whose registered office is Fanum House, Basing View, Basingstoke, Hampshire RG21 4EA, UK. Registered number 06112600).

ISBN: 978 0 7495 7118 4

A CIP Catalogue record for this book is available from the British Library.

Disclaimer:
The contents of this atlas are believed to be correct at the time of the latest revision, it will not include any subsequent amended, new or temporary information including diversions and traffic control or enforcement systems. The publishers cannot be held responsible or liable for any loss or damage occasioned to any person acting or refraining from action as a result of any use or reliance on material in this atlas, nor for any errors, omissions or changes in such material. This does not affect your statutory rights.

The publishers would welcome information to correct any errors or omissions and to keep this atlas up to date. Please write to the Atlas Editor, AA Publishing, The Automobile Association, Fanum House, Basing View, Basingstoke, Hampshire RG21 4EA, UK.
Email: *roadatlasfeedback@theaa.com*

Printer:
Printed and bound in Thailand by Sirivatana Interprint Public Co. Ltd.

GLO...
BRITAIN
WITH 85 TOWN PLANS

Atlas contents

Map pages	II
Road map symbols	1
Road atlas Britain 1:500,000 scale	2–65
Index to places in Britain	66–81
County, administrative area map	66–67
Mileage charts	68 & 90
Britain	68
Ireland	90
Road atlas Ireland 1:1 million scale	82–89
Index to places in Ireland	91–94
Town plan section	95–191
Index to town plans	95
Key to town plans	96
Central London	97–107
Town plans	108–191
Major airports	192–197
Channel tunnel	198

Map pages

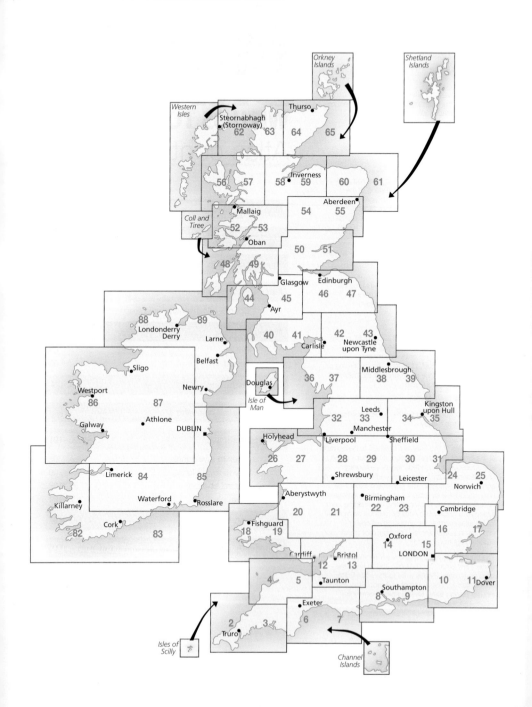

Britain

M4	Motorway with number	5	Distance in miles between symbols
TOLL T4	Toll motorway with junction	TOLL	Road toll
40	Motorway junction with and without number	or V	Vehicle ferry
40	Restricted motorway junction		Vehicle ferry - fast catamaran
Fleet S	Motorway service area		National boundary
	Motorway under construction		County, administrative boundary
A40	Primary route single/dual carriageway	H	Heliport
26	Primary junction with and without number	BRISTOL	Airport
25	Restricted Primary junction		Viewpoint
S	Primary route service area	SNAEFELL 620	Spot height in metres
A33	Other A road single/dual carriageway		River, lake and coastline
B4224	B road		
	Unclassified road		National Park or National Scenic Area
	Road under construction		
	Narrow Primary, other A or B road with passing places (Scotland)	27	Page overlap with number

1: 500 000

0   5   10 miles
0   5   10   15 kilometres

8 miles to 1 inch

Ireland

M1	Motorway	A2	Primary route (Northern Ireland)
M1 Toll	Toll motorway and booth	A42	A road (Northern Ireland)
3	Motorway junctions with and without number	B176	B road (Northern Ireland)
3	Restricted motorway junctions	7	Distance in miles between symbols (Northern Ireland)
	Motorway under construction		Minor Road
N7	National primary route (Republic of Ireland)		Road under construction
N81	National secondary route (Republic of Ireland)		International boundary
R116	Regional road (Republic of Ireland)	Roscoff	Vehicle ferry
7	Distance in kilometres between symbols (Republic of Ireland)	Troon	Vehicle ferry- fast catamaran
	Gaeltacht (Irish language area)		

1: 1 000 000

0   10   20 miles
0   10   20   30 kilometres

16 miles to 1 inch

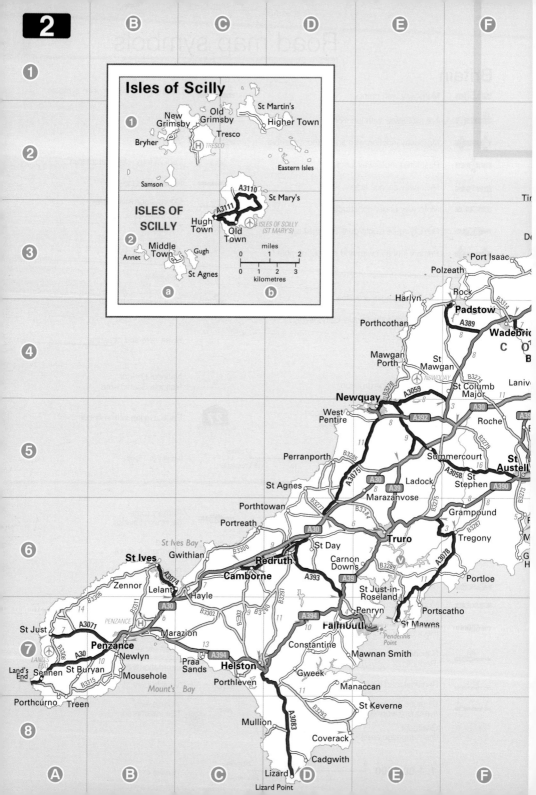

2

A B C D E F

Isles of Scilly

ISLES OF SCILLY

New Grimsby
Old Grimsby
St Martin's
Higher Town
Bryher
Tresco
Samson
Eastern Isles
A3110
St Mary's
A3111
ISLES OF SCILLY (ST MARY'S)
Hugh Town
Old Town
Annet
Middle Town
Gugh
St Agnes

miles
0 1 2
kilometres
0 1 2 3

a b

Port Isaac
Polzeath
Harlyn
Rock
B3314
Padstow
Porthcothan
A389
Wadebri
C O
B
Mawgan Porth
St Mawgan
NEWQUAY
B3276
St Columb Major
Lanive
A30
A39
Newquay
A3059
Roche
West Pentire
A392
8
8
3
B3279
Perranporth
B3285
A3075
Summercourt
St Austell
A30
A39
Ladock
A3058
St Stephen
A390
Marazanvose
B3275
St Agnes
Porthtowan
B3277
B3284
Grampound
B3287
Portreath
A30
St Day
Truro
Tregony
A3078
St Ives
Gwithian
B3300
Redruth
Carnon Downs
A3289
Portloe
Zennor
A3074
Camborne
A393
A39
V
Lelant
Hayle
St Just-in-Roseland
Portscatho
A30
B3302
B3280
B3301
Penryn
St Mawes
St Just
A3071
PENZANCE
B3311
Marazion
A394
Falmouth
Pendennis Point
Penzance
A30
Newlyn
Praa Sands
Constantine
Mawnan Smith
Land's End
St Buryan
B3315
Mousehole
Helston
Gweek
Manaccan
Porthcurno
Treen
Mount's Bay
Porthleven
St Keverne
Mullion
A3083
B3293
Coverack
Cadgwith
Lizard
Lizard Point

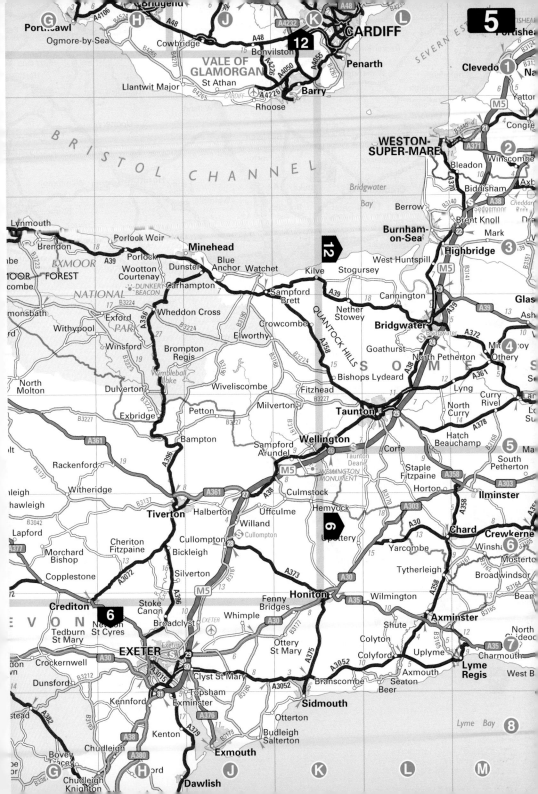

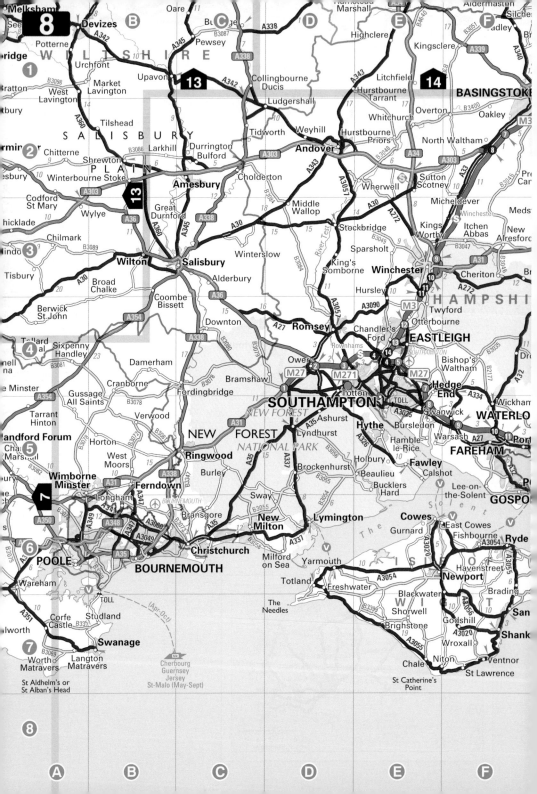

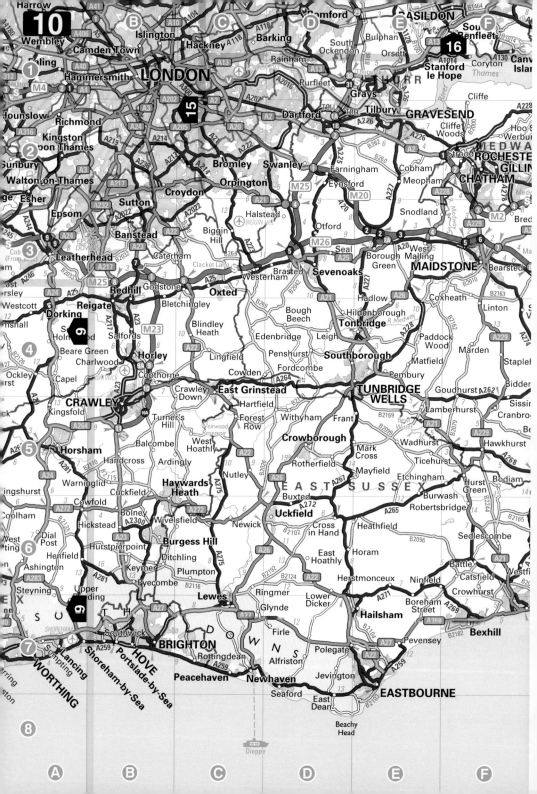

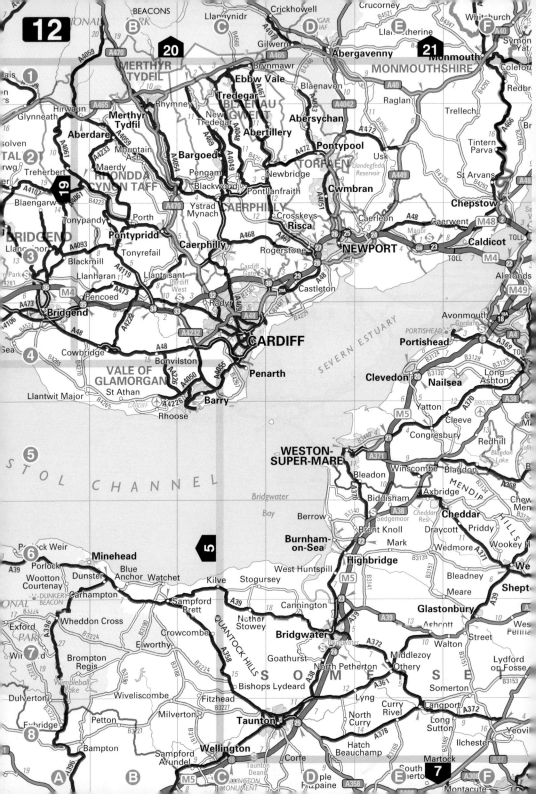

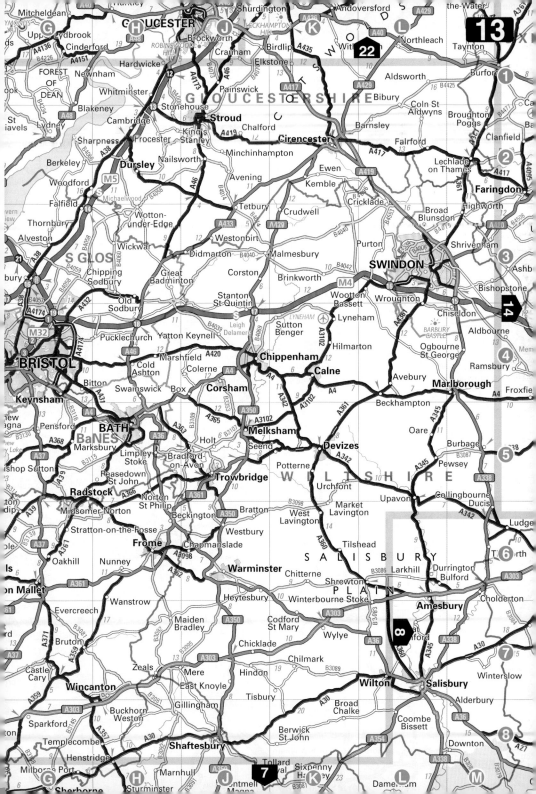

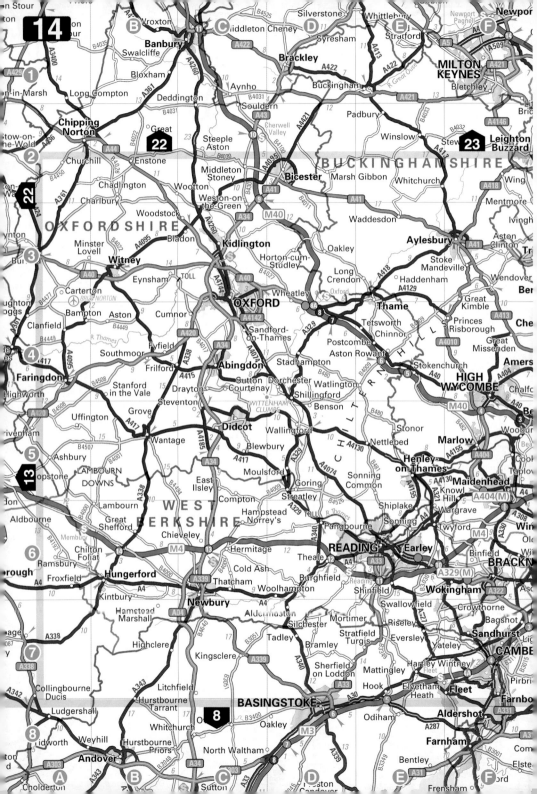

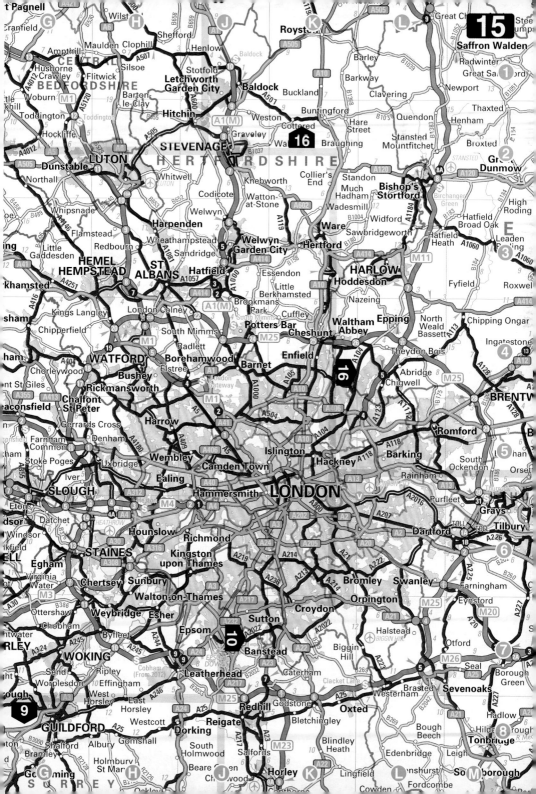

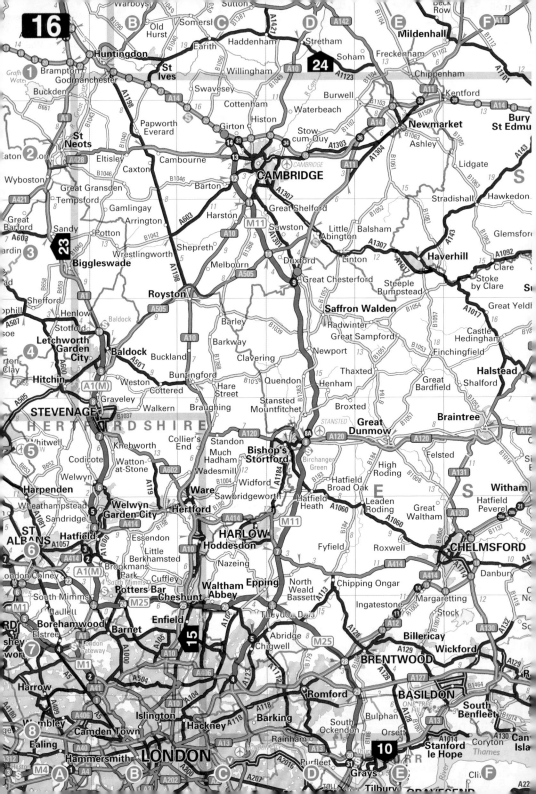

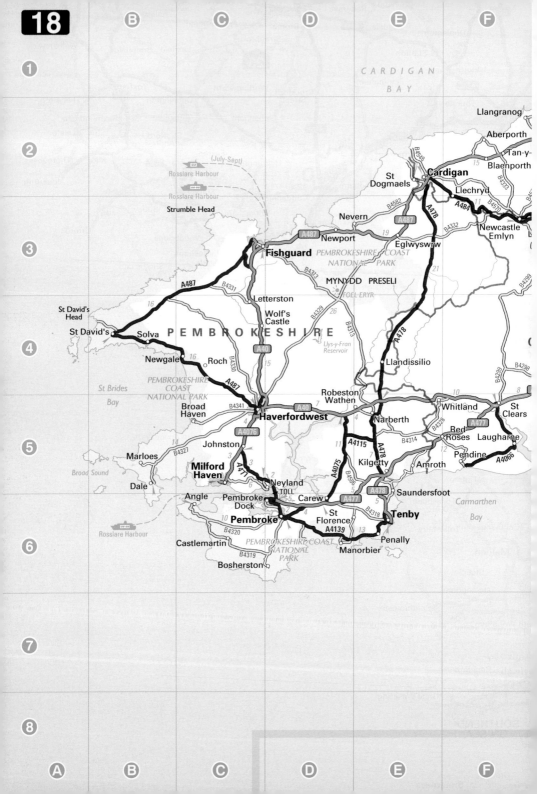

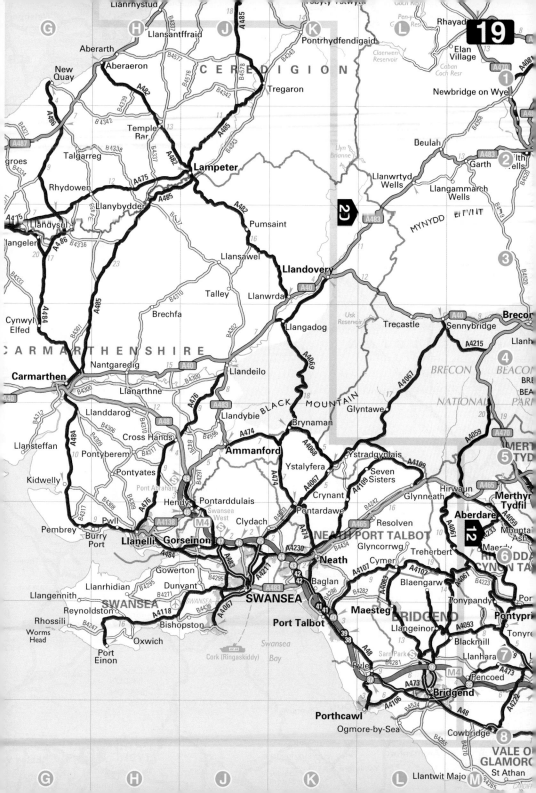

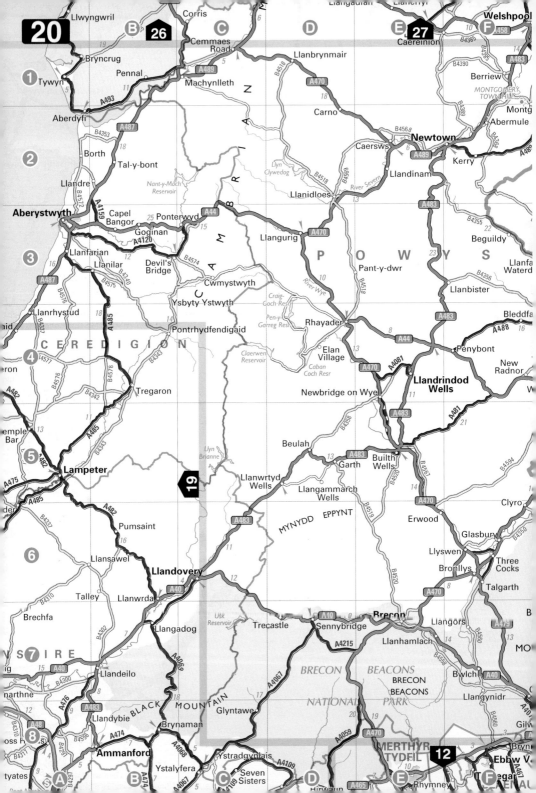

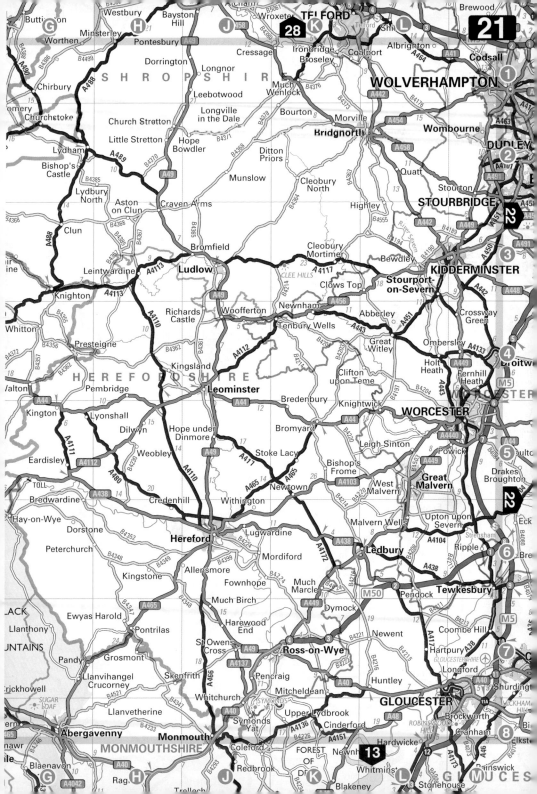

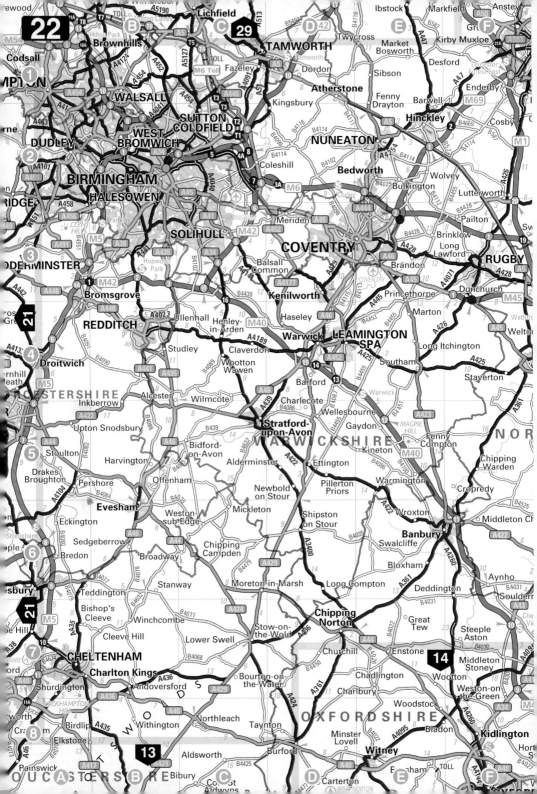

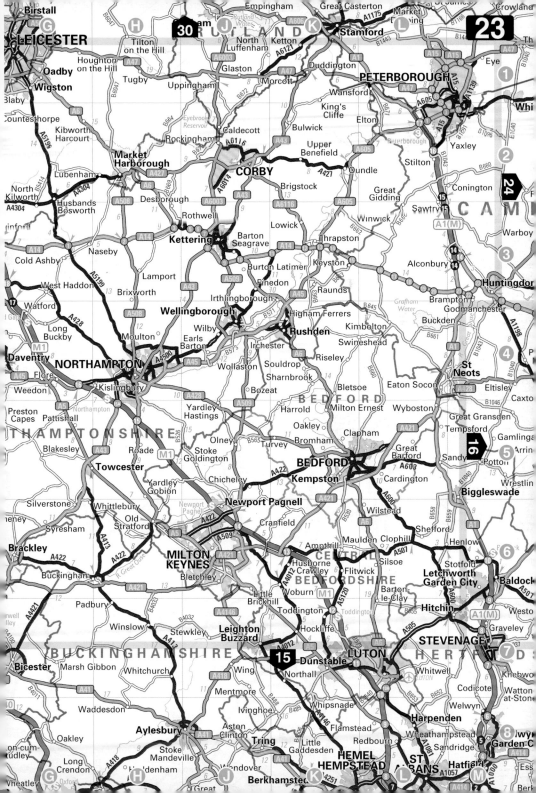

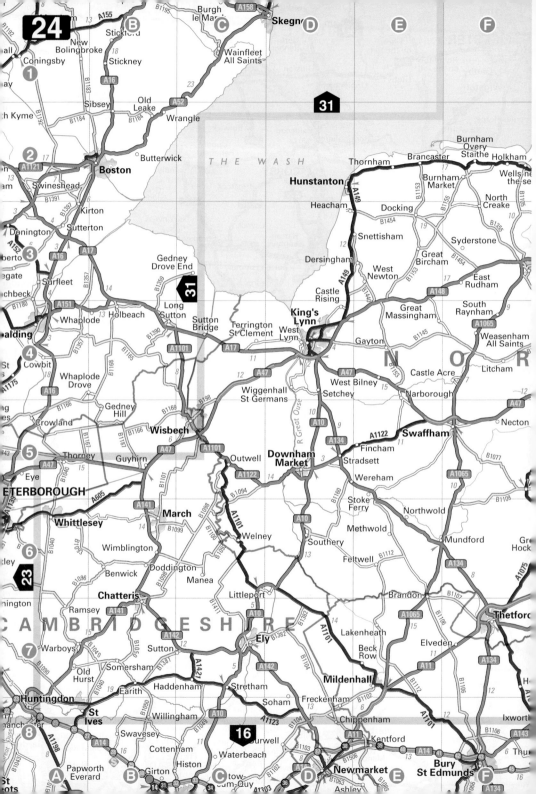

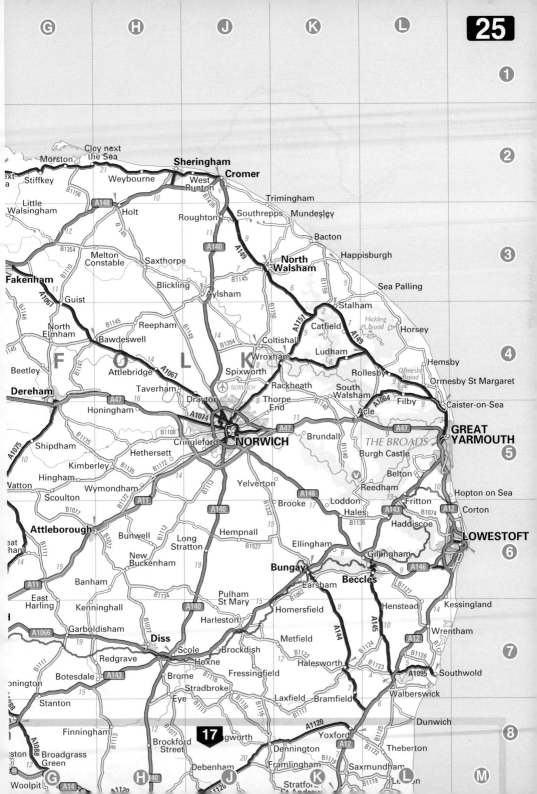

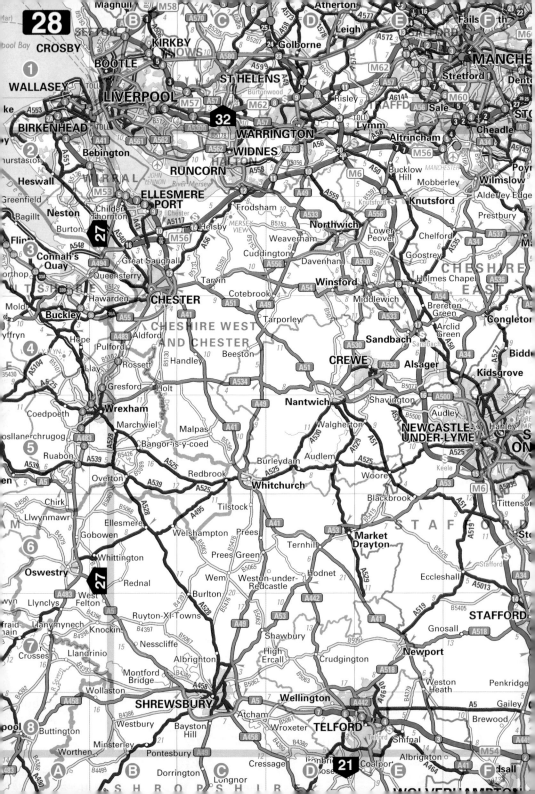

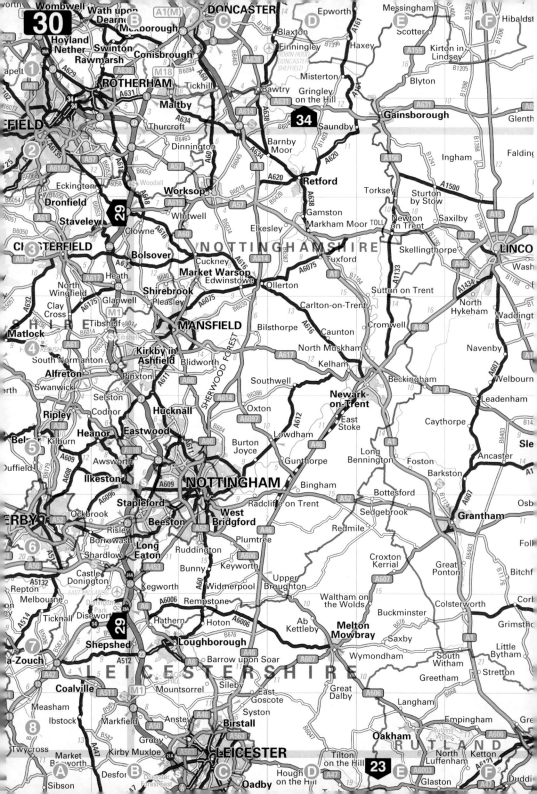

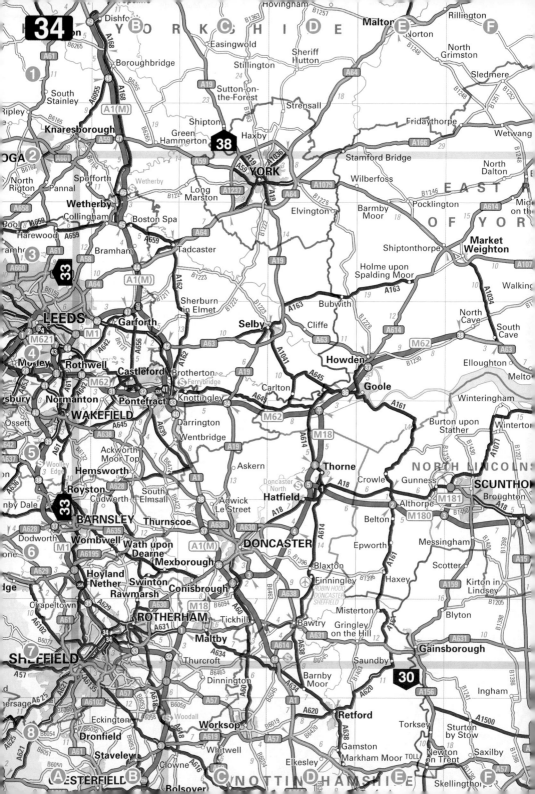

35

①

②

③

④

⑤

⑥

⑦

⑧

G   H   J   K   L

Burton Fleming
Bempton
Flamborough Head
Rudston
Carnaby
Flamborough
Langtoft
Bridlington
Kilham
B1255
Burton Agnes
A614
B1229
B1253
B1249
12
B1253
Driffield
Barmston
A165
16
Skipsea
15
North Frodingham
Beeford
B1242
39
13
Brandesburton
Atwick
Rainton
Wolds
Leven
Hornsea
letton
the Wolds
B1244
6
Beverley
A1035
B1243
Aldbrough
A1174
A165
13
B1238
Sproatley
A164
7
Cottingham
B1239
17
B1240
B1231
A1033
KINGSTON UPON HULL
Hedon
Withernsea
Hessle
A63
TOLL
B1362
North Ferriby
New Holland
16
A1033
4
1077
Barton-upon-Humber
Goxhill
Patrington
B1445
Easington
B1206
Immingham Dock
River Humber
B1218
B204
Wootton
Ulceby
A160
B1211
A15
Immingham
Spurn Head
SHIRE
A180
Keelby
A180
RPE
5
GRIMSBY
Wrawby
HUMBERSIDE
NE
Cleethorpes
Barnetby le Wold
12
A18
Laceby
Humberston
Rotterdam (Europoort) Zeebrugge
Brigg
A1084
A1173
A46
Waltham
Scawby
Swallow
Holton le Clay
Hibaldstow
Caistor
Tetney
B1203
A18
A16
North Cotes
B1434
Ludborough
B1201
A1031
North Somercotes
B1205
B1225
Grainthorpe
29
A46
B1203
Binbrook
17
Saltfleet
9
Middle Rasen
2
14
B1200
Glentham
A631
A631
Market Rasen
A157
Louth
A631
15
Legbourne
A1031
Mablethorpe
Faldingworth
31
B1200
A46
Lissington
15
Withern
A157
A52
Sutton on Sea
A157
East Barkwith
A153
A111
16
B1399
A202
Wragby
Scamblesby
A16
Alford
Huttoft
Langworth
A158
10
Bilsby
A158
Baumber
Tetford
B1373
Chapel St Leonards
18
B1201
Edlington
A1028
A1104
Hogsthorpe
B1196

G   H   J   K   L   M

LINCOL   LINCOLNSHIRE

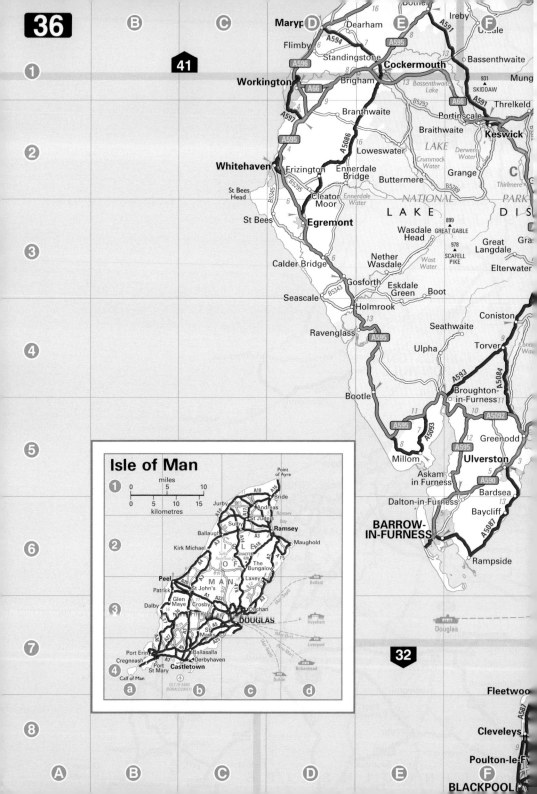

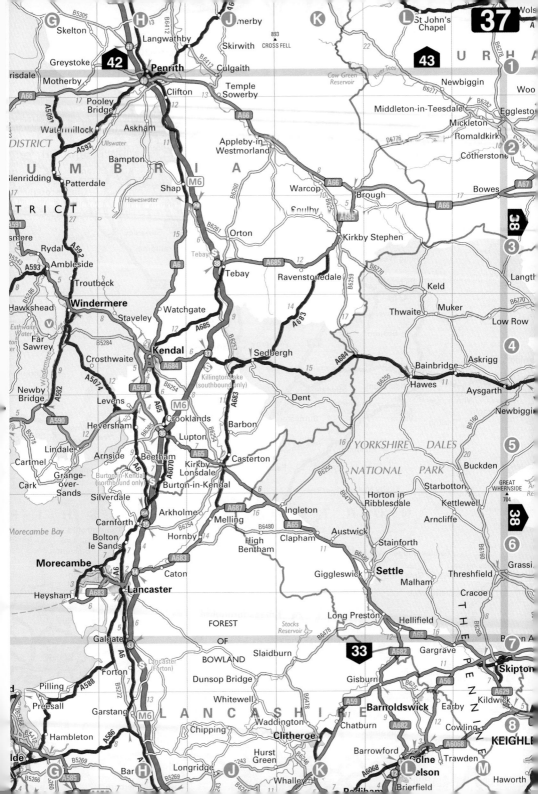

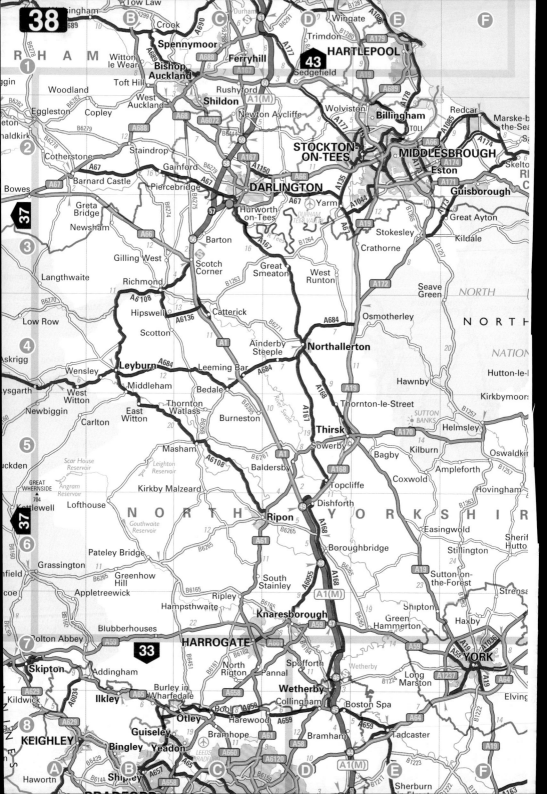

40

44

Ayr
Ochiltre
Au
Alloway
Coylton
Dunure
Dalrymple
Kirkmichael
Patna
EAST
AYRSHI
Maybole
Turnberry
Kirkoswald
Crosshill
Straiton
Dalmellington
Kirkmichael
Dailly
Loch Doon
Ailsa Craig
SOUTH
AYRSHIRE
Girvan
Barr
Carsphairn
Lendalfoot
MERRICK
842
CORSERINE
813
Pinwherry
St Joh
Colmonell
Barrhill
Loch Moan
Ballantrae
Loch Dee
Loch Enoch
(Mar-Oct)
Larne
Larne
Loch Maberry
Clatteringshaws Loch
Belfast
Belfast
Loch Grannoch
Stena Line to relocate from Stranraer Autumn 2011
Cairnryan
New Luce
Newton Stewart
CAIRNSMORE OF FLEET
710
Kirkcolm
Kirkcowan
Creetown
Leswalt
Gate
of F
Stranraer
Dunragit
Glenluce
Wigtown
Portpatrick
Stoneykirk
Kirkinner
Sandhead
Whauphill
Mochrum
Sorbie
Garlieston
Ardwell
Luce Bay
Wigtown Bay
Port William
Whithorn
Port Logan
Drummore
Isle of Whithorn
Burrow Head
Mull of Galloway

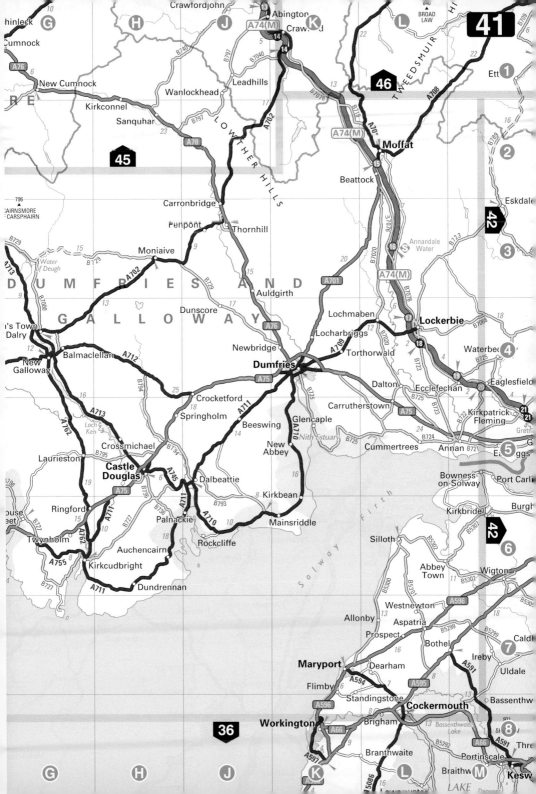

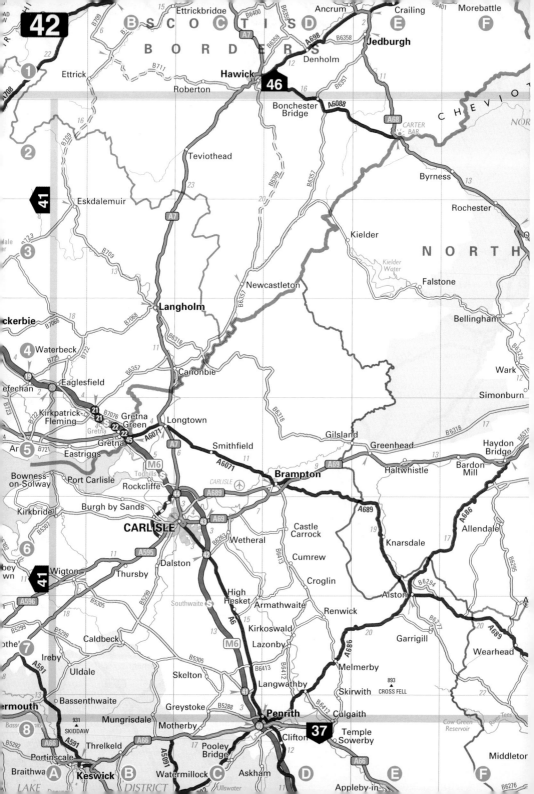

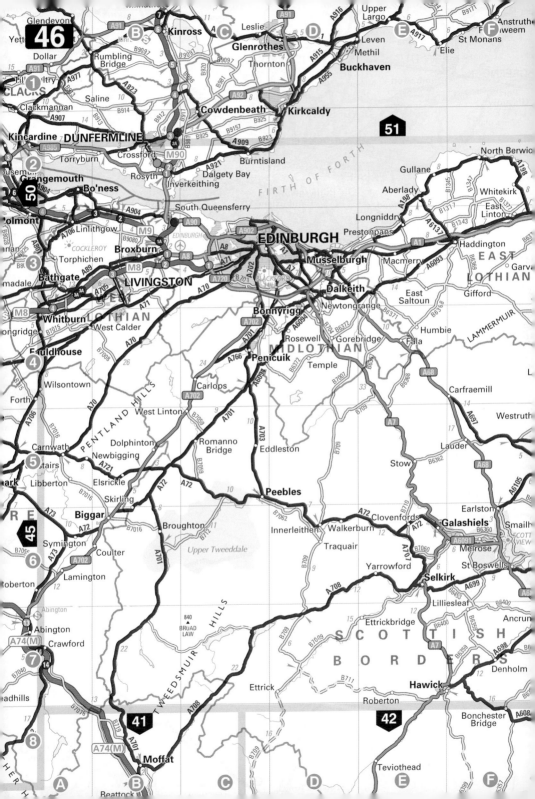

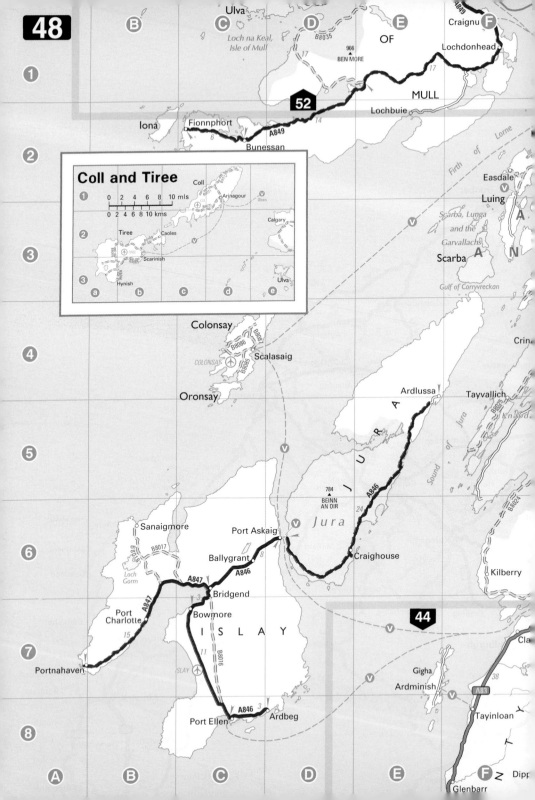

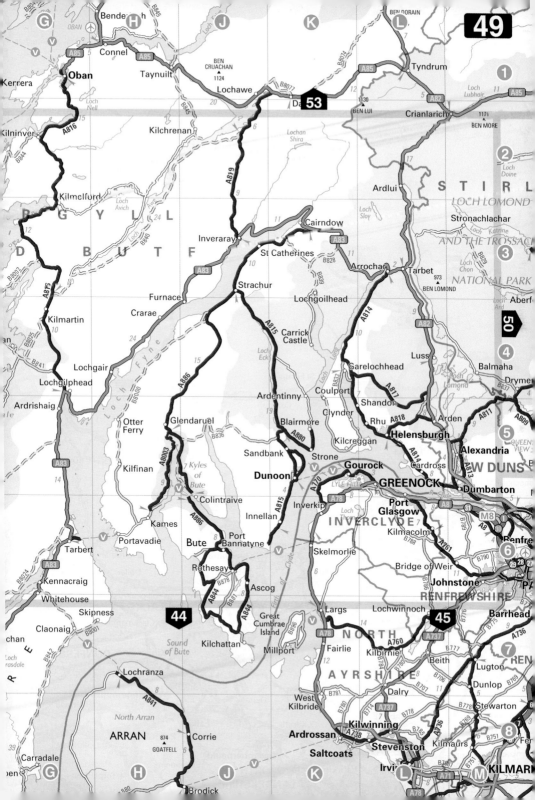

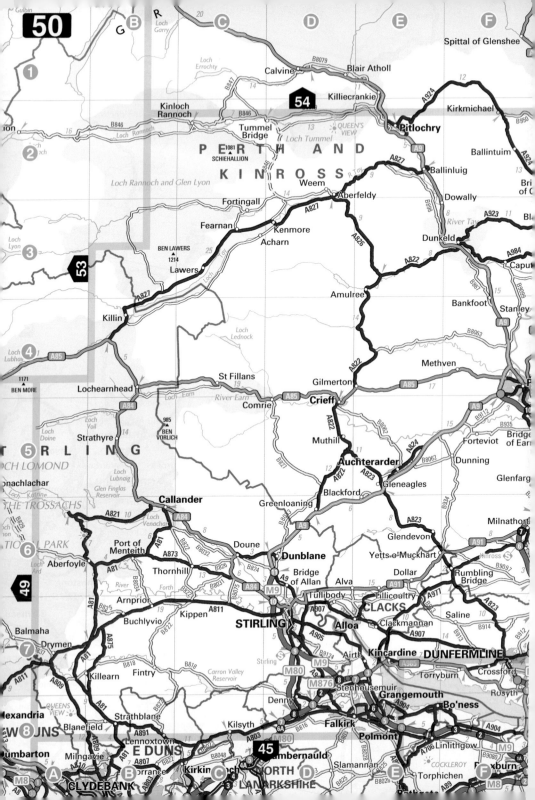

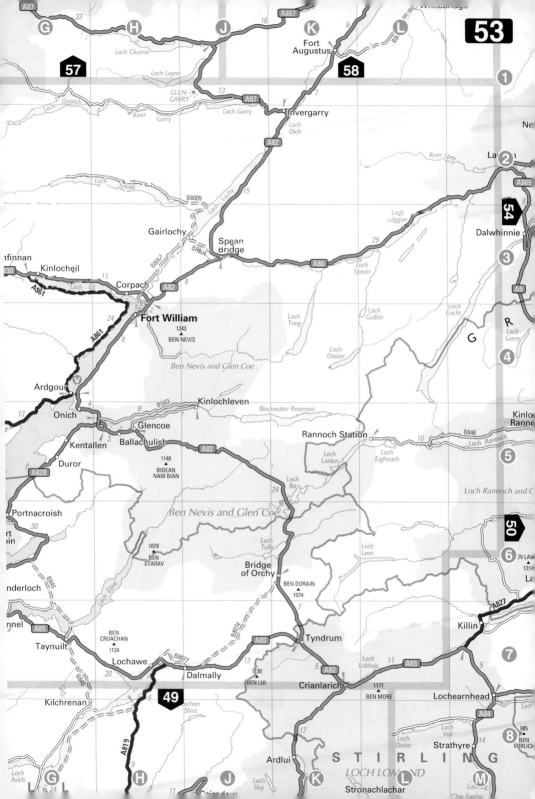

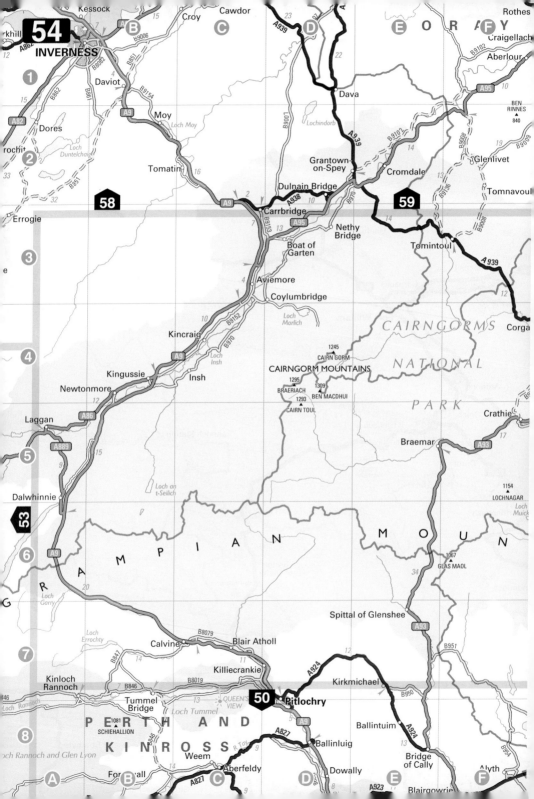

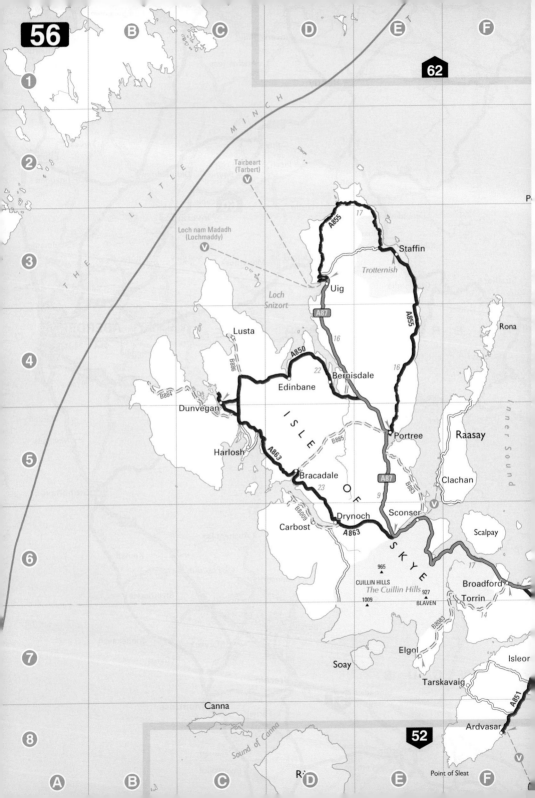

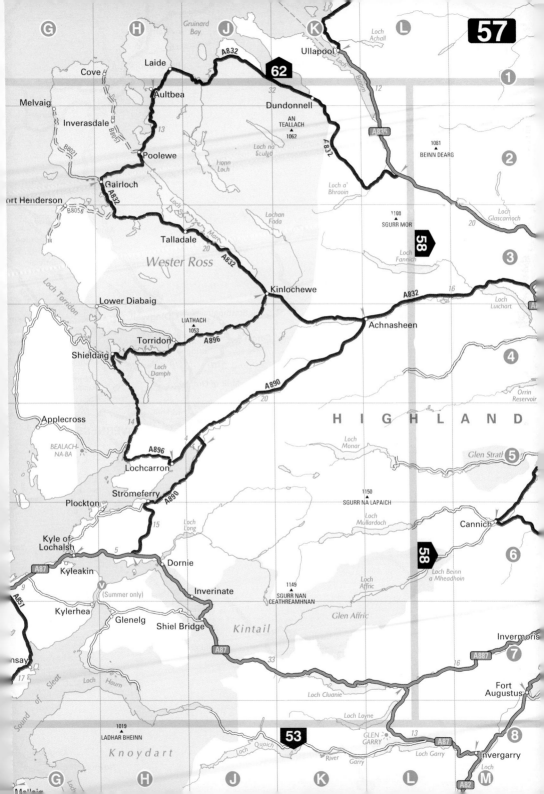

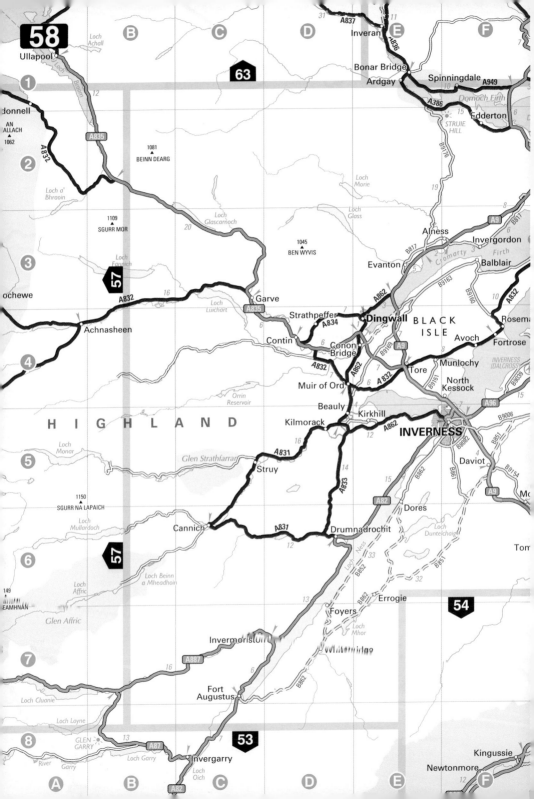

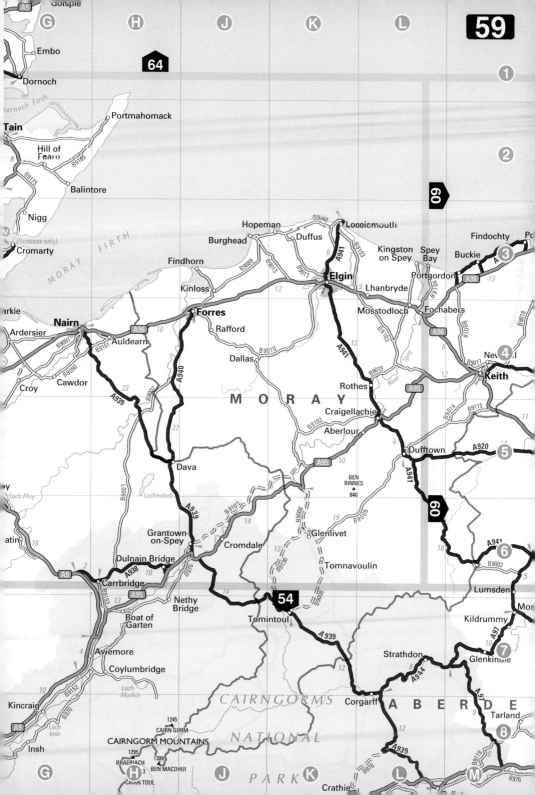

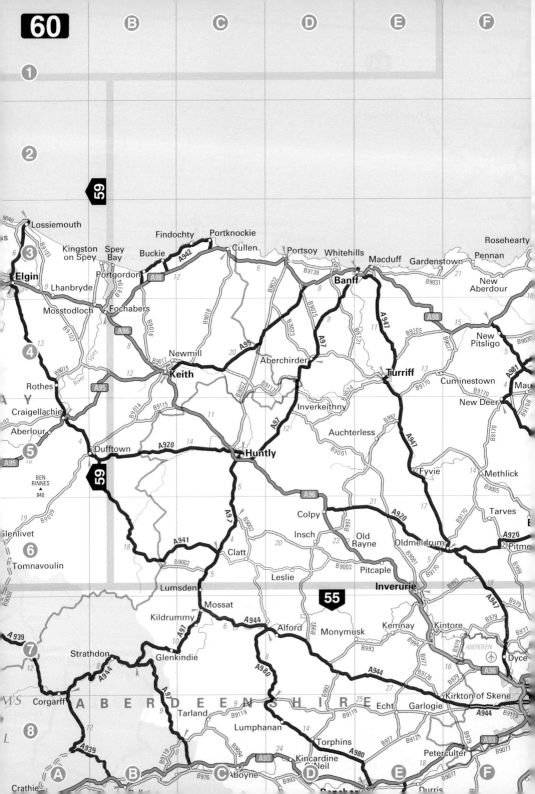

G H J K L

① ② ③ ④ ⑤ ⑥ ⑦ ⑧

Sandhaven
Fraserburgh
Inverallochy
St Combs
Memsie
B9032   B9033
Rathen
A90
Crimond
Strichen
A951   12
B9093   18
St Fergus
A952   12
A950
Mintlaw   6
PETERHEAD
Old Deer   A950   ⒽPETERHEAD
Longside   9   **Peterhead**
Stuartfield
B9030
Clola   Boddam
A952   14
Hatton   A90
A948   12
Cruden Bay
A975
llon   17
den   A975   32   Collieston
B9000
Newburgh
17
Balmedie
A90
ⓋKirkwall
Lerwick
ABERDEEN
A956
ortlethen

G H J K L M

Shetland Islands

| 0 | 5 | 10 | 15 mls | *Herma Ness*
| 0 | 5 | 10 | 15 | 20 kms |

① Haroldswick
Unst   A968   Baltasound
② Uyesound
Gutcher   Ⓥ
Yell   Mid
West   Yell   Fetlar
Sandwick   A968
③ Ⓥ   Burravoe   Out Skerries
Ollaberry   B9078   Ulsta
Hillswick   SHETLAND   Toft
Brae   A970
④ Muckle   Vidlin   Whalsay
Roe   Voe   Ⓥ
Sandness   ISLANDS   Symbister
⑤   A971   A970   25
Walls   KIRKWALL   Lerwick
Scalloway   Kirkabister
⑥   Bressay
MAINLAND   Ⓥ Fladdabister
⑦   A970   Sandwick   Ⓥ
Kirkwall
Aberdeen
⑧   SUMBURGH
Sumburgh Head

ⓐ ⓑ ⓒ ⓓ ⓔ

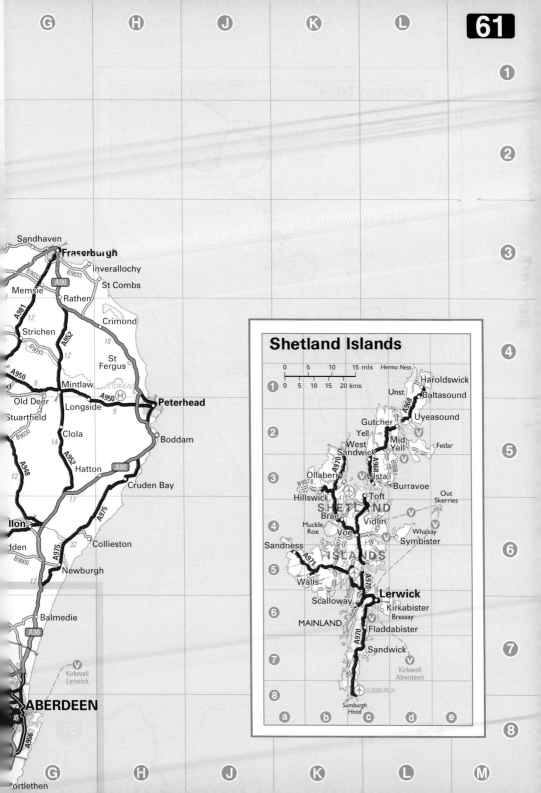

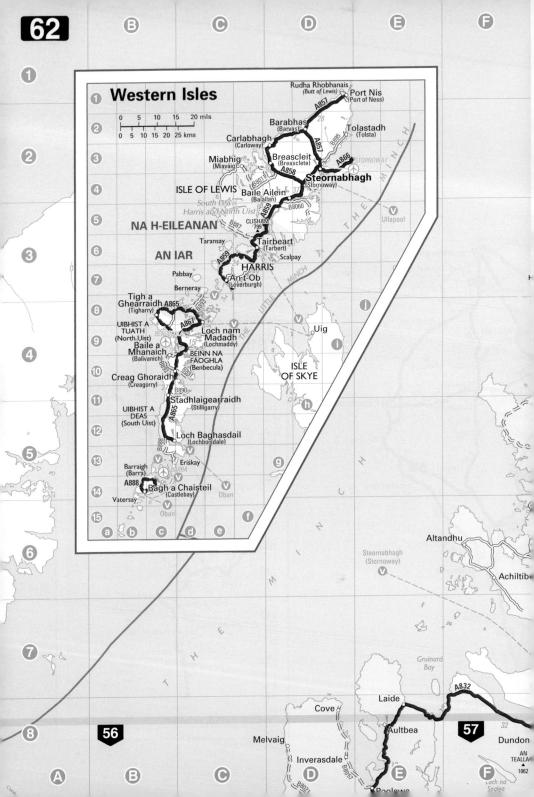

Western Isles

0 5 10 15 20 mls
0 5 10 15 20 25 kms

Rudha Rhobhanais
(Butt of Lewis)
Port Nis
(Port of Ness)
A857

Barabhas
(Barvas)
28

Carlabhagh
(Carloway)
Tolastadh
(Tolsta)
A857
B895

Breascleit
(Breasclete)
A858
A866
STORNOWAY

Miabhig
(Miavaig)
B8011
Steornabhagh
(Stornoway)

ISLE OF LEWIS
Baile Ailein
(Balallan)
37

South Lewis
Harris and North Uist
A859
B8060

NA H-EILEANAN
CLISHAM
799
B887
V
Ullapool

Taransay
Tairbeart
(Tarbert)
THE MINCH

AN IAR
A859
Scalpay

Pabbay
HARRIS
An t-Ob
(Leverburgh)
24

Berneray
LITTLE MINCH
V

Tigh a
Ghearraidh
(Tigharry)
A865
V
j

UIBHIST A
TUATH
(North Uist)
A867
Loch nam
Madadh
(Lochmaddy)
V
Uig

Baile a
Mhanaich
(Balivanich)
BENBECULA
15
i
ISLE
OF SKYE

Creag Ghoraidh
(Creagorry)
BEINN NA
FAOGHLA
(Benbecula)

Stadhlaigearraidh
(Stilligarry)
B890
h

UIBHIST A
DEAS
(South Uist)
A865

Loch Baghasdail
(Lochboisdale)
V

B888
Eriskay
g

Barraigh
(Barra)
V
BARRA
Oban

A888
Bagh a Chaisteil
(Castlebay)
V
Oban

Vatersay
Oban
f

a b c d e

Altandhu

Steornabhagh
(Stornoway)
V
Achiltib

Gruinard
Bay

A832
Laide

Cove
57

Aultbea
Dundon

Melvaig
AN
TEALLA
1062

Inverasdale
E
F

B8021
Loch na
Seglea

Poolewe

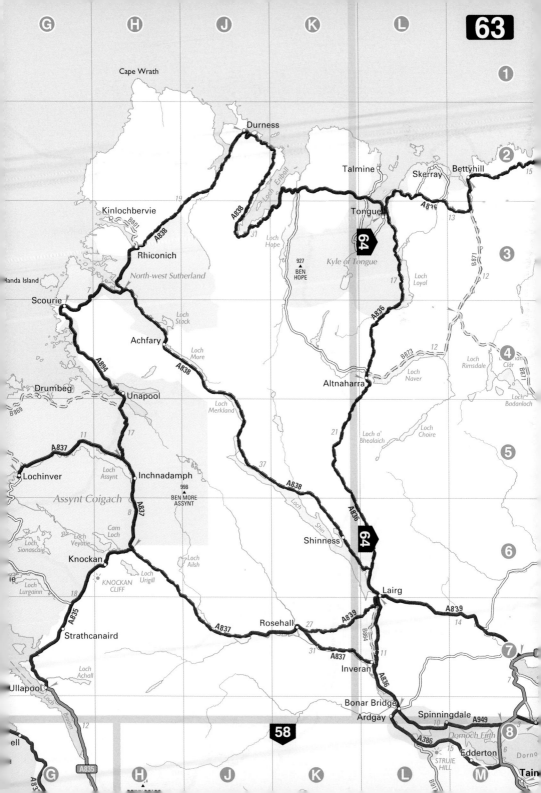

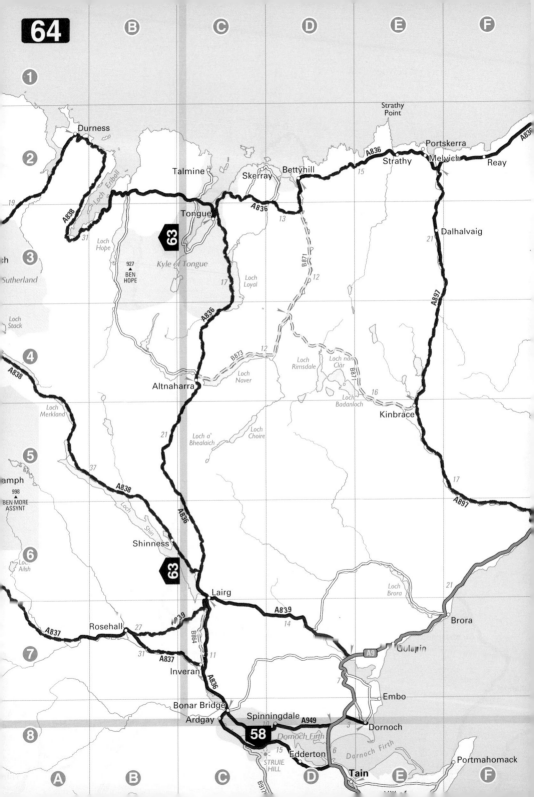

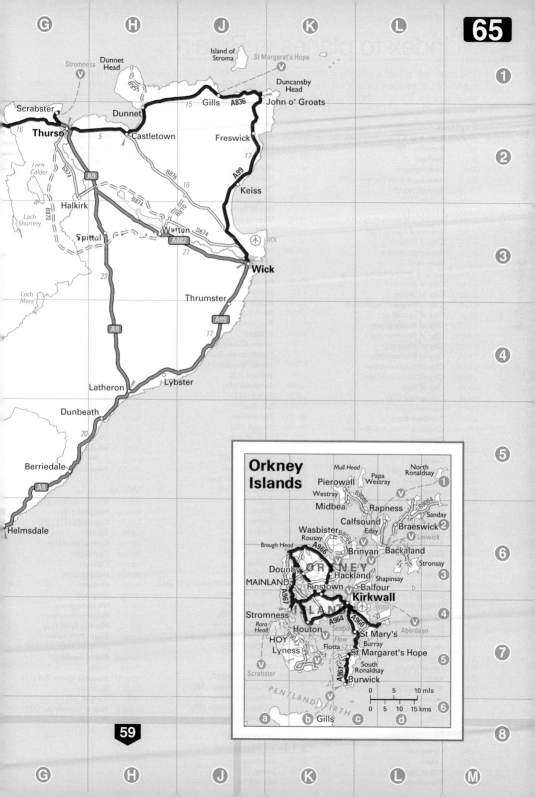

Index to places in Britain

This index lists places appearing in the main-map section of the atlas in alphabetical order. The reference before each name gives the atlas page number and grid reference of the square in which the place appears. The map shows counties, unitary authorities and administrative areas, together with a list of the abbreviated name forms used in the index.

England

BaNES	Bath & N E Somerset (18)
Barns	Barnsley (19)
Bed	Bedford
Birm	Birmingham
Bl w D	Blackburn with Darwen (20)
Bmouth	Bournemouth
Bolton	Bolton (21)
Bpool	Blackpool
Br & H	Brighton & Hove (22)
Br For	Bracknell Forest (23)
Bristl	City of Bristol
Bucks	Buckinghamshire
Bury	Bury (24)
C Beds	Central Bedfordshire
C Brad	City of Bradford
C Derb	City of Derby
C KuH	City of Kingston upon Hull
C Leic	City of Leicester
C Nott	City of Nottingham
C Pete	City of Peterborough
C Plym	City of Plymouth
C Port	City of Portsmouth
C Sotn	City of Southampton
C Stke	City of Stoke-on-Trent
C York	City of York
Calder	Calderdale (25)
Cambs	Cambridgeshire
Ches E	Cheshire East
Ches W	Cheshire West and Chester
Cnwll	Cornwall
Covtry	Coventry
Cumb	Cumbria
Darltn	Darlington (26)
Derbys	Derbyshire
Devon	Devon
Donc	Doncaster (27)
Dorset	Dorset
Dudley	Dudley (28)
Dur	Durham
E R Yk	East Riding of Yorkshire
E Susx	East Sussex
Essex	Essex
Gatesd	Gateshead (29)
Gloucs	Gloucestershire
Gt Lon	Greater London
Halton	Halton (30)
Hants	Hampshire
Hartpl	Hartlepool (31)
Herefs	Herefordshire
Herts	Hertfordshire
IoS	Isles of Scilly
IoW	Isle of Wight
Kent	Kent
Kirk	Kirklees (32)
Knows	Knowsley (33)
Lancs	Lancashire
Leeds	Leeds
Leics	Leicestershire
Lincs	Lincolnshire
Lpool	Liverpool
Luton	Luton
M Keyn	Milton Keynes
Manch	Manchester

Medway	Medway
Middsb	Middlesbrough
NE Lin	North East Lincolnshire
N Linc	North Lincolnshire
N Som	North Somerset (34)
N Tyne	North Tyneside (35)
N u Ty	Newcastle upon Tyne
N York	North Yorkshire
Nhants	Northamptonshire
Norfk	Norfolk
Notts	Nottinghamshire
Nthumb	Northumberland
Oldham	Oldham (36)
Oxon	Oxfordshire
Poole	Poole
R & Cl	Redcar & Cleveland
Readg	Reading
Rochdl	Rochdale (37)
Rothm	Rotherham (38)
Rutlnd	Rutland
S Glos	South Gloucestershire (39)
S on T	Stockton-on-Tees (40)
S Tyne	South Tyneside (41)
Salfd	Salford (42)
Sandw	Sandwell (43)
Sefton	Sefton (44)
Sheff	Sheffield
Shrops	Shropshire
Slough	Slough (45)
Solhll	Solihull (46)
Somset	Somerset
St Hel	St Helens (47)
Staffs	Staffordshire
Sthend	Southend-on-Sea
Stockp	Stockport (48)
Suffk	Suffolk
Sundld	Sunderland
Surrey	Surrey
Swindn	Swindon
Tamesd	Tameside (49)
Thurr	Thurrock (50)
Torbay	Torbay
Traffd	Trafford (51)
W & M	Windsor and Maidenhead (52)
W Berk	West Berkshire
W Susx	West Sussex
Wakefd	Wakefield (53)
Warrtn	Warrington (54)
Warwks	Warwickshire
Wigan	Wigan (55)
Wilts	Wiltshire
Wirral	Wirral (56)
Wokham	Wokingham (57)
Wolves	Wolverhampton (58)
Worcs	Worcestershire
Wrekin	Telford & Wrekin (59)
Wsall	Walsall (60)

Channel Islands & Isle of Man

Guern	Guernsey
Jersey	Jersey
IoM	Isle of Man

Scotland

Abers	Aberdeenshire
Ag & B	Argyll and Bute
Angus	Angus
Border	Scottish Borders
C Aber	City of Aberdeen
C Dund	City of Dundee
C Edin	City of Edinburgh
C Glas	City of Glasgow
Clacks	Clackmannanshire (1)
D & G	Dumfries & Galloway
E Ayrs	East Ayrshire
E Duns	East Dunbartonshire (2)
E Loth	East Lothian
E Rens	East Renfrewshire (3)
Falk	Falkirk
Fife	Fife
Highld	Highland
Inver	Inverclyde (4)
Mdloth	Midlothian (5)
Moray	Moray
N Ayrs	North Ayrshire
N Lans	North Lanarkshire (6)
Ork	Orkney Islands
P & K	Perth & Kinross
Rens	Renfrewshire (7)
S Ayrs	South Ayrshire
Shet	Shetland Islands
S Lans	South Lanarkshire
Stirlg	Stirling
W Duns	West Dunbartonshire (8)
W Isls	Western Isles (Na h-Eileanan an Iar)
W Loth	West Lothian

Wales

Blae G	Blaenau Gwent (9)
Brdgnd	Bridgend (10)
Caerph	Caerphilly (11)
Cardif	Cardiff
Carmth	Carmarthenshire
Cerdgn	Ceredigion
Conwy	Conwy
Denbgs	Denbighshire
Flints	Flintshire
Gwynd	Gwynedd
IoA	Isle of Anglesey
Mons	Monmouthshire
Myr Td	Merthyr Tydfil (12)
Neath	Neath Port Talbot (13)
Newpt	Newport (14)
Pembks	Pembrokeshire
Powys	Powys
Rhondd	Rhondda Cynon Taff (15)
Swans	Swansea
Torfn	Torfaen (16)
V Glam	Vale of Glamorgan (17)
Wrexhm	Wrexham

Mileage chart - Britain

The mileage chart shows distances in miles between two towns along AA-recommended routes. Using motorways and other main roads this is normally the fastest route, though not necessarily the shortest.

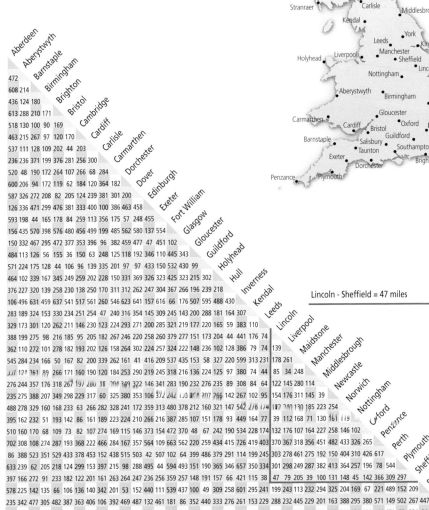

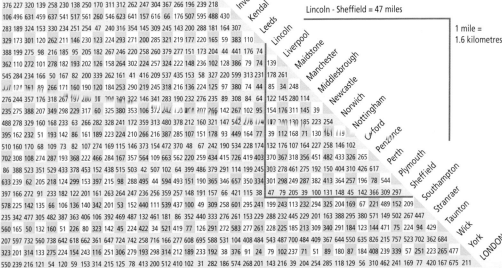

Lincoln - Sheffield = 47 miles

1 mile = 1.6 kilometres

Distances (in miles) between the towns listed below. Each row is headed by its town name:

```
Aberdeen
Aberystwyth    472
Barnstaple     608 214
Birmingham     436 124 180
Brighton       613 288 210 171
Bristol        518 130 100 90 169
Cambridge      463 215 267 97 120 170
Cardiff        537 111 128 109 202 44 203
Carlisle       236 236 371 199 376 281 256 300
Carmarthen     520 48 190 172 264 107 266 68 284
Dorchester     600 206 94 172 119 62 184 120 364 182
Dover          587 326 272 208 82 205 124 239 381 301 200
Edinburgh      126 336 471 299 476 381 333 400 100 386 463 458
Exeter         593 198 44 165 178 84 259 113 356 175 57 248 455
Fort William   156 435 570 398 576 480 456 499 199 485 562 580 137 554
Glasgow        150 332 467 295 472 377 353 396 96 382 459 477 47 451 102
Gloucester     484 113 126 56 155 36 150 63 248 125 118 192 346 110 445 343
Guildford      571 224 175 128 44 106 96 139 335 201 97 97 433 150 532 430 99
Holyhead       464 102 339 167 345 249 259 202 228 150 331 369 326 323 425 323 215 302
Hull           376 227 320 139 258 230 138 250 170 311 312 262 247 304 367 266 196 239 218
Inverness      106 496 631 459 637 541 517 561 260 546 623 641 157 616 66 176 507 595 488 430
Kendal         283 189 324 153 330 234 251 254 47 240 316 354 145 309 245 143 200 288 181 164 307
Leeds          329 173 301 120 262 211 146 230 123 224 293 271 200 285 321 219 177 220 165 59 383 110
Lincoln        388 199 275 98 216 185 95 205 182 267 246 220 258 260 379 277 151 173 204 44 441 176 74
Liverpool      362 110 272 101 278 182 193 202 126 158 264 302 224 257 324 222 148 236 102 128 386 79 74 139
Maidstone      545 284 234 166 50 167 82 200 339 262 161 41 416 209 537 435 153 58 327 220 599 313 231 178 261
Manchester     337 124 261 89 266 171 160 190 120 184 253 290 219 245 318 216 136 224 125 97 380 74 44 85 34 248
Middlesbrough  276 244 357 176 318 267 197 280 31 304 349 322 146 341 283 190 232 276 235 89 308 84 64 122 145 280 114
Newcastle      235 275 388 207 349 298 229 317 60 325 380 353 106 372 242 133 307 266 142 267 102 95 154 176 311 145 39
Norwich        488 278 329 160 168 233 63 266 282 328 241 172 359 313 480 378 212 160 321 147 542 276 174 107 240 130 185 223 254
Nottingham     395 162 232 51 193 142 86 161 189 223 224 210 266 216 387 285 107 151 178 93 449 164 77 39 112 168 71 130 161 119
Oxford         510 160 170 68 109 73 82 107 274 169 115 146 373 154 472 370 48 67 242 190 534 228 174 132 176 107 164 227 258 146 102
Penzance       702 308 108 274 287 193 368 222 466 284 167 357 564 109 663 562 220 259 434 415 726 419 403 370 367 318 356 451 482 433 326 265
Perth          86 388 523 351 529 433 378 453 152 438 515 503 42 507 102 64 399 486 379 291 114 199 245 303 278 461 275 192 150 404 310 426 617
Plymouth       633 239 62 205 218 124 299 153 397 215 98 288 495 44 594 493 151 190 365 346 657 350 334 301 298 249 287 382 413 364 257 196 78 544
Sheffield      397 166 272 91 233 182 122 201 161 263 264 247 236 256 359 257 148 191 157 66 421 115 38 47 79 205 39 100 131 148 45 142 366 309 297
Southampton    578 225 142 135 66 106 136 140 342 201 53 152 440 111 539 437 100 49 309 258 601 295 241 199 243 113 232 294 325 204 169 67 221 489 152 209
Stranraer      235 342 477 305 482 387 363 406 106 392 469 487 132 461 181 86 352 440 333 276 261 153 229 288 232 445 229 92 141 59 214 314 523 339 57 251 223 265 447
Taunton        560 165 50 132 160 51 226 80 323 142 45 224 422 34 521 419 77 126 291 272 583 277 261 228 225 185 213 309 340 291 184 123 144 471 75 224 94 429
Wick           207 597 732 560 738 642 618 662 361 647 724 742 258 716 166 277 608 695 588 531 104 408 484 543 487 700 484 409 367 644 550 635 826 215 757 523 702 362 684
York           323 201 314 133 275 224 154 243 116 251 306 279 193 298 314 212 189 233 192 38 376 91 24 79 102 237 71 51 89 180 87 184 408 239 339 57 251 223 265 477
LONDON         550 239 216 121 54 120 59 153 314 215 125 78 413 200 512 410 102 31 282 186 574 268 201 143 216 39 204 254 285 118 129 56 310 462 241 169 77 420 167 675 211
```

A

21 L4 Abberley Worcs
41 L6 Abbey Town Cumb
29 H7 Abbots Bromley Staffs
19 H1 Aberaeron Cerdgn
19 H1 Aberarth Cerdgn
60 D4 Aberchirder Abers
12 B2 Aberdare Rhondd
26 B6 Aberdaron Gwynd
55 M4 Aberdeen C Aber
20 A2 Aberdyfi Gwynd
50 D2 Aberfeldy P & K
26 C3 Aberffraw IoA
50 B6 Aberfoyle Stirlg
21 G8 Abergavenny Mons
27 H3 Abergele Conwy
46 E2 Aberlady E Loth
59 L5 Aberlour Moray
20 F2 Abermule Powys
51 G5 Abernethy P & K
18 F2 Aberporth Cerdgn
26 C6 Abersoch Gwynd
12 D1 Abersychan Torfn
12 D2 Abertillery Blae G
20 A3 Aberystwyth Cerdgn
14 C4 Abingdon Oxon
45 M5 Abington S Lans
30 D7 Ab Kettleby Leics
55 J4 Aboyne Abers
16 D7 Abridge Essex
33 G4 Accrington Lancs
52 D4 Acharacle Highld
50 C3 Acharn P & K
63 H4 Achfary Highld
62 F6 Achiltibuie Highld
52 F6 Achnacroish Ag & B
57 L4 Achnasheen Highld
34 B5 Ackworth Moor Top Wakefd
25 K5 Acle Norfk
29 G7 Acton Trussell Staffs
33 J2 Addingham C Brad
34 C6 Adwick Le Street Donc
38 D4 Ainderby Steeple N York
45 L2 Airdrie N Lans
50 E7 Airth Falk
21 L1 Albrighton Shrops
28 C7 Albrighton Shrops
9 K2 Albury Surrey
22 B4 Alcester Warwks
23 M3 Alconbury Cambs
14 A6 Aldbourne Wilts
35 J3 Aldbrough E R Yk
17 M2 Aldeburgh Suffk
8 C3 Alderbury Wilts
28 F3 Alderley Edge Ches E
14 D7 Aldermaston W Berk
22 D5 Alderminster Warwks
9 H2 Aldershot Hants
28 B4 Aldford Ches W
17 G5 Aldham Essex
13 L1 Aldsworth Gloucs
49 M5 Alexandria W Duns
9 K3 Alfold Surrey
55 J3 Alford Abers
31 K3 Alford Lincs
29 L4 Alfreton Derbys
10 D7 Alfriston E Susx
11 K4 Alkham Kent
47 H4 Allanton Border
42 F6 Allendale Nthumb
42 F7 Allenheads Nthumb
21 J6 Allensmore Herefs
50 E7 Alloa Clacks
41 L7 Allonby Cumb
45 G6 Alloway S Ayrs
13 G3 Almondsbury S Glos
58 F3 Alness Highld
43 K2 Alnmouth Nthumb
47 L7 Alnwick Nthumb
29 J7 Alrewas Staffs
28 E4 Alsager Ches E
42 E6 Alston Cumb
62 F6 Altandhu Highld
34 E5 Althorpe N Linc
64 C4 Altnaharra Highld
9 G2 Alton Hants
7 K2 Alton Pancras Dorset
28 E2 Altrincham Traffd
50 E6 Alva Clacks
13 G3 Alveston S Glos
51 G3 Alyth P & K
9 K4 Amberley W Susx
43 K2 Amble Nthumb
37 G3 Ambleside Cumb
15 G4 Amersham Bucks

8 C2 Amesbury Wilts
26 D1 Amlwch IoA
19 J5 Ammanford Carmth
38 F5 Ampleforth N York
23 K6 Ampthill C Beds
18 E5 Amroth Pembks
50 E3 Amulree P & K
30 F5 Ancaster Lincs
47 K5 Ancroft Nthumb
47 G7 Ancrum Border
8 D2 Andover Hants
22 B7 Andoversford Gloucs
30 c1 Andreas IoM
18 C6 Angle Pembks
9 K5 Angmering W Susx
41 M5 Annan D & G
43 J6 Annfield Plain Dur
30 C8 Anstey Leics
51 K6 Anstruther Fife
62 e7 An t-Ob W Isls
31 G5 Anwick Lincs
37 J2 Appleby-in-Westmorland Cumb
57 G5 Applecross Highld
4 D4 Appledore Devon
11 H5 Appledore Kent
38 A7 Appletreewick N York
51 L3 Arbroath Angus
28 E4 Arclid Green Ches E
48 D8 Ardbeg Ag & B
49 L5 Arden Ag & B
49 K4 Ardentinny Ag & B
59 G4 Ardersier Highld
64 C8 Ardgay Highld
53 G4 Ardgour Highld
10 C5 Ardingly W Susx
17 H4 Ardleigh Essex
49 L2 Ardlui Ag & B
48 F4 Ardlussa Ag & B
44 A3 Ardminish Ag & B
49 G5 Ardrishaig Ag & B
44 F4 Ardrossan N Ayrs
52 D1 Ardvasar Highld
40 C7 Ardwell D & G
48 d1 Arinagour Ag & B
52 D3 Arisaig Highld
37 J6 Arkholme Lancs
45 M2 Armadale W Loth
42 C7 Armathwaite Cumb
37 M6 Arncliffe N York
50 B7 Arnprior Stirlg
37 H5 Arnside Cumb
16 B3 Arrington Cambs
49 L3 Arrochar Ag & B
9 K5 Arundel W Susx
49 J6 Ascog Ag & B
15 G6 Ascot W & M
11 K3 Ash Kent
29 J5 Ashbourne Derbys
26 B3 Ashburton Devon
14 A5 Ashbury Oxon
29 K7 Ashby-de-la-Zouch Leics
12 E7 Ashcott Somset
11 H4 Ashford Kent
43 K3 Ashington Nthumb
9 L4 Ashington W Susx
16 E2 Ashley Cambs
33 H6 Ashton-under-Lyne Tamesd
8 D5 Ashurst Hants
4 D7 Ashwater Devon
36 F5 Askam in Furness Cumb
34 C5 Askern Donc
37 H2 Askham Cumb
37 M4 Askrigg N York
41 L7 Aspatria Cumb
14 B4 Aston Oxon
21 H3 Aston Clinton Bucks
21 H3 Aston on Clun Shrops
14 E4 Aston Rowant Oxon
28 C8 Atcham Shrops
22 D1 Atherstone Warwks
32 F6 Atherton Wigan
25 H4 Attleborough Norfk
25 H4 Attlebridge Norfk
11 K3 Atwick E R Yk
55 K6 Auchenblae Abers
45 J5 Auchencairn D & G
60 E5 Auchterless Abers
60 E5 Auchterless Abers
51 H4 Auchtermuchty Fife
28 D5 Audlem Ches E
28 E5 Audley Staffs
59 H4 Auldearn Highld
45 J5 Auldgirth D & G
57 H1 Aultbea Highld
37 K6 Austwick N York

13 L4 Avebury Wilts
13 J2 Avening Gloucs
6 A6 Aveton Gifford Devon
54 C3 Aviemore Highld
58 F4 Avoch Highld
12 F4 Avonmouth Bristl
30 B5 Awsworth Notts
12 E5 Axbridge Somset
6 F3 Axminster Devon
6 F3 Axmouth Devon
15 H3 Aylesbury Bucks
11 K3 Aylsham Kent
25 J3 Aylsham Norfk
22 F6 Aynho Nhants
45 G5 Ayr S Ayrs
38 A4 Aysgarth N York
47 J4 Ayton Border

B

65 d2 Backaland Ork
25 K3 Bacton Norfk
32 H4 Bacup Lancs
38 E5 Bagby N York
b14 Bagh a Chaisteil W Isls
27 K3 Bagillt Flints
19 K6 Bagnan Neath
14 F7 Bagshot Surrey
62 g4 Baile Ailein W Isls
62 c10 Baile a Mhanaich W Isls
37 M4 Bainbridge N York
34 F2 Bainton E R Yk
29 J3 Bakewell Derbys
27 H6 Bala Gwynd
62 g4 Balallan W Isls
58 F3 Balblair Highld
10 B5 Balcombe W Susx
38 D5 Baldersby N York
16 B4 Baldock Herts
65 c3 Balfour Ork
59 G2 Balintore Highld
62 c10 Balivanich W Isls
53 H5 Ballachulish Highld
40 B4 Ballantrae S Ayrs
36 b4 Ballasalla IoM
55 G5 Ballater Abers
36 c2 Ballaugh IoM
50 E2 Ballinluig P & K
50 F2 Ballintuim P & K
48 C6 Ballygrant Ag & B
41 G4 Balmaclellan D & G
49 M4 Balmaha Stirlg
55 M3 Balmedie Abers
23 K7 Balsall Common Solhll
16 E3 Balsham Cambs
61 d1 Baltasound Shet
32 E4 Bamber Bridge Lancs
47 L6 Bamburgh Nthumb
29 J2 Bamford Derbys
37 H2 Bampton Cumb
5 H5 Bampton Devon
14 A4 Bampton Oxon
22 E6 Banbury Oxon
55 K5 Banchory Abers
60 E3 Banff Abers
26 E3 Bangor Gwynd
26 E3 Bangor-is-y-coed Wrexhm
25 H6 Banham Norfk
50 F4 Bankfoot P & K
10 B3 Banstead Surrey
62 h2 Barabhas W Isls
37 J5 Barbon Cumb
31 G3 Bardney Lincs
42 F5 Bardon Mill Nthumb
36 F5 Bardsea Cumb
22 D4 Barford Warwks
12 C2 Bargoed Caerph
16 C8 Barking Gt Lon
30 F5 Barkston Lincs
16 C3 Barkway Herts
34 E2 Barmby Moor E R Yk
21 M7 Barmouth Gwynd
38 A2 Barnard Castle Dur
30 D2 Barnby Moor Notts
15 J4 Barnet Gt Lon
35 G4 Barnetby le Wold N Linc
33 H3 Barnoldswick Lancs
33 M6 Barnsley Barns
13 L2 Barnsley Gloucs
4 E4 Barnstaple Devon
40 D3 Barr S Ayrs
43 G4 Barrasford Nthumb

45 H3 Barrhead E Rens
40 D4 Barrhill S Ayrs
33 H3 Barrowford Lancs
36 E6 Barrow-in-Furness Cumb
30 C7 Barrow upon Soar Leics
5 K1 Barry V Glam
16 C2 Barton Cambs
32 E3 Barton Lancs
38 C3 Barton N York
23 I7 Barton-le-Clay C Beds
25 J3 Barton Seagrave Nhants
29 J7 Barton-under-Needwood Staffs
35 G5 Barton-upon-Humber N Linc
62 h2 Barvas W Isls
22 E2 Barwell Leics
16 F7 Basildon Essex
9 G1 Basingstoke Hants
29 J3 Baslow Derbys
42 A8 Bassenthwaite Cumb
31 G7 Baston Lincs
13 H5 Bath BaNES
46 A3 Bathgate W Loth
33 L4 Batley Kirk
10 F6 Battle E Susx
31 H3 Baumber Lincs
25 H4 Bawdeswell Norfk
17 L4 Bawdsey Suffk
34 D7 Bawtry Donc
36 F6 Baycliff Cumb
28 C8 Bayston Hill Shrops
15 G5 Beaconsfield Bucks
47 L6 Beadnell Nthumb
4 E5 Beaford Devon
47 K5 Beal Nthumb
7 H2 Beaminster Dorset
9 L2 Beare Green Surrey
10 F3 Bearsted Kent
41 L2 Beattock D & G
8 E5 Beaulieu Hants
58 D5 Beauly Highld
26 E3 Beaumaris IoA
7 b2 Beaumont Jersey
4 D7 Beaworthy Devon
27 L2 Bebington Wirral
25 L6 Beccles Suffk
13 L4 Beckhampton Wilts
30 E4 Beckingham Lincs
13 H6 Beckington Somset
24 E7 Beck Row Suffk
38 C4 Bedale N York
26 E5 Beddgelert Gwynd
23 K5 Bedford Bed
43 K4 Bedlington Nthumb
22 E2 Bedworth Warwks
35 H2 Beeford E R Yk
29 J3 Beeley Derbys
6 F3 Beer Devon
6 B7 Beesands Devon
28 C4 Beeston Ches W
30 B6 Beeston Notts
41 J5 Beeswing D & G
37 H5 Beetham Cumb
25 G4 Beetley Norfk
20 F3 Beguildy Powys
45 G3 Beith N Ayrs
47 L6 Belford Nthumb
42 F4 Bellingham Nthumb
44 A5 Bellochantuy Ag & B
45 K2 Bellshill N Lans
29 K5 Belper Derbys
43 H4 Belsay Nthumb
34 E6 Belton N Linc
25 L5 Belton Norfk
9 G6 Bembridge IoW
39 L6 Bempton E R Yk
52 F6 Benderloch Ag & B
10 F5 Benenden Kent
26 D2 Benllech IoA
14 D5 Benson Oxon
9 H2 Bentley Hants
24 B6 Benwick Cambs
3 K4 Bere Alston Devon
3 K4 Bere Ferrers Devon
7 L3 Bere Regis Dorset
13 G2 Berkeley Gloucs
15 G3 Berkhamsted Herts
56 D4 Bernisdale Highld
65 G5 Berriedale Highld
20 F1 Berriew Powys
12 D6 Berrow Somset
13 K8 Berwick St John Wilts
47 K4 Berwick-upon-Tweed Nthumb
11 G4 Bethersden Kent
26 E3 Bethesda Gwynd

64 D2 **Bettyhill** Highld
27 G4 **Betws-y-Coed** Conwy
27 H3 **Betws-yn-Rhos** Conwy
20 D5 **Beulah** Powys
35 G3 **Beverley** E R Yk
21 L3 **Bewdley** Worcs
10 F7 **Bexhill** E Susx
13 L1 **Bibury** Gloucs
14 D2 **Bicester** Oxon
5 H6 **Bickleigh** Devon
11 G4 **Biddenden** Kent
12 E6 **Biddisham** Somset
28 F4 **Biddulph** Staffs
4 D5 **Bideford** Devon
22 C5 **Bidford-on-Avon** Warwks
3 M6 **Bigbury-on-Sea** Devon
46 B6 **Biggar** S Lans
10 C3 **Biggin Hill** Gt Lon
23 M5 **Biggleswade** C Beds
17 H3 **Bildeston** Suffk
16 E7 **Billericay** Essex
31 G6 **Billingborough** Lincs
38 E2 **Billingham** S on T
31 H4 **Billinghay** Lincs
9 K3 **Billingshurst** W Susx
31 K3 **Bilsby** Lincs
30 C4 **Bilsthorpe** Notts
35 H7 **Binbrook** Lincs
14 F6 **Binfield** Br For
30 D5 **Bingham** Notts
33 K3 **Bingley** C Brad
22 A8 **Birdlip** Gloucs
32 C7 **Birkenhead** Wirral
22 B2 **Birmingham** Birm
30 C8 **Birstall** Leics
43 K6 **Birtley** Gatesd
38 C1 **Bishop Auckland** Dur
21 G2 **Bishop's Castle** Shrops
22 A7 **Bishop's Cleeve** Gloucs
21 K5 **Bishop's Frome** Herefs
12 C7 **Bishops Lydeard** Somset
16 D5 **Bishop's Stortford** Herts
6 C4 **Bishopsteignton** Devon
19 J7 **Bishopston** Swans
13 M3 **Bishopstone** Swindn
13 G5 **Bishop Sutton** BaNES
8 F4 **Bishop's Waltham** Hants
30 F6 **Bitchfield** Lincs
13 G4 **Bitton** S Glos
22 F1 **Blaby** Leics
28 E6 **Blackbrook** Staffs
32 F4 **Blackburn** Bl w D
50 E6 **Blackford** P & K
19 M7 **Blackmill** Brdgnd
32 C3 **Blackpool** Bpool
4 D6 **Black Torrington** Devon
8 F6 **Blackwater** IoW
44 C5 **Blackwaterfoot** N Ayrs
12 C2 **Blackwood** Caerph
45 L4 **Blackwood** S Lans
14 C3 **Bladon** Oxon
26 F5 **Blaenau Ffestiniog** Gwynd
12 D1 **Blaenavon** Torfn
19 L6 **Blaengarw** Brdgnd
18 F2 **Blaenporth** Cerdgn
12 F5 **Blagdon** N Som
54 C7 **Blair Atholl** P & K
51 G3 **Blairgowrie** P & K
49 K5 **Blairmore** Ag & B
13 G1 **Blakeney** Gloucs
23 G5 **Blakesley** Nhants
43 G6 **Blanchland** Nthumb
7 L2 **Blandford Forum** Dorset
50 B8 **Blanefield** Stirlg
34 D6 **Blaxton** Donc
43 J5 **Blaydon** Gatesd
12 F6 **Bleadney** Somset
12 E5 **Bleadon** N Som
11 J3 **Blean** Kent
20 F4 **Bleddfa** Powys
10 B3 **Bletchingley** Surrey
23 J6 **Bletchley** M Keyn
23 K4 **Bletsoe** Bed
14 C5 **Blewbury** Oxon
25 J3 **Blickling** Norfk
30 C4 **Blidworth** Notts
10 C4 **Blindley Heath** Surrey

3 G4 **Blisland** Cnwll
22 E6 **Bloxham** Oxon
38 B7 **Blubberhouses** N York
5 J3 **Blue Anchor** Somset
43 K4 **Blyth** Nthumb
34 E7 **Blyton** Lincs
54 D3 **Boat of Garten** Highld
61 H5 **Boddam** Abers
27 J3 **Bodfari** Denbgs
26 C6 **Bodfuan** Gwynd
10 F5 **Bodiam** E Susx
3 G4 **Bodmin** Cnwll
9 J6 **Bognor Regis** W Susx
29 G3 **Bollington** Ches E
10 B6 **Bolney** W Susx
29 L3 **Bolsover** Derbys
32 F6 **Bolton** Bolton
33 J2 **Bolton Abbey** N York
37 H6 **Bolton le Sands** Lancs
3 H3 **Bolventor** Cnwll
64 C8 **Bonar Bridge** Highld
42 D1 **Bonchester Bridge** Border
46 A2 **Bo'ness** Falk
46 D4 **Bonnyrigg** Mdloth
26 D4 **Bontnewydd** Gwynd
12 B4 **Bonvilston** V Glam
36 E3 **Boot** Cumb
36 E4 **Bootle** Cumb
32 C7 **Bootle** Sefton
6 b1 **Bordeaux** Guern
10 E6 **Boreham Street** E Susx
15 J4 **Borehamwood** Herts
38 D6 **Boroughbridge** N York
10 E3 **Borough Green** Kent
29 L6 **Borrowash** Derbys
20 A2 **Borth** Cerdgn
26 E6 **Borth-y-Gest** Gwynd
3 G2 **Boscastle** Cnwll
9 H5 **Bosham** W Susx
18 D6 **Bosherston** Pembks
31 J5 **Boston** Lincs
34 B3 **Boston Spa** Leeds
25 H7 **Botesdale** Suffk
41 M7 **Bothel** Cumb
30 E6 **Bottesford** Leics
10 D4 **Bough Beech** Kent
11 H3 **Boughton Street** Kent
47 M7 **Boulmer** Nthumb
31 G7 **Bourne** Lincs
8 B6 **Bournemouth** Bmouth
21 K2 **Bourton** Shrops
22 C7 **Bourton-on-the-Water** Gloucs
6 B4 **Bovey Tracey** Devon
37 M3 **Bowes** Dur
48 C7 **Bowmore** Ag & B
41 M5 **Bowness-on-Solway** Cumb
13 J4 **Box** Wilts
17 H4 **Boxford** Suffk
23 J4 **Bozeat** Nhants
56 D5 **Bracadale** Highld
23 G6 **Brackley** Nhants
14 F6 **Bracknell** Br For
33 K4 **Bradford** C Brad
13 J5 **Bradford-on-Avon** Wilts
8 F6 **Brading** IoW
29 J2 **Bradwell** Derbys
17 H6 **Bradwell-on-Sea** Essex
4 C6 **Bradworthy** Devon
61 b4 **Brae** Shet
54 E8 **Braemar** Abers
65 d2 **Bragar** W Isls
45 L3 **Braidwood** S Lans
29 J5 **Brailsford** Derbys
16 F5 **Braintree** Essex
36 F2 **Braithwaite** Cumb
8 F3 **Bramdean** Hants
25 K7 **Bramfield** Suffk
34 B3 **Bramham** Leeds
33 L3 **Bramhope** Leeds
14 D7 **Bramley** Hants
9 K2 **Bramley** Surrey
23 M3 **Brampton** Cambs
42 D5 **Brampton** Cumb
8 D4 **Bramshaw** Hants
25 J6 **Brancaster** Norfk
35 H3 **Brandesburton** E R Yk
43 J7 **Brandon** Dur
24 E6 **Brandon** Suffk
22 E3 **Brandon** Warwks
6 E3 **Branscombe** Devon
8 C6 **Bransgore** Hants
30 F3 **Branston** Lincs

36 D2 **Branthwaite** Cumb
29 J4 **Brassington** Derbys
10 D3 **Brasted** Kent
13 J6 **Bratton** Wilts
3 K2 **Bratton Clovelly** Devon
4 F4 **Bratton Fleming** Devon
16 C5 **Braughing** Herts
4 E4 **Braunton** Devon
4 F4 **Brayford** Devon
62 g3 **Breasc"te** W Isls
62 g3 **Breasclete** W Isls
19 H4 **Brechfa** Carmth
55 J7 **Brechin** Angus
20 E7 **Brecon** Powys
11 G6 **Brede** E Susx
21 K5 **Bredenbury** Herefs
10 F3 **Bredhurst** Kent
22 A6 **Bredon** Worcs
21 G6 **Bredwardine** Herefs
5 G3 **Brendon** Devon
12 E6 **Brent Knoll** Somset
16 E7 **Brentwood** Essex
11 H5 **Brenzett** Kent
28 E4 **Brereton Green** Ches E
28 F8 **Brewood** Staffs
36 c1 **Bride** IoM
3 L2 **Bridestowe** Devon
11 J3 **Bridge** Kent
48 C6 **Bridgend** Ag & B
19 L7 **Bridgend** Brdgnd
50 D6 **Bridge of Allan** Stirlg
51 G2 **Bridge of Cally** P & K
51 G5 **Bridge of Earn** P & K
53 K6 **Bridge of Orchy** Ag & B
49 M6 **Bridge of Weir** Rens
21 L2 **Bridgnorth** Shrops
12 D7 **Bridgwater** Somset
39 L6 **Bridlington** E R Yk
7 H3 **Bridport** Dorset
33 H3 **Brierfield** Lancs
35 G6 **Brigg** N Linc
41 L8 **Brigham** Cumb
33 K4 **Brighouse** Calder
8 E7 **Brighstone** IoW
17 J5 **Brightlingsea** Essex
10 B7 **Brighton** Br & H
23 K2 **Brigstock** Nhants
22 E3 **Brinklow** Warwks
13 K3 **Brinkworth** Wilts
65 c3 **Brinyan** Ork
13 G4 **Bristol** Bristl
6 C6 **Brixham** Torbay
3 L5 **Brixton** Devon
23 H3 **Brixworth** Nhants
13 L3 **Broad Blunsdon** Swindn
13 K8 **Broad Chalke** Wilts
6 D3 **Broadclyst** Devon
56 F6 **Broadford** Highld
18 C5 **Broad Haven** Pembks
11 L2 **Broadstairs** Kent
22 C6 **Broadway** Worcs
7 G2 **Broadwindsor** Dorset
25 J7 **Brockdish** Norfk
8 D5 **Brockenhurst** Hants
17 J1 **Brockford Street** Suffk
21 M8 **Brockworth** Gloucs
44 D4 **Brodick** N Ayrs
25 H7 **Brome** Suffk
21 J3 **Bromfield** Shrops
23 K5 **Bromham** Beds
10 C2 **Bromley** Gt Lon
39 J5 **Brompton-by-Sawdon** N York
5 H4 **Brompton Regis** Somset
22 A3 **Bromsgrove** Worcs
21 K5 **Bromyard** Herefs
20 F6 **Bronllys** Powys
25 K6 **Brooke** Norfk
11 H5 **Brookland** Kent
15 J4 **Brookmans Park** Herts
43 K2 **Broomhill** Nthumb
64 F7 **Brora** Highld
21 K1 **Broseley** Shrops
34 B4 **Brotherton** N York
39 G2 **Brotton** R & Cl
37 K2 **Brough** Cumb
46 B6 **Broughton** Border
34 F6 **Broughton** N Linc
36 F5 **Broughton-in-Furness** Cumb

13 M2 **Broughton Poggs** Oxon
29 H8 **Brownhills** Wsall
46 B3 **Broxburn** W Loth
16 D5 **Broxted** Essex
25 K5 **Brundall** Norfk
13 G7 **Bruton** Somset
19 K5 **Brynamman** Carmth
20 A1 **Bryncrug** Gwynd
12 C1 **Brynmawr** Blae G
34 D3 **Bubwith** E R Yk
50 B7 **Buchlyvie** Stirlg
23 M4 **Buckden** Cambs
37 M5 **Buckden** N York
6 B5 **Buckfastleigh** Devon
51 H6 **Buckhaven** Fife
13 H8 **Buckhorn Weston** Dorset
60 B3 **Buckie** Moray
23 G6 **Buckingham** Bucks
16 C4 **Buckland** Herts
8 E5 **Bucklers Hard** Hants
27 L4 **Buckley** Flints
28 E2 **Bucklow Hill** Ches E
30 E7 **Buckminster** Leics
4 B6 **Bude** Cnwll
6 D4 **Budleigh Salterton** Devon
2 F5 **Bugle** Cnwll
20 E5 **Builth Wells** Powys
8 C2 **Bulford** Wilts
22 E2 **Bulkington** Warwks
16 E8 **Bulphan** Thurr
23 K2 **Bulwick** Nhants
48 C2 **Bunessan** Ag & B
25 K6 **Bungay** Suffk
30 C6 **Bunny** Notts
16 C4 **Buntingford** Herts
25 H6 **Bunwell** Norfk
13 M5 **Burbage** Wilts
17 G4 **Bures** Essex
13 M1 **Burford** Oxon
10 B6 **Burgess Hill** W Susx
42 B6 **Burgh by Sands** Cumb
25 L5 **Burgh Castle** Norfk
59 J3 **Burghead** Moray
14 D6 **Burghfield** W Berk
31 K4 **Burgh le Marsh** Lincs
8 C5 **Burley** Hants
28 D5 **Burleydam** Ches E
33 K3 **Burley in Wharfedale** C Brad
28 C7 **Burlton** Shrops
38 C5 **Burneston** N York
24 F2 **Burnham Market** Norfk
17 H7 **Burnham-on-Crouch** Essex
12 D6 **Burnham-on-Sea** Somset
24 F2 **Burnham Overy Staithe** Norfk
33 G4 **Burnley** Lancs
43 J6 **Burnopfield** Dur
46 C2 **Burntisland** Fife
61 d3 **Burravoe** Shet
51 G3 **Burrelton** P & K
4 F5 **Burrington** Devon
19 H6 **Burry Port** Carmth
32 D5 **Burscough Bridge** Lancs
8 E5 **Bursledon** Hants
27 L3 **Burton** Ches W
39 K6 **Burton Agnes** E R Yk
7 H3 **Burton Bradstock** Dorset
39 K6 **Burton Fleming** E R Yk
37 H5 **Burton-in-Kendal** Cumb
30 C5 **Burton Joyce** Notts
23 J3 **Burton Latimer** Nhants
34 F5 **Burton upon Stather** N Linc
29 J7 **Burton upon Trent** Staffs
10 E5 **Burwash** E Susx
16 E1 **Burwell** Cambs
65 c6 **Burwick** Ork
33 G5 **Bury** Bury
17 G2 **Bury St Edmunds** Suffk
15 H4 **Bushey** Herts
17 L3 **Butley** Suffk
36 E2 **Buttermere** Cumb
31 J5 **Butterwick** Lincs
27 K8 **Buttington** Powys
10 D6 **Buxted** E Susx

29 H3 **Buxton** Derbys
20 F7 **Bwlch** Powys
15 H7 **Byfleet** Surrey
27 H4 **Bylchau** Conwy
42 F2 **Byrness** Nthumb

C

2 D8 **Cadgwith** Cnwll
12 E3 **Caerleon** Newpt
26 D4 **Caernarfon** Gwynd
12 C3 **Caerphilly** Caerph
20 E2 **Caersws** Powys
12 F3 **Caerwent** Mons
27 J3 **Caerwys** Flints
49 K3 **Cairndow** Ag & B
40 B5 **Cairnryan** D & G
25 L5 **Caister-on-Sea** Norfk
35 H6 **Caistor** Lincs
42 B7 **Caldbeck** Cumb
23 J2 **Caldecott** Rutlnd
36 D3 **Calder Bridge** Cumb
45 L2 **Caldercruix** N Lans
12 F3 **Caldicot** Mons
65 d2 **Calfsound** Ork
52 B5 **Calgary** Ag & B
50 B6 **Callander** Stirlg
3 J4 **Callington** Cnwll
13 K4 **Calne** Wilts
8 E5 **Calshot** Hants
54 C7 **Calvine** P & K
11 H6 **Camber** E Susx
14 F7 **Camberley** Surrey
43 H4 **Cambo** Nthumb
2 C6 **Camborne** Cnwll
16 B2 **Cambourne** Cambs
16 C2 **Cambridge** Cambs
13 H2 **Cambridge** Gloucs
45 K2 **Cambuslang** S Lans
15 K5 **Camden Town** Gt Lon
3 G3 **Camelford** Cnwll
44 B5 **Campbeltown** Ag & B
31 K3 **Candlesby** Lincs
58 C6 **Cannich** Highld
12 D7 **Cannington** Somset
29 G8 **Cannock** Staffs
42 C4 **Canonbie** D & G
11 J3 **Canterbury** Kent
16 F8 **Canvey Island** Essex
48 b2 **Caoles** Ag & B
9 L2 **Capel** Surrey
20 B3 **Capel Bangor** Cerdgn
26 F4 **Capel Curig** Conwy
17 J4 **Capel St Mary** Suffk
50 F3 **Caputh** P & K
56 D6 **Carbost** Highld
12 C4 **Cardiff** Cardif
18 E2 **Cardigan** Cerdgn
23 L5 **Cardington** Bed
49 L5 **Cardross** Ag & B
18 D6 **Carew** Pembks
46 F4 **Carfraemill** Border
5 J3 **Carhampton** Somset
37 G5 **Cark** Cumb
62 g3 **Carlabhagh** W Isls
42 C6 **Carlisle** Cumb
46 C4 **Carlops** Border
62 g3 **Carloway** W Isls
34 D4 **Carlton** N York
38 A5 **Carlton** N York
30 E4 **Carlton-on-Trent** Notts
45 L3 **Carluke** S Lans
19 G4 **Carmarthen** Carmth
39 K6 **Carnaby** E R Yk
37 H6 **Carnforth** Lancs
20 D2 **Carno** Powys
2 E6 **Carnon Downs** Cnwll
51 K4 **Carnoustie** Angus
46 A5 **Carnwath** S Lans
44 C4 **Carradale** Ag & B
59 H6 **Carrbridge** Highld
7 b1 **Carrefour** Jersey
49 K4 **Carrick Castle** Ag & B
41 J3 **Carronbridge** D & G
41 L5 **Carrutherstown** D & G
40 F3 **Carsphairn** D & G
45 M3 **Carstairs** S Lans
14 A3 **Carterton** Oxon
37 G5 **Cartmel** Cumb
6 a2 **Castel** Guern
37 J5 **Casterton** Cumb
24 F4 **Castle Acre** Norfk
62 b14 **Castlebay** W Isls
42 D6 **Castle Carrock** Cumb
13 G7 **Castle Cary** Somset
29 L6 **Castle Donington** Leics

41 H5 **Castle Douglas** D & G
34 B4 **Castleford** Wakefd
16 F4 **Castle Hedingham** Essex
18 C6 **Castlemartin** Pembks
24 D4 **Castle Rising** Norfk
43 H6 **Castleside** Dur
29 H2 **Castleton** Derbys
39 G3 **Castleton** N York
12 D3 **Castleton** Newpt
65 H2 **Castletown** Highld
36 b4 **Castletown** IoM
10 C3 **Caterham** Surrey
25 K4 **Catfield** Norfk
37 H6 **Caton** Lancs
45 J5 **Catrine** E Ayrs
10 F6 **Catsfield** E Susx
38 C4 **Catterick** N York
30 D4 **Caunton** Notts
59 G4 **Cawdor** Highld
3 K5 **Cawsand** Cnwll
16 B2 **Caxton** Cambs
30 F5 **Caythorpe** Lincs
39 K5 **Cayton** N York
26 C1 **Cemaes** IoA
20 C1 **Cemmaes Road** Powys
51 J5 **Ceres** Fife
7 J2 **Cerne Abbas** Dorset
27 H5 **Cerrigydrudion** Conwy
33 H6 **Chadderton** Oldham
14 B2 **Chadlington** Oxon
6 A3 **Chagford** Devon
8 E7 **Chale** IoW
15 G4 **Chalfont St Giles** Bucks
15 G5 **Chalfont St Peter** Bucks
13 J2 **Chalford** Gloucs
4 F3 **Challacombe** Devon
11 H3 **Challock** Kent
8 E4 **Chandler's Ford** Hants
29 H2 **Chapel-en-le-Frith** Derbys
31 L3 **Chapel St Leonards** Lincs
34 A6 **Chapeltown** Sheff
13 J6 **Chapmanslade** Wilts
6 F2 **Chard** Somset
11 H4 **Charing** Kent
14 B2 **Charlbury** Oxon
22 D5 **Charlecote** Warwks
22 A7 **Charlton Kings** Gloucs
7 L2 **Charlton Marshall** Dorset
10 B4 **Charlwood** Surrey
7 G3 **Charmouth** Dorset
11 J3 **Chartham** Kent
33 G3 **Chatburn** Lancs
10 F2 **Chatham** Medway
24 B7 **Chatteris** Cambs
47 K6 **Chatton** Nthumb
4 F6 **Chawleigh** Devon
9 G3 **Chawton** Hants
29 G5 **Cheadle** Staffs
33 H7 **Cheadle** Stockp
12 F6 **Cheddar** Somset
29 G5 **Cheddleton** Staffs
28 F3 **Chelford** Ches E
16 F6 **Chelmsford** Essex
22 A7 **Cheltenham** Gloucs
12 F3 **Chepstow** Mons
8 F3 **Cheriton** Hants
5 H6 **Cheriton Fitzpaine** Devon
15 G6 **Chertsey** Surrey
15 G4 **Chesham** Bucks
15 K4 **Cheshunt** Herts
28 B3 **Chester** Ches W
29 K3 **Chesterfield** Derbys
43 K6 **Chester-le-Street** Dur
13 G5 **Chew Magna** BaNES
13 G6 **Chewton Mendip** Somset
23 J5 **Chicheley** M Keyn
9 H5 **Chichester** W Susx
7 J4 **Chickerell** Dorset
13 J7 **Chicklade** Wilts
9 J3 **Chiddingfold** Surrey
14 C6 **Chieveley** W Berk
16 C7 **Chigwell** Essex
28 B3 **Childer Thornton** Ches W
11 J3 **Chilham** Kent
13 K7 **Chilmark** Wilts
4 C6 **Chilsworthy** Devon
14 A6 **Chilton Foliat** Wilts
14 E4 **Chinnor** Oxon

16 E1 **Chippenham** Cambs
13 J4 **Chippenham** Wilts
15 G4 **Chipperfield** Herts
32 F3 **Chipping** Lancs
22 C6 **Chipping Campden** Gloucs
22 D7 **Chipping Norton** Oxon
16 D6 **Chipping Ongar** Essex
13 H3 **Chipping Sodbury** S Glos
22 F5 **Chipping Warden** Nhants
21 G1 **Chirbury** Shrops
27 L6 **Chirk** Wrexhm
47 J4 **Chirnside** Border
13 M4 **Chiseldon** Swindn
13 K6 **Chitterne** Wilts
4 F5 **Chittlehamholt** Devon
15 G7 **Chobham** Surrey
8 C2 **Cholderton** Wilts
32 E5 **Chorley** Lancs
15 G4 **Chorleywood** Herts
8 C6 **Christchurch** Dorset
6 C4 **Chudleigh** Devon
6 C4 **Chudleigh Knighton** Devon
4 F6 **Chulmleigh** Devon
14 A2 **Churchill** Oxon
21 G2 **Churchstoke** Powys
21 H2 **Church Stretton** Shrops
6 C6 **Churston Ferrers** Torbay
9 H3 **Churt** Surrey
21 K8 **Cinderford** Gloucs
13 K2 **Cirencester** Gloucs
44 B3 **Clachan** Ag & B
56 E5 **Clachan** Highld
50 E7 **Clackmannan** Clacks
17 J5 **Clacton-on-Sea** Essex
14 A4 **Clanfield** Oxon
44 C3 **Claonaig** Ag & B
23 K5 **Clapham** Bed
37 K6 **Clapham** N York
16 F3 **Clare** Suffk
60 C6 **Clatt** Abers
22 C4 **Claverdon** Warwks
16 D4 **Clavering** Essex
4 C7 **Clawton** Devon
29 K4 **Clay Cross** Derbys
17 J3 **Claydon** Suffk
36 D2 **Cleator Moor** Cumb
35 J6 **Cleethorpes** NE Lin
12 F5 **Cleeve** N Som
22 B7 **Cleeve Hill** Gloucs
21 K3 **Cleobury Mortimer** Shrops
21 K2 **Cleobury North** Shrops
12 E4 **Clevedon** N Som
32 C3 **Cleveleys** Lancs
25 G2 **Cley next the Sea** Norfk
10 F2 **Cliffe** Medway
34 D4 **Cliffe** N York
10 F2 **Cliffe Woods** Medway
37 H2 **Clifton** Cumb
21 L4 **Clifton upon Teme** Worcs
9 K5 **Climping** W Susx
33 G3 **Clitheroe** Lancs
61 G5 **Clola** Abers
23 L6 **Clophill** C Beds
7 H2 **Closworth** Somset
39 J4 **Cloughton** N York
55 G6 **Clova** Angus
4 C5 **Clovelly** Devon
46 E6 **Clovenfords** Border
30 B3 **Clowne** Derbys
21 L3 **Clows Top** Worcs
21 J6 **Clun** Shrops
19 J6 **Clydach** Swans
45 J2 **Clydebank** W Duns
49 K5 **Clynder** Ag & B
26 D5 **Clynnog-fawr** Gwynd
20 F6 **Clyro** Powys
6 D3 **Clyst St Mary** Devon
21 K1 **Coalport** Wrekin
29 J2 **Coalville** Leics
45 K2 **Coatbridge** N Lans
12 B4 **Cobham** Kent
47 H3 **Cockburnspath** Border
41 L8 **Cockermouth** Cumb
9 K5 **Cocking** W Susx
17 J2 **Coddenham** Suffk
22 F3 **Codford St Mary** Wilts
15 J3 **Codicote** Herts
29 L5 **Codnor** Derbys

21 M1 **Codsall** Staffs
27 L5 **Coedpoeth** Wrexhm
17 G5 **Coggeshall** Essex
17 H5 **Colchester** Essex
14 C6 **Cold Ash** W Berk
23 G3 **Cold Ashby** Nhants
13 H4 **Cold Ashton** S Glos
47 J3 **Coldingham** Border
17 G7 **Cold Norton** Essex
47 H5 **Coldstream** Border
13 G1 **Coleford** Gloucs
13 J4 **Colerne** Wilts
22 C2 **Coleshill** Warwks
49 J6 **Colintraive** Ag & B
15 K2 **Collier's End** Herts
61 G6 **Collieston** Abers
13 M6 **Collingbourne Ducis** Wilts
34 B3 **Collingham** Leeds
40 C3 **Colmonell** S Ayrs
33 H3 **Colne** Lancs
17 G4 **Colne Engaine** Essex
13 L2 **Coln St Aldwyns** Gloucs
60 D6 **Colpy** Abers
30 F7 **Colsterworth** Lincs
25 J4 **Coltishall** Norfk
43 G4 **Colwell** Nthumb
27 G2 **Colwyn Bay** Conwy
6 F3 **Colyford** Devon
6 F3 **Colyton** Devon
4 E3 **Combe Martin** Devon
9 J2 **Compton** Surrey
14 C5 **Compton** W Berk
50 D5 **Comrie** P & K
28 F4 **Congleton** Ches E
12 E5 **Congresbury** N Som
31 H4 **Coningsby** Lincs
23 M2 **Conington** Cambs
34 C6 **Conisbrough** Donc
36 F4 **Coniston** Cumb
27 L3 **Connah's Quay** Flints
52 F7 **Connel** Ag & B
58 E4 **Conon Bridge** Highld
43 H6 **Consett** Dur
2 D7 **Constantine** Cnwll
58 D4 **Contin** Highld
27 G3 **Conwy** Conwy
14 F5 **Cookham** W & M
9 L4 **Coolham** W Susx
21 M7 **Coombe Bissett** Wilts
17 G5 **Copdock** Suffk
17 G5 **Copford Green** Essex
38 B2 **Copley** Dur
6 C3 **Copplestone** Devon
10 B4 **Copthorne** W Susx
7 a2 **Corbiere** Jersey
43 G5 **Corbridge** Nthumb
23 J2 **Corby** Nhants
30 F7 **Corby Glen** Lincs
6 F1 **Corfe** Somset
7 M4 **Corfe Castle** Dorset
55 G4 **Corgarff** Abers
47 H5 **Cornhill-on-Tweed** Nthumb
3 L5 **Cornwood** Devon
53 H3 **Corpach** Highld
44 D4 **Corrie** N Ayrs
26 F3 **Corris** Gwynd
13 J4 **Corsham** Wilts
13 J3 **Corston** Wilts
25 M6 **Corton** Suffk
7 G3 **Corwen** Denbgs
16 F8 **Coryton** Thurr
12 F2 **Cosby** Leics
28 D4 **Cotebrook** Ches W
38 A2 **Cotherstone** Dur
16 C1 **Cottenham** Cambs
16 B4 **Cottered** Herts
35 G4 **Cottingham** E R Yk
49 K5 **Coulport** Ag & B
46 B6 **Coulter** S Lans
23 G2 **Countesthorpe** Leics
51 G3 **Coupar Angus** P & K
62 D8 **Cove** Highld
22 E3 **Coventry** Covtry
2 D8 **Coverack** Cnwll
31 H7 **Cowbit** Lincs
12 B4 **Cowbridge** V Glam
10 D4 **Cowden** Kent
51 G7 **Cowdenbeath** Fife
8 E6 **Cowes** IoW
9 L4 **Cowfold** W Susx
33 J3 **Cowling** N York
10 F3 **Coxheath** Kent
38 E5 **Coxwold** N York
45 H6 **Coylton** S Ayrs
54 D3 **Coylumbridge** Highld

4 B7 **Crackington Haven** Cnwll
37 M7 **Cracoe** N York
3 J5 **Crafthole** Cnwll
59 L5 **Craigellachie** Moray
48 D6 **Craighouse** Ag & B
52 E6 **Craignure** Ag & B
51 J5 **Craigrothie** Fife
51 L6 **Crail** Fife
47 G7 **Crailing** Border
43 K4 **Cramlington** Nthumb
8 B4 **Cranborne** Dorset
10 F5 **Cranbrook** Kent
23 K6 **Cranfield** C Beds
21 M8 **Cranham** Gloucs
9 K2 **Cranleigh** Surrey
47 G4 **Cranshaws** Border
49 H4 **Crarae** Ag & B
47 M7 **Craster** Nthumb
54 F5 **Crathie** Abers
38 E3 **Crathorne** N York
21 H3 **Craven Arms** Shrops
46 A7 **Crawford** S Lans
45 M5 **Crawfordjohn** S Lans
10 B5 **Crawley** W Susx
10 B4 **Crawley Down** W Susx
62 C10 **Creag Ghoraidh** W Isls
62 C10 **Creagorry** W Isls
21 H6 **Credenhill** Herefs
5 G7 **Crediton** Devon
40 F6 **Creetown** D & G
36 a4 **Cregneash** IoM
21 K1 **Cressage** Shrops
28 E4 **Crewe** Ches E
7 G2 **Crewkerne** Somset
53 K7 **Crianlarich** Stirlg
26 D6 **Criccieth** Gwynd
20 F7 **Crickhowell** Powys
13 L3 **Cricklade** Wilts
50 D5 **Crieff** P & K
61 H4 **Crimond** Abers
49 G4 **Crinan** Ag & B
25 J5 **Cringleford** Norfk
6 B3 **Crockernwell** Devon
41 J4 **Crocketford** D & G
42 D6 **Croglin** Cumb
59 G3 **Cromarty** Highld
59 J6 **Cromdale** Highld
25 J2 **Cromer** Norfk
29 K4 **Cromford** Derbys
30 E4 **Cromwell** Notts
43 J7 **Crook** Dur
37 H5 **Crooklands** Cumb
22 F5 **Cropredy** Oxon
39 G4 **Cropton** N York
36 b3 **Crosby** IoM
32 C6 **Crosby** Sefton
46 B2 **Crossford** Fife
45 L3 **Crossford** S Lans
19 H5 **Cross Hands** Carmth
45 G6 **Crosshill** S Ayrs
10 D6 **Cross in Hand** E Susx
12 D3 **Crosskeys** Caerph
41 H5 **Crossmichael** D & G
21 M4 **Crossway Green** Worcs
37 G4 **Crosthwaite** Cumb
10 D5 **Crowborough** E Susx
5 K4 **Crowcombe** Somset
10 F6 **Crowhurst** E Susx
31 H8 **Crowland** Lincs
34 E5 **Crowle** N Linc
14 F7 **Crowthorne** Wokham
30 E6 **Croxton Kerrial** Leics
60 C4 **Croy** Highld
4 D4 **Croyde** Devon
15 K7 **Croydon** Gt Lon
61 H5 **Cruden Bay** Abers
28 D7 **Crudgington** Wrekin
13 K3 **Crudwell** Wilts
19 K5 **Crynant** Neath
10 B5 **Cuckfield** W Susx
30 C3 **Cuckney** Notts
28 D3 **Cuddington** Ches W
34 B6 **Cudworth** Barns
15 K4 **Cuffley** Herts
37 J1 **Culgaith** Cumb
60 C3 **Cullen** Moray
5 J6 **Cullompton** Devon
5 K6 **Culmstock** Devon
45 L1 **Cumbernauld** N Lans
60 E4 **Cuminestown** Abers
41 L5 **Cummertrees** D & G
45 J5 **Cumnock** E Ayrs
14 C4 **Cumnor** Oxon
42 D6 **Cumrew** Cumb
51 J5 **Cupar** Fife

12 E8 **Curry Rivel** Somset
12 D2 **Cwmbran** Torfn
20 C3 **Cwmystwyth** Cerdgn
19 L6 **Cymer** Neath
19 G4 **Cynwyl Elfed** Carmth

D

40 D2 **Dailly** S Ayrs
51 J5 **Dairsie** Fife
41 J5 **Dalbeattie** D & G
36 a3 **Dalby** IoM
18 B5 **Dale** Pembks
46 C2 **Dalgety Bay** Fife
64 E3 **Dalhalvaig** Highld
46 D3 **Dalkeith** Mdloth
59 J4 **Dallas** Moray
53 J7 **Dalmally** Ag & B
45 H7 **Dalmellington** E Ayrs
45 G3 **Dalry** N Ayrs
45 G6 **Dalrymple** E Ayrs
42 B6 **Dalston** Cumb
41 L4 **Dalton** D & G
36 F6 **Dalton-in-Furness** Cumb
54 A5 **Dalwhinnie** Highld
8 B4 **Damerham** Hants
16 F6 **Danbury** Essex
38 C2 **Darlington** Darltn
43 J5 **Darras Hall** Nthumb
34 B5 **Darrington** Wakefd
10 D2 **Dartford** Kent
6 B5 **Dartington** Devon
6 C6 **Dartmouth** Devon
45 J4 **Darvel** E Ayrs
32 F5 **Darwen** Bl w D
15 G6 **Datchet** W & M
59 H5 **Dava** Highld
28 D3 **Davenham** Ches W
23 G4 **Daventry** Nhants
58 F5 **Daviot** Highld
6 C4 **Dawlish** Devon
11 L3 **Deal** Kent
41 L7 **Dearham** Cumb
17 J2 **Debenham** Suffk
22 F6 **Deddington** Oxon
17 H4 **Dedham** Essex
31 H8 **Deeping St James**
31 H7 **Deeping St Nicholas** Lincs
27 G2 **Deganwy** Conwy
3 G3 **Delabole** Cnwll
27 J3 **Denbigh** Denbgs
33 L6 **Denby Dale** Kirk
15 G5 **Denham** Bucks
46 F7 **Denholm** Border
9 G5 **Denmead** Hants
17 K1 **Dennington** Suffk
50 D8 **Denny** Falk
11 K4 **Densole** Kent
37 K5 **Dent** Cumb
33 H7 **Denton** Tamesd
29 K6 **Derby** C Derb
36 b4 **Derbyhaven** IoM
25 G4 **Dereham** Norfk
24 E3 **Dersingham** Norfk
52 B5 **Dervaig** Ag & B
23 H3 **Desborough** Nhants
22 F1 **Desford** Leics
20 B3 **Devil's Bridge** Cerdgn
13 K5 **Devizes** Wilts
33 L5 **Dewsbury** Kirk
9 L4 **Dial Post** W Susx
14 C5 **Didcot** Oxon
13 J3 **Didmarton** Gloucs
31 G4 **Digby** Lincs
21 H5 **Dilwyn** Herefs
27 G7 **Dinas-Mawddwy** Gwynd
58 E4 **Dingwall** Highld
30 B2 **Dinnington** Rothm
44 C4 **Dippen** Ag & B
29 L7 **Diseworth** Leics
38 D6 **Dishforth** N York
29 G2 **Disley** Ches E
25 H7 **Diss** Norfk
10 B6 **Ditchling** E Susx
6 C6 **Dittisham** Devon
21 K2 **Ditton Priors** Shrops
3 H4 **Dobwalls** Cnwll
24 E3 **Docking** Norfk
24 B6 **Doddington** Cambs
11 G3 **Doddington** Kent
47 K6 **Doddington** Nthumb
33 L6 **Dodworth** Barns
26 F7 **Dolgellau** Gwynd

50 E6 **Dollar** Clacks
46 B5 **Dolphinton** S Lans
4 E6 **Dolton** Devon
26 F5 **Dolwyddelan** Conwy
34 C6 **Doncaster** Donc
31 H6 **Donington** Lincs
7 K3 **Dorchester** Dorset
14 D4 **Dorchester** Oxon
22 D1 **Dordon** Warwks
58 E5 **Dores** Highld
9 L2 **Dorking** Surrey
57 H6 **Dornie** Highld
59 G1 **Dornoch** Highld
21 J1 **Dorrington** Shrops
21 G6 **Dorstone** Herefs
36 c3 **Douglas** IoM
45 L5 **Douglas** S Lans
65 b3 **Dounby** Ork
50 C6 **Doune** Stirlg
3 L4 **Dousland** Devon
11 L4 **Dover** Kent
29 H6 **Doveridge** Derbys
50 E3 **Dowally** P & K
3 J5 **Downderry** Cnwll
24 D5 **Downham Market** Norfk
8 C4 **Downton** Wilts
22 A5 **Drakes Broughton** Worcs
12 F6 **Draycott** Somset
25 J4 **Drayton** Norfk
14 C4 **Drayton** Oxon
39 J7 **Driffield** E R Yk
52 C5 **Drimnin** Highld
22 A4 **Droitwich** Worcs
29 K3 **Dronfield** Derbys
8 F4 **Droxford** Hants
63 G4 **Drumbeg** Highld
40 C7 **Drummore** D & G
58 D6 **Drumnadrochit** Highld
50 A7 **Drymen** Stirlg
56 D6 **Drynoch** Highld
23 K1 **Duddington** Nhants
22 A2 **Dudley** Dudley
29 K5 **Duffield** Derbys
59 L5 **Dufftown** Moray
59 K3 **Duffus** Moray
59 H6 **Dulnain Bridge** Highld
5 H4 **Dulverton** Somset
49 M5 **Dumbarton** W Duns
41 K4 **Dumfries** D & G
47 G2 **Dunbar** E Loth
65 H5 **Dunbeath** Highld
50 D6 **Dunblane** Stirlg
22 F3 **Dunchurch** Warwks
51 J4 **Dundee** C Dund
45 G4 **Dundonald** S Ayrs
57 K1 **Dundonnell** Highld
41 H6 **Dundrennan** D & G
46 B2 **Dunfermline** Fife
50 F3 **Dunkeld** P & K
45 H3 **Dunlop** E Ayrs
65 H2 **Dunnet** Highld
50 F5 **Dunning** P & K
49 K5 **Dunoon** Ag & B
40 C6 **Dunragit** D & G
47 H4 **Duns** Border
41 J4 **Dunscore** D & G
9 K3 **Dunsfold** Surrey
6 B3 **Dunsford** Devon
32 F2 **Dunsop Bridge** Lancs
15 G2 **Dunstable** C Beds
5 J3 **Dunster** Somset
7 K2 **Duntish** Dorset
44 F6 **Dunure** S Ayrs
19 J6 **Dunvant** Swans
56 C4 **Dunvegan** Highld
25 L8 **Dunwich** Suffk
43 K7 **Durham** Dur
63 J2 **Durness** Highld
53 G5 **Duror** Highld
13 J2 **Durrington** Wilts
55 L5 **Durris** Abers
13 H2 **Dursley** Gloucs
16 D3 **Duxford** Cambs
55 M3 **Dyce** C Aber
26 E7 **Dyffryn Ardudwy** Gwynd
11 J5 **Dymchurch** Kent
21 K7 **Dymock** Gloucs

E

42 A4 **Eaglesfield** D & G
43 J3 **Eaglesham** E Rens
15 J5 **Ealing** Gt Lon
33 H3 **Earby** Lancs

21 G5 **Eardisley** Herefs
24 B7 **Earith** Cambs
14 E6 **Earley** Wokham
23 J4 **Earls Barton** Nhants
17 G4 **Earls Colne** Essex
46 F6 **Earlston** Border
25 K6 **Earsham** Norfk
48 F7 **Easdale** Ag & B
9 J4 **Easebourne** W Susx
43 L7 **Easington** Dur
35 K5 **Easington** E R Yk
38 E6 **Easingwold** N York
39 J5 **East Ayton** N York
31 H2 **East Barkwith** Lincs
17 J4 **East Bergholt** Suffk
10 E7 **Eastbourne** E Susx
7 H1 **East Chinnock** Somset
11 H2 **Eastchurch** Kent
8 E6 **East Cowes** IoW
10 D8 **East Dean** E Susx
9 J4 **East Dean** W Susx
30 C7 **East Goscote** Leics
10 C4 **East Grinstead** W Susx
25 G6 **East Harling** Norfk
10 D6 **East Hoathly** E Susx
15 H8 **East Horsley** Surrey
14 C5 **East Ilsley** W Berk
45 J3 **East Kilbride** S Lans
13 J7 **East Knoyle** Wilts
9 H5 **East Lavant** W Susx
8 E4 **Eastleigh** Hants
46 F3 **East Linton** E Loth
7 L4 **East Lulworth** Dorset
17 K2 **Easton** Suffk
6 B7 **East Prawle** Devon
9 K5 **East Preston** W Susx
42 A5 **Eastriggs** D & G
24 F3 **East Rudham** Norfk
11 L3 **Eastry** Kent
46 E3 **East Saltoun** E Loth
30 D5 **East Stoke** Notts
9 H6 **East Wittering** W Susx
38 B5 **East Witton** N York
29 L5 **Eastwood** Notts
23 L4 **Eaton Socon** Cambs
12 C1 **Ebbw Vale** Blae G
43 H6 **Ebchester** Dur
41 M4 **Ecclefechan** D & G
47 H5 **Eccles** Border
22 C3 **Eccleshall** Staffs
55 K4 **Echt** Abers
29 L2 **Eckington** Derbys
22 A6 **Eckington** Worcs
58 F2 **Edderton** Highld
46 C5 **Eddleston** Border
10 C4 **Edenbridge** Kent
56 D4 **Edinbane** Highld
46 C3 **Edinburgh** C Edin
31 H3 **Edlington** Lincs
43 H6 **Edmundbyers** Dur
47 G6 **Ednam** Border
30 C3 **Edwinstowe** Notts
55 J7 **Edzell** Angus
15 H7 **Effingham** Surrey
4 F6 **Eggesford** Devon
37 M2 **Eggleston** Dur
15 G6 **Egham** Surrey
47 K7 **Eglingham** Nthumb
18 E3 **Eglwyswrw** Pembks
36 D3 **Egremont** Cumb
39 H3 **Egton Bridge** N York
20 D4 **Elan Village** Powys
59 K3 **Elgin** Moray
56 E7 **Elgol** Highld
11 J4 **Elham** Kent
51 K6 **Elie** Fife
30 D3 **Elkesley** Notts
13 K1 **Elkstone** Gloucs
33 K5 **Elland** Calder
28 B6 **Ellesmere** Shrops
28 B3 **Ellesmere Port** Ches W
25 K6 **Ellingham** Norfk
61 G6 **Ellon** Abers
34 F4 **Elloughton** E R Yk
17 H5 **Elmstead Market** Essex
43 G3 **Elsdon** Nthumb
46 B5 **Elsrickle** S Lans
9 J2 **Elstead** Surrey
15 J4 **Elstree** Herts
37 G3 **Elterwater** Cumb
16 B2 **Eltisley** Cambs
16 B2 **Elton** Cambs
24 F7 **Elveden** Suffk
14 E7 **Elvetham Heath** Hants
34 D3 **Elvington** C York
5 J4 **Elworthy** Somset
24 C7 **Ely** Cambs

47 M7	Embleton	Nthumb
64 E8	Embo	Highld
30 F8	Empingham	Rutlnd
9 H5	Emsworth	Hants
22 F1	Enderby	Leics
15 K4	Enfield	Gt Lon
36 D2	Ennerdale Bridge	Cumb
14 B2	Enstone	Oxon
16 C6	Epping	Essex
15 J7	Epsom	Surrey
34 E6	Epworth	N Linc
58 E6	Errogie	Highld
51 H4	Errol	P & K
20 E6	Erwood	Powys
15 H7	Esher	Surrey
36 E4	Eskdale Green	Cumb
42 A3	Eskdalemuir	D & G
31 G8	Essendine	Rutlnd
15 J3	Essendon	Herts
38 E2	Eston	R & Cl
47 J6	Etal	Nthumb
10 F5	Etchingham	E Susx
15 G6	Eton	W & M
22 D5	Ettington	Warwks
46 D7	Ettrick	Border
46 E7	Ettrickbridge	Border
58 E3	Evanton	Highld
13 G7	Evercreech	Somset
14 E7	Eversley	Hants
22 B6	Evesham	Worcs
13 K2	Ewen	Gloucs
9 K2	Ewhurst	Surrey
21 H7	Ewyas Harold	Herefs
5 H5	Exbridge	Somset
6 C3	Exeter	Devon
5 H4	Exford	Somset
6 C3	Exminster	Devon
6 D4	Exmouth	Devon
23 M1	Eye	C Pete
25 H7	Eye	Suffk
47 J4	Eyemouth	Border
10 D2	Eynsford	Kent
14 B3	Eynsham	Oxon

F

33 H6	Failsworth	Oldham
26 E8	Fairbourne	Gwynd
13 L2	Fairford	Gloucs
44 F3	Fairlie	N Ayrs
11 G6	Fairlight	E Susx
24 F3	Fakenham	Norfk
46 E4	Fala	Mdloth
31 G2	Faldingworth	Lincs
13 G3	Falfield	S Glos
50 E8	Falkirk	Falk
51 H6	Falkland	Fife
2 E7	Falmouth	Cnwll
42 E3	Falstone	Nthumb
8 F5	Fareham	Hants
14 A4	Faringdon	Oxon
14 F7	Farnborough	Hants
51 L2	Farnell	Angus
9 H2	Farnham	Surrey
15 G5	Farnham Common	Bucks
10 D2	Farningham	Kent
37 G4	Far Sawrey	Cumb
45 M2	Fauldhouse	W Loth
11 H3	Faversham	Kent
8 E5	Fawley	Hants
22 C1	Fazeley	Staffs
50 C3	Fearnan	P & K
17 K4	Felixstowe	Suffk
16 E5	Felsted	Essex
43 J2	Felton	Nthumb
24 E6	Feltwell	Norfk
29 J5	Fenny Bentley	Derbys
6 E3	Fenny Bridges	Devon
22 E5	Fenny Compton	Warwks
22 E1	Fenny Drayton	Leics
45 H4	Fenwick	E Ayrs
8 B5	Ferndown	Dorset
21 M4	Fernhill Heath	Worcs
9 J3	Fernhurst	W Susx
29 G3	Fernilee	Derbys
9 K5	Ferring	W Susx
43 K8	Ferryhill	Dur
55 K6	Fettercairn	Abers
26 F5	Ffestiniog	Gwynd
25 L4	Filby	Norfk
39 K5	Filey	N York
24 E5	Fincham	Norfk
16 E4	Finchingfield	Essex
59 J3	Findhorn	Moray
60 C3	Findochty	Moray

9 L5	Findon	W Susx
23 J3	Finedon	Nhants
17 H1	Finningham	Suffk
34 D6	Finningley	Donc
65 b4	Finstown	Ork
50 B7	Fintry	Stirlg
48 C2	Fionnphort	Ag & B
10 D7	Firle	E Susx
8 F6	Fishbourne	IoW
18 C3	Fishguard	Pembks
9 K4	Fittleworth	W Susx
5 K4	Fitzhead	Somset
7 C2	Five Oaks	Jersey
61 c6	Fladdabister	Shet
39 L6	Flamborough	E R Yk
15 H3	Flamstead	Herts
14 F7	Fleet	Hants
32 C3	Fleetwood	Lancs
41 K7	Flimby	Cumb
27 K3	Flint	Flints
23 K6	Flitwick	C Beds
39 K5	Flixton	N York
23 G4	Flore	Nhants
59 L4	Fochabers	Moray
11 K5	Folkestone	Kent
31 G6	Folkingham	Lincs
7 L1	Fontmell Magna	Dorset
9 J5	Fontwell	W Susx
47 J6	Ford	Nthumb
10 D4	Fordcombe	Kent
8 C4	Fordingbridge	Hants
55 K6	Fordoun	Abers
11 J3	Fordwich	Kent
6 a2	Forest	Guern
10 C5	Forest Row	E Susx
51 J2	Forfar	Angus
32 C6	Formby	Sefton
59 J4	Forres	Moray
58 C7	Fort Augustus	Highld
50 F5	Forteviot	P & K
45 M3	Forth	S Lans
50 C3	Fortingall	P & K
32 E2	Forton	Lancs
58 F4	Fortrose	Highld
7 J4	Fortuneswell	Dorset
53 H4	Fort William	Highld
30 E5	Foston	Lincs
27 L7	Four Crosses	Powys
9 G3	Four Marks	Hants
3 G5	Fowey	Cnwll
21 J6	Fownhope	Herefs
36 b3	Foxdale	IoM
58 D7	Foyers	Highld
17 K2	Framlingham	Suffk
7 J3	Frampton	Dorset
10 E5	Frant	E Susx
61 G3	Fraserburgh	Abers
24 D8	Freckenham	Suffk
32 D4	Freckleton	Lancs
9 H2	Frensham	Surrey
8 D6	Freshwater	IoW
25 J7	Fressingfield	Suffk
65 J2	Freswick	Highld
39 H7	Fridaythorpe	E R Yk
14 B4	Frilford	Oxon
17 K5	Frinton-on-Sea	Essex
51 K2	Friockheim	Angus
25 L5	Fritton	Norfk
36 D2	Frizington	Cumb
13 H2	Frocester	Gloucs
28 C3	Frodsham	Ches W
13 H6	Frome	Somset
14 A6	Froxfield	Wilts
9 H5	Funtington	W Susx
49 J4	Furnace	Ag & B
29 G2	Furness Vale	Derbys
16 D6	Fyfield	Essex
14 B4	Fyfield	Oxon
60 E5	Fyvie	Abers

G

28 F8	Gailey	Staffs
38 B2	Gainford	Dur
34 E7	Gainsborough	Lincs
57 H2	Gairloch	Highld
53 J3	Gairlochy	Highld
46 E6	Galashiels	Border
37 H7	Galgate	Lancs
45 H4	Galston	E Ayrs
16 B3	Gamlingay	Cambs
30 D3	Gamston	Notts
26 F7	Ganllwyd	Gwynd
25 G7	Garboldisham	Norfk
60 E3	Gardenstown	Abers
49 K4	Garelochhead	Ag & B
34 B4	Garforth	Leeds

33 H2	Gargrave	N York
40 F6	Garlieston	D & G
55 L4	Garlogie	Abers
42 E7	Garrigill	Cumb
32 E3	Garstang	Lancs
20 D5	Garth	Powys
46 F3	Garvald	E Loth
58 C3	Garve	Highld
41 G6	Gatehouse of Fleet	D & G
43 K5	Gateshead	Gatesd
22 F5	Gaydon	Warwks
24 B4	Gayton	Norfk
31 K6	Gedney Drove End	Lincs
31 J8	Gedney Hill	Lincs
4 D4	Georgeham	Devon
15 G5	Gerrards Cross	Bucks
46 F3	Gifford	E Loth
37 L6	Giggleswick	N York
13 H8	Gillingham	Dorset
10 F2	Gillingham	Medway
25 L6	Gillingham	Norfk
38 B3	Gilling West	N York
65 J1	Gills	Highld
50 E4	Gilmerton	P & K
42 D4	Gilsland	Nthumb
21 G8	Gilwern	Mons
16 C2	Girton	Cambs
40 C3	Girvan	S Ayrs
33 G2	Gisburn	Lancs
51 J3	Glamis	Angus
47 K7	Glanton	Nthumb
30 B3	Glapwell	Derbys
20 F6	Glasbury	Powys
45 J2	Glasgow	C Glas
23 J1	Glaston	Rutlnd
12 F7	Glastonbury	Somset
17 G3	Glemsford	Suffk
44 A4	Glenbarr	Ag & B
52 D5	Glenborrodale	Highld
41 K5	Glencaple	D & G
53 H5	Glencoe	Highld
49 H5	Glendaruel	Ag & B
50 E6	Glendevon	P & K
50 E5	Gleneagles	P & K
57 H7	Glenelg	Highld
50 D6	Glenfarg	P & K
52 F3	Glenfinnan	Highld
55 H3	Glenkindie	Abers
59 K6	Glenlivet	Moray
40 C6	Glenluce	D & G
36 b3	Glen Maye	IoM
37 G2	Glenridding	Cumb
51 H6	Glenrothes	Fife
35 G7	Glentham	Lincs
33 J7	Glossop	Derbys
21 M7	Gloucester	Gloucs
27 K6	Glyn Ceiriog	Wrexhm
19 L6	Glyncorrwg	Neath
10 C7	Glynde	E Susx
19 L5	Glynneath	Neath
20 C8	Glyntawe	Powys
29 H5	Gnosall	Staffs
39 H3	Goathland	N York
5 H3	Goathurst	Somset
27 L6	Gobowen	Shrops
9 J2	Godalming	Surrey
23 M4	Godmanchester	Cambs
8 F7	Godshill	IoW
10 C3	Godstone	Surrey
20 B3	Goginan	Cerdgn
32 F6	Golborne	Wigan
17 G6	Goldhanger	Essex
64 E7	Golspie	Highld
9 K2	Gomshall	Surrey
34 E4	Goole	E R Yk
28 E3	Goostrey	Ches E
47 G5	Gordon	Border
46 D4	Gorebridge	Mdloth
7 C1	Gorey	Jersey
14 D5	Goring	Oxon
19 J6	Gorseinon	Swans
31 H6	Gosberton	Lincs
36 D3	Gosforth	Cumb
43 J5	Gosforth	N u Ty
8 F5	Gosport	Hants
64 E7	Goudhurst	Kent
49 K5	Gourock	Inver
19 J6	Gowerton	Swans
35 H5	Goxhill	N Linc
11 G2	Grain	Medway
35 K6	Grainthorpe	Lincs
62 d9	Gramsdal	W Isls
62 d9	Gramsdale	W Isls
6 a1	Grandes Rocques	Guern

36 F2	Grange	Cumb
50 E8	Grangemouth	Falk
37 G5	Grange-over-Sands	Cumb
30 F6	Grantham	Lincs
59 J6	Grantown-on-Spey	Highld
47 H4	Grantshouse	Border
37 G3	Grasmere	Cumb
38 A6	Grassington	N York
16 B4	Graveley	Herts
10 E2	Gravesend	Kent
10 E1	Grays	Thurr
38 F3	Great Ayton	N York
13 H3	Great Badminton	S Glos
16 E4	Great Bardfield	Essex
23 L5	Great Barford	Bed
24 E3	Great Bircham	Norfk
17 J3	Great Blakenham	Suffk
30 F8	Great Casterton	Rutlnd
16 D3	Great Chesterford	Essex
30 D7	Great Dalby	Leics
16 E5	Great Dunmow	Essex
8 B3	Great Durnford	Wilts
23 L3	Great Gidding	Cambs
16 B2	Great Gransden	Cambs
9 H3	Greatham	Hants
33 G4	Great Harwood	Lancs
29 G7	Great Haywood	Staffs
25 G6	Great Hockham	Norfk
14 F3	Great Kimble	Bucks
36 F3	Great Langdale	Cumb
21 L5	Great Malvern	Worcs
24 E4	Great Massingham	Norfk
14 F4	Great Missenden	Bucks
30 F6	Great Ponton	Lincs
16 E4	Great Sampford	Essex
28 B3	Great Saughall	Ches W
14 B6	Great Shefford	W Berk
16 C3	Great Shelford	Cambs
38 D3	Great Smeaton	N York
22 E7	Great Tew	Oxon
4 E5	Great Torrington	Devon
17 G8	Great Wakering	Essex
16 E6	Great Waltham	Essex
21 L4	Great Witley	Worcs
25 L5	Great Yarmouth	Norfk
16 F4	Great Yeldham	Essex
27 K3	Greenfield	Flints
38 E7	Green Hammerton	N York
42 E5	Greenhead	Nthumb
38 B6	Greenhow Hill	N York
47 G5	Greenlaw	Border
50 D6	Greenloaning	P & K
49 L5	Greenock	Inver
36 F5	Greenodd	Cumb
30 F7	Greetham	Rutlnd
27 L4	Gresford	Wrexhm
38 B3	Greta Bridge	Dur
42 B5	Gretna	D & G
42 B5	Gretna Green	D & G
42 C5	Greystoke	Cumb
35 J5	Grimsby	NE Lin
31 G7	Grimsthorpe	Lincs
29 J3	Grindleford	Derbys
34 E7	Gringley on the Hill	Notts
30 B8	Groby	Leics
21 H7	Grosmont	Mons
7 c2	Grouville	Jersey
14 B5	Grove	Oxon
51 J5	Guardbridge	Fife
11 G6	Guestling Green	E Susx
9 K2	Guildford	Surrey
38 F2	Guisborough	R & Cl
33 K3	Guiseley	Leeds
25 G4	Guist	Norfk
46 E2	Gullane	E Loth
34 E5	Gunness	N Linc
3 K4	Gunnislake	Cnwll
30 D5	Gunthorpe	Notts
8 E6	Gurnard	IoW
8 A5	Gussage All Saints	Dorset
61 d2	Gutcher	Shet
24 B5	Guyhirn	Cambs
2 D7	Gweek	Cnwll
27 K4	Gwernymynydd	Flints

2 C6 **Gwithian** Cnwll
27 J5 **Gwyddelwern** Denbgs

H

65 b3 **Hackland** Ork
39 J4 **Hackness** N York
15 K5 **Hackney** Gt Lon
14 E3 **Haddenham** Bucks
24 C7 **Haddenham** Cambs
46 F3 **Haddington** E Loth
25 L6 **Haddiscoe** Norfk
17 H3 **Hadleigh** Suffk
10 E4 **Hadlow** Kent
31 J3 **Hagworthingham** Lincs
10 E7 **Hailsham** E Susx
5 J6 **Halberton** Devon
25 K6 **Hales** Norfk
22 A3 **Halesowen** Dudley
25 K7 **Halesworth** Suffk
33 K4 **Halifax** Calder
65 G2 **Halkirk** Highld
16 F4 **Halstead** Essex
10 D3 **Halstead** Kent
42 E5 **Haltwhistle** Nthumb
6 B6 **Halwell** Devon
4 D7 **Halwill Junction** Devon
9 G4 **Hambledon** Hants
8 E5 **Hamble-le-Rice** Hants
32 D3 **Hambleton** Lancs
45 K3 **Hamilton** S Lans
15 J6 **Hammersmith** Gt Lon
14 C6 **Hampstead Norreys** W Berk
38 C7 **Hampsthwaite** N York
14 B7 **Hamstead Marshall** W Berk
11 H5 **Hamstreet** Kent
10 B5 **Handcross** W Susx
28 C4 **Handley** Ches W
28 F5 **Hanley** C Stke
25 K3 **Happisburgh** Norfk
6 B6 **Harbertonford** Devon
13 H1 **Hardwicke** Gloucs
16 C4 **Hare Street** Herts
33 L3 **Harewood** Leeds
21 J7 **Harewood End** Herefs
26 E6 **Harlech** Gwynd
25 J7 **Harleston** Norfk
56 C5 **Harlosh** Highld
16 C6 **Harlow** Essex
2 E4 **Harlyn** Cnwll
61 d1 **Haroldswick** Shet
15 H3 **Harpenden** Herts
33 L2 **Harrogate** N York
23 K5 **Harrold** Bed
15 H5 **Harrow** Gt Lon
16 C3 **Harston** Cambs
43 H3 **Hartburn** Nthumb
17 G3 **Hartest** Suffk
10 D5 **Hartfield** E Susx
29 H4 **Hartington** Derbys
4 C5 **Hartland** Devon
43 M8 **Hartlepool** Hartpl
14 E7 **Hartley Wintney** Hants
21 L7 **Hartpury** Gloucs
22 B5 **Harvington** Worcs
17 K4 **Harwich** Essex
22 D4 **Haseley** Warwks
9 J3 **Haslemere** Surrey
10 F7 **Hastings** E Susx
12 D8 **Hatch Beauchamp** Somset
34 D5 **Hatfield** Donc
15 J3 **Hatfield** Herts
16 D5 **Hatfield Broad Oak** Essex
16 D5 **Hatfield Heath** Essex
16 F6 **Hatfield Peverel** Essex
4 E6 **Hatherleigh** Devon
30 B7 **Hathern** Leics
29 J2 **Hathersage** Derbys
61 H5 **Hatton** Abers
9 G5 **Havant** Hants
8 F6 **Havenstreet** IoW
18 C5 **Haverfordwest** Pembks
16 E3 **Haverhill** Suffk
27 L3 **Hawarden** Flints
37 L4 **Hawes** N York
46 F7 **Hawick** Border
16 F3 **Hawkedon** Suffk
10 F5 **Hawkhurst** Kent
11 K4 **Hawkinge** Kent

37 G4 **Hawkshead** Cumb
38 E4 **Hawnby** N York
33 J3 **Haworth** C Brad
38 F7 **Haxby** C York
34 E6 **Haxey** N Linc
42 F5 **Haydon Bridge** Nthumb
2 C6 **Hayle** Cnwll
21 G6 **Hay-on-Wye** Powys
10 B6 **Haywards Heath** W Susx
28 F2 **Hazel Grove** Stockp
24 D3 **Heacham** Norfk
11 G4 **Headcorn** Kent
29 L5 **Heanor** Derbys
29 L3 **Heath** Derbys
10 E6 **Heathfield** E Susx
29 G8 **Heath Hayes & Wimblebury** Staffs
31 G5 **Heckington** Lincs
8 E4 **Hedge End** Hants
29 G8 **Hednesford** Staffs
35 H4 **Hedon** E R Yk
49 L5 **Helensburgh** Ag & B
37 L7 **Hellifield** N York
17 K2 **Helmingham** Suffk
65 G6 **Helmsdale** Highld
38 F5 **Helmsley** N York
31 G5 **Helpringham** Lincs
28 C3 **Helsby** Ches W
2 C7 **Helston** Cnwll
15 H3 **Hemel Hempstead** Herts
25 J6 **Hempnall** Norfk
25 L4 **Hemsby** Norfk
34 B5 **Hemsworth** Wakefd
5 K6 **Hemyock** Devon
19 J6 **Hendy** Carmth
9 L4 **Henfield** W Susx
16 D4 **Henham** Essex
22 C4 **Henley-in-Arden** Warwks
14 E5 **Henley-on-Thames** Oxon
27 J3 **Henllan** Denbgs
23 L6 **Henlow** C Beds
25 L7 **Henstead** Suffk
7 K1 **Henstridge** Somset
21 J6 **Hereford** Herefs
14 C6 **Hermitage** W Berk
11 J2 **Herne Bay** Kent
11 K3 **Hersden** Kent
10 E6 **Herstmonceux** E Susx
15 K3 **Hertford** Herts
35 G4 **Hessle** E R Yk
27 L2 **Heswall** Wirral
25 H5 **Hethersett** Norfk
37 H5 **Heversham** Cumb
43 G5 **Hexham** Nthumb
3 M4 **Hexworthy** Devon
3 K6 **Heybrook Bay** Devon
37 G7 **Heysham** Lancs
13 J6 **Heytesbury** Wilts
35 G6 **Hibaldstow** N Linc
10 B6 **Hickstead** W Susx
23 K4 **Higham Ferrers** Nhants
4 E6 **Highampton** Devon
37 J6 **High Bentham** N York
12 D6 **Highbridge** Somset
14 B7 **Highclere** Hants
28 D7 **High Ercall** Wrekin
2 b1 **Higher Town** IoS
11 G5 **High Halden** Kent
42 C7 **High Hesket** Cumb
21 L3 **Highley** Shrops
16 E5 **High Roding** Essex
13 M3 **Highworth** Swindn
14 E4 **High Wycombe** Bucks
10 D4 **Hildenborough** Kent
9 H3 **Hill Brow** Hants
59 G2 **Hill of Fearn** Highld
61 b3 **Hillswick** Shet
13 K4 **Hilmarton** Wilts
22 E2 **Hinckley** Leics
39 G2 **Hinderwell** N York
13 J7 **Hindhead** Surrey
13 J7 **Hindon** Wilts
25 G5 **Hingham** Norfk
38 B4 **Hipswell** N York
12 A2 **Hirwaun** Rhondd
16 C2 **Histon** Cambs
17 H3 **Hitcham** Suffk
23 M7 **Hitchin** Herts
17 G7 **Hockley** Essex
23 K7 **Hockliffe** C Beds
15 K3 **Hoddesdon** Herts
28 D6 **Hodnet** Shrops
31 L3 **Hogsthorpe** Lincs
31 L3 **Holbeach** Lincs

3 L5 **Holbeton** Devon
17 J4 **Holbrook** Suffk
8 E5 **Holbury** Hants
24 F2 **Holkham** Norfk
11 G3 **Hollingbourne** Kent
9 L2 **Holmbury St Mary** Surrey
28 E3 **Holmes Chapel** Ches E
34 E3 **Holme upon Spalding Moor** E R Yk
33 K6 **Holmfirth** Kirk
36 D4 **Holmrook** Cumb
6 A5 **Holne** Devon
4 C6 **Holsworthy** Devon
25 H3 **Holt** Norfk
13 J5 **Holt** Wilts
28 B4 **Holt** Wrexhm
21 L4 **Holt Heath** Worcs
35 J6 **Holton le Clay** Lincs
26 B2 **Holyhead** IoA
47 L5 **Holy Island** Nthumb
45 L2 **Holytown** N Lans
7 J2 **Holywell** Dorset
27 K3 **Holywell** Flints
25 J7 **Homersfield** Suffk
25 H5 **Honingham** Norfk
24 F7 **Honington** Suffk
6 E2 **Honiton** Devon
14 E7 **Hook** Hants
13 J5 **Hook Norton** Oxon
10 F2 **Hoo St Werburgh** Medway
29 J2 **Hope** Derbys
6 A7 **Hope** Devon
27 L4 **Hope** Flints
21 J2 **Hope Bowdler** Shrops
59 K3 **Hopeman** Moray
21 J5 **Hope under Dinmore** Herefs
25 M5 **Hopton on Sea** Norfk
10 D6 **Horam** E Susx
10 B4 **Horley** Surrey
37 J6 **Hornby** Lancs
31 H3 **Horncastle** Lincs
9 G4 **Horndean** Hants
4 D5 **Horns Cross** Devon
35 H3 **Hornsea** E R Yk
3 L4 **Horrabridge** Devon
25 L4 **Horsey** Norfk
9 L3 **Horsham** W Susx
43 H5 **Horsley** Nthumb
8 B5 **Horton** Dorset
6 F1 **Horton** Somset
14 D3 **Horton-cum-Studley** Oxon
37 L6 **Horton in Ribblesdale** N York
32 F5 **Horwich** Bolton
30 C7 **Hoton** Leics
43 K6 **Houghton-le-Spring** Sundld
23 G1 **Houghton on the Hill** Leics
15 H6 **Hounslow** Gt Lon
65 b4 **Houton** Ork
10 B7 **Hove** Br & H
38 F5 **Hovingham** N York
34 E4 **Howden** E R Yk
25 J7 **Hoxne** Suffk
32 B7 **Hoylake** Wirral
34 B6 **Hoyland Nether** Barns
30 B5 **Hucknall** Notts
33 K5 **Huddersfield** Kirk
2 a2 **Hugh Town** IoS
35 J6 **Humberston** NE Lin
46 E4 **Humbie** E Loth
47 G5 **Hume** Border
14 B6 **Hungerford** W Berk
39 K5 **Hunmanby** N York
24 D2 **Hunstanton** Norfk
23 M3 **Huntingdon** Cambs
21 L7 **Huntley** Gloucs
60 C5 **Huntly** Abers
8 E4 **Hursley** Hants
8 E2 **Hurstbourne Priors** Hants
14 B7 **Hurstbourne Tarrant** Hants
10 F5 **Hurst Green** E Susx
32 F3 **Hurst Green** Lancs
10 B6 **Hurstpierpoint** W Susx
38 C3 **Hurworth-on-Tees** Darltn
23 G2 **Husbands Bosworth** Leics
23 K6 **Husborne Crawley** C Beds
31 L3 **Huttoft** Lincs
39 G4 **Hutton-le-Hole** N York
33 H7 **Hyde** Tamesd
48 b3 **Hynish** Ag & B

8 E5 **Hythe** Hants
11 J5 **Hythe** Kent

I

29 K8 **Ibstock** Leics
6 C4 **Ideford** Devon
12 F8 **Ilchester** Somset
4 E3 **Ilfracombe** Devon
29 L5 **Ilkeston** Derbys
33 K3 **Ilkley** C Brad
7 G1 **Ilminster** Somset
35 H5 **Immingham** NE Lin
35 H5 **Immingham Dock** NE Lin
63 H5 **Inchnadamph** Highld
16 E7 **Ingatestone** Essex
30 F2 **Ingham** Lincs
37 K6 **Ingleton** N York
31 L3 **Ingoldmells** Lincs
22 B5 **Inkberrow** Worcs
49 K6 **Innellan** Ag & B
46 D6 **Innerleithen** Border
60 D6 **Insch** Abers
54 C4 **Insh** Highld
4 D4 **Instow** Devon
61 G3 **Inverallochy** Abers
64 C7 **Inveran** Highld
49 J3 **Inveraray** Ag & B
57 H2 **Inverarish** Highld
55 L6 **Inverbervie** Abers
53 K2 **Invergarry** Highld
58 F3 **Invergordon** Highld
51 H4 **Invergowrie** P & K
57 J6 **Inverinate** Highld
51 L2 **Inverkeilor** Angus
46 B2 **Inverkeithing** Fife
60 D5 **Inverkeithny** Abers
49 K6 **Inverkip** Inver
58 D7 **Invermoriston** Highld
58 F5 **Inverness** Highld
55 L3 **Inverurie** Abers
6 B5 **Ipplepen** Devon
29 G5 **Ipstones** Staffs
17 J3 **Ipswich** Suffk
23 J4 **Irchester** Nhants
42 A7 **Ireby** Cumb
21 K1 **Ironbridge** Wrekin
23 K3 **Irthlingborough** Nhants
45 G4 **Irvine** N Ayrs
40 F7 **Isle of Whithorn** D & G
57 G7 **Isleornsay** Highld
15 K5 **Islington** Gt Lon
8 F3 **Itchen Abbas** Hants
15 G5 **Iver** Bucks
15 G3 **Ivinghoe** Bucks
3 M5 **Ivybridge** Devon
11 G2 **Iwade** Kent
7 L1 **Iwerne Minster** Dorset
25 G8 **Ixworth** Suffk

J

43 K5 **Jarrow** S Tyne
47 G7 **Jedburgh** Border
6 b2 **Jerbourg** Guern
10 D7 **Jevington** E Susx
65 J1 **John o' Groats** Highld
55 L7 **Johnshaven** Abers
18 C5 **Johnston** Pembks
49 M6 **Johnstone** Rens
36 c1 **Jurby** IoM

K

49 H6 **Kames** Ag & B
35 H5 **Keelby** Lincs
30 B6 **Kegworth** Leics
33 J3 **Keighley** C Brad
65 J2 **Keiss** Highld
60 B4 **Keith** Moray
37 L3 **Keld** N York
30 D4 **Kelham** Notts
47 G6 **Kelso** Border
17 G5 **Kelvedon** Essex
13 K2 **Kemble** Gloucs
55 K3 **Kemnay** Abers
23 K5 **Kempston** Bed
37 H4 **Kendal** Cumb
22 D3 **Kenilworth** Warwks
50 D3 **Kenmore** P & K
49 G6 **Kennacraig** Ag & B

6 C3 Kennford Devon
25 G7 Kenninghall Norfk
53 G5 Kentallen Highld
16 F2 Kentford Suffk
6 C4 Kenton Devon
20 F2 Kerry Powys
25 L6 Kessingland Suffk
36 F2 Keswick Cumb
23 J3 Kettering Nhants
37 M6 Kettlewell N York
23 K1 Ketton Rutlnd
10 B6 Keymer W Susx
13 G4 Keynsham BaNES
23 K3 Keyston Cambs
30 C6 Keyworth Notts
23 G2 Kibworth Harcourt Leics
21 M3 Kidderminster Worcs
14 C3 Kidlington Oxon
28 F4 Kidsgrove Staffs
19 G5 Kidwelly Carmth
42 D3 Kielder Nthumb
48 F6 Kilberry Ag & B
45 G3 Kilbirnie N Ayrs
29 K5 Kilburn Derbys
38 E5 Kilburn N York
44 E3 Kilchattan Ag & B
52 C4 Kilchoan Highld
49 J2 Kilchrenan Ag & B
49 K5 Kilcreggan Ag & B
38 F3 Kildale N York
55 H3 Kildrummy Abers
33 J3 Kildwick N York
49 H5 Kilfinan Ag & B
18 E5 Kilgetty Pembks
39 K6 Kilham E R Yk
44 B5 Kilkenzie Ag & B
4 C6 Kilkhampton Cnwll
50 B7 Killearn Stirlg
54 D7 Killiecrankie P & K
50 B4 Killin Stirlg
49 L6 Kilmacolm Inver
51 J5 Kilmany Fife
45 H4 Kilmarnock E Ayrs
49 G4 Kilmartin Ag & B
45 H4 Kilmaurs E Ayrs
49 G3 Kilmelford Ag & B
58 D5 Kilmorack Highld
49 G2 Kilninver Ag & B
50 C8 Kilsyth N Lans
5 K3 Klive Somset
45 G4 Kilwinning N Ayrs
25 H5 Kimberley Norfk
23 L4 Kimbolton Cambs
64 E5 Kinbrace Highld
50 E7 Kincardine Fife
55 J4 Kincardine O'Neil Abers
54 C4 Kincraig Highld
22 E5 Kineton Warwks
51 K5 Kingsbarns Fife
6 B7 Kingsbridge Devon
22 D2 Kingsbury Warwks
14 C7 Kingsclere Hants
23 K1 King's Cliffe Nhants
11 L4 Kingsdown Kent
9 L3 Kingsfold W Susx
6 C5 Kingskerswell Devon
21 H4 Kingsland Herefs
15 H4 Kings Langley Herts
29 G5 Kingsley Staffs
24 D4 King's Lynn Norfk
6 a2 King's Mills Guern
11 H4 Kingsnorth Kent
8 D3 King's Somborne Hants
7 K2 King's Stag Dorset
13 H2 King's Stanley Gloucs
6 C4 Kingsteignton Devon
21 H6 Kingstone Herefs
59 L3 Kingston on Spey Moray
35 G4 Kingston upon Hull C KuH
15 J6 Kingston upon Thames Gt Lon
6 C6 Kingswear Devon
8 E3 Kings Worthy Hants
21 G5 Kington Herefs
54 B4 Kingussie Highld
63 H3 Kinlochbervie Highld
53 G3 Kinlocheil Highld
57 J3 Kinlochewe Highld
53 J5 Kinlochleven Highld
50 C2 Kinloch Rannoch P & K
59 J3 Kinloss Moray
55 L6 Kinloss Abers
50 F6 Kinross P & K
14 B6 Kintbury W Berk

55 L3 Kintore Abers
50 C7 Kippen Stirlg
39 G5 Kirby Misperton N York
22 F1 Kirby Muxloe Leics
61 c6 Kirkabister Shet
41 K6 Kirkbean D & G
42 A6 Kirkbride Cumb
33 K5 Kirkburton Kirk
32 D6 Kirkby Knows
30 B4 Kirkby in Ashfield Notts
37 J5 Kirkby Lonsdale Cumb
38 C5 Kirkby Malzeard N York
39 G5 Kirkbymoorside N York
37 K3 Kirkby Stephen Cumb
51 H7 Kirkcaldy Fife
40 B5 Kirkcolm D & G
45 K6 Kirkconnel D & G
40 D5 Kirkcowan D & G
41 G6 Kirkcudbright D & G
32 D4 Kirkham Lancs
58 E5 Kirkhill Highld
40 E6 Kirkinner D & G
45 K1 Kirkintilloch E Duns
29 K6 Kirk Langley Derbys
36 b2 Kirk Michael IoM
50 F2 Kirkmichael P & K
45 G6 Kirkmichael S Ayrs
47 J6 Kirknewton Nthumb
42 D7 Kirkoswald Cumb
44 F6 Kirkoswald S Ayrs
42 B5 Kirkpatrick-Fleming D & G
55 L4 Kirkton of Skene Abers
65 c4 Kirkwall IoA
43 H4 Kirkwhelpington Nthumb
51 J2 Kirriemuir Angus
31 J6 Kirton Lincs
34 F6 Kirton in Lindsey N Linc
23 H4 Kislingbury Nhants
38 D7 Knaresborough N York
42 E6 Knarsdale Nthumb
15 J2 Knebworth Herts
21 G3 Knighton Powys
21 L5 Knightwick Worcs
63 H6 Knockan Highld
27 L7 Knockin Shrops
34 C4 Knottingley Wakefd
14 F5 Knowl Hill W & M
28 E3 Knutsford Ches E
57 G6 Kyleakin Highld
57 G6 Kyle of Lochalsh Highld
57 G7 Kylerhea Highld

L

35 H6 Laceby NE Lin
2 E5 Ladock Cnwll
51 H5 Ladybank Fife
54 A5 Laggan Highld
7 a1 La Greve de Lecq Jersey
62 E8 Laide Highld
64 C6 Lairg Highld
24 E7 Lakenheath Suffk
10 E5 Lamberhurst Kent
14 B6 Lambourn W Berk
3 K3 Lamerton Devon
46 A6 Lamington S Lans
44 D5 Lamlash N Ayrs
19 J2 Lampeter Cerdgn
23 H3 Lamport Nhants
45 M4 Lanark S Lans
37 H6 Lancaster Lancs
43 J6 Lanchester Dur
9 L5 Lancing W Susx
6 b1 L'Ancresse Guern
3 J5 Landrake Cnwll
30 E8 Langham Rutlnd
42 B4 Langholm D & G
12 E8 Langport Somset
38 A3 Langthwaite N York
39 J6 Langtoft E R Yk
8 A7 Langton Matravers Dorset
42 D7 Langwathby Cumb
31 G3 Langworth Lincs
3 G4 Lanivet Cnwll

5 G6 Lapford Devon
51 J6 Largoward Fife
44 F2 Largs N Ayrs
45 L3 Larkhall S Lans
8 B2 Larkhill Wilts
39 G4 Lastingham N York
17 G7 Latchingdon Essex
65 H4 Latheron Highld
46 F5 Lauder Border
18 F5 Laugharne Carmth
3 J3 Launceston Cnwll
55 K6 Laurencekirk Abers
41 G5 Laurieston D & G
17 G3 Lavenham Suffk
50 C3 Lawers P & K
36 c3 Laxey IoM
25 K8 Laxfield Suffk
42 D7 Lazonby Cumb
30 F5 Leadenham Lincs
16 E6 Leaden Roding Essex
43 J6 Leadgate Dur
45 M6 Leadhills S Lans
22 D4 Leamington Spa Warwks
15 J7 Leatherhead Surrey
13 M2 Lechlade on Thames Gloucs
21 L6 Ledbury Herefs
4 E3 Lee Devon
21 J1 Leebotwood Shrops
33 L4 Leeds Leeds
29 G4 Leek Staffs
38 C4 Leeming Bar N York
8 F5 Lee-on-the-Solent Hants
31 J2 Legbourne Lincs
23 G1 Leicester C Leic
10 D4 Leigh Kent
32 F6 Leigh Wigan
21 L5 Leigh Sinton Worcs
23 J7 Leighton Buzzard C Beds
21 H3 Leintwardine Herefs
17 M2 Leiston Suffk
2 C6 Lelant Cnwll
40 C3 Lendalfoot S Ayrs
11 G3 Lenham Kent
50 B8 Lennoxtown E Duns
21 J4 Leominster Herefs
6 a2 L'Eree Guern
61 c6 Lerwick Shet
60 D6 Leslie Abers
51 H6 Leslie Fife
45 L4 Lesmahagow S Lans
40 B5 Leswalt D & G
7 a1 L'Etacq Jersey
16 B4 Letchworth Garden City Herts
51 K3 Letham Angus
18 C4 Letterston Pembks
51 J5 Leuchars Fife
35 H3 Leven E R Yk
51 J6 Leven Fife
37 H5 Levens Cumb
10 C7 Leverburgh W Isls
35 B4 Leyburn N York
32 E5 Leyland Lancs
11 H2 Leysdown-on-Sea Kent
59 L3 Lhanbryde Moray
46 A5 Libberton S Lans
29 H8 Lichfield Staffs
16 F2 Lidgate Suffk
3 J3 Lifton Devon
15 G7 Lightwater Surrey
46 F7 Lilliesleaf Border
13 H5 Limpley Stoke Wilts
30 F3 Lincoln Lincs
37 G5 Lindale Cumb
10 C4 Lingfield Surrey
46 A3 Linlithgow W Loth
16 D3 Linton Cambs
10 F4 Linton Kent
9 H3 Liphook Hants
3 H4 Liskeard Cnwll
9 H1 Liss Hants
31 G2 Lissington Lincs
14 C7 Litcham Norfk
14 C7 Litchfield Hants
22 D8 Little Abington Cambs
15 K3 Little Berkhamsted Herts
33 H5 Littleborough Rochdl
26 B2 Little Brickhill M Keyn
30 F7 Little Bytham Lincs
17 J5 Little Clacton Essex
15 G3 Little Gaddesden Herts

9 K5 Littlehampton W Susx
24 D6 Littleport Cambs
21 H2 Little Stretton Shrops
4 E5 Little Torrington Devon
25 G3 Little Walsingham Norfk
32 C7 Liverpool Lpool
46 B3 Livingston W Loth
2 D8 Lizard Cnwll
26 C5 Llanaelhaearn Gwynd
27 K6 Llanarmon Dyffryn Ceiriog Wrexhm
19 H4 Llanarthne Carmth
26 E6 Llanbedr Gwynd
27 K4 Llanbedr-Dyffryn-Clwyd Denbgs
26 C6 Llanbedrog Gwynd
26 E4 Llanberis Gwynd
20 F3 Llanbister Powys
20 D1 Llanbrynmair Powys
19 H5 Llanddarog Carmth
27 H6 Llandderfel Gwynd
27 H3 Llandduias Conwy
19 J4 Llandeilo Carmth
20 E2 Llandinam Powys
18 E4 Llandissilio Pembks
19 K3 Llandovery Carmth
20 B2 Llandre Cerdgn
27 J6 Llandrillo Denbgs
20 E4 Llandrindod Wells Powys
27 L7 Llandrinio Powys
27 J5 Llandudno Conwy
26 D4 Llandwrog Gwynd
19 J5 Llandybie Carmth
19 G3 Llandysul Cerdgn
19 H6 Llanelli Carmth
26 D2 Llanerchymedd IoA
27 J8 Llanerfyl Powys
26 C2 Llanfachraeth IoA
27 J8 Llanfair Caereinion Powys
27 J4 Llanfair Dyffryn Clwyd Denbgs
26 F3 Llanfairfechan Conwy
26 D3 Llanfair P G IoA
27 H3 Llanfair Talhaiarn Conwy
21 G3 Llanfair Waterdine Shrops
20 A3 Llanfarian Cerdgn
27 K7 Llanfyllin Powys
27 H8 Llangadfan Powys
19 K4 Llangadog Carmth
20 D5 Llangammarch Wells Powys
27 K7 Llangedwyn Powys
26 D3 Llangefni IoA
19 L1 Llangeinor Brdgnd
19 G3 Llangeler Carmth
19 G6 Llangennith Swans
27 G3 Llangernyw Conwy
26 E2 Llangoed IoA
27 K5 Llangollen Denbgs
27 J5 Llangors Powys
18 F2 Llangranog Cerdgn
20 F7 Llangurig Powys
27 J7 Llangynidr Powys
27 J7 Llangynog Powys
20 E7 Llanhamlach Powys
12 B3 Llanharan Rhondd
20 D2 Llanidloes Powys
20 B3 Llanilar Cerdgn
26 E3 Llanllechid Gwynd
27 H3 Llannefydd Conwy
27 J7 Llanrhaeadr-ym-Mochnant Powys
19 H6 Llanrhidian Swans
20 A4 Llanrhystud Cerdgn
26 E4 Llanrug Gwynd
27 G4 Llanrwst Conwy
27 G3 Llansanffraid Glan Conwy Conwy
27 H3 Llansannan Conwy
27 H1 Llansantffraid Cerdgn
27 K7 Llansantffraid-ym-Mechain Powys
19 J3 Llansawel Carmth
19 G5 Llansteffan Carmth
21 G7 Llanthony Mons
12 B3 Llantrisant Rhondd
5 J1 Llantwit Major V Glam
27 G5 Llanuwchllyn Gwynd
21 H8 Llanvetherine Mons
21 G7 Llanvihangel Crucorney Mons
27 J7 Llanwddyn Powys
26 D4 Llanwnda Gwynd

19 K3	**Llanwrda** Carmth	
20 D5	**Llanwrtyd Wells** Powys	
19 H2	**Llanybydder** Carmth	
27 L7	**Llanymynech** Powys	
26 D6	**Llanystumdwy** Gwynd	
27 L4	**Llay** Wrexhm	
18 F3	**Llechryd** Cerdgn	
26 E8	**Llwyngwril** Gwynd	
27 K6	**Llwynmawr** Wrexhm	
27 L7	**Llynclys** Shrops	
20 F6	**Llyswen** Powys	
52 E3	**Lochailort** Highld	
52 D6	**Lochaline** Highld	
41 K4	**Locharbriggs** D & G	
53 H7	**Lochawe** Ag & B	
62 c12	**Loch Baghasdail** W Isls	
62 c12	**Lochboisdale** W Isls	
52 D7	**Lochbuie** Ag & B	
57 H5	**Lochcarron** Highld	
52 E7	**Lochdonhead** Ag & B	
50 B4	**Lochearnhead** Stirlg	
49 H4	**Lochgair** Ag & B	
49 G4	**Lochgilphead** Ag & B	
49 K3	**Lochgoilhead** Ag & B	
63 G5	**Lochinver** Highld	
41 L4	**Lochmaben** D & G	
62 d8	**Lochmaddy** W Isls	
62 d8	**Loch nam Madadh** W Isls	
44 D3	**Lochranza** N Ayrs	
45 c2	**Lochwinnoch** Rens	
41 L4	**Lockerbie** D & G	
39 H4	**Lockton** N York	
25 K6	**Loddon** Norfk	
38 B6	**Lofthouse** N York	
39 G2	**Loftus** R & Cl	
15 J5	**London** Gt Lon	
15 J4	**London Colney** Herts	
12 F4	**Long Ashton** N Som	
30 E5	**Long Bennington** Lincs	
23 G4	**Long Buckby** Nhants	
7 J1	**Longburton** Dorset	
22 D6	**Long Compton** Warwks	
14 E3	**Long Crendon** Bucks	
30 B6	**Long Eaton** Derbys	
21 M7	**Longford** Gloucs	
47 G4	**Longformacus** Border	
43 J2	**Longframlington** Nthumb	
8 B6	**Longham** Dorset	
43 J3	**Longhorsley** Nthumb	
47 M7	**Longhoughton** Nthumb	
22 E4	**Long Itchington** Warwks	
22 F3	**Long Lawford** Warwks	
34 C2	**Long Marston** N York	
17 G3	**Long Melford** Suffk	
46 E3	**Longniddry** E Loth	
21 J1	**Longnor** Shrops	
29 H4	**Longnor** Staffs	
37 L7	**Long Preston** N York	
32 F3	**Longridge** Lancs	
45 M2	**Longridge** W Loth	
61 G5	**Longside** Abers	
25 J6	**Long Stratton** Norfk	
31 K7	**Long Sutton** Lincs	
12 F8	**Long Sutton** Somset	
32 D4	**Longton** Lancs	
42 B5	**Longtown** Cumb	
21 J2	**Longville in the Dale** Shrops	
3 H5	**Looe** Cnwll	
59 K3	**Lossiemouth** Moray	
7 C5	**Lostwithiel** Cnwll	
30 B7	**Loughborough** Leics	
31 J2	**Louth** Lincs	
30 D5	**Lowdham** Notts	
57 H4	**Lower Diabaig** Highld	
10 D6	**Lower Dicker** E Susx	
28 E3	**Lower Peover** Ches E	
22 C7	**Lower Swell** Gloucs	
25 M6	**Lowestoft** Suffk	
36 E2	**Loweswater** Cumb	
23 K3	**Lowick** Nhants	
47 K5	**Lowick** Nthumb	
37 M4	**Low Row** N Yk	
23 H2	**Lubenham** Leics	
35 J7	**Luddington** Lincs	
8 D2	**Ludgershall** Wilts	
25 K4	**Ludham** Norfk	
21 J3	**Ludlow** Shrops	
45 H3	**Lugton** E Ayrs	
21 J6	**Lugwardine** Herefs	
55 J4	**Lumphanan** Abers	
55 H3	**Lumsden** Abers	
51 L2	**Lunan** Angus	
37 H5	**Lupton** Cumb	
49 L4	**Luss** Ag & B	
56 C4	**Lusta** Highld	
15 H2	**Luton** Luton	
22 F2	**Lutterworth** Leics	
65 H4	**Lybster** Highld	
21 H2	**Lydbury North** Shrops	
11 H6	**Lydd** Kent	
1 L3	**Lydford** Devon	
12 F7	**Lydford on Fosse** Somset	
21 G2	**Lydham** Shrops	
13 G2	**Lydney** Gloucs	
7 G3	**Lyme Regis** Dorset	
11 J4	**Lyminge** Kent	
8 D6	**Lymington** Hants	
28 E2	**Lymm** Warrtn	
11 J5	**Lympne** Kent	
8 D5	**Lyndhurst** Hants	
13 K4	**Lyneham** Wilts	
65 b5	**Lyness** Ork	
12 E7	**Lyng** Somset	
5 G3	**Lynmouth** Devon	
4 F3	**Lynton** Devon	
21 G5	**Lyonshall** Herefs	
32 C4	**Lytham St Anne's** Lancs	
39 H3	**Lythe** N York	

M

31 K2	**Mablethorpe** Lincs	
28 F3	**Macclesfield** Ches E	
60 E3	**Macduff** Abers	
44 A5	**Machrihanish** Ag & B	
20 C1	**Machynlleth** Powys	
46 E3	**Macmerry** E Loth	
26 F5	**Maentwrog** Gwynd	
12 B2	**Maerdy** Rhondd	
19 L7	**Maesteg** Brdgnd	
32 D6	**Maghull** Sefton	
13 H7	**Maiden Bradley** Wilts	
6 C5	**Maidencombe** Torbay	
14 F5	**Maidenhead** W & M	
7 J3	**Maiden Newton** Dorset	
10 F3	**Maidstone** Kent	
41 K6	**Mainsriddle** D & G	
6 A7	**Malborough** Devon	
17 G6	**Maldon** Essex	
37 L6	**Malham** N York	
52 D2	**Mallaig** Highld	
27 G8	**Mallwyd** Gwynd	
13 J3	**Malmesbury** Wilts	
28 C5	**Malpas** Ches W	
34 C7	**Maltby** Rothm	
39 G6	**Malton** N York	
21 L6	**Malvern Wells** Worcs	
2 D7	**Manaccan** Cnwll	
33 G6	**Manchester** Manch	
24 C6	**Manea** Cambs	
17 J4	**Manningtree** Essex	
18 D6	**Manorbier** Pembks	
30 B4	**Mansfield** Notts	
2 E5	**Marazanvose** Cnwll	
2 B7	**Marazion** Cnwll	
24 B6	**March** Cambs	
28 B5	**Marchwiel** Wrexhm	
10 F4	**Marden** Kent	
31 J4	**Mareham le Fen** Lincs	
16 E6	**Margaretting** Essex	
11 L2	**Margate** Kent	
12 E6	**Mark** Somset	
10 E5	**Mark Cross** E Susx	
22 E1	**Market Bosworth** Leics	
31 G8	**Market Deeping** Lincs	
28 D6	**Market Drayton** Shrops	
23 H2	**Market Harborough** Leics	
13 K6	**Market Lavington** Wilts	
35 H7	**Market Rasen** Lincs	
30 C3	**Market Warsop** Notts	
34 F7	**Market Weighton** E R Yk	
30 B8	**Markfield** Leics	
30 D3	**Markham Moor** Notts	
13 G5	**Marksbury** BaNES	
17 G5	**Marks Tey** Essex	
13 M4	**Marlborough** Wilts	
18 B5	**Marloes** Pembks	
14 F5	**Marlow** Bucks	
7 K1	**Marnhull** Dorset	
13 G1	**Marshfield** S Glos	
14 D2	**Marsh Gibbon** Bucks	
38 F2	**Marske-by-the-Sea** R & Cl	
31 G4	**Martin** Lincs	
7 J3	**Martinstown** Dorset	
17 K3	**Martlesham Heath** Suffk	
7 H1	**Martock** Somset	
22 E4	**Marton** Warwks	
55 K7	**Marykirk** Abers	
41 K7	**Maryport** Cumb	
1 L3	**Mary Tavy** Devon	
55 J5	**Marywell** Abers	
38 C5	**Masham** N York	
10 E4	**Matfield** Kent	
29 K4	**Matlock** Derbys	
14 E7	**Mattingley** Hants	
45 H5	**Mauchline** E Ayrs	
60 F4	**Maud** Abers	
36 d2	**Maughold** IoM	
23 K6	**Maulden** C Beds	
2 E4	**Mawgan Porth** Cnwll	
2 D7	**Mawnan Smith** Cnwll	
45 G6	**Mayble** S Ayrs	
10 E5	**Mayfield** E Susx	
29 H5	**Mayfield** Staffs	
12 F6	**Meare** Somset	
29 K8	**Measham** Leics	
9 G3	**Medstead** Hants	
4 E6	**Meeth** Devon	
27 K8	**Meifod** Powys	
51 H3	**Meigle** P & K	
16 C3	**Melbourn** Cambs	
29 K7	**Melbourne** Derbys	
27 J2	**Meliden** Denbgs	
13 J5	**Melksham** Wilts	
37 J6	**Melling** Lancs	
42 D7	**Melmerby** Cumb	
46 F6	**Melrose** Border	
33 K5	**Meltham** Kirk	
34 F4	**Melton** E R Yk	
25 H3	**Melton Constable** Norfk	
30 D7	**Melton Mowbray** Leics	
57 G2	**Melvaig** Highld	
64 E2	**Melvich** Highld	
61 G3	**Memsie** Abers	
51 J2	**Memus** Angus	
26 E3	**Menai Bridge** IoA	
14 F7	**Mentmore** Bucks	
10 E2	**Meopham** Kent	
13 H7	**Mere** Wilts	
22 D3	**Meriden** Solhll	
12 B2	**Merthyr Tydfil** Myr Td	
4 E6	**Merton** Devon	
34 F6	**Messingham** N Linc	
25 K7	**Metfield** Suffk	
51 J6	**Methil** Fife	
60 F5	**Methlick** Abers	
50 F4	**Methven** P & K	
24 E6	**Methwold** Norfk	
2 F6	**Mevagissey** Cnwll	
34 B6	**Mexborough** Donc	
62 f3	**Miabhig** W Isls	
62 f3	**Miavaig** W Isls	
8 F2	**Micheldever** Hants	
37 M2	**Mickleton** Dur	
22 C6	**Mickleton** Gloucs	
65 c2	**Midbea** Ork	
38 B4	**Middleham** N York	
35 G7	**Middle Rasen** Lincs	
38 E2	**Middlesbrough** Middsb	
22 F6	**Middleton Cheney** Nhants	
37 M2	**Middleton-in-Teesdale** Dur	
9 J5	**Middleton-on-Sea** W Susx	
34 F7	**Middleton on the Wolds** E R Yk	
14 C2	**Middleton Stoney** Oxon	
2 a2	**Middle Town** IoS	
8 D3	**Middle Wallop** Hants	
28 E3	**Middlewich** Ches E	
12 E7	**Middlezoy** Somset	
9 J4	**Midhurst** W Susx	
13 G6	**Midsomer Norton** BaNES	
61 d2	**Mid Yell** Shet	
7 J1	**Milborne Port** Somset	
24 E7	**Mildenhall** Suffk	
47 J6	**Milfield** Nthumb	
18 C5	**Milford Haven** Pembks	
8 D6	**Milford on Sea** Hants	
3 K5	**Millbrook** Cnwll	
7 b3	**Millbrook** Jersey	
36 E5	**Millom** Cumb	
44 F3	**Millport** N Ayrs	
50 F6	**Milnathort** P & K	
45 J1	**Milngavie** E Duns	
7 K2	**Milton Abbas** Dorset	
3 K3	**Milton Abbot** Devon	
4 D6	**Milton Damerel** Devon	
23 K5	**Milton Ernest** Bed	
23 J6	**Milton Keynes** M Keyn	
5 K5	**Milverton** Somset	
13 J2	**Minchinhampton** Gloucs	
5 J3	**Minehead** Somset	
11 H2	**Minster** Kent	
11 L2	**Minster** Kent	
28 B8	**Minsterley** Shrops	
14 A3	**Minster Lovell** Oxon	
61 G4	**Mintlaw** Abers	
33 K5	**Mirfield** Kirk	
34 E7	**Misterton** Notts	
7 H2	**Misterton** Somset	
21 K7	**Mitcheldean** Gloucs	
28 E2	**Mobberley** Ches E	
40 E6	**Mochrum** D & G	
3 M5	**Modbury** Devon	
41 L2	**Moffat** D & G	
27 K4	**Mold** Flints	
41 H3	**Moniaive** D & G	
51 K4	**Monifieth** Angus	
4 D5	**Monkleigh** Devon	
45 G5	**Monkton** S Ayrs	
21 J8	**Monmouth** Mons	
7 H1	**Montacute** Somset	
28 B7	**Montford Bridge** Shrops	
20 F1	**Montgomery** Powys	
51 L2	**Montrose** Angus	
6 a2	**Mont Saint** Guern	
29 H3	**Monyash** Derbys	
55 K3	**Monymusk** Abers	
5 G6	**Morchard Bishop** Devon	
23 J1	**Morcott** Rutlnd	
21 J6	**Mordiford** Herefs	
47 H7	**Morebattle** Border	
37 G6	**Morecambe** Lancs	
7 K3	**Moreton** Dorset	
6 B3	**Moretonhampstead** Devon	
22 C6	**Moreton-in-Marsh** Gloucs	
26 B5	**Morfa Nefyn** Gwynd	
33 L4	**Morley** Leeds	
43 J3	**Morpeth** Nthumb	
25 G2	**Morston** Norfk	
4 D3	**Mortehoe** Devon	
14 D7	**Mortimer** W Berk	
21 K2	**Morville** Shrops	
4 B5	**Morwenstow** Cnwll	
55 H3	**Mossat** Abers	
59 L4	**Mosstodloch** Moray	
7 H2	**Mosterton** Dorset	
27 K2	**Mostyn** Flints	
37 G1	**Motherby** Cumb	
45 K3	**Motherwell** N Lans	
14 D5	**Moulsford** Oxon	
23 H4	**Moulton** Nhants	
12 B2	**Mountain Ash** Rhondd	
30 C7	**Mountsorrel** Leics	
2 B7	**Mousehole** Cnwll	
58 F5	**Moy** Highld	
55 M5	**Muchalls** Abers	
21 J7	**Much Birch** Herefs	
16 C5	**Much Hadham** Herts	
21 K6	**Much Marcle** Herefs	
21 K1	**Much Wenlock** Shrops	
4 E4	**Muddiford** Devon	
51 K3	**Muirdrum** Angus	
51 H4	**Muirhead** Angus	
45 K5	**Muirkirk** E Ayrs	
58 D4	**Muir of Ord** Highld	
57 L4	**Mulben** Moray	
2 D8	**Mullion** Cnwll	
25 K3	**Mundesley** Norfk	
24 E6	**Mundford** Norfk	
42 B8	**Mungrisdale** Cumb	
58 E4	**Munlochy** Highld	
21 J2	**Munslow** Shrops	
46 D3	**Musselburgh** E Loth	
50 D5	**Muthill** P & K	

N

17 K4	**Nacton** Suffk	
12 F4	**Nailsea** N Som	
13 J2	**Nailsworth** Gloucs	
59 G4	**Nairn** Highld	
19 H4	**Nantgaredig** Carmth	

28 D5 **Nantwich** Ches E
18 E5 **Narberth** Pembks
24 E4 **Narborough** Norfk
23 G3 **Naseby** Nhants
30 F4 **Navenby** Lincs
17 H4 **Nayland** Suffk
16 C6 **Nazeing** Essex
19 K6 **Neath** Neath
24 F5 **Necton** Norfk
17 J2 **Needham Market** Suffk
26 C5 **Nefyn** Gwynd
33 H3 **Nelson** Lancs
20 B7 **Nesscliffe** Shrops
27 L3 **Neston** Ches W
12 C7 **Nether Stowey** Somset
36 E3 **Nether Wasdale** Cumb
54 D3 **Nethy Bridge** Highld
14 E5 **Nettlebed** Oxon
18 E3 **Nevern** Pembks
41 K5 **New Abbey** D & G
60 F3 **New Aberdour** Abers
8 F3 **New Alresford** Hants
30 E4 **Newark-on-Trent** Notts
45 L2 **Newarthill** N Lans
37 L1 **Newbiggin** Dur
38 A5 **Newbiggin** N York
43 K3 **Newbiggin-by-the-Sea** Nthumb
46 A5 **Newbigging** S Lans
22 D5 **Newbold on Stour** Warwks
31 J4 **New Bolingbroke** Lincs
26 D4 **Newborough** IoA
12 C2 **Newbridge** Caerph
41 K4 **Newbridge** D & G
20 E4 **Newbridge on Wye** Powys
25 H6 **New Buckenham** Norfk
61 G6 **Newburgh** Abers
51 G5 **Newburgh** Fife
14 C6 **Newbury** W Berk
37 G5 **Newby Bridge** Cumb
18 F3 **Newcastle Emlyn** Carmth
42 C3 **Newcastleton** Border
28 F5 **Newcastle-under-Lyme** Staffs
43 K5 **Newcastle upon Tyne** N u Ty
45 J6 **New Cumnock** S Ayrs
60 F5 **New Deer** Abers
21 L7 **Newent** Gloucs
18 C4 **Newgale** Pembks
41 G4 **New Galloway** D & G
2 a1 **New Grimsby** IoS
10 C7 **Newhaven** E Susx
35 G4 **New Holland** N Linc
10 C6 **Newick** E Susx
40 C5 **New Luce** D & G
2 B7 **Newlyn** Cnwll
45 L3 **Newmains** N Lans
16 E2 **Newmarket** Suffk
60 B4 **Newmill** Moray
8 C6 **New Milton** Hants
13 G1 **Newnham** Gloucs
21 K4 **Newnham** Worcs
60 F4 **New Pitsligo** Abers
16 D4 **Newport** Essex
8 E6 **Newport** IoW
12 D3 **Newport** Newpt
18 D3 **Newport** Pembks
28 E7 **Newport** Wrekin
51 J4 **Newport-on-Tay** Fife
23 J6 **Newport Pagnell** M Keyn
19 G1 **New Quay** Cerdgn
2 E5 **Newquay** Cnwll
20 F4 **New Radnor** Powys
11 H5 **New Romney** Kent
38 B3 **Newsham** N York
6 C5 **Newton Abbot** Devon
38 C2 **Newton Aycliffe** Dur
3 L6 **Newton Ferrers** Devon
62 d8 **Newton Ferry** W Isls
46 D4 **Newtongrange** Mdloth
45 J3 **Newton Mearns** E Rens
54 B4 **Newtonmore** Highld
43 J2 **Newton-on-the-Moor** Nthumb
30 E3 **Newton on Trent** Lincs

6 C3 **Newton St Cyres** Devon
29 J7 **Newton Solney** Derbys
40 E5 **Newton Stewart** D & G
21 K5 **Newtown** Herefs
20 F2 **Newtown** Powys
12 C2 **New Tredegar** Caerph
51 H3 **Newtyle** Angus
18 D5 **Neyland** Pembks
59 G3 **Nigg** Highld
10 C **Ninfield** E Susx
0 F7 **Niton** IoW
31 G4 **Nocton** Lincs
47 J5 **Norham** Nthumb
34 B4 **Normanton** Wakefd
15 G2 **Northall** Bucks
38 D4 **Northallerton** N York
4 D4 **Northam** Devon
23 H4 **Northampton** Nhants
46 F2 **North Berwick** E Loth
34 F4 **North Cave** E R Yk
9 J3 **Northchapel** W Susx
7 K3 **North Chideock** Dorset
35 K6 **North Cotes** Lincs
24 F3 **North Creake** Norfk
12 D8 **North Curry** Somset
34 F2 **North Dalton** E R Yk
25 G4 **North Elmham** Norfk
35 G4 **North Ferriby** E R Yk
35 H2 **North Frodingham** E R Yk
39 H6 **North Grimston** N York
9 G5 **North Hayling** Hants
30 F3 **North Hykeham** Lincs
11 G6 **Northiam** E Susx
58 F4 **North Kessock** Highld
23 G3 **North Kilworth** Leics
31 H4 **North Kyme** Lincs
22 C8 **Northleach** Gloucs
23 J1 **North Luffenham** Rutlnd
5 G4 **North Molton** Devon
30 E4 **North Muskham** Notts
27 K3 **Northop** Flints
12 D7 **North Petherton** Somset
33 L2 **North Rigton** N York
43 K5 **North Shields** N Tyne
35 K6 **North Somercotes** Lincs
25 J3 **North Walsham** Norfk
8 F2 **North Waltham** Hants
16 D6 **North Weald Bassett** Essex
28 D3 **Northwich** Ches W
29 K4 **North Wingfield** Derbys
24 E6 **Northwold** Norfk
39 G6 **Norton** N York
13 H5 **Norton St Philip** Somset
25 J5 **Norwich** Norfk
30 C5 **Nottingham** C Nott
22 E2 **Nuneaton** Warwks
13 H6 **Nunney** Somset
10 C5 **Nutley** E Susx

O

23 G1 **Oadby** Leics
30 E8 **Oakham** Rutlnd
13 G6 **Oakhill** Somset
23 K5 **Oakley** Bed
14 D3 **Oakley** Bucks
8 F2 **Oakley** Hants
13 L5 **Oare** Wilts
52 F7 **Oban** Ag & B
45 H5 **Ochiltree** E Ayrs
29 L6 **Ockbrook** Derbys
9 L2 **Ockley** Surrey
9 G2 **Odiham** Hants
22 B5 **Ogbourne St George** Wilts
13 M4 **Ogbourne St George** Wilts
19 L8 **Ogmore-by-Sea** V Glam
4 E7 **Okehampton** Devon
61 G4 **Old Deer** Abers
2 a1 **Old Grimsby** IoS
33 H6 **Oldham** Oldham
24 A7 **Old Hurst** Cambs
31 K5 **Old Leake** Lincs
60 F6 **Oldmeldrum** Abers
60 D6 **Old Rayne** Abers

13 H3 **Old Sodbury** S Glos
23 H6 **Old Stratford** Nhants
2 b2 **Old Town** IoS
15 G6 **Old Windsor** W & M
61 b3 **Ollaberry** Shet
30 C3 **Ollerton** Notts
23 J5 **Olney** M Keyn
21 M4 **Ombersley** Worcs
36 c3 **Onchan** IoM
53 G5 **Onich** Highld
17 L3 **Orford** Suffk
25 L4 **Ormesby St Margaret** Norfk
32 D6 **Ormskirk** Lancs
10 D2 **Orpington** Gt Lon
10 E1 **Orsett** Thurr
37 J3 **Orton** Cumb
31 G6 **Osbournby** Lincs
7 K4 **Osmington** Dorset
38 E4 **Osmotherley** N York
11 H3 **Ospringe** Kent
33 L5 **Ossett** Wakefd
38 F5 **Oswaldkirk** N York
27 L6 **Oswestry** Shrops
10 D3 **Otford** Kent
12 E7 **Othery** Somset
33 K3 **Otley** Leeds
8 E4 **Otterbourne** Hants
43 G3 **Otterburn** Nthumb
49 H5 **Otter Ferry** Ag & B
15 G7 **Ottershaw** Surrey
6 E4 **Otterton** Devon
6 E3 **Ottery St Mary** Devon
23 K2 **Oundle** Nhants
24 C5 **Outwell** Norfk
29 K7 **Overseal** Derbys
8 F2 **Overton** Hants
28 B5 **Overton** Wrexhm
8 D4 **Ower** Hants
14 C3 **Oxford** Oxon
10 C3 **Oxted** Surrey
30 C5 **Oxton** Notts
19 H7 **Oxwich** Swans

P

23 H7 **Padbury** Bucks
10 E4 **Paddock Wood** Kent
33 G4 **Padiham** Lancs
2 F4 **Padstow** Cnwll
6 C5 **Paignton** Torbay
22 F3 **Pailton** Warwks
13 J1 **Painswick** Gloucs
45 H2 **Paisley** Rens
41 J6 **Palnackie** D & G
21 G7 **Pandy** Mons
14 D6 **Pangbourne** W Berk
33 L2 **Pannal** N York
20 E3 **Pant-y-dwr** Powys
16 B2 **Papworth Everard** Cambs
4 F3 **Parracombe** Devon
38 B6 **Pateley Bridge** N York
45 H6 **Patna** E Ayrs
36 b3 **Patrick** IoM
35 J4 **Patrington** E R Yk
37 G2 **Patterdale** Cumb
23 G5 **Pattishall** Nhants
10 C7 **Peacehaven** E Susx
13 H5 **Peasedown St John** BaNES
11 G6 **Peasmarsh** E Susx
46 C5 **Peebles** Border
36 b3 **Peel** IoM
3 H5 **Pelynt** Cnwll
19 G6 **Pembrey** Carmth
21 H4 **Pembridge** Herefs
18 D6 **Pembroke** Pembks
18 D6 **Pembroke Dock** Pembks
10 E4 **Pembury** Kent
18 E6 **Penally** Pembks
12 C4 **Penarth** V Glam
12 A3 **Pencoed** Brdgnd
21 J7 **Pencraig** Herefs
18 F5 **Pendine** Carmth
21 L6 **Pendock** Worcs
3 G3 **Pendoggett** Cnwll
12 C2 **Pengam** Caerph
46 C4 **Penicuik** Mdloth
33 L6 **Penistone** Barns
27 G5 **Penkridge** Staffs
26 F3 **Penmaenmawr** Conwy
20 B1 **Pennal** Gwynd
60 F3 **Pennan** Abers
41 J3 **Penpont** D & G

26 E6 **Penrhyndeudraeth** Gwynd
42 D8 **Penrith** Cumb
2 E7 **Penryn** Cnwll
13 G5 **Pensford** BaNES
10 D4 **Penshurst** Kent
3 J4 **Pensilva** Cnwll
2 F6 **Pentewan** Cnwll
26 D3 **Pentraeth** IoA
27 G5 **Pentrefoelas** Conwy
20 F4 **Penybont** Powys
27 I7 **Pen-y bont-fawr** Powys
26 D4 **Penygroes** Gwynd
2 B7 **Penzance** Cnwll
2 D5 **Perranporth** Cnwll
22 A5 **Pershore** Worcs
50 F4 **Perth** P & K
23 M1 **Peterborough** C Pete
21 H6 **Peterchurch** Herefs
55 L4 **Peterculter** C Aber
61 H5 **Peterhead** Abers
43 L7 **Peterlee** Dur
9 H4 **Petersfield** Hants
3 J5 **Petton** Devon
9 J4 **Petworth** W Susx
10 E7 **Pevensey** E Susx
13 L5 **Pewsey** Wilts
39 G5 **Pickering** N York
38 C2 **Piercebridge** Darltn
65 C1 **Pierowall** Ork
3 J4 **Pillaton** Cnwll
22 D5 **Pillerton Priors** Warwks
32 D3 **Pilling** Lancs
31 H7 **Pinchbeck** Lincs
40 C3 **Pinwherry** S Ayrs
29 L4 **Pinxton** Derbys
15 G7 **Pirbright** Surrey
60 E6 **Pitcaple** Abers
50 E2 **Pitlochry** P & K
60 F6 **Pitmedden** Abers
51 K6 **Pittenweem** Fife
30 B4 **Pleasley** Derbys
57 H6 **Plockton** Highld
11 G4 **Pluckley** Kent
10 C6 **Plumpton** E Susx
30 C6 **Plumtree** Notts
3 K5 **Plymouth** C Plym
3 L5 **Plympton** C Plym
34 E2 **Pocklington** E R Yk
3 J5 **Polbathic** Cnwll
10 D7 **Polegate** E Susx
50 E8 **Polmont** Falk
3 H5 **Polperro** Cnwll
5 G4 **Polruan** Cnwll
2 F3 **Polzeath** Cnwll
19 K6 **Pontardawe** Neath
19 J6 **Pontarddulais** Swans
34 B5 **Pontefract** Wakefd
43 J4 **Ponteland** Nthumb
20 C3 **Ponterwyd** Cerdgn
28 B8 **Pontesbury** Shrops
12 C2 **Pontllanfraith** Caerph
19 K1 **Pontrhydfendigaid** Cerdgn
21 H7 **Pontrilas** Herefs
19 H5 **Pontyates** Carmth
19 H5 **Pontyberem** Carmth
12 D2 **Pontypool** Torfn
12 B3 **Pontypridd** Rhondd
33 L3 **Pool** Leeds
8 A6 **Poole** Poole
57 H2 **Poolewe** Highld
37 H2 **Pooley Bridge** Cumb
5 H3 **Porlock** Somset
5 H3 **Porlock Weir** Somset
52 F6 **Port Appin** Ag & B
48 D6 **Port Askaig** Ag & B
49 H6 **Portavadie** Ag & B
49 J6 **Port Bannatyne** Ag & B
42 A5 **Port Carlisle** Cumb
48 B7 **Port Charlotte** Ag & B
8 F5 **Portchester** Hants
48 C7 **Port Einon** Swans
48 C8 **Port Ellen** Ag & B
36 a4 **Port Erin** IoM
7 J3 **Portesham** Dorset
49 L5 **Port Glasgow** Inver
60 B3 **Portgordon** Moray
12 B3 **Porth** Rhondd
19 L8 **Porthcawl** Brdgnd
2 E4 **Porthcothan** Cnwll
2 A8 **Porthcurno** Cnwll
57 G3 **Port Henderson** Highld
2 C7 **Porthleven** Cnwll
26 E6 **Porthmadog** Gwynd
2 D6 **Porthtowan** Cnwll

Ref	Place
36 F2	Portinscale Cumb
2 F3	Port Isaac Cnwll
12 F4	Portishead N Som
60 C3	Portknockie Moray
55 M5	Portlethen Abers
2 F6	Portloe Cnwll
40 C7	Port Logan D & G
59 H2	Portmahomack Highld
53 G6	Portnacroish Ag & B
48 A7	Portnahaven Ag & B
62 d8	Port nan Long W Isls
62 i1	Port Nis W Isls
50 B6	Port of Menteith Stirlg
62 i1	Port of Ness W Isls
40 B6	Portpatrick D & G
2 C6	Portreath Cnwll
56 E5	Portree Highld
36 a4	Port St Mary IoM
2 E7	Portscatho Cnwll
64 E2	Portskerra Highld
10 B7	Portslade-by-Sea Br & H
9 G5	Portsmouth C Port
60 D3	Portsoy Abers
19 K7	Port Talbot Neath
40 E7	Port William D & G
3 M3	Postbridge Devon
14 E4	Postcombe Oxon
13 K5	Potterne Wilts
15 J4	Potters Bar Herts
16 B3	Potton C Beds
32 C3	Poulton-le-Fylde Lancs
47 K7	Powburn Nthumb
21 M5	Powick Worcs
28 F2	Poynton Ches E
2 C7	Praa Sands Cnwll
28 C6	Prees Shrops
32 D3	Preesall Lancs
28 C6	Prees Green Shrops
26 E5	Prenteg Gwynd
27 J2	Prestatyn Denbgs
28 F3	Prestbury Ches E
21 G4	Presteigne Powys
47 H4	Preston Border
32 E4	Preston Lancs
8 F2	Preston Candover Hants
22 F5	Preston Capes Nhants
46 E3	Prestonpans E Loth
33 G6	Prestwich Bury
45 G5	Prestwick S Ayrs
12 F6	Priddy Somset
14 F4	Princes Risborough Bucks
22 E3	Princethorpe Warwks
3 L4	Princetown Devon
41 L7	Prospect Cumb
43 H5	Prudhoe Nthumb
13 H4	Pucklechurch S Glos
7 K3	Puddletown Dorset
33 L4	Pudsey Leeds
9 K4	Pulborough W Susx
28 B4	Pulford Ches W
25 J7	Pulham St Mary Norfk
19 J3	Pumsaint Carmth
10 D1	Purfleet Thurr
13 L3	Purton Wilts
19 H6	Pwll Carmth
26 C6	Pwllheli Gwynd
10 B6	Pyecombe W Susx
19 L7	Pyle Brdgnd

Q

21 L2	Quatt Shrops
27 L3	Queensferry Flints
16 D4	Quendon Essex

R

5 H5	Rackenford Devon
25 J4	Rackheath Norfk
30 C6	Radcliffe on Trent Notts
15 H4	Radlett Herts
13 G5	Radstock BaNES
16 E4	Radwinter Essex
12 C4	Radyr Cardif
59 J4	Rafford Moray
12 E1	Raglan Mons
10 D1	Rainham Gt Lon
36 F6	Rampside Cumb
14 A6	Ramsbury Wilts
24 A7	Ramsey Cambs
36 c2	Ramsey IoM
11 L2	Ramsgate Kent
53 L5	Rannoch Station P & K
65 c2	Rapness Ork
61 G3	Rathen Abers
23 K3	Raunds Nhants
36 E4	Ravenglass Cumb
39 J3	Ravenscar N York
37 K3	Ravenstonedale Cumb
34 B7	Rawmarsh Rothm
33 G4	Rawtenstall Lancs
16 F7	Rayleigh Essex
14 E6	Reading Readg
64 F2	Reay Highld
11 K2	Reculver Kent
15 H3	Redbourn Herts
12 F1	Redbrook Gloucs
28 C5	Redbrook Wrexhm
38 F2	Redcar R & Cl
22 B4	Redditch Worcs
25 G7	Redgrave Suffk
12 F5	Redhill N Som
10 B4	Redhill Surrey
30 E6	Redmile Leics
28 B6	Rednal Shrops
18 F5	Red Roses Carmth
43 K2	Red Row Nthumb
2 D6	Redruth Cnwll
26 D2	Red Wharf Bay IoA
25 L5	Reedham Norfk
25 H4	Reepham Norfk
10 B4	Reigate Surrey
39 K5	Reighton N York
30 C7	Rempstone Notts
45 H2	Renfrew Rens
42 D7	Renwick Cumb
29 K6	Repton Derbys
19 L6	Resolven Neath
30 D2	Retford Notts
19 H7	Reynoldston Swans
20 D4	Rhayader Powys
63 H3	Rhiconich Highld
5 J2	Rhoose V Glam
27 L5	Rhoslanerchrugog Wrexhm
26 C3	Rhosneigr IoA
27 G2	Rhôs-on-Sea Conwy
19 G7	Rhossili Swans
49 L5	Rhu Ag & B
27 J3	Rhuddlan Denbgs
26 E4	Rhyd-Ddu Gwynd
19 G2	Rhydowen Cerdgn
27 H2	Rhyl Denbgs
12 C1	Rhymney Caerph
21 J4	Richards Castle Herefs
15 J6	Richmond Gt Lon
38 B3	Richmond N York
15 H4	Rickmansworth Herts
43 H5	Riding Mill Nthumb
43 G4	Ridsdale Nthumb
39 H5	Rillington N York
41 G6	Ringford D & G
10 C6	Ringmer E Susx
8 C5	Ringwood Hants
29 K5	Ripley Derbys
38 C7	Ripley N York
15 H7	Ripley Surrey
38 D6	Ripon N York
21 M6	Ripple Worcs
33 J5	Ripponden Calder
12 D3	Risca Caerph
31 H6	Risegate Lincs
23 K4	Riseley Bed
14 E7	Riseley Wokham
29 L6	Risley Derbys
32 E7	Risley Warrtn
23 H5	Roade Nhants
46 E7	Roberton Border
45 M5	Roberton S Lans
10 F6	Robertsbridge E Susx
18 E5	Robeston Wathen Pembks
39 J3	Robin Hood's Bay N York
29 H6	Rocester Staffs
18 C4	Roch Pembks
33 H5	Rochdale Rochdl
2 F5	Roche Cnwll
10 F2	Rochester Medway
42 F3	Rochester Nthumb
17 G7	Rochford Essex
2 F3	Rock Cnwll
42 B5	Rockcliffe Cumb
41 J6	Rockcliffe D & G
23 J2	Rockingham Nhants
9 H4	Rogate W Susx
12 D3	Rogerstone Newpt
25 L4	Rollesby Norfk
11 G5	Rolvenden Kent
37 M2	Romaldkirk Dur
46 C5	Romanno Bridge Border
16 D7	Romford Gt Lon
8 D4	Romsey Hants
43 G7	Rookhope Dur
9 G3	Ropley Hants
39 G4	Rosedale Abbey N York
63 K7	Rosehall Highld
61 G3	Rosehearty Abers
58 F4	Rosemarkie Highld
46 D4	Rosewell Mdloth
28 B4	Rossett Wrexhm
21 K7	Ross-on-Wye Herefs
46 B2	Rosyth Fife
43 H2	Rothbury Nthumb
10 D5	Rotherfield E Susx
34 B7	Rotherham Rothm
59 L4	Rothes Moray
49 J6	Rothesay Ag & B
33 M4	Rothwell Leeds
23 H3	Rothwell Nhants
10 C7	Rottingdean Br & H
25 J3	Roughton Norfk
9 G5	Rowland's Castle Hants
43 J6	Rowland's Gill Gatesd
29 J3	Rowsley Derbys
47 G6	Roxburgh Border
16 E6	Roxwell Essex
34 A5	Royston Barns
16 C4	Royston Herts
7 c1	Rozel Jersey
27 L5	Ruabon Wrexhm
30 C6	Ruddington Notts
9 K3	Rudgwick W Susx
39 K6	Rudston E R Yk
32 D5	Rufford Lancs
22 F3	Rugby Warwks
29 G7	Rugeley Staffs
50 F6	Rumbling Bridge P & K
28 C2	Runcorn Halton
23 K4	Rushden Nhants
38 C1	Rushyford Dur
31 G5	Ruskington Lincs
9 K5	Rustington W Susx
39 H3	Ruswarp N York
45 J2	Rutherglen S Lans
27 J4	Ruthin Denbgs
28 B7	Ruyton-XI-Towns Shrops
37 G3	Rydal Cumb
8 F6	Ryde IoW
11 G6	Rye E Susx

S

44 B5	Saddell Ag & B
16 D4	Saffron Walden Essex
47 J3	St Abbs Border
2 D5	St Agnes Cnwll
15 H3	St Albans Herts
6 a2	St Andrew Guern
51 K5	St Andrews Fife
12 F2	St Arvans Mons
27 J3	St Asaph Denbgs
5 J1	St Athan V Glam
7 b2	St Aubin Jersey
2 F5	St Austell Cnwll
36 D3	St Bees Cumb
3 G5	St Blazey Cnwll
46 F6	St Boswells Border
7 a2	St Brelade Jersey
7 a3	St Brelade's Bay Jersey
12 F2	St Briavels Gloucs
3 H4	St Cleer Cnwll
7 c2	St Clement Jersey
2 F4	St Columb Major Cnwll
61 H3	St Combs Abers
55 K7	St Cyrus Abers
18 B4	St David's Pembks
2 D6	St Day Cnwll
18 E2	St Dogmaels Pembks
61 H4	St Fergus Abers
50 C4	St Fillans P & K
18 E6	St Florence Pembks
9 G6	St Helens IoW
32 E7	St Helens St Hel
7 b2	St Helier Jersey
24 A8	St Ives Cambs
2 B6	St Ives Cnwll
7 b1	St John Jersey
36 b3	St John's IoM
43 G7	St John's Chapel Dur
41 G4	St John's Town of Dalry D & G
36 c2	St Jude's IoM
2 A7	St Just Cnwll
2 E7	St Just-in-Roseland Cnwll
2 E8	St Keverne Cnwll
3 H5	St Keyne Cnwll
8 F7	St Lawrence IoW
7 b1	St Lawrence Jersey
11 L4	St Margaret's at Cliffe Kent
65 c5	St Margaret's Hope Ork
36 b3	St Marks IoM
6 a2	St Martin Guern
7 c1	St Martin Jersey
7 b1	St Mary Jersey
65 c4	St Mary's Ork
11 J5	St Mary's Bay Kent
2 E7	St Mawes Cnwll
2 E4	St Mawgan Cnwll
51 K6	St Monans Fife
23 M4	St Neots Cambs
17 J5	St Osyth Essex
7 a1	St Ouen Jersey
21 J7	St Owens Cross Herefs
7 b1	St Peter Jersey
6 b2	St Peter Port Guern
6 a2	St Peter's Guern
6 b1	St Sampson Guern
6 a2	St Saviour Guern
7 b2	St Saviour Jersey
2 F5	St Stephen Cnwll
3 G3	St Tudy Cnwll
6 B7	Salcombe Devon
33 G7	Sale Traffd
52 D6	Salen Ag & B
52 E4	Salen Highld
10 B4	Salfords Surrey
50 F7	Saline Fife
8 C3	Salisbury Wilts
3 K5	Saltash Cnwll
38 F2	Saltburn-by-the-Sea R & Cl
44 F4	Saltcoats N Ayrs
35 K7	Saltfleet Lincs
5 K5	Sampford Arundel Somset
5 J3	Sampford Brett Somset
48 B6	Sanaigmore Ag & B
28 E4	Sandbach Ches E
49 K5	Sandbank Ag & B
14 C4	Sandford-on-Thames Oxon
61 G3	Sandhaven Abers
40 C6	Sandhead D & G
14 F7	Sandhurst Br For
61 a5	Sandness Shet
29 G6	Sandon Staffs
8 F7	Sandown IoW
15 J3	Sandridge Herts
39 H3	Sandsend N York
11 L3	Sandwich Kent
61 c7	Sandwick Shet
23 L5	Sandy C Beds
45 L6	Sanquhar D & G
26 B6	Sarn Gwynd
11 K2	Sarre Kent
34 E7	Saundby Notts
18 E5	Saundersfoot Pembks
4 D4	Saunton Devon
16 D5	Sawbridgeworth Herts
16 D3	Sawston Cambs
23 L3	Sawtry Cambs
30 E7	Saxby Leics
30 E3	Saxilby Lincs
17 L2	Saxmundham Suffk
25 H3	Saxthorpe Norfk
48 C4	Scalasaig Ag & B
39 J4	Scalby N York
61 c6	Scalloway Shet
31 J3	Scamblesby Lincs
39 K4	Scarborough N York
48 b2	Scarinish Ag & B
34 F6	Scawby N Linc
25 H7	Scole Norfk
51 G4	Scone P & K
55 H3	Sconser Highld
38 F7	Scotch Corner N York
34 F6	Scotter Lincs
38 B4	Scotton N York

25 G5 **Scoulton** Norfk
63 G4 **Scourie** Highld
65 G2 **Scrabster** Highld
34 F5 **Scunthorpe** N Linc
10 D7 **Seaford** E Susx
43 L6 **Seaham** Dur
47 L6 **Seahouses** Nthumb
10 D3 **Seal** Kent
39 J5 **Seamer** N York
25 L3 **Sea Palling** Norfk
36 D3 **Seascale** Cumb
36 F4 **Seathwaite** Cumb
6 F3 **Seaton** Devon
43 K4 **Seaton Delaval**
       Nthumb
38 F4 **Seave Green** N York
9 G6 **Seaview** IoW
37 J4 **Sedbergh** Cumb
22 B6 **Sedgeberrow** Worcs
30 E4 **Sedgebrook** Lincs
38 D1 **Sedgefield** Dur
10 F6 **Sedlescombe** E Susx
13 K5 **Seend** Wilts
9 G3 **Selborne** Hants
34 D4 **Selby** N York
46 E6 **Selkirk** Border
11 J4 **Sellindge** Kent
9 H6 **Selsey** W Susx
29 L4 **Selston** Notts
15 G7 **Send** Surrey
2 A7 **Sennen** Cnwll
20 D7 **Sennybridge** Powys
24 D4 **Setchey** Norfk
37 L6 **Settle** N York
10 D3 **Sevenoaks** Kent
19 L5 **Seven Sisters** Neath
13 J8 **Shaftesbury** Dorset
16 F4 **Shalford** Essex
9 K2 **Shalford** Surrey
49 K5 **Shandon** Ag & B
8 F7 **Shanklin** IoW
37 H2 **Shap** Cumb
29 L6 **Shardlow** Derbys
23 K4 **Sharnbrook** Bed
13 G2 **Sharpness** Gloucs
3 L4 **Shaugh Prior** Devon
28 E5 **Shavington** Ches E
28 C7 **Shawbury** Shrops
4 D6 **Shebbear** Devon
4 E6 **Sheepwash** Devon
11 G2 **Sheerness** Kent
29 K2 **Sheffield** Sheff
23 L6 **Shefford** C Beds
16 C3 **Shepreth** Cambs
30 B7 **Shepshed** Leics
13 G6 **Shepton Mallet**
       Somset
7 J1 **Sherborne** Dorset
39 J5 **Sherburn** N York
34 C4 **Sherburn in Elmet**
       N York
14 D7 **Sherfield on Loddon**
       Hants
38 F6 **Sheriff Hutton** N York
25 H2 **Sheringham** Norfk
57 J7 **Shiel Bridge** Highld
57 H4 **Shieldaig** Highld
28 E8 **Shifnal** Shrops
38 C2 **Shildon** Dur
14 D4 **Shillingford** Oxon
7 L2 **Shillingstone** Dorset
14 E6 **Shinfield** Wokham
63 K6 **Shinness** Highld
25 G5 **Shipdham** Norfk
14 E6 **Shiplake** Oxon
33 K3 **Shipley** C Brad
22 D6 **Shipston on Stour**
       Warwks
38 E7 **Shipton** N York
34 E3 **Shiptonthorpe** E R Yk
30 B3 **Shirebrook** Derbys
9 L5 **Shoreham-by-Sea**
       W Susx
8 E7 **Shorwell** IoW
17 K4 **Shotley** Suffk
17 L3 **Shottisham** Suffk
45 L2 **Shotts** N Lans
28 C8 **Shrewsbury** Shrops
13 L6 **Shrewton** Wilts
13 M3 **Shrivenham** Oxon
22 A7 **Shurdington** Gloucs
6 F3 **Shute** Devon
31 J5 **Sibsey** Lincs
22 E1 **Sibson** Leics
6 E3 **Sidmouth** Devon
14 D7 **Silchester** Hants
30 C7 **Sileby** Leics
31 G5 **Silk Willoughby** Lincs
41 L6 **Silloth** Cumb
23 L6 **Silsoe** C Beds

37 H5 **Silverdale** Lancs
16 F5 **Silver End** Essex
23 G6 **Silverstone** Nhants
5 H6 **Silverton** Devon
42 F4 **Simonburn** Nthumb
5 G4 **Simonsbath** Somset
9 J4 **Singleton** W Susx
10 F4 **Sissinghurst** Kent
11 G3 **Sittingbourne** Kent
8 A4 **Sixpenny Handley**
       Dorset
31 L4 **Skegness** Lincs
30 F3 **Skellingthorpe** Lincs
32 D6 **Skelmersdale** Lancs
49 K6 **Skelmorlie** N Ayrs
42 C7 **Skelton** Cumb
38 F2 **Skelton** R & Cl
21 H7 **Skenfrith** Mons
64 C2 **Skerray** Highld
44 C3 **Skipness** Ag & B
35 H2 **Skipsea** E R Yk
33 J2 **Skipton** N York
46 B6 **Skirling** Border
42 D8 **Skirwith** Cumb
32 F2 **Slaidburn** Lancs
43 G6 **Slaley** Nthumb
45 L1 **Slamannan** Falk
6 B7 **Slapton** Devon
31 G5 **Sleaford** Lincs
39 J6 **Sledmere** E R Yk
39 H3 **Sleights** N York
39 G5 **Slingsby** N York
15 G5 **Slough** Slough
47 G6 **Smailholm** Border
11 G4 **Smarden** Kent
42 C5 **Smithfield** Cumb
39 J5 **Snainton** N York
17 L2 **Snape** Suffk
24 E3 **Snettisham** Norfk
10 E3 **Snodland** Kent
24 D7 **Soham** Cambs
22 C3 **Solihull** Solhll
18 B4 **Solva** Pembks
24 B7 **Somersham** Cambs
12 F7 **Somerton** Somset
9 L5 **Sompting** W Susx
14 E6 **Sonning** Wokham
14 E5 **Sonning Common**
       Oxon
40 E6 **Sorbie** D & G
37 K3 **Soulby** Cumb
22 F6 **Souldern** Oxon
23 K4 **Souldrop** Bed
3 L2 **Sourton** Devon
22 E4 **Southam** Warwks
8 E5 **Southampton** C Sotn
16 F8 **South Benfleet** Essex
10 D4 **Southborough** Kent
6 A5 **South Brent** Devon
34 F4 **South Cave** E R Yk
34 B5 **South Elmsall** Wakefd
44 B6 **Southend** Ag & B
17 G8 **Southend-on-Sea**
       Sthend
24 D6 **Southery** Norfk
9 H4 **South Harting** W Susx
9 G5 **South Hayling** Hants
9 L2 **South Holmwood**
       Surrey
31 H5 **South Kyme** Lincs
15 J4 **South Mimms** Herts
17 H7 **Southminster** Essex
4 F5 **South Molton** Devon
14 B4 **Southmoor** Oxon
29 L4 **South Normanton**
       Derbys
16 E8 **South Ockendon**
       Thurr
7 G1 **South Petherton**
       Somset
32 C5 **Southport** Sefton
46 B3 **South Queensferry**
       C Edin
24 F4 **South Raynham** Norfk
25 J3 **Southrepps** Norfk
9 G6 **Southsea** C Port
43 L5 **South Shields** S Tyne
38 C6 **South Stainley** N York
25 K4 **South Walsham** Norfk
30 D4 **Southwell** Notts
9 G5 **Southwick** Hants
10 B7 **Southwick** W Susx
30 F7 **South Witham** Lincs
25 L7 **Southwold** Suffk
16 F7 **South Woodham**
       Ferrers** Essex
3 M2 **South Zeal** Devon
38 D5 **Sowerby** N York
33 J4 **Sowerby Bridge**
       Calder

31 H7 **Spalding** Lincs
13 G8 **Sparkford** Somset
8 E3 **Sparsholt** Hants
53 J3 **Spean Bridge** Highld
43 K7 **Spennymoor** Dur
7 L2 **Spetisbury** Dorset
60 B3 **Spey Bay** Moray
31 K3 **Spilsby** Lincs
58 F1 **Spinningdale** Highld
65 H3 **Spittal** Highld
54 E7 **Spittal of Glenshee**
       P & K
25 I4 **Spixworth** Norfk
54 A2 **Spofforth** N York
41 H5 **Springholm** D & G
35 H4 **Sproatley** E R Yk
14 D4 **Stadhampton** Oxon
62 C11 **Stadhlaigearraidh**
       W Isls
56 E3 **Staffin** Highld
28 F7 **Stafford** Staffs
38 B2 **Staindrop** Dur
15 G6 **Staines** Surrey
37 L6 **Stainforth** N York
39 G2 **Staithes** N York
25 K4 **Stalham** Norfk
31 G8 **Stamford** Lincs
39 G7 **Stamford Bridge**
       E R Yk
43 H5 **Stamfordham**
       Nthumb
41 K7 **Standingstone** Cumb
32 E5 **Standish** Wigan
16 C5 **Standon** Herts
14 B4 **Stanford in the Vale**
       Oxon
10 E1 **Stanford le Hope**
       Thurr
43 G7 **Stanhope** Dur
43 J6 **Stanley** Dur
50 F4 **Stanley** P & K
43 J4 **Stannington** Nthumb
16 D5 **Stansted**
       Mountfitchet Essex
25 G7 **Stanton** Suffk
13 J4 **Stanton St Quintin**
       Wilts
22 B6 **Stanway** Gloucs
6 F1 **Staple Fitzpaine**
       Somset
30 B6 **Stapleford** Notts
10 F4 **Staplehurst** Kent
37 M5 **Starbotton** N York
37 H4 **Staveley** Cumb
29 L3 **Staveley** Derbys
22 F4 **Staverton** Nhants
39 J5 **Staxton** N York
17 G6 **Steeple** Essex
22 F7 **Steeple Aston** Oxon
16 E3 **Steeple Bumpstead**
       Essex
50 D8 **Stenhousemuir** Falk
62 h3 **Steornabhagh** W Isls
16 B5 **Stevenage** Herts
44 F4 **Stevenston** N Ayrs
14 C5 **Steventon** Oxon
45 H3 **Stewarton** E Ayrs
23 J7 **Stewkley** Bucks
9 L5 **Steyning** W Susx
4 D5 **Stibb Cross** Devon
31 J4 **Stickford** Lincs
31 J4 **Stickney** Lincs
25 G2 **Stiffkey** Norfk
62 C11 **Stilligarry** W Isls
38 F6 **Stillington** N York
23 L2 **Stilton** Cambs
50 D7 **Stirling** Stirlg
16 E7 **Stock** Essex
8 D3 **Stockbridge** Hants
33 H7 **Stockport** Stockp
33 L6 **Stocksbridge** Sheff
38 E2 **Stockton-on-Tees**
       S on T
12 C6 **Stogursey** Somset
16 F3 **Stoke by Clare** Suffk
17 H4 **Stoke-by-Nayland**
       Suffk
6 C3 **Stoke Canon** Devon
24 E5 **Stoke Ferry** Norfk
6 C6 **Stoke Fleming** Devon
6 C6 **Stoke Gabriel** Devon
23 J5 **Stoke Goldington**
       M Keyn
21 K5 **Stoke Lacy** Herefs
14 F3 **Stoke Mandeville**
       Bucks
14 E4 **Stokenchurch** Bucks
28 F5 **Stoke-on-Trent** C Stke
15 G5 **Stoke Poges** Bucks
38 E3 **Stokesley** N York

28 F6 **Stone** Staffs
55 L5 **Stonehaven** Abers
13 H2 **Stonehouse** Gloucs
45 K3 **Stonehouse** S Lans
40 B6 **Stoneykirk** D & G
14 E5 **Stonor** Oxon
62 h3 **Stornoway** W Isls
9 K4 **Storrington** W Susx
16 A4 **Stotfold** C Beds
22 A5 **Stoulton** Worcs
21 M3 **Stourbridge** Dudley
7 L2 **Stourpaine** Dorset
21 L3 **Stourport-on-Severn**
       Worcs
21 M2 **Stourton** Staffs
46 E5 **Stow** Border
16 D2 **Stow-cum-Quy** Cambs
17 H2 **Stowmarket** Suffk
22 C7 **Stow-on-the-Wold**
       Gloucs
55 K5 **Strachan** Abers
49 J3 **Strachur** Ag & B
16 F3 **Stradishall** Suffk
24 D5 **Stradsett** Norfk
45 G7 **Straiton** S Ayrs
40 B5 **Stranraer** D & G
14 E7 **Stratfield Turgis** Hants
17 L2 **Stratford St Andrew**
       Suffk
22 C5 **Stratford-upon-Avon**
       Warwks
45 K4 **Strathaven** S Lans
50 B8 **Strathblane** Stirlg
55 G3 **Strathdon** Abers
58 D4 **Strathpeffer** Highld
64 D2 **Strathy** Highld
50 B5 **Strathyre** Stirlg
4 B6 **Stratton** Cnwll
13 G6 **Stratton-on-the-**
       Fosse Somset
14 D5 **Streatley** W Berk
12 F7 **Street** Somset
38 F7 **Strensall** C York
6 C6 **Strete** Devon
33 G7 **Stretford** Traffd
24 C7 **Stretham** Cambs
30 F7 **Stretton** Rutlnd
61 G4 **Strichen** Abers
57 H5 **Stromeferry** Highld
65 b4 **Stromness** Ork
49 M3 **Stronachlachar** Stirlg
49 K5 **Strone** Ag & B
52 F5 **Strontian** Highld
10 F2 **Strood** Medway
13 J2 **Stroud** Gloucs
58 C5 **Struy** Highld
61 G5 **Stuartfield** Abers
22 B4 **Studland** Dorset
22 B4 **Studley** Warwks
7 K1 **Sturminster Newton**
       Dorset
11 J3 **Sturry** Kent
30 E2 **Sturton by Stow** Lincs
29 H6 **Sudbury** Derbys
17 G3 **Sudbury** Suffk
36 C2 **Sulby** IoM
2 E5 **Summercourt** Cnwll
15 H6 **Sunbury** Surrey
43 L6 **Sunderland** Sundld
31 H6 **Surfleet** Lincs
31 J6 **Sutterton** Lincs
24 C7 **Sutton** Cambs
10 B2 **Sutton** Gt Lon
13 K4 **Sutton Benger** Wilts
24 C4 **Sutton Bridge** Lincs
22 C2 **Sutton Coldfield** Birm
14 C4 **Sutton Courtenay**
       Oxon
31 L2 **Sutton on Sea** Lincs
38 F6 **Sutton-on-the-Forest**
       N York
30 E3 **Sutton on Trent** Notts
8 E2 **Sutton Scotney** Hants
10 F4 **Sutton Valence** Kent
29 K7 **Swadlincote** Derbys
24 F5 **Swaffham** Norfk
13 H4 **Swainswick** BaNES
22 E6 **Swalcliffe** Oxon
35 H6 **Swallow** Lincs
8 B7 **Swallowfield** Wokham
8 B7 **Swanage** Dorset
10 E2 **Swanley** Kent
19 J6 **Swansea** Swans
29 K4 **Swanwick** Derbys
8 F5 **Swanwick** Hants
5 J4 **Swaton** Lincs
16 C1 **Swavesey** Cambs
8 D6 **Sway** Hants

13 L3 **Swindon** Swindn
23 K4 **Swineshead** Bed
31 H5 **Swineshead** Lincs
22 F3 **Swinford** Leics
47 H5 **Swinton** Border
34 B6 **Swinton** Rothm
24 F3 **Syderstone** Norfk
61 d4 **Symbister** Shet
45 G5 **Symington** S Ayrs
46 A6 **Symington** S Lans
21 J8 **Symonds Yat** Herefs
23 G6 **Syresham** Nhants
30 C8 **Syston** Leics

T

34 B3 **Tadcaster** N York
14 D7 **Tadley** Hants
59 G2 **Tain** Highld
62 f6 **Tairbeart** W Isls
19 G2 **Talgarreg** Cerdgn
20 F6 **Talgarth** Powys
57 J3 **Talladale** Highld
19 J3 **Talley** Carmth
64 C2 **Talmine** Highld
28 E6 **Talsarnau** Gwynd
20 B2 **Tal-y-bont** Cerdgn
26 F3 **Tal-y-Bont** Conwy
26 E7 **Tal-y-bont** Gwynd
27 G3 **Tal-y-Cafn** Conwy
22 C1 **Tamworth** Staffs
51 J2 **Tannadice** Angus
18 F2 **Tan-y-groes** Cerdgn
14 F5 **Taplow** Bucks
49 G6 **Tarbert** Ag & B
62 f6 **Tarbert** W Isls
49 L3 **Tarbet** Ag & B
45 H5 **Tarbolton** S Ayrs
55 H4 **Tarland** Abers
32 D5 **Tarleton** Lancs
28 C4 **Tarporley** Ches W
7 M2 **Tarrant Hinton** Dorset
56 F7 **Tarskavaig** Highld
60 F6 **Tarves** Abers
28 C3 **Tarvin** Ches W
31 H4 **Tattershall** Lincs
12 D8 **Taunton** Somset
25 H4 **Taverham** Norfk
3 K4 **Tavistock** Devon
44 B3 **Tayinloan** Ag & B
22 D8 **Taynton** Oxon
53 G7 **Taynuilt** Ag & B
51 J4 **Tayport** Fife
48 F5 **Tayvallich** Ag & B
37 J3 **Tebay** Cumb
6 B3 **Tedburn St Mary** Devon
22 A6 **Teddington** Gloucs
6 C4 **Teignmouth** Devon
28 E8 **Telford** Wrekin
46 D4 **Temple** Mdloth
19 H2 **Temple Bar** Cerdgn
13 H8 **Templecombe** Somset
37 J1 **Temple Sowerby** Cumb
23 L5 **Tempsford** C Beds
21 K4 **Tenbury Wells** Worcs
18 E6 **Tenby** Pembks
11 G5 **Tenterden** Kent
28 D6 **Ternhill** Shrops
24 C4 **Terrington St Clement** Norfk
13 J3 **Tetbury** Gloucs
31 J3 **Tetford** Lincs
35 J6 **Tetney** Lincs
14 E4 **Tetsworth** Oxon
42 C2 **Teviothead** Border
21 M6 **Tewkesbury** Gloucs
11 H3 **Teynham** Kent
14 E3 **Thame** Oxon
14 C6 **Thatcham** W Berk
16 E4 **Thaxted** Essex
14 D6 **Theale** W Berk
17 M2 **Theberton** Suffk
36 C2 **The Bungalow** IoM
24 F7 **Thetford** Norfk
16 C7 **Theydon Bois** Essex
38 D5 **Thirsk** N York
13 G3 **Thornbury** S Glos
34 D5 **Thorne** Donc
24 A5 **Thorney** C Pete
24 E2 **Thornham** Norfk
41 J3 **Thornhill** D & G
50 C6 **Thornhill** Stirlg
43 L7 **Thornley** Dur
51 H6 **Thornton** Fife
39 H5 **Thornton le Dale** N York

38 D5 **Thornton-le-Street** N York
38 C5 **Thornton Watlass** N York
25 J5 **Thorpe End** Norfk
17 J5 **Thorpe-le-Soken**
17 M2 **Thorpeness** Suffk
17 J5 **Thorrington** Essex
23 K3 **Thrapston** Nhants
20 F6 **Three Cocks** Powys
31 G6 **Threekingham** Lincs
36 F2 **Threlkeld** Cumb
37 M6 **Threshfield** N York
43 H2 **Thropton** Nthumb
65 J4 **Thrumster** Highld
34 C7 **Thurcroft** Rothm
6 A7 **Thurlestone** Devon
34 B6 **Thurnscoe** Barns
42 B6 **Thursby** Cumb
65 G2 **Thurso** Highld
27 K2 **Thurstaston** Wirral
17 G2 **Thurston** Suffk
37 L4 **Thwaite** N York
29 L4 **Tibshelf** Derbys
10 E5 **Ticehurst** E Susx
34 C7 **Tickhill** Donc
29 K7 **Ticknall** Derbys
29 H3 **Tideswell** Derbys
8 C2 **Tidworth** Wilts
62 c8 **Tigh a Ghearraidh** W Isls
62 c8 **Tigharry** W Isls
10 E2 **Tilbury** Thurr
9 J2 **Tilford** Surrey
50 E6 **Tillicoultry** Clacks
13 K6 **Tilshead** Wilts
28 C6 **Tilstock** Shrops
30 D8 **Tilton on the Hill** Leics
3 G3 **Tintagel** Cnwll
12 F2 **Tintern Parva** Mons
17 G5 **Tiptree** Essex
13 K7 **Tisbury** Wilts
29 J5 **Tissington** Derbys
28 F6 **Tittensor** Staffs
5 H6 **Tiverton** Devon
52 C5 **Tobermory** Ag & B
23 K7 **Toddington** C Beds
33 H4 **Todmorden** Calder
61 c3 **Toft** Shet
38 B1 **Toft Hill** Dur
62 i2 **Tolastadh** W Isls
7 M1 **Tollard Royal** Wilts
17 H6 **Tollesbury** Essex
17 G6 **Tolleshunt D'Arcy** Essex
7 K3 **Tolpuddle** Dorset
62 i2 **Tolsta** W Isls
59 G6 **Tomatin** Highld
59 K6 **Tomintoul** Moray
59 K6 **Tomnavoulin** Moray
10 E4 **Tonbridge** Kent
64 C3 **Tongue** Highld
12 B3 **Tonypandy** Rhondd
12 B3 **Tonyrefail** Rhondd
38 D5 **Topcliffe** N York
6 D3 **Topsham** Devon
44 C5 **Torbeg** N Ayrs
6 B7 **Torcross** Devon
58 E4 **Tore** Highld
30 E3 **Torksey** Lincs
46 A3 **Torphichen** W Loth
55 J4 **Torphins** Abers
3 K5 **Torpoint** Cnwll
6 C5 **Torquay** Torbay
45 J1 **Torrance** E Duns
57 H4 **Torridon** Highld
56 F7 **Torrin** Highld
46 B2 **Torryburn** Fife
41 K4 **Torthorwald** D & G
36 F4 **Torver** Cumb
6 D6 **Totland** IoW
6 B5 **Totnes** Devon
3 D4 **Totton** Hants
23 G5 **Towcester** Nhants
43 J7 **Tow Law** Dur
47 H6 **Town Yetholm** Border
46 D6 **Traquair** Border
33 H3 **Trawden** Lancs
26 F6 **Trawsfynydd** Gwynd
26 B2 **Trearddur Bay** IoA
20 D7 **Trecastle** Powys
12 C1 **Tredegar** Blae G
2 A8 **Treen** Cnwll
27 G4 **Trefriw** Conwy
19 J1 **Tregaron** Cerdgn
2 F6 **Tregony** Cnwll
19 M6 **Treherbert** Rhondd
12 F2 **Trellech** Mons
26 E5 **Tremadog** Gwynd

43 L7 **Trimdon** Dur
25 J3 **Trimingham** Norfk
14 F3 **Tring** Herts
7 b1 **Trinity** Jersey
45 G5 **Troon** S Ayrs
9 H4 **Trotton** W Susx
37 G3 **Troutbeck** Cumb
13 J5 **Trowbridge** Wilts
2 E6 **Truro** Cnwll
23 H1 **Tugby** Leics
50 D7 **Tullibody** Clacks
50 D2 **Tummel Bridge** P & K
10 E4 **Tunbridge Wells** Kent
17 L2 **Tunstall** Suffk
44 F7 **Turnberry** S Ayrs
29 K5 **Turnditch** Derbys
10 B5 **Turner's Hill** W Susx
60 E4 **Turriff** Abers
23 K5 **Turvey** Bed
29 J6 **Tutbury** Staffs
30 D3 **Tuxford** Notts
22 E1 **Twycross** Leics
8 E4 **Twyford** Hants
14 E6 **Twyford** Wokham
41 G6 **Twynholm** D & G
53 K7 **Tyndrum** Stirlg
43 L5 **Tynemouth** N Tyne
6 F2 **Tytherleigh** Devon
20 A1 **Tywyn** Gwynd

U

10 D6 **Uckfield** E Susx
5 J6 **Uffculme** Devon
14 A5 **Uffington** Oxon
6 A6 **Ugborough** Devon
56 D3 **Uig** Highld
35 H5 **Ulceby** N Linc
42 A7 **Uldale** Cumb
63 G7 **Ullapool** Highld
22 C4 **Ullenhall** Warwks
36 E4 **Ulpha** Cumb
61 c3 **Ulsta** Shet
36 F5 **Ulverston** Cumb
4 F5 **Umberleigh** Devon
63 H4 **Unapool** Highld
13 L5 **Upavon** Wilts
6 F3 **Uplyme** Devon
6 E2 **Uppottery** Devon
9 L5 **Upper Beeding** W Susx
23 K2 **Upper Benefield** Nhants
30 D7 **Upper Broughton** Notts
51 J6 **Upper Largo** Fife
21 K8 **Upper Lydbrook** Gloucs
29 G5 **Upper Tean** Staffs
23 J1 **Uppingham** Rutlnd
11 K3 **Upstreet** Kent
22 A5 **Upton Snodsbury** Worcs
21 M6 **Upton upon Severn** Worcs
13 K5 **Urchfont** Wilts
12 E2 **Usk** Mons
29 H6 **Uttoxeter** Staffs
15 H5 **Uxbridge** Gt Lon
61 d2 **Uyeasound** Shet

V

6 b1 **Vale** Guern
8 F7 **Ventnor** IoW
8 A7 **Verwood** Dorset
61 c4 **Vidlin** Shet
15 G6 **Virginia Water** Surrey
61 c4 **Voe** Shet

W

14 E3 **Waddesdon** Bucks
33 G3 **Waddington** Lancs
30 F4 **Waddington** Lincs
2 F4 **Wadebridge** Cnwll
15 K3 **Wadesmill** Herts
10 E5 **Wadhurst** E Susx
31 K4 **Wainfleet All Saints** Lincs
33 M5 **Wakefield** Wakefd
25 L7 **Walberswick** Suffk
28 E5 **Walgherton** Ches E
46 D6 **Walkerburn** Border

16 B5 **Walkern** Herts
35 G3 **Walkington** E R Yk
32 C7 **Wallasey** Wirral
14 D5 **Wallingford** Oxon
61 b5 **Walls** Shet
22 B1 **Walsall** Wsall
35 J6 **Waltham** NE Lin
16 C7 **Waltham Abbey** Essex
30 E7 **Waltham on the Wolds** Leics
21 G4 **Walton** Powys
12 F7 **Walton** Somset
15 H6 **Walton-on-Thames** Surrey
17 K5 **Walton on the Naze** Essex
45 L6 **Wanlockhead** D & G
23 L1 **Wansford** C Pete
13 H6 **Wanstrow** Somset
14 B5 **Wantage** Oxon
24 A7 **Warboys** Cambs
37 K2 **Warcop** Cumb
29 J3 **Wardlow** Derbys
15 K3 **Ware** Herts
7 L3 **Wareham** Dorset
47 L6 **Warenford** Nthumb
14 E6 **Wargrave** Wokham
42 F4 **Wark** Nthumb
47 H6 **Wark** Nthumb
43 K2 **Warkworth** Nthumb
22 E5 **Warmingham** Ches W
13 J6 **Warminster** Wilts
9 L5 **Warninglid** W Susx
32 F7 **Warrington** Warrtn
8 E5 **Warsash** Hants
29 H4 **Warslow** Staffs
32 D4 **Warton** Lancs
22 D4 **Warwick** Warwks
65 b2 **Wasbister** Ork
36 E3 **Wasdale Head** Cumb
30 F3 **Washingborough** Lincs
43 K6 **Washington** Sundld
5 J3 **Watchet** Somset
37 H4 **Watchgate** Cumb
16 D2 **Waterbeach** Cambs
42 A4 **Waterbeck** D & G
29 H5 **Waterhouses** Staffs
9 G5 **Waterlooville** Hants
37 G2 **Watermillock** Cumb
15 H4 **Watford** Herts
23 G4 **Watford** Nhants
34 B6 **Wath upon Dearne** Rothm
14 E4 **Watlington** Oxon
65 H3 **Watten** Highld
24 F5 **Watton** Norfk
15 K2 **Watton-at-Stone** Herts
42 F7 **Wearhead** Dur
24 F4 **Weasenham All Saints** Norfk
28 D3 **Weaverham** Ches W
12 E6 **Wedmore** Somset
23 G4 **Weedon** Nhants
4 B7 **Week St Mary** Cnwll
50 D2 **Weem** P & K
30 F4 **Welbourn** Lincs
22 D5 **Wellesbourne** Warwks
23 J4 **Wellingborough** Nhants
5 K5 **Wellington** Somset
28 D8 **Wellington** Wrekin
12 F6 **Wells** Somset
24 F2 **Wells-next-the-sea** Norfk
24 C6 **Welney** Norfk
28 B6 **Welshampton** Shrops
27 K8 **Welshpool** Powys
23 G4 **Welton** Nhants
16 J7 **Welwyn** Herts
15 J3 **Welwyn Garden City** Herts
28 C6 **Wem** Shrops
15 J5 **Wembley** Gt Lon
3 L6 **Wembury** Devon
14 F3 **Wendover** Bucks
38 B4 **Wensley** N York
34 B5 **Wentbridge** Wakefd
21 H5 **Weobley** Herefs
24 D5 **Wereham** Norfk
38 B2 **West Auckland** Dur
7 H3 **West Bay** Dorset
7 H3 **West Bexington** Dorset
24 E4 **West Bilney** Norfk
30 C6 **West Bridgford** Notts
22 B2 **West Bromwich** Sandw
28 B8 **Westbury** Shrops

13 J6 **Westbury** Wilts
46 A4 **West Calder** W Loth
9 K4 **West Chiltington** W Susx
9 L2 **Westcott** Surrey
10 C3 **Westerham** Kent
27 L7 **West Felton** Shrops
10 F6 **Westfield** E Susx
23 G3 **West Haddon** Nhants
10 C5 **West Hoathly** W Susx
15 H8 **West Horsley** Surrey
12 D6 **West Huntspill** Somset
44 F3 **West Kilbride** N Ayrs
27 K2 **West Kirby** Wirral
13 K6 **West Lavington** Wilts
46 C5 **West Linton** Border
7 L4 **West Lulworth** Dorset
24 D4 **West Lynn** Norfk
10 E3 **West Malling** Kent
21 L5 **West Malvern** Worcs
9 G4 **West Meon** Hants
17 H6 **West Mersea** Essex
8 B5 **West Moors** Dorset
41 L7 **Westnewton** Cumb
24 E3 **West Newton** Norfk
16 B4 **Weston** Herts
29 G6 **Weston** Staffs
13 J3 **Westonbirt** Gloucs
28 E7 **Weston Heath** Shrops
14 C3 **Weston-on-the-Green** Oxon
22 C6 **Weston-sub-Edge** Gloucs
12 D5 **Weston-super-Mare** N Som
28 D6 **Weston-under-Redcastle** Shrops
12 F7 **West Pennard** Somset
2 D5 **West Pentire** Cnwll
38 D3 **West Rounton** N York
25 J2 **West Runton** Norfk
47 G5 **Westruther** Border
61 c3 **West Sandwick** Shet
4 D4 **Westward Ho!** Devon
9 H6 **West Wittering** W Susx
38 A4 **West Witton** N York
43 G3 **West Woodburn** Nthumb
42 C6 **Wetheral** Cumb
34 B3 **Wetherby** Leeds
39 J7 **Wetwang** E R Yk
25 H2 **Weybourne** Norfk
15 H7 **Weybridge** Surrey
8 D2 **Weyhill** Hants
7 J4 **Weymouth** Dorset
29 G2 **Whaley Bridge** Derbys
33 G3 **Whalley** Lancs
31 J7 **Whaplode** Lincs
31 J7 **Whaplode Drove** Lincs
40 E6 **Whauphill** D & G
15 J3 **Wheathampstead** Herts
14 D3 **Wheatley** Oxon
5 H4 **Wheddon Cross** Somset
17 G2 **Whepstead** Suffk
8 E2 **Wherwell** Hants
43 J5 **Whickham** Gatesd
6 A3 **Whiddon Down** Devon
6 D3 **Whimple** Devon
15 G3 **Whipsnade** C Beds
46 A4 **Whitburn** W Loth
39 H3 **Whitby** N York
14 E2 **Whitchurch** Bucks
8 E2 **Whitchurch** Hants
21 J8 **Whitchurch** Herefs
28 C5 **Whitchurch** Shrops
58 D7 **Whitebridge** Highld
36 D2 **Whitehaven** Cumb
9 H3 **Whitehill and Bordon** Hants
60 D3 **Whitehills** Abers
49 G6 **Whitehouse** Ag & B
46 F2 **Whitekirk** E Loth
32 F3 **Whitewell** Lancs
40 E7 **Whithorn** D & G
44 E5 **Whiting Bay** N Ayrs
18 E5 **Whitland** Carmth
43 K5 **Whitley Bay** N Tyne
43 G6 **Whitley Chapel** Nthumb
13 H1 **Whitminster** Gloucs
11 J2 **Whitstable** Kent
27 L6 **Whittington** Shrops
23 G6 **Whittlebury** Nhants
24 A6 **Whittlesey** Cambs
21 G4 **Whitton** Powys
30 B3 **Whitwell** Derbys

15 J2 **Whitwell** Herts
65 J3 **Wick** Highld
16 F7 **Wickford** Essex
8 F5 **Wickham** Hants
17 K2 **Wickham Market** Suffk
13 H3 **Wickwar** S Glos
43 K3 **Widdrington** Nthumb
6 A4 **Widecombe in the Moor** Devon
3 J5 **Widegates** Cnwll
4 B6 **Widemouth Bay** Cnwll
16 C5 **Widford** Herts
30 C6 **Widmerpool** Notts
28 C2 **Widnes** Halton
32 E6 **Wigan** Wigan
24 D4 **Wiggenhall St Germans** Norfk
23 G1 **Wigston** Leics
42 A6 **Wigton** Cumb
40 E6 **Wigtown** D & G
34 D2 **Wilberfoss** E R Yk
23 J4 **Wilby** Nhants
5 J6 **Willand** Devon
24 B8 **Willingham** Cambs
22 C4 **Wilmcote** Warwks
6 F2 **Wilmington** Devon
28 F2 **Wilmslow** Ches E
46 A4 **Wilsontown** S Lans
23 L6 **Wilstead** Bed
13 L7 **Wilton** Wilts
24 B6 **Wimblington** Cambs
8 A5 **Wimborne Minster** Dorset
13 H7 **Wincanton** Somset
22 B7 **Winchcombe** Gloucs
11 G6 **Winchelsea** E Susx
8 E3 **Winchester** Hants
37 G4 **Windermere** Cumb
15 G6 **Windsor** W & M
14 F2 **Wing** Bucks
43 L7 **Wingate** Dur
11 K3 **Wingham** Kent
14 F6 **Winkfield** Br For
4 F6 **Winkleigh** Devon
12 E5 **Winscombe** N Som
28 D3 **Winsford** Ches W
5 H4 **Winsford** Somset
7 G2 **Winsham** Somset
23 H7 **Winslow** Bucks
29 J4 **Winster** Derbys
7 J3 **Winterborne Monkton** Dorset
7 L2 **Winterborne Stickland** Dorset
7 L2 **Winterborne Whitechurch** Dorset
7 J3 **Winterborne Abbas** Dorset
13 L7 **Winterbourne Stoke** Wilts
34 F5 **Winteringham** N Linc
8 C3 **Winterslow** Wilts
34 F5 **Winterton** N Linc
23 L3 **Winwick** Cambs
29 J4 **Wirksworth** Derbys
31 K8 **Wisbech** Cambs
9 K3 **Wisborough Green** W Susx
45 L3 **Wishaw** N Lans
16 F5 **Witham** Essex
5 G6 **Witheridge** Devon
31 K2 **Withern** Lincs
35 K4 **Withernsea** E R Yk
22 B8 **Withington** Gloucs
21 J6 **Withington** Herefs
10 D5 **Withyham** E Susx
5 H4 **Withypool** Somset
17 J3 **Witnesham** Suffk
14 B3 **Witney** Oxon
11 G5 **Wittersham** Kent
43 J8 **Witton le Wear** Dur
5 J4 **Wiveliscombe** Somset
10 C6 **Wivelsfield** E Susx
17 H5 **Wivenhoe** Essex
17 J4 **Wix** Essex
23 K6 **Woburn** C Beds
15 G7 **Woking** Surrey
14 F6 **Wokingham** Wokham
18 C4 **Wolf's Castle** Pembks
23 J4 **Wollaston** Nhants
27 L8 **Wollaston** Shrops
43 H7 **Wolsingham** Dur
21 M1 **Wolverhampton** Wolves
22 C4 **Wolvey** Warwks
38 E2 **Wolviston** S on T
21 M2 **Wombourne** Staffs
34 B6 **Wombwell** Barns
14 F5 **Wooburn** Bucks

17 K3 **Woodbridge** Suffk
11 G5 **Woodchurch** Kent
13 G2 **Woodford** Gloucs
31 H4 **Woodhall Spa** Lincs
38 B2 **Woodland** Dur
14 C3 **Woodstock** Oxon
21 J4 **Woofferton** Shrops
12 F6 **Wookey Hole** Somset
7 L3 **Wool** Dorset
4 D3 **Woolacombe** Devon
47 K6 **Wooler** Nthumb
14 D6 **Woolhampton** W Berk
17 H2 **Woolpit** Suffk
28 E5 **Woore** Shrops
35 G5 **Wootton** N Linc
14 B2 **Wootton** Oxon
13 L3 **Wootton Bassett** Wilts
5 H3 **Wootton Courtenay** Somset
22 C4 **Wootton Wawen** Warwks
21 M5 **Worcester** Worcs
36 D1 **Workington** Cumb
30 C2 **Worksop** Notts
17 K1 **Worlingworth** Suffk
51 J4 **Wormit** Fife
15 G7 **Worplesdon** Surrey
21 G1 **Worthen** Shrops
9 L5 **Worthing** W Susx
7 M4 **Worth Matravers** Dorset
13 H3 **Wotton-under-Edge** Gloucs
31 G3 **Wragby** Lincs
6 A6 **Wrangaton** Devon
31 K5 **Wrangle** Lincs
35 G6 **Wrawby** N Linc
39 G5 **Wrelton** N York
25 L7 **Wrentham** Suffk
16 B3 **Wrestlingworth** C Beds
27 L5 **Wrexham** Wrexhm
13 L4 **Wroughton** Swindn
8 F7 **Wroxall** IoW
28 D8 **Wroxeter** Shrops
25 K4 **Wroxham** Norfk
22 E6 **Wroxton** Oxon
23 L5 **Wyboston** Bed
11 H4 **Wye** Kent
13 K7 **Wylye** Wilts
30 E7 **Wymondham** Leics
25 H5 **Wymondham** Norfk

Y

6 F2 **Yarcombe** Devon
23 H5 **Yardley Gobion** Nhants
23 J5 **Yardley Hastings** Nhants
38 D3 **Yarm** S on T
8 D6 **Yarmouth** IoW
46 E6 **Yarrowford** Border
14 F7 **Yateley** Hants
12 E5 **Yatton** N Som
13 J4 **Yatton Keynell** Wilts
23 M2 **Yaxley** Cambs
33 K3 **Yeadon** Leeds
3 L5 **Yealmpton** Devon
3 L4 **Yelverton** Devon
25 K5 **Yelverton** Norfk
7 H1 **Yeovil** Somset
12 F8 **Yeovilton** Somset
50 E6 **Yetts o'Muckhart** Clacks
26 D3 **Y Felinheli** Gwynd
27 J5 **Y Maerdy** Conwy
34 C2 **York** C York
29 J4 **Youlgreave** Derbys
29 H7 **Yoxall** Staffs
17 L1 **Yoxford** Suffk
26 B6 **Y Rhiw** Gwynd
20 B3 **Ysbyty Ystwyth** Cerdgn
19 K5 **Ystalyfera** Neath
19 K5 **Ystradgynlais** Powys
12 C2 **Ystrad Mynach** Caerph

Z

13 H7 **Zeals** Wilts
2 B6 **Zennor** Cnwll

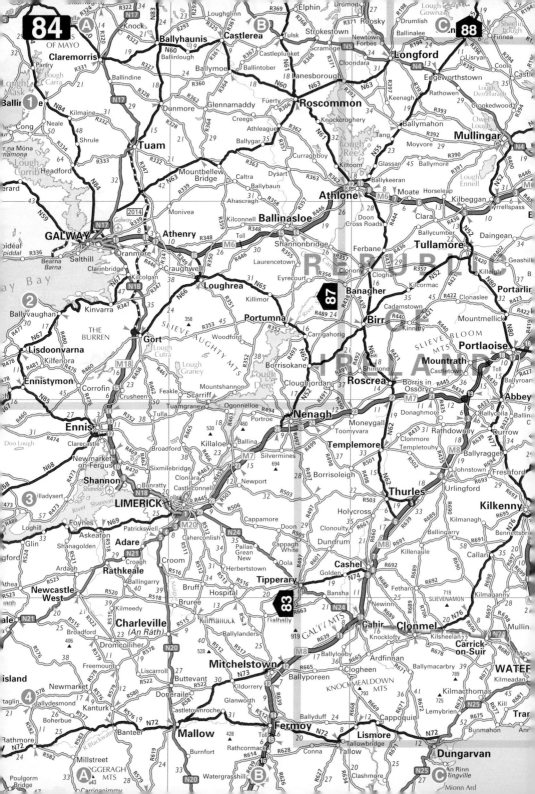

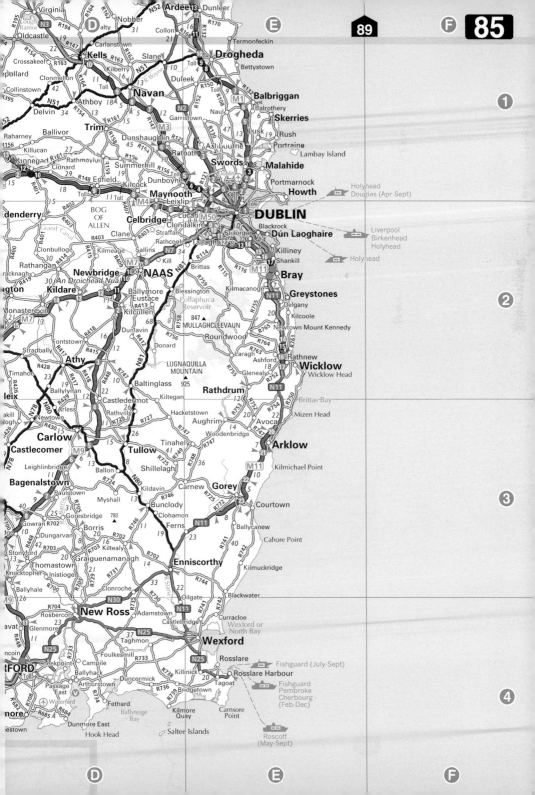

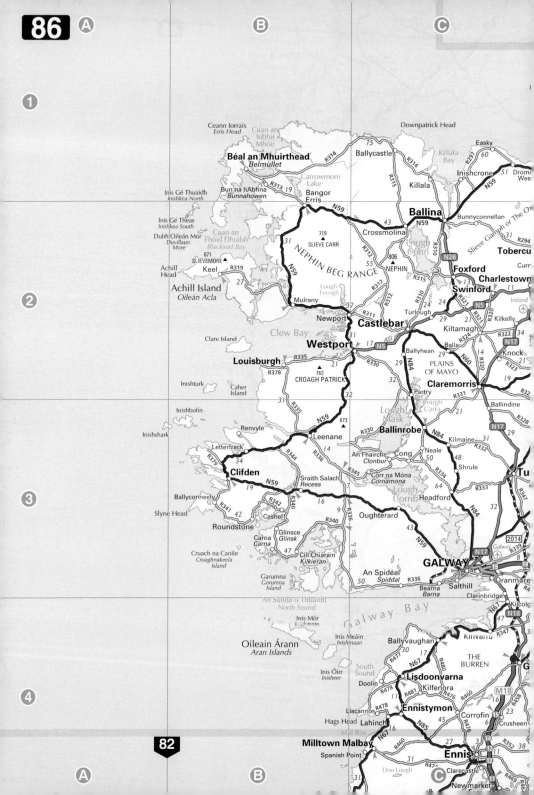

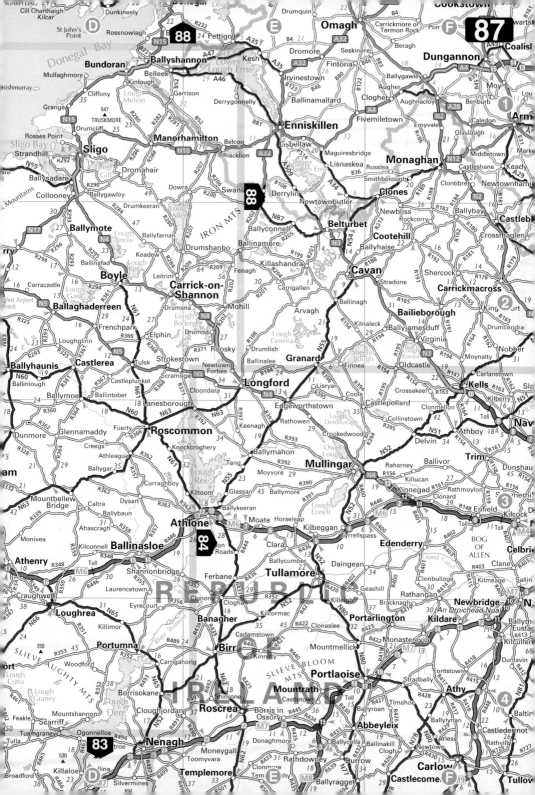

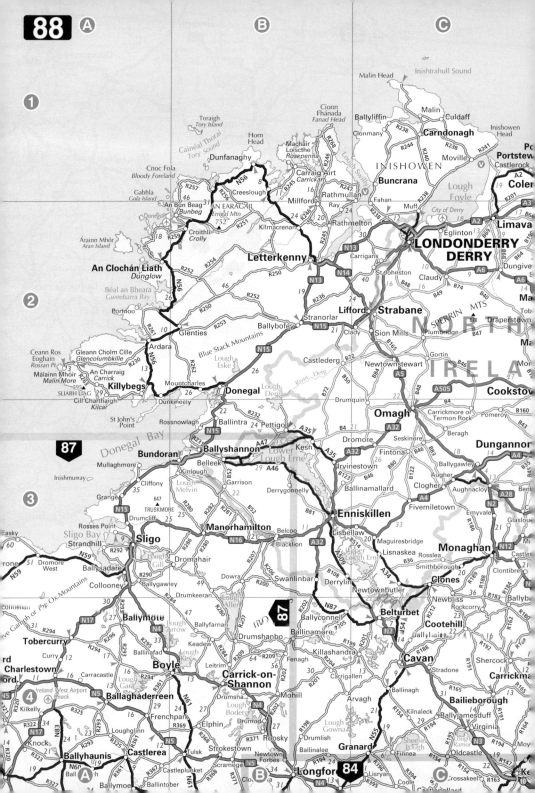

Mileage chart - Ireland

The mileage chart shows distances in miles between two towns along AA-recommended routes. Using motorways and other main roads this is normally the fastest route, though not necessarily the shortest.

Map of Ireland with towns marked:
Carraig Airt / Carrickart, Portrush, Londonderry / Derry, Larne, Donegal, Omagh, BELFAST, Enniskillen, Armagh, Downpatrick, Béal an Mhuirthead / Belmullet, Sligo, Cavan, Dundalk, Roscommon, Trim, Clifden, Athlone, Tullamore, DUBLIN, Galway, Portlaoise, Wicklow, Kilkee, Shannon, Limerick, Kilkenny, Tipperary, Wexford, Tralee, Waterford, Mallow, Killarney, An Coireán / Waterville, Cork

Limerick- Waterford = 78miles

1 mile = 1.6 kilometres

Distance chart (miles):

| Armagh |
Athlone	99
Belfast	41	139
Belmullet / Béal an Mhuirthead	168	123	202
Carrickart / Carraig Airt	95	166	117	168
Cavan	47	52	88	148	117
Clifden	196	106	230	91	196	160
Cork	246	136	264	231	300	187	178
Donegal	84	113	116	116	53	69	144	248
Downpatrick	47	138	22	212	138	94	240	257	127
Dublin	86	78	105	189	175	68	186	162	136	98
Dundalk	33	93	51	195	123	61	201	213	111	44	53
Enniskillen	50	84	84	118	85	32	146	219	37	95	99	64
Galway	150	57	191	111	180	103	50	128	128	196	136	152	114
Kilkee	202	103	242	178	248	155	126	94	196	242	181	197	187	76
Kilkenny	160	76	178	199	241	121	155	92	190	171	76	127	153	105	133
Killarney	239	142	271	236	306	193	184	56	254	264	192	220	225	134	63	122
Larne	62	161	22	223	120	109	251	286	113	44	126	73	106	212	264	203	293
Limerick	171	74	203	167	237	125	114	64	184	196	124	152	157	65	57	75	70	225
Londonderry / Derry	71	145	72	161	45	93	189	279	46	94	151	99	61	173	241	220	299	75	229
Mallow	233	115	252	210	280	166	157	22	227	245	150	200	198	108	73	80	42	273	43	259
Omagh	37	111	70	144	58	59	172	245	47	80	117	65	27	141	214	186	251	75	183	34	225
Portlaoise	138	45	156	169	207	90	142	108	159	149	54	105	122	93	125	31	136	178	68	183	95	149
Portrush	68	160	63	199	82	109	227	326	84	85	167	113	98	210	263	244	301	55	233	40	314	71	218
Roscommon	101	20	142	103	145	55	98	156	93	146	96	102	65	49	121	96	162	164	94	126	136	92	66	163
Shannon	180	81	221	157	227	133	104	76	174	209	136	164	165	55	47	88	82	242	13	220	56	192	81	242	99
Sligo	92	74	125	76	92	70	104	208	40	136	133	105	41	88	156	150	214	147	144	85	187	68	119	122	53	135
Tipperary	197	82	215	192	261	133	139	64	209	208	114	164	165	90	82	51	92	237	25	226	51	192	59	278	103	37	169
Tralee	235	138	267	232	302	189	179	76	250	260	188	243	239	130	43	139	20	288	65	281	61	247	132	297	158	78	210	88
Trim	78	56	97	166	158	50	164	160	118	90	26	45	81	114	160	83	182	118	114	134	147	100	52	159	73	126	110	111	178
Tullamore	109	24	133	147	185	68	125	129	138	126	66	81	100	76	121	51	137	154	69	161	116	127	21	177	44	82	98	80	133	44
Waterford	187	105	206	229	268	163	184	80	219	199	104	154	194	135	135	30	119	227	78	244	78	210	60	268	126	90	180	53	139	108	81
Waterville / An Coireán	280	182	312	277	347	233	224	99	294	305	233	260	265	175	96	172	50	333	110	326	92	292	177	342	203	123	255	133	53	223	178	170
Wexford	173	116	192	239	262	162	203	118	230	185	87	140	193	154	173	48	157	213	116	238	116	204	70	254	136	128	190	91	177	99	91	38	208
Wicklow	116	111	135	222	205	103	219	160	172	128	30	83	135	169	208	77	199	156	151	181	158	147	81	197	129	163	166	133	215	62	93	80	250	59

A

82 C2　**Abbeydorney** Kerry
82 C2　**Abbeyfeale** Limrck
84 C3　**Abbeyleix** Laois
85 D4　**Adamstown** Wexfd
83 D2　**Adare** Limrck
82 C3　**Adrigole** Cork
89 D2　**Aghadowey** Lderry
87 D3　**Ahascragh** Galway
89 D2　**Ahoghill** Antrim
82 B3　**Allihies** Cork
82 B2　**Anascaul** Kerry
88 B2　**An Bun Beag** Donegl
88 A2　**An Charraig** Donegl
88 A2　**An Clochán Liath** Donegl
82 B3　**An Coireán** Kerry
82 B2　**An Daingean** Kerry
86 C3　**An Fhairche** Galway
89 E4　**Annalong** Down
84 C4　**Annestown** Watfd
83 F3　**An Rinn** Watfd
86 C3　**An Spidéal** Galway
89 D2　**Antrim** Antrim
83 D2　**Ardagh** Limrck
88 A2　**Ardara** Donegl
89 D4　**Ardee** Louth
82 C2　**Ardfert** Kerry
84 C4　**Ardfinnan** Tippry
89 E3　**Ardglass** Down
82 B3　**Ardgroom** Cork
83 E3　**Ardmore** Watfd
85 E3　**Arklow** Wicklw
85 D3　**Arless** Laois
89 D3　**Armagh** Armagh
89 D1　**Armoy** Antrim
85 D4　**Arthurstown** Wexfd
88 B4　**Arvagh** Cavan
85 E1　**Ashbourne** Meath
85 E2　**Ashford** Wicklw
83 D1　**Askeaton** Limrck
85 D1　**Athboy** Meath
82 C2　**Athea** Limrck
87 D3　**Athenry** Galway
87 D3　**Athleague** Roscom
84 C1　**Athlone** Wmeath
85 D2　**Athy** Kildre
88 C3　**Augher** Tyrone
88 C3　**Aughnacloy** Tyrone
85 E3　**Aughrim** Wicklw
85 E3　**Avoca** Wicklw

B

85 D3　**Bagenalstown** Carlow
82 C3　**Baile Mhic Íre** Cork
88 C4　**Bailieborough** Cavan
85 E1　**Balbriggan** Dublin
86 C2　**Balla** Mayo
87 D2　**Ballaghaderreen** Roscom
86 C2　**Ballina** Mayo
83 D1　**Ballina** Tippry
87 D2　**Ballinafad** Sligo
88 C4　**Ballinagh** Cavan
84 C3　**Ballinakill** Laois
88 B4　**Ballinalee** Longfd
88 B3　**Ballinamallard** Ferman
88 B4　**Ballinamore** Leitrm
83 D3　**Ballinascarty** Cork

84 B2　**Ballinasloe** Galway
86 C3　**Ballindine** Mayo
83 D3　**Ballineen** Cork
83 D2　**Ballingarry** Limrck
84 C3　**Ballingarry** Tippry
82 C3　**Ballingeary** Cork
83 D3　**Ballinhassig** Cork
87 D2　**Ballinlough** Roscom
86 C3　**Ballinrobe** Mayo
83 D3　**Ballinspittle** Cork
87 D2　**Ballintober** Roscom
88 B3　**Ballintra** Donegl
85 D1　**Ballivor** Meath
85 D3　**Ballon** Carlow
87 D3　**Ballybaun** Galway
88 C4　**Ballybay** Monhan
88 B2　**Ballybofey** Donegl
82 C2　**Ballybunion** Kerry
85 E3　**Ballycanew** Wexfd
89 E2　**Ballycarry** Antrim
89 D1　**Ballycastle** Antrim
86 C4　**Ballycastle** Mayo
89 E2　**Ballyclare** Antrim
84 C3　**Ballycolla** Laois
86 B3　**Ballyconneely** Galway
88 B4　**Ballyconnell** Cavan
83 E3　**Ballycotton** Cork
84 C2　**Ballycumber** Offaly
82 C4　**Ballydehob** Cork
82 C2　**Ballydesmond** Cork
82 C2　**Ballyduff** Kerry
84 B4　**Ballyduff** Watfd
87 D2　**Ballyfarnan** Roscom
89 E2　**Ballygalley** Antrim
87 D3　**Ballygar** Galway
87 D1　**Ballygawley** Sligo
88 C3　**Ballygawley** Tyrone
89 E3　**Ballygowan** Down
85 D4　**Ballyhack** Wexfd
88 C4　**Ballyhaise** Cavan
85 D3　**Ballyhale** Kilken
87 D2　**Ballyhaunis** Mayo
86 C2　**Ballyhean** Mayo
82 B2　**Ballyheige** Kerry
88 C4　**Ballyjamesduff** Cavan
84 C1　**Ballykeeran** Wmeath
83 E2　**Ballylanders** Limrck
82 C3　**Ballylickey** Cork
88 C1　**Ballyliffin** Donegl
82 C2　**Ballylongford** Kerry
84 B4　**Ballylooby** Tippry
85 D2　**Ballylynan** Laois
84 C4　**Ballymacarbry** Watfd
84 C1　**Ballymahon** Longfd
82 C3　**Ballymakeery** Cork
89 D2　**Ballymena** Antrim
87 D2　**Ballymoe** Galway
89 D2　**Ballymoney** Antrim
84 C1　**Ballymore** Wmeath
85 D2　**Ballymore Eustace** Kildre
87 D2　**Ballymote** Sligo
89 E3　**Ballynahinch** Down
89 E2　**Ballynure** Antrim
84 B4　**Ballyporeen** Tippry
85 D3　**Ballyragget** Kilken
84 C2　**Ballyroan** Laois
89 D2　**Ballyronan** Lderry
84 B4　**Ballysadare** Sligo
87 D1　**Ballyshannon** Donegl
86 C4　**Ballyvaughan** Clare
89 E3　**Ballywalter** Down
85 E1　**Balrothery** Dublin
82 C4　**Baltimore** Cork
85 D2　**Baltinglass** Wicklw

84 B2　**Banagher** Offaly
89 D3　**Banbridge** Down
83 D3　**Bandon** Cork
89 E2　**Bangor** Down
86 B2　**Bangor Erris** Mayo
84 B3　**Bansha** Tippry
83 D2　**Banteer** Cork
82 C3　**Bantry** Cork
86 C3　**Barna** Galway
86 B1　**Béal an Mhuirthead** Mayo
82 C3　**Béal Átha an Ghaorthaidh** Cork
86 C3　**Bearna** Galway
82 C3　**Beaufort** Kerry
87 E1　**Belcoo** Ferman
89 E3　**Belfast** Belfst
83 D3　**Belgooly** Cork
89 D2　**Bellaghy** Lderry
87 D1　**Belleek** Ferman
86 B1　**Belmullet** Mayo
88 C4　**Belturbet** Cavan
89 D3　**Benburb** Tyrone
85 D3　**Bennettsbridge** Kilken
88 C3　**Beragh** Tyrone
85 E1　**Bettystown** Meath
84 C2　**Birr** Offaly
87 E1　**Blacklion** Cavan
85 E1　**Blackrock** Dublin
85 E3　**Blackwater** Wexfd
83 D3　**Blarney** Cork
85 D2　**Blessington** Wicklw
83 D2　**Boherbue** Cork
85 D3　**Borris** Carlow
84 C2　**Borris in Ossory** Laois
87 D4　**Borrisokane** Tippry
84 C3　**Borrisoleigh** Tippry
87 D2　**Boyle** Roscom
85 D2　**Bracknagh** Offaly
85 E2　**Bray** Wicklw
85 D4　**Bridgetown** Wexfd
85 E2　**Brittas** Dublin
83 D1　**Broadford** Clare
83 D2　**Broadford** Limrck
89 D2　**Broughshane** Antrim
83 D2　**Bruff** Limrck
83 D2　**Bruree** Limrck
88 B2　**Bunbeg** Donegl
85 D3　**Bunclody** Wexfd
88 C1　**Buncrana** Donegl
87 D1　**Bundoran** Donegl
84 C4　**Bunmahon** Watfd
86 B1　**Bun na hAbhna** Mayo
86 B1　**Bunnahowen** Mayo
86 C2　**Bunnyconnellan** Mayo
83 D1　**Bunratty** Clare
83 D3　**Burnfort** Cork
89 D1　**Bushmills** Antrim
83 D2　**Buttevant** Cork

C

84 C2　**Cadamstown** Offaly
83 D1　**Caherconlish** Limrck
82 B3　**Caherdaniel** Kerry
82 B3　**Cahersiveen** Kerry
84 C4　**Cahir** Tippry
88 C3　**Caledon** Tyrone
84 C3　**Callan** Kilken
87 D3　**Caltra** Galway
82 B2　**Camp** Kerry

85 D4　**Campile** Wexfd
84 B3　**Cappagh White** Tippry
83 E1　**Cappamore** Limrck
84 C4　**Cappoquin** Watfd
85 D1　**Carlanstown** Meath
89 D4　**Carlingford** Louth
85 D3　**Carlow** Carlow
86 B3　**Carna** Galway
88 C1　**Carndonagh** Donegl
85 E3　**Carnew** Wicklw
89 E2　**Carnlough** Antrim
87 D2　**Carracastle** Mayo
88 B1　**Carraig Airt** Donegl
88 A2　**Carrick** Donegl
88 B1　**Carrickart** Donegl
89 E2　**Carrickfergus** Antrim
89 D4　**Carrickmacross** Monhan
88 C3　**Carrickmore or Termon Rock** Tyrone
87 D2　**Carrick-on-Shannon** Leitrm
84 C4　**Carrick-on-Suir** Tippry
87 D4　**Carrigahorig** Tippry
83 D3　**Carrigaline** Cork
88 B4　**Carrigallen** Leitrm
83 D3　**Carriganimmy** Cork
88 C2　**Carrigans** Donegl
83 E3　**Carrigtohill** Cork
89 E3　**Carryduff** Down
86 B3　**Cashel** Galway
84 C3　**Cashel** Tippry
86 C2　**Castlebar** Mayo
89 D4　**Castlebellingham** Louth
89 D4　**Castleblayney** Monhan
85 E4　**Castlebridge** Wexfd
85 D3　**Castlecomer** Kilken
83 D1　**Castleconnell** Limrck
88 B2　**Castlederg** Tyrone
85 D2　**Castledermot** Kildre
82 B2　**Castlegregory** Kerry
82 C2　**Castleisland** Kerry
82 C2　**Castlemaine** Kerry
83 E3　**Castlemartyr** Cork
87 D2　**Castleplunket** Roscom
84 C1　**Castlepollard** Wmeath
87 D2　**Castlerea** Roscom
88 C1　**Castlerock** Lderry
88 C3　**Castleshane** Monhan
84 C2　**Castletown** Laois
82 B3　**Castletown Bearhaven** Cork
83 D2　**Castletownroche** Cork
82 C4　**Castletownshend** Cork
89 E3　**Castlewellan** Down
82 B3　**Cathair Dónall** Kerry
82 C2　**Causeway** Kerry
88 C4　**Cavan** Cavan
85 D2　**Celbridge** Kildre
86 C2　**Charlestown** Mayo
83 D2　**Charleville** Cork
85 D4　**Cheekpoint** Watfd
88 A2　**Cill Charthaigh** Donegl
86 B3　**Cill Chiaráin** Galway
88 C2　**Clady** Tyrone
85 D2　**Clane** Kildre
84 C2　**Clara** Offaly

83 D1　**Clarecastle** Clare
86 C2　**Claremorris** Mayo
86 C3　**Clarinbridge** Galway
83 E3　**Clashmore** Watfd
88 C2　**Claudy** Lderry
86 B3　**Clifden** Galway
87 D1　**Cliffony** Sligo
85 D3　**Clogh** Kilken
84 C2　**Cloghan** Offaly
84 B4　**Clogheen** Tippry
88 C3　**Clogher** Tyrone
85 D3　**Clohamon** Wexfd
83 D4　**Clonakilty** Cork
85 D1　**Clonard** Meath
84 C2　**Clonaslee** Laois
85 D2　**Clonbulloge** Offaly
86 C3　**Clonbur** Galway
85 E2　**Clondalkin** Dublin
88 C3　**Clones** Monhan
83 D1　**Clonlara** Clare
88 C1　**Clonmany** Donegl
84 C4　**Clonmel** Tippry
85 D1　**Clonmellon** Wmeath
84 C3　**Clonmore** Tippry
84 C2　**Clonony** Offaly
84 C3　**Clonoulty** Tippry
85 D3　**Clonroche** Wexfd
88 C3　**Clontibret** Monhan
84 C1　**Cloondara** Longfd
89 E3　**Clough** Down
87 E4　**Cloughjordan** Tippry
83 E3　**Cloyne** Cork
89 D2　**Coagh** Tyrone
89 D3　**Coalisland** Tyrone
83 E3　**Cobh** Cork
89 D1　**Coleraine** Lderry
85 D1　**Collinstown** Wmeath
89 D4　**Collon** Louth
87 D1　**Collooney** Sligo
89 E3　**Comber** Down
86 C3　**Cong** Mayo
83 E3　**Conna** Cork
89 D2　**Cookstown** Tyrone
84 C1　**Coole** Wmeath
82 C1　**Cooraclare** Clare
88 C4　**Cootehill** Cavan
83 D3　**Cork** Cork
86 C3　**Cornamona** Galway
86 C3　**Corr na Móna** Galway
86 C4　**Corrofin** Clare
83 D3　**Courtmacsherry** Cork
85 E3　**Courtown** Wexfd
89 D3　**Craigavon** Armagh
87 D3　**Craughwell** Galway
89 E2　**Crawfordsburn** Down
87 D3　**Creegs** Galway
88 B1　**Creeslough** Donegl
83 D2　**Croagh** Limrck
88 B2　**Croithlí** Donegl
88 B2　**Crolly** Donegl
84 C1　**Crookedwood** Wmeath
82 C4　**Crookhaven** Cork
83 D3　**Crookstown** Cork
83 D2　**Croom** Limrck
85 D1　**Crossakeel** Meath
83 D3　**Cross Barry** Cork
83 E3　**Crosshaven** Cork
89 D4　**Crossmaglen** Armagh
86 C2　**Crossmolina** Mayo
89 D2　**Crumlin** Antrim
86 C4　**Crusheen** Clare
88 C1　**Culdaff** Donegl
89 D2　**Cullybackey** Antrim
85 E4　**Curracloe** Wexfd

87 D3　**Curraghboy** Roscom
87 D2　**Curry** Sligo
89 D2　**Cushendall** Antrim
89 D1　**Cushendun** Antrim

D

84 C2　**Daingean** Offaly
85 E2　**Delgany** Wicklw
85 D1　**Delvin** Wmeath
88 C2　**Derry** Lderry
87 E1　**Derrygonnelly** Ferman
88 B3　**Derrylin** Ferman
89 D1　**Dervock** Antrim
82 B2　**Dingle** Kerry
89 D2　**Doagh** Antrim
89 E2　**Donaghadee** Down
84 C3　**Donaghmore** Laois
85 D2　**Donard** Wicklw
88 B2　**Donegal** Donegl
83 D2　**Doneraile** Cork
86 C4　**Doolin** Clare
83 E1　**Doon** Limrck
82 C1　**Doonbeg** Clare
84 C2　**Doon Cross Roads** Offaly
83 D3　**Douglas** Cork
89 E3　**Downpatrick** Down
87 E1　**Dowra** Cavan
89 D2　**Draperstown** Lderry
82 C3　**Drimoleague** Cork
83 D3　**Dripsey** Cork
85 E1　**Drogheda** Louth
87 D1　**Dromahair** Leitrm
83 D2　**Dromcolliher** Limrck
89 D3　**Dromore** Down
88 C3　**Dromore** Tyrone
86 C1　**Dromore West** Sligo
87 D1　**Drumcliff** Sligo
89 D4　**Drumcondra** Meath
87 D1　**Drumkeeran** Leitrm
88 B4　**Drumlish** Longfd
87 E2　**Drumod** Leitrm
88 C3　**Drumquin** Tyrone
87 E2　**Drumshanbo** Leitrm
87 E2　**Drumsna** Leitrm
82 B2　**Duagh** Kerry
85 E2　**Dublin** Dublin
85 E1　**Duleek** Meath
85 E1　**Dunboyne** Meath
85 D4　**Duncormick** Wexfd
89 D4　**Dundalk** Louth
83 D3　**Dunderrow** Cork
89 E3　**Dundonald** Down
89 E3　**Dundrum** Down
84 B3　**Dundrum** Tippry
88 B1　**Dunfanaghy** Donegl
89 D3　**Dungannon** Tyrone
85 D3　**Dungarvan** Kilken
83 F3　**Dungarvan** Watfd
88 C2　**Dungiven** Lderry
88 A2　**Dunglow** Donegl
83 E3　**Dungourney** Cork
88 A2　**Dunkineely** Donegl
85 E2　**Dún Laoghaire** Dublin
85 D2　**Dunlavin** Wicklw
89 D4　**Dunleer** Louth
89 D2　**Dunloy** Antrim
82 C3　**Dunmanway** Cork
87 D3　**Dunmore** Galway
85 D4　**Dunmore East** Watfd
89 E3　**Dunmurry** Antrim

85 D1　**Dunshaughlin** Meath
84 C3　**Durrow** Laois
82 C4　**Durrus** Cork
87 D3　**Dysart** Roscom

E

86 C1　**Easky** Sligo
85 D2　**Edenderry** Offaly
84 C1　**Edgeworthstown** Longfd
88 C2　**Eglinton** Lderry
87 D2　**Elphin** Roscom
88 C3　**Emyvale** Monhan
85 D1　**Enfield** Meath
83 D1　**Ennis** Clare
85 D3　**Enniscorthy** Wexfd
83 D3　**Enniskean** Cork
88 B3　**Enniskillen** Ferman
86 C4　**Ennistymon** Clare
87 D4　**Eyrecourt** Galway

F

88 C2　**Fahan** Donegl
82 C2　**Farranfore** Kerry
87 D4　**Feakle** Clare
87 E2　**Fenagh** Leitrm
84 C2　**Ferbane** Offaly
83 E2　**Fermoy** Cork
85 E3　**Ferns** Wexfd
84 C3　**Fethard** Tippry
85 D4　**Fethard** Wexfd
88 C4　**Finnea** Wmeath
88 C3　**Fintona** Tyrone
88 C3　**Fivemiletown** Tyrone
85 D2　**Fontstown** Kildre
85 D4　**Foulkesmill** Wexfd
86 C2　**Foxford** Mayo
83 D1　**Foynes** Limrck
83 D2　**Freemount** Cork
87 D2　**Frenchpark** Roscom
84 C3　**Freshford** Kilken
87 D3　**Fuerty** Roscom

G

83 E2　**Galbally** Limrck
86 C3　**Galway** Galway
87 D1　**Garrison** Ferman
85 E1　**Garristown** Dublin
83 E3　**Garryvoe** Cork
89 D2　**Garvagh** Lderry
84 C2　**Geashill** Offaly
89 D3　**Gilford** Down
82 C4　**Glandore** Cork
83 D3　**Glanmire** Cork
83 E2　**Glanworth** Cork
88 C3　**Glaslough** Monhan
84 C1　**Glassan** Wmeath
88 A2　**Gleann Cholm Cille** Donegl
89 E2　**Glenarm** Antrim
89 D3　**Glenavy** Antrim
82 B3　**Glenbeigh** Kerry
88 A2　**Glencolumbkille** Donegl
85 E2　**Glenealy** Wicklw
82 C3　**Glengarriff** Cork

85 D4　**Glenmore** Kilken
87 D3　**Glennamaddy** Galway
88 B2　**Glenties** Donegl
82 C2　**Glin** Limrck
86 B3　**Glinsce** Galway
86 B3　**Glinsk** Galway
84 B3　**Golden** Tippry
82 C4　**Goleen** Cork
85 D3　**Goresbridge** Kilken
85 E3　**Gorey** Wexfd
86 C4　**Gort** Galway
88 C2　**Gortin** Tyrone
85 D3　**Gowran** Kilken
85 D3　**Graiguenamanagh** Kilken
88 C4　**Granard** Longfd
87 D1　**Grange** Sligo
89 D4　**Greenore** Louth
89 E3　**Greyabbey** Down
85 E2　**Greystones** Wicklw
89 D2　**Gulladuff** Lderry

H

85 D3　**Hacketstown** Carlow
86 C3　**Headford** Galway
83 D2　**Herbertstown** Limrck
89 D3　**Hillsborough** Down
89 D3　**Hilltown** Down
84 C3　**Holycross** Tippry
89 E2　**Holywood** Down
84 C1　**Horseleap** Wmeath
83 D2　**Hospital** Limrck
85 E1　**Howth** Dublin

I

82 B2　**Inch** Kerry
82 C3　**Inchigeelagh** Cork
83 D3　**Inishannon** Cork
86 C1　**Inishcrone** Sligo
85 D3　**Inistioge** Kilken
88 B3　**Irvinestown** Ferman

J

84 C3　**Johnstown** Kilken

K

83 D2　**Kanturk** Cork
87 D2　**Keadew** Roscom
89 D3　**Keady** Armagh
86 B2　**Keel** Mayo
84 C1　**Keenagh** Longfd
89 D2　**Kells** Antrim
85 D1　**Kells** Meath
82 C3　**Kenmare** Kerry
88 B3　**Kesh** Ferman
84 C2　**Kilbeggan** Wmeath
85 D1　**Kilberry** Meath
83 D3　**Kilbrittain** Cork
88 A2　**Kilcar** Donegl
85 D1　**Kilcock** Kildre
86 C4　**Kilcolgan** Galway
87 D3　**Kilconnell** Galway
85 E2　**Kilcoole** Wicklw

84 C2 **Kilcormac** Offaly
85 D2 **Kilcullen** Kildre
89 D4 **Kilcurry** Louth
85 D2 **Kildare** Kildre
85 D3 **Kildavin** Carlow
83 D2 **Kildorrery** Cork
86 C4 **Kilfenora** Clare
82 C3 **Kilgarvan** Kerry
82 C1 **Kilkee** Clare
89 E4 **Kilkeel** Down
86 C2 **Kilkelly** Mayo
84 C3 **Kilkenny** Kilken
86 B3 **Kilkieran** Galway
82 C2 **Kilkinlea Lower** Limrck
85 D2 **Kill** Kildre
84 C4 **Kill** Watfd
83 D1 **Killadysert** Clare
86 C1 **Killala** Mayo
83 D1 **Killaloe** Clare
82 C3 **Killarney** Kerry
88 C4 **Killashandra** Cavan
83 E3 **Killeagh** Cork
84 C2 **Killeigh** Offaly
84 C3 **Killenaule** Tippry
82 C1 **Killimer** Clare
87 D4 **Killimor** Galway
85 E2 **Killiney** Dublin
85 E4 **Killinick** Wexfd
82 C2 **Killorglin** Kerry
89 E3 **Killough** Down
85 D1 **Killucan** Wmeath
88 A2 **Killybegs** Donegl
89 E3 **Killyleagh** Down
85 E2 **Kilmacanoge** Wicklw
88 B2 **Kilmacrenan** Donegl
84 C4 **Kilmacthomas** Watfd
84 C3 **Kilmaganny** Kilken
86 C3 **Kilmaine** Mayo
83 D2 **Kilmallock** Limrck
84 C3 **Kilmanagh** Kilken
84 C4 **Kilmeadan** Watfd
85 D2 **Kilmeage** Kildre
83 D2 **Kilmeedy** Limrck
83 D3 **Kilmichael** Cork
85 D4 **Kilmore Quay** Wexfd
85 E3 **Kilmuckridge** Wexfd
88 C4 **Kilnaleck** Cavan
89 D2 **Kilrea** Lderry
82 C1 **Kilrush** Clare
84 C4 **Kilsheelan** Tippry
86 C2 **Kiltamagh** Mayo
85 D3 **Kiltealy** Wexfd
85 D3 **Kiltegan** Wicklw
87 E3 **Kiltoom** Roscom
89 D4 **Kingscourt** Cavan
87 D1 **Kinlough** Leitrm
85 D1 **Kinnegad** Wmeath
84 C2 **Kinnitty** Offaly
83 D3 **Kinsale** Cork
86 C4 **Kinvarra** Galway
89 E3 **Kircubbin** Down
86 C2 **Knock** Mayo
87 D3 **Knockcroghery** Roscom
84 C4 **Knocklofty** Tippry
85 D3 **Knocktopher** Kilken

86 C4 **Lahinch** Clare

84 B1 **Lanesborough** Roscom
85 E2 **Laragh** Wicklw
89 E2 **Larne** Antrim
82 C3 **Lauragh** Kerry
87 D3 **Laurencetown** Galway
82 C4 **Leap** Cork
86 B3 **Leenane** Galway
85 D3 **Leighlinbridge** Carlow
87 D2 **Leitrim** Leitrm
85 D2 **Leixlip** Kildre
84 C4 **Lemybrien** Watfd
86 B3 **Letterfrack** Galway
88 B2 **Letterkenny** Donegl
88 C2 **Lifford** Donegl
88 C2 **Limavady** Lderry
83 D1 **Limerick** Limrck
88 C3 **Lisbellaw** Ferman
89 D3 **Lisburn** Antrim
86 C4 **Liscannor** Clare
83 D2 **Liscarroll** Cork
84 C4 **Lisdoonvarna** Clare
84 C4 **Lismore** Watfd
88 C3 **Lisnaskea** Ferman
84 C1 **Lisryan** Longfd
82 C2 **Listowel** Kerry
82 C1 **Loghill** Limrck
88 C2 **Londonderry** Lderry
84 C1 **Longford** Longfd
89 D3 **Loughbrickland** Down
89 D3 **Loughgall** Armagh
87 D2 **Loughglinn** Roscom
87 D4 **Loughrea** Galway
86 B2 **Louisburgh** Mayo
85 E2 **Lucan** Dublin
89 D3 **Lurgan** Armagh
85 E1 **Lusk** Dublin

88 B1 **Machair Loisce** Donegl
83 D3 **Macroom** Cork
89 E3 **Maghera** Down
89 D2 **Maghera** Lderry
89 D2 **Magherafelt** Lderry
88 C3 **Maguiresbridge** Ferman
85 E1 **Malahide** Dublin
88 A2 **Málainn Mhóir** Donegl
88 C1 **Malin** Donegl
88 A2 **Malin More** Donegl
83 D2 **Mallow** Cork
87 D1 **Manorhamilton** Leitrm
89 D3 **Markethill** Armagh
89 D2 **Martinstown** Antrim
85 D1 **Maynooth** Kildre
89 D3 **Mazetown** Antrim
88 C3 **Middletown** Armagh
83 E3 **Midleton** Cork
88 B2 **Millford** Donegl
83 D3 **Millstreet** Cork
82 C2 **Milltown** Kerry
82 C1 **Milltown Malbay** Clare
83 E2 **Mitchelstown** Cork
84 C1 **Moate** Wmeath
87 E2 **Mohill** Leitrm
88 C3 **Monaghan** Monhan
85 D2 **Monasterevin** Kildre
84 C3 **Moneygall** Offaly

89 D2 **Moneymore** Lderry
87 D3 **Monivea** Galway
84 C4 **Mooncoin** Kilken
89 D2 **Moorfields** Antrim
87 D3 **Mountbellew Bridge** Galway
88 B2 **Mountcharles** Donegl
84 C2 **Mountmellick** Laois
84 C2 **Mountrath** Laois
87 D4 **Mountshannon** Clare
88 C1 **Moville** Donegl
88 C4 **Moy** Tyrone
88 C4 **Moynalty** Meath
84 C1 **Moyvore** Wmeath
82 C3 **Muckross** Kerry
88 C2 **Muff** Donegl
87 D1 **Mullaghmore** Sligo
85 D4 **Mullinavat** Kilken
84 C1 **Mullingar** Wmeath
86 B2 **Mulrany** Mayo
85 D3 **Myshall** Carlow

85 D2 **Naas** Kildre
85 E1 **Naul** Dublin
85 D1 **Navan** Meath
86 C3 **Neale** Mayo
83 E1 **Nenagh** Tippry
88 C3 **Newbliss** Monhan
85 D2 **Newbridge** Kildre
89 E3 **Newcastle** Down
83 D2 **Newcastle West** Limrck
84 C4 **Newinn** Tippry
83 D2 **Newmarket** Cork
83 D1 **Newmarket-on-Fergus** Clare
86 B2 **Newport** Mayo
83 D1 **Newport** Tippry
85 D4 **New Ross** Wexfd
89 D3 **Newry** Down
85 D3 **Newtown** Laois
89 E2 **Newtownabbey** Antrim
89 E3 **Newtownards** Down
88 C3 **Newtownbutler** Ferman
84 C1 **Newtown Forbes** Longfd
89 D3 **Newtownhamilton** Armagh
85 E2 **Newtown Mount Kennedy** Wicklw
88 C2 **Newtownstewart** Tyrone
89 D4 **Nobber** Meath

83 D1 **Ogonnelloe** Clare
85 D4 **Oilgate** Wexfd
88 C4 **Oldcastle** Meath
88 C3 **Omagh** Tyrone
89 D4 **Omeath** Louth
83 E2 **Oola** Limrck
86 C3 **Oranmore** Galway
86 C3 **Oughterard** Galway

83 D3 **Ovens** Cork

83 E2 **Pallas Green New** Limrck
82 B3 **Parknasilla** Kerry
86 C2 **Partry** Mayo
85 D4 **Passage East** Watfd
83 E3 **Passage West** Cork
83 D1 **Patrickswell** Limrck
85 D3 **Paulstown** Kilken
88 B3 **Pettigo** Donegl
88 C2 **Plumbridge** Tyrone
88 C3 **Pomeroy** Tyrone
89 D3 **Portadown** Armagh
89 E3 **Portaferry** Down
85 D2 **Portarlington** Laois
89 E3 **Portavogie** Down
89 D1 **Portballintrae** Antrim
89 D2 **Portglenone** Antrim
84 C2 **Portlaoise** Laois
85 E1 **Portmarnock** Dublin
88 A2 **Portnoo** Donegl
85 E1 **Portraine** Dublin
83 E1 **Portroe** Tippry
89 D1 **Portrush** Antrim
89 D1 **Portstewart** Lderry
87 D4 **Portumna** Galway
82 C3 **Poulgorm Bridge** Kerry
89 D3 **Poyntz Pass** Armagh

85 D1 **Raharney** Wmeath
89 D2 **Randalstown** Antrim
89 D2 **Rasharkin** Antrim
85 D2 **Rathangan** Kildre
85 E2 **Rathcoole** Dublin
83 E3 **Rathcormack** Cork
84 C3 **Rathdowney** Laois
85 E2 **Rathdrum** Wicklw
89 D3 **Rathfriland** Down
83 D2 **Rathkeale** Limrck
88 B2 **Rathmelton** Donegl
82 C3 **Rathmore** Kerry
85 D1 **Rathmoylon** Meath
88 C1 **Rathmullan** Donegl
85 E2 **Rathnew** Wicklw
84 C1 **Rathowen** Wmeath
85 D3 **Rathvilly** Carlow
85 E1 **Ratoath** Meath
88 B2 **Ray** Donegl
86 B3 **Recess** Galway
86 B3 **Renvyle** Galway
83 E3 **Ringaskiddy** Cork
83 F3 **Ringville** Watfd
88 C4 **Rockcorry** Monhan
87 E2 **Roosky** Roscom
85 D4 **Rosbercon** Wexfd
87 D3 **Roscommon** Roscom
84 C2 **Roscrea** Tippry
88 B1 **Rosepenna** Donegl
83 D4 **Ross Carbery** Cork
87 D1 **Rosses Point** Sligo
85 E4 **Rosslare** Wexfd
85 E4 **Rosslare Harbour** Wexfd
88 C3 **Rosslea** Ferman
88 B3 **Rossnowlagh** Donegl

89 D4	**Rostrevor** Down	
86 B3	**Roundstone** Galway	
85 E2	**Roundwood** Wicklw	
85 E1	**Rush** Dublin	

S

89 E3	**Saintfield** Down	
88 C2	**St Johnston** Donegl	
85 D2	**Sallins** Kildre	
86 C3	**Salthill** Galway	
87 D4	**Scarriff** Clare	
82 C2	**Scartaglin** Kerry	
89 D3	**Scarva** Down	
82 C4	**Schull** Cork	
87 D2	**Scramoge** Roscom	
88 C3	**Seskinore** Tyrone	
83 E3	**Shanagarry** Cork	
83 D1	**Shanagolden** Limrck	
85 E2	**Shankill** Dublin	
83 D1	**Shannon** Clare	
87 D3	**Shannonbridge** Offaly	
88 C4	**Shercock** Cavan	
85 D3	**Shillelagh** Wicklw	
84 C2	**Shinrone** Offaly	
86 C3	**Shrule** Mayo	
83 E1	**Silvermines** Tippry	
88 C2	**Sion Mills** Tyrone	
83 D1	**Sixmilebridge** Clare	
85 E1	**Skerries** Dublin	
82 C4	**Skibbereen** Cork	
85 D1	**Slane** Meath	
87 D1	**Sligo** Sligo	
88 C3	**Smithborough** Monhan	
82 B3	**Sneem** Kerry	

82 C1	**Spanish Point** Clare	
86 C3	**Spiddal** Galway	
86 B3	**Sraith Salach** Galway	
89 D3	**Stewartstown** Tyrone	
85 E2	**Stillorgan** Dublin	
85 D3	**Stonyford** Kilken	
88 C2	**Strabane** Tyrone	
85 D2	**Stradbally** Laois	
88 C4	**Stradone** Cavan	
85 D2	**Straffan** Kildre	
87 D1	**Strandhill** Sligo	
89 E3	**Strangford** Down	
88 B2	**Stranorlar** Donegl	
87 D2	**Strokestown** Roscom	
85 D1	**Summerhill** Meath	
88 B3	**Swanlinbar** Cavan	
89 D2	**Swatragh** Lderry	
86 C2	**Swinford** Mayo	
85 E1	**Swords** Dublin	

T

85 D4	**Taghmon** Wexfd	
85 E4	**Tagoat** Wexfd	
82 B3	**Tahilla** Kerry	
85 E2	**Tallaght** Dublin	
83 E3	**Tallow** Watfd	
84 B4	**Tallowbridge** Watfd	
89 D3	**Tandragee** Armagh	
84 C1	**Tang** Wmeath	
82 C1	**Tarbert** Kerry	
84 C3	**Templemore** Tippry	
84 C3	**Templetouhy** Tippry	
89 D4	**Termonfeckin** Louth	
85 D3	**Thomastown** Kilken	
84 C3	**Thurles** Tippry	

85 D2	**Timahoe** Laois	
83 D3	**Timoleague** Cork	
85 E3	**Tinahely** Wicklw	
84 B3	**Tipperary** Tippry	
87 D2	**Tobercurry** Sligo	
89 D2	**Tobermore** Lderry	
84 B3	**Toomyvara** Tippry	
82 C4	**Toormore** Cork	
82 C2	**Tralee** Kerry	
85 D4	**Tramore** Watfd	
85 D1	**Trim** Meath	
86 C3	**Tuam** Galway	
83 D1	**Tuamgraney** Clare	
83 D1	**Tulla** Clare	
84 C2	**Tullamore** Offaly	
85 D3	**Tullow** Carlow	
87 D2	**Tulsk** Roscom	
86 C2	**Turlough** Mayo	
84 C1	**Tyrrellspass** Wmeath	

U

84 C3	**Urlingford** Kilken	

V

88 C4	**Virginia** Cavan	

W

89 D4	**Warrenpoint** Down	
85 D4	**Waterford** Watfd	

83 E3	**Watergrasshill** Cork	
82 B3	**Waterville** Kerry	
86 C2	**Westport** Mayo	
85 E4	**Wexford** Wexfd	
83 E3	**Whitegate** Cork	
89 E2	**Whitehead** Antrim	
85 E2	**Wicklow** Wicklw	
85 E3	**Woodenbridge** Wicklw	
87 D4	**Woodford** Galway	

Y

83 E3	**Youghal** Cork	

GLOVEBOX ATLAS
TOWN PLANS

Atlas contents

Key to town plans	96
Town plans	97–191
Major airports	192–197
Channel Tunnel	198

Index to town plans

Aberdeen	108	Edinburgh	133	Newquay	157	Swindon	182
Aberystwyth	109	Exeter	134	Northampton	158	Taunton	183
Basingstoke	110	Glasgow	135	Norwich	159	Torquay	184
Bath	111	Gloucester	136	Nottingham	160	Tunbridge Wells	185
Birmingham	112	Great Yarmouth	137	Oldham	161	Warwick	186
Blackpool	113	Guildford	138	Oxford	162	Watford	187
Bournemouth	114	Harrogate	139	Perth	163	Winchester	188
Bradford	115	Huddersfield	140	Peterborough	164	Wolverhampton	189
Brighton	116	Inverness	141	Plymouth	165	Worcester	190
Bristol	117	Ipswich	142	Portsmouth	166	York	191
Cambridge	118	Kingston upon Hull	143	Preston	167		
Canterbury	119	Lancaster	144	Reading	168		
Cardiff	120	Leeds	145	St Andrews	169		
Carlisle	121	Leicester	146	Salisbury	170		
Cheltenham	122	Lincoln	147	Scarborough	171		
Chester	123	Liverpool	148	Sheffield	172		
Colchester	124	Llandudno	149	Shrewsbury	173		
Coventry	125	London	97-107	Southampton	174		
Darlington	126	Luton	150	Southend-on-Sea	175		
Derby	127	Maidstone	151	Stirling	176		
Doncaster	128	Manchester	152	Stockton-on-Tees	177		
Dover	129	Middlesbrough	153	Stoke-on-Trent	178		
Dundee	130	Milton Keynes	154	Stratford-upon-Avon	179		
Durham	131	Newcastle upon Tyne	155	Sunderland	180		
Eastbourne	132	Newport	156	Swansea	181		

Airports

London Heathrow	192
London Gatwick	192
London Stansted	193
London Luton	193
London City	194
Birmingham Int'l	194
East Midlands	195
Manchester	195
Leeds Bradford	196
Aberdeen	196
Edinburgh	197
Glasgow	197

Key to town plans

Town plan legend

M8	Motorway with number
	Primary Road
	A Road
	B Road
	Local / other road
	Restricted road / pedestrians only
- - - -	Footpath
COLLEGE ■	Building of interest
†	Church
	Park and open space
P	Car park
	Toilet
←	One-way street
	Shopmobility
P+	Park and Ride
◉	World Heritage Site (UNESCO)
H	24-hour Accident & Emergency hospital
i	Tourist Information Centre
	Light rapid transit system
	Central London Congestion Charging Zone

Inverness

Aberdeen

Dundee
Perth
St Andrews
Stirling
Glasgow
Edinburgh

Newcastle upon Tyne
Carlisle
Durham
Sunderland
Stockton-on-Tees
Middlesbrough
Darlington
Scarborough

Lancaster
Harrogate
Leeds
York
Blackpool
Bradford
Leeds
Kingston upon Hull
Preston
Huddersfield
Oldham
Liverpool
Manchester
Doncaster
Llandudno
Sheffield
Chester
Lincoln
Stoke-on-Trent (Hanley)
Shrewsbury
Derby
Nottingham
Wolverhampton
East Midlands
Norwich
Leicester
Peterborough
Great Yarmouth
Birmingham
Coventry
Aberystwyth
Birmingham
Northampton
Warwick
Cambridge
Ipswich
Worcester
Stratford-upon-Avon
Milton Keynes
Cheltenham
Stansted
Colchester
Gloucester
Oxford
Luton
Swansea
Newport
Watford
Southend-on-Sea
Swindon
Reading
LONDON
City
Cardiff
Bristol
Heathrow
Bath
Basingstoke
Salisbury
Winchester
Guildford
Maidstone
Canterbury
Taunton
Gatwick
Dover
Tunbridge Wells
Channel Tunnel Terminal
Southampton
Brighton
Portsmouth
Exeter
Bournemouth
Eastbourne
Newquay
Torquay
Plymouth

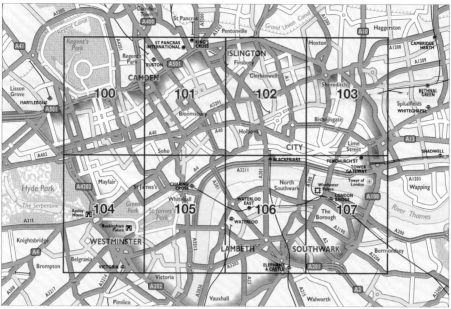

105 F6 Abbey Orchard Street
107 K6 Abbey Street
107 G1 Abchurch Lane
107 H7 Aberdour Street
105 H6 Abingdon Street
101 J2 Acton Street
104 B2 Adam's Row
105 J2 Adam Street
105 K5 Addington Street
101 G5 Adeline Place
102 C3 Agdon Street
104 E2 Air Street
106 B4 Alaska Street
100 C1 Albany Street
102 A4 Albemarle Street
102 D4 Albion Place
101 F1 Aldenham Street
103 F6 Aldermanbury
102 E4 Aldersgate Street
104 B3 Aldford Street
103 J7 Aldgate
103 K6 Aldgate High Street
101 K7 Aldwych
101 F5 Alfred Place
107 H7 Alice Street
103 K7 Alie Street
107 F2 All Hallows Lane
104 D6 Allington Street
107 K7 Alscot Road
104 E7 Ambrosden Avenue
106 E4 America Street
101 J2 Ampton Street
102 B1 Amwell Street
107 G2 Angel Lane
102 E6 Angel Street
104 A5 Ann's Close
105 F3 Apple Tree Yard
103 H4 Appold Street
106 B3 Aquinas Street
106 E7 Arch Street
101 H2 Argyle Square
101 H2 Argyle Street
100 E7 Argyll Street
104 E3 Arlington Street
102 C1 Arlington Way
101 H6 Arne Street
103 K2 Arnold Circus
107 G2 Arthur Street
103 J5 Artillery Lane
105 F6 Artillery Row
106 A1 Arundel Street
103 H2 Ashby Street
103 H2 Ashford Street
104 E7 Ashley Place
100 D1 Augustus Street
103 J2 Austin Street
106 C7 Austral Street
102 D6 Ave Maria Lane
104 C1 Avery Row
100 B5 Aybrook Street
102 C3 Aylesbury Street
106 E4 Ayres Street
105 F3 Babmaes Street
103 G2 Bache's Street
102 B4 Back Hill
107 J7 Bacon Grove
106 G6 Bainbridge Street
102 B3 Baker's Row
100 A4 Baker Street
102 B1 Balderton Street
102 B5 Baldwin's Gardens

104 B2 Balfour Place
102 E3 Baltic Street East
102 E4 Baltic Street West
107 F3 Bank East
106 E2 Bankside
103 F3 Banner Street
106 C3 Barge House Street
104 D2 Barlow Place
100 E1 Barnby Street
107 J4 Barnham Street
106 C5 Baron's Place
100 B7 Barrett Street
101 H6 Barter Street
102 E5 Bartholomew Close
103 G6 Bartholomew Lane
101 G7 Bartholomew Row
102 C6 Bartlett Court
103 F6 Basinghall Lane
103 F6 Basinghall Street
102 E3 Bastwick Street
101 F6 Bateman's Buildings
103 J3 Bateman's Row
101 F7 Bateman Street
103 F2 Bath Street
106 E6 Bath Terrace
107 H3 Battle Bridge Lane
101 F5 Bayley Street
106 B5 Baylis Road
104 E1 Beak Street
106 D3 Bear Lane
100 E3 Beaumont Place
100 B4 Beaumont Street
107 G6 Beckett Street
107 G3 Bedale Street
101 G5 Bedford Avenue
105 H2 Bedfordbury
101 H5 Bedford Place
101 G5 Bedford Square
105 H2 Bedford Street
101 G3 Bedford Way
102 E4 Beech Street
102 D6 Beeston Place
104 B6 Belgrave Place
104 B6 Belgrave Square
101 H1 Belgrove Street
103 J5 Bell Lane
102 B6 Bell Yard
105 K5 Belvedere Road
100 B6 Benjamin Street
100 B6 Bentinck Street
104 C2 Berkeley Square
104 D3 Berkeley Street
107 H5 Bermondsey Street
101 H4 Bernard Street
101 F6 Berners Place
100 E6 Berners Street
102 D3 Berry Street
101 F7 Berwick Street
103 K3 Bethnal Green Road
101 H6 Betterton Street
103 G1 Bevenden Street
103 J6 Bevis Marks
100 A4 Bickenhall Street
101 G2 Bidborough Street
103 J7 Billiter Street
100 B4 Bingham Place
103 J2 Binney Street
103 G7 Birchin Lane
105 F5 Birdcage Walk
102 C7 Bride Lane
100 B7 Bird Street

101 H1 Birkenhead Street
103 H5 Bishopsgate
106 E5 Bittern Street
103 H3 Blackall Street
104 B2 Blackburne's Mews
106 D1 Black Friars Lane
106 C5 Blackfriars Road
107 G6 Blackhorse Court
106 A6 Blandford Street
100 C7 Blenheim Street
103 F1 Bletchley Street
103 G5 Blomfield Street
101 H5 Bloomsbury Square
100 C5 Bloomsbury Street
101 H6 Bloomsbury Way
104 E3 Blue Ball Yard
100 D4 Bolsover Street
104 D3 Bolton Street
103 G4 Bonhill Street
103 H2 Boot Street
106 E5 Borough High Street
106 D6 Borough Road
104 B7 Boscobel Place
107 H2 Botolph Lane
106 C4 Boundary Row
103 J2 Boundary Street
104 C2 Bourdon Street
102 C7 Bouverie Street
103 F7 Bow Lane
102 B3 Bowling Green Lane
101 J4 Boswell Street
101 J7 Bow Street
106 D5 Boyfield Street
103 K6 Braham Street
102 E7 Bread Street
102 B6 Bream's Buildings
106 D6 Bressenden Place
104 E2 Brewer Street
103 K3 Brick Lane
104 C4 Brick Street
102 C7 Bridewell Place
105 H5 Bridge Street
106 E1 Bridge Street
101 G1 Brill Place
102 C4 Briset Street
101 J1 Britannia Street
103 F1 Britannia Walk
103 F1 Britannia Way
102 C4 Britton Street
104 C2 Broadbent Street
104 D3 Broadley Street
105 G5 Broad Sanctuary
102 A5 Broadstone Place
100 B1 Broad Walk
104 B3 Broad Walk
106 C3 Broadwall
105 F6 Broadway
101 F7 Broadwick Street
107 F6 Brockham Street
106 C7 Brook Drive
102 B5 Brook Street
104 C1 Brook Street
104 B1 Brown Heart Gardens
101 K3 Brownlow Mews
102 A5 Brownlow Street
103 K5 Brune Street
103 J5 Brunswick Close
103 G2 Brunswick Place
101 H3 Brunswick Square
101 H2 Brunswick Street
103 J5 Brushfield Street

104 D2 Bruton Lane
104 D2 Bruton Place
104 D2 Bruton Street
100 A7 Bryanston Street
104 D6 Buckingham Gate
104 C7 Buckingham Palace Road
104 E6 Buckingham Place
100 B6 Bulstrode Street
103 F3 Bunhill Row
106 B6 Burdett Street
107 G6 Burge Street
104 E2 Burlington Arcade
104 D2 Burlington Gardens
106 D3 Burrell Street
101 G2 Burton Street
101 H5 Bury Place
103 J6 Bury Street
104 E3 Bury Street
107 G2 Bush Lane
103 G2 Buttesland Street
101 F4 Byng Place
107 J2 Byward Street
104 A7 Cadogan Gate
104 A7 Cadogan Lane
104 A6 Cadogan Place
101 J1 Caledonian Road
101 H1 Caledonia Street
101 K3 Calthorpe Street
103 J2 Calvert Avenue
103 K4 Calvin Street
100 C3 Cambridge Gate
100 D3 Cambridge Gate Mews
100 C2 Cambridge Terrace
103 K3 Camlet Street
103 H6 Camomile Street
107 F1 Cannon Street
105 H5 Canon Row
101 F4 Capper Street
100 D4 Carburton Street
100 E2 Cardington Street
102 A6 Carey Street
106 A6 Carlisle Lane
104 E7 Carlisle Place
101 F6 Carlisle Street
104 C2 Carlos Place
105 F4 Carlton Gardens
105 F3 Carlton House Terrace
106 C1 Carmelite Street
100 E7 Carnaby Street
104 C2 Carpenter Street
104 C3 Carrington Street
105 F5 Carteret Street
102 D7 Carter Lane
105 J2 Carting Lane
101 G2 Cartwright Gardens
104 E6 Castle Lane
104 E6 Catherine Place
105 J1 Catherine Street
100 D6 Cavendish Place
100 C6 Cavendish Square
105 F6 Caxton Street
103 F2 Cayton Street
106 A6 Centaur Street
104 E2 Central Street
102 C1 Chadwell Street
105 F7 Chadwick Street
101 G1 Chalton Street
103 K2 Chambord Street
106 D3 Chancel Street
102 B6 Chancery Lane
103 K3 Chance Street

105 H2 Chandos Place
100 D5 Chandos Street
106 B6 Chapel Street
106 C5 Chaplin Close
101 G6 Charing Cross Road
105 F3 Charles II Street
103 H2 Charles Square
103 J2 Charles Street
103 H2 Charlotte Road
100 E5 Charlotte Street
102 C4 Charterhouse Square
102 C5 Charterhouse Street
103 G2 Chart Street
102 E6 Cheapside
101 F5 Chenies Street
103 F3 Chequer Street
103 F4 Chequer Street
104 B7 Chesham Close
104 A7 Chesham Place
104 A7 Chesham Street
100 C1 Chester Close North
100 D2 Chester Close South
104 C3 Chesterfield Gardens
104 C3 Chesterfield Hill
104 C3 Chesterfield Street
100 C2 Chester Gate
104 C6 Chester Mews
100 C1 Chester Place
100 C2 Chester Road
104 C7 Chester Square
104 C6 Chester Street
100 C2 Chester Terrace
105 K4 Chicheley Street
100 A5 Chiltern Street
103 F4 Chiswell Street
100 E4 Chitty Street
103 H3 Christina Street
103 J4 Christopher Street
101 G2 Church Way
102 D1 City Garden Row
102 D1 City Road
103 G3 City Road
102 B1 Claremont Square
100 D2 Clarence Gardens
104 D3 Clarges Street
100 A5 Clay Street
107 G1 Clements Lane
103 G3 Clere Street
102 C4 Clerkenwell Green
102 C3 Clerkenwell Lane
102 B3 Clerkenwell Road
104 E3 Cleveland Place
104 E4 Cleveland Row
100 D4 Cleveland Street
104 D2 Clifford Street
107 F3 Clink Street
100 D4 Clipstone Street
107 F1 Cloak Lane
102 D5 Cloth Fair
102 C5 Cloth Street
103 K3 Club Row
107 H6 Cluny Place
103 J6 Cobb Street
100 E1 Cobourg Street
104 E7 Cobourg Close
105 G3 Cockspur Street
106 B3 Coin Street
106 E6 Coleman Street
107 F5 Cole Street
106 C4 College Street
106 K3 Colnbrook Street

103 G5 Moorgate
103 F5 Moor Lane
103 F2 Mora Street
102 D2 Moreland Street
107 H4 Morgan's Lane
106 B6 Morley Street
107 H5 Morocco Street
104 E7 Morpeth Terrace
100 E5 Mortimer Street
101 F5 Morwell Street
104 A6 Motcomb Street
102 A4 Mount Pleasant
104 C2 Mount Row
104 B2 Mount Street
100 B5 Moxon Street
103 H2 Mundy Street
100 D3 Munster Square
107 F7 Munton Road
106 B5 Murphy Street
103 F1 Murray Grove
101 H5 Museum Street
102 B1 Myddelton Passage
102 B2 Myddelton Square
102 C2 Myddelton Street
102 B2 Naoroji Street
100 D2 Nash Street
100 E5 Nassau Street
103 J3 Navarre Street
101 H6 Neal Street
107 K6 Neckinger
102 D1 Nelson Place
106 D4 Nelson Square
102 D1 Nelson Terrace
100 E2 Netley Street
100 C7 New Bond Street
102 C7 New Bridge Street
103 G5 New Broad Street
104 E2 New Burlington Street
102 E5 Newbury Street
100 C5 New Cavendish Street
102 E7 New Change
107 F4 Newcomen Street
102 B6 New Fetter Lane
102 D6 Newgate Street
103 K6 New Goulston Street
107 J6 Newham's Row
106 E6 Newington Causeway
103 J3 New Inn Street
103 J3 New Inn Yard
107 F7 New Kent Road
101 F5 Newman Street
103 H3 New North Place
103 G1 New North Road
101 J4 New North Street
101 G6 New Oxford Street
105 H2 New Row
102 A6 New Square
103 J5 New Street
102 C6 New Street Square
101 J6 Newton Street
103 F5 New Union Street
107 G1 Nicholas Lane
106 C4 Nicholson Street
103 F1 Nile Street
102 E6 Noble Street
100 E6 Noel Street
102 E2 Norman Street
102 B3 Northampton Road
102 D2 Northampton Square
104 B1 North Audley Street
102 D3 Northburgh Street
100 E2 North Gower Street
101 K4 Northington Street
102 A4 North Mews
104 A1 North Row
103 J7 Northumberland Alley
105 H3 Northumberland Avenue
105 H3 Northumberland Street
103 J4 Norton Folgate
102 B6 Norwich Street
100 B4 Nottingham Place
100 B4 Nottingham Street
107 F4 O'Meara Street
100 E5 Ogle Street
102 D6 Old Bailey
104 A5 Old Barrack Yard
104 D2 Old Bond Street
103 G6 Old Broad Street
104 D2 Old Burlington Street
100 B4 Oldbury Place
103 K6 Old Castle Street
100 C6 Old Cavendish Street
105 F1 Old Compton Street
101 H4 Old Gloucester Street
103 F7 Old Jewry
103 J3 Old Nichol Street
101 J5 Old North Street
105 J7 Old Paradise Street
104 C4 Old Park Lane
105 F6 Old Pye Street
105 G5 Old Queen Street
102 A6 Old Square
102 E3 Old Street
101 J1 Omega Place
106 D6 Ontario Street
105 G2 Orange Street
100 B6 Orchard Street
101 J4 Ordehall Street
106 C7 Orient Street
100 D3 Osnaburgh Street
100 D3 Osnaburgh Terrace
101 G1 Ossulston Street
106 D7 Oswin Street
100 B3 Outer Circle
100 C1 Outer Circle
102 C1 Owen Street
105 F2 Oxendon Street
100 B7 Oxford Street
100 A5 Paddington Street
107 J7 Page's Walk
105 G7 Page Street
102 A2 Pakenham Street
104 E6 Palace Street
105 F3 Pall Mall
105 G3 Pall Mall East
105 F6 Palmer Street
105 F2 Panton Street
107 G6 Pardoner Street
106 C3 Paris Garden
100 C4 Park Crescent
101 H6 Parker Street
104 A2 Park Lane
104 E3 Park Place
100 C3 Park Square East
100 C3 Park Square West
104 A1 Park Street
106 E3 Park Street
105 H5 Parliament Square
105 H5 Parliament Street
103 H3 Paul Street
104 A7 Pavilion Road
104 A7 Pavilion Street
106 B6 Pearman Street
102 C3 Pear Tree Court
102 E3 Pear Tree Street
103 F2 Peerless Street
103 K2 Pelter Street
102 B6 Pemberton Row
104 B5 Pembroke Close
101 K1 Penton Rise
101 J1 Pentonville Road
106 E4 Pepper Street
107 J2 Pepys Street
102 D3 Percival Street
102 A2 Percy Circus
101 F5 Percy Street
105 F1 Peter Street
100 D3 Peto Place
103 J5 Petticoat Lane
105 F6 Petty France
107 J2 Petty Wales
107 H2 Philpot Lane
103 H3 Phipp Street
102 A3 Phoenix Place
101 F1 Phoenix Road
101 G7 Phoenix Street
104 D4 Piccadilly
104 E3 Piccadilly Arcade
105 F2 Piccadilly Circus
102 D1 Pickard Street
107 F5 Pilgrimage Street
103 H4 Pindar Street
102 B3 Pine Street
103 H1 Pitfield Street
103 H2 Pitfield Street
103 J4 Plough Yard
106 D5 Pocock Street
100 E7 Poland Street
101 F1 Polygon Road
104 A6 Pont Street
107 J5 Pope Street
107 G5 Porlock Street
100 A4 Porter Street
106 F3 Porter Street
100 C4 Portland Place
100 A6 Portman Close
100 A6 Portman Square
100 A7 Portman Street
102 B4 Portpool Lane
101 K6 Portsmouth Street
107 K1 Portsoken Street
101 K6 Portugal Street
107 G6 Potier Street
103 F7 Poultry
107 K1 Prescot Street
103 H4 Primrose Street
103 G6 Prince's Street
103 K4 Princelet Street
106 D7 Princess Street
100 D7 Princes Street
101 J5 Princeton Street
107 G7 Prioress Street
101 J5 Proctor Street
104 B1 Provident Court
103 G1 Provost Street
107 G2 Pudding Lane
107 J6 Purbrook Street
103 K4 Quaker Street
104 E4 Queen's Walk
107 J3 Queen's Walk
105 F5 Queen Anne's Gate
100 C6 Queen Ann Street
107 K4 Queen Elizabeth Street
101 H4 Queen Square
103 F7 Queen Street
104 C3 Queen Street
107 F2 Queen Street Place
103 F7 Queen Victoria Street
106 E1 Queen Victoria Street
107 J6 Radcliffe Road
103 F2 Radnor Street
107 G3 Railway Approach
100 E6 Ramillies Place
100 E6 Ramillies Street
101 F6 Rathbone Place
101 F5 Rathbone Street
103 K1 Ravenscroft Street
102 C2 Rawstone Street
103 J3 Redchurch Street
107 F4 Redcross Way
100 D1 Redhill Street
101 J5 Red Lion Square
101 K5 Red Lion Street
104 E2 Regent Place
101 H2 Regent Square
100 D7 Regent Street
105 F2 Regent Street
102 D1 Remington Street
101 J6 Remnant Street
106 C3 Rennie Street
103 K3 Rhoda Street
105 H4 Richmond Terrace
101 F4 Ridgemount Gardens
101 F4 Ridgemount Street
100 D5 Riding House Street
107 J6 Riley Road
106 D4 Risborough Street
102 B2 River Street
103 H2 Rivington Street
100 A6 Robert Adam Street
100 D2 Robert Street
103 K2 Rochelle Street
105 F7 Rochester Row
105 F7 Rochester Street
106 E7 Rockingham Street
100 A5 Rodmarton Street
107 F7 Rodney Place
101 K4 Roger Street
105 G1 Romilly Street
105 G7 Romney Street
107 H2 Rood Lane
103 F5 Ropemaker Street
107 J5 Roper Lane
103 F3 Roscoe Street
106 E3 Rose Alley
102 B3 Rosebery Avenue
106 D6 Rotary Street
107 H6 Rothsay Street
106 B4 Roupell Street
107 H5 Royal Oak Yard
105 K6 Royal Street
101 J4 Rugby Street
105 F1 Rupert Street
106 D5 Rushworth Street
101 H4 Russell Square
105 J1 Russell Street
104 E3 Ryder Street
104 E2 Sackville Street
102 C4 Saffron Hill
102 C4 Saffron Street
106 A7 Sail Street
105 F2 St Alban's Street
100 C3 St Andrew's Place
106 D1 St Andrews Hill
102 C5 St Andrew Street
105 G6 St Ann's Street
101 F7 St Anne's Court
104 C1 St Anselm's Place
103 J6 St Botolph Street
102 C6 St Bride Street
101 H1 St Chads Street
101 K6 St Clements Lane
102 B4 St Cross Street
107 H2 St Dunstan's Hill
106 C6 St George's Circus
106 C6 St George's Road
104 D1 St George Street
101 G6 St Giles High Street
104 E4 St James's Place
105 F3 St James's Square
104 E3 St James's Street
102 C3 St James Way
102 D4 St John's Lane
102 C4 St John's Square
102 C2 St John Street
105 G2 St Martin's Lane
102 E6 St Martin's Le Grand
105 G2 St Martin's Place
107 H2 St Mary at Hill
103 H6 St Mary Axe
105 F6 St Matthew Street
102 D7 St Paul's Churchyard
107 G1 St Swithin's Lane
107 G4 St Thomas Street
100 B5 St Vincent Street
102 C7 Salisbury Court
101 K5 Sandland Street
101 H2 Sandwich Street
102 C3 Sans Walk
101 J6 Sardinia Street
104 D1 Savile Row
105 J2 Savoy Hill
105 J2 Savoy Place
105 J2 Savoy Street
106 E4 Sawyer Street
103 K3 Sclater Street
106 D4 Scoresby Street
103 H3 Scrutton Street
107 G7 Searles Road
102 D2 Sebastian Street
106 B4 Secker Street
101 K2 Seddon Street
107 J2 Seething Lane
102 C3 Sekforde Street
102 A6 Serle Street
104 A4 Serpentine Road
101 G7 Seven Dials
104 A5 Seville Street
102 E2 Seward Street
100 B6 Seymour Mews
100 A7 Seymour Street
107 K4 Shad Thames
101 G7 Shaftesbury Avenue
107 H4 Shand Street
103 J1 Shenfield Street
103 F1 Shepherdess Walk
104 C3 Shepherd Street
107 H5 Ship and Mermaid Row
102 C6 Shoe Lane
103 J2 Shoreditch High Street
107 K2 Shorter Street
101 H7 Shorts Gardens
106 C4 Short Street
101 J2 Sidmouth Street
106 D5 Silex Street
103 F5 Silk Street
107 F5 Silvester Street
103 G2 Singer Street
102 C3 Skinner Street
104 A6 Sloane Street
102 D5 Smithfield Street
105 H7 Smith Square
102 C5 Snow Hill
107 G4 Snowsfields
101 F6 Soho Square
101 F6 Soho Street
107 F5 Southall Place
102 A5 Southampton Buildings
101 H5 Southampton Place
101 H4 Southampton Row
105 H2 Southampton Street
104 B2 South Audley Street
100 C7 South Molton Lane
100 C7 South Molton Street
103 G5 South Place
102 A5 South Square
104 B3 South Street
106 E5 Southwark Bridge Road
106 D3 Southwark Street
107 K7 Spa Road
102 C2 Spencer Street
104 E6 Spenser Street
103 J4 Spital Square
105 G3 Spring Gardens
107 F6 Spurgeon Street
106 B5 Spur Road
104 E4 Stable Yard Road
101 G6 Stacey Street
104 D6 Stafford Place
104 D3 Stafford Street
107 G4 Stainer Street
106 B3 Stamford Street
104 B3 Stanhope Gate
104 C4 Stanhope Row
100 D1 Stanhope Street
107 G5 Staple Street
100 E2 Starcross Street
100 E3 Stephenson Way
101 F6 Stephen Street
107 J6 Stevens Street
106 E2 Stew Lane
102 A5 Stone Buildings
102 C6 Stonecutter Street
103 J6 Stoney Lane
107 F3 Stoney Street
101 F5 Store Street
105 G5 Storey's Gate
105 H2 Strand
100 C6 Stratford Place
104 D3 Stratton Street
103 J5 Strype Street
101 H6 Stukeley Street
106 E5 Sudrey Street
107 G2 Suffolk Lane
106 D3 Sumner Street
103 H4 Sun Street
106 D4 Surrey Row
106 A1 Surrey Street
101 F6 Sutton Row
103 F4 Suttons Way
104 E2 Swallow Street
103 K2 Swanfield Street
107 G2 Swan Lane
107 H7 Swan Mead
107 F6 Swan Street
107 K5 Sweeney Crescent
101 J2 Swinton Street
102 G6 Tabard Street
103 G4 Tabernacle Street
107 J5 Tanner Street
103 F1 Taplow Street
101 H3 Tavistock Place
101 G3 Tavistock Square
105 J2 Tavistock Street
101 F3 Taviton Street
106 C1 Temple Avenue
102 B7 Temple Lane
106 A2 Temple Place
107 F4 Tennis Street
100 C7 Tenterden Street
104 D7 Terminus Place
101 H2 Thanet Street
100 B6 Thayer Street
106 C4 The Cut
106 B4 Theed Street
107 J6 The Grange
104 E4 The Mall
101 J5 Theobald's Road
107 G7 Theobald Street
104 E7 Thirleby Road
102 E1 Thoresby Street
106 E3 Thrale Street
103 K5 Thrawl Street
103 G6 Threadneedle Street
103 G6 Throgmorton Avenue
103 G6 Throgmorton Street
106 E6 Tiverton Street
101 H2 Tonbridge Street
107 G3 Tooley Street
107 J4 Tooley Street
101 F4 Torrington Place
101 G4 Torrington Square
105 G6 Tothill Street
100 E4 Tottenham Court Road
100 E5 Tottenham Street
106 E5 Toulmin Street
107 K2 Tower Bridge Approach
107 H7 Tower Bridge Road
107 J2 Tower Hill
107 J2 Tower Place
101 G7 Tower Street
103 K5 Toynbee Street
105 G3 Trafalgar Square
104 C3 Trebeck Street
107 F6 Trinity Church Square
107 J2 Trinity Square
107 F6 Trinity Street
103 F6 Trump Street
106 C1 Tudor Street
105 G6 Tufton Street
102 C4 Turnmill Street
107 H5 Tyers Gate
106 C5 Ufford Street
100 C4 Ulster Place
103 H6 Undershaft
103 F1 Underwood Street
106 D4 Union Street
103 J1 Union Walk
100 E4 University Street
104 B6 Upper Belgrave Street
104 A2 Upper Brook Street
104 A2 Upper Grosvenor Street
106 B3 Upper Ground
100 C3 Upper Harley Street
104 E1 Upper James Street
104 E1 Upper John Street
105 K6 Upper Marsh
105 G1 Upper St Martin's
106 E2 Upper Thames Street
100 C4 Upper Wimpole Street
101 G2 Upper Woburn Place
106 C5 Valentine Place
105 F6 Vandon Passage
104 E6 Vandon Street
103 H4 Vandy Street
100 D2 Varndell Street
107 K7 Vauban Street
104 E7 Vauxhall Bridge Road
100 C6 Vere Street
101 H5 Vernon Place
101 K1 Vernon Rise
102 B5 Verulam Street
103 G2 Vestry Street
105 H4 Victoria Embankment
104 D6 Victoria Square
104 D7 Victoria Street
104 E2 Vigo Street
105 H3 Villiers Street
105 F7 Vincent Square
103 G2 Vince Street
103 J7 Vine Street
103 K2 Virginia Road
102 E4 Viscount Street
101 H2 Wakefield Street
102 D1 Wakley Street
107 F1 Walbrook
106 B7 Walcot Square
106 B7 Walnut Tree Walk
106 E4 Warden's Grove
101 F7 Wardour Street
102 B4 Warner Street
100 D4 Warren Street
105 G3 Warwick House Street
102 D6 Warwick Lane
104 D6 Warwick Row
104 E2 Warwick Street
105 F3 Waterloo Place
106 B5 Waterloo Road
103 J2 Waterson Street
102 E7 Watling Street
104 C3 Waverton Street
107 J4 Weavers Lane
106 C5 Webber Row
106 C5 Webber Street
107 H7 Webb Street
104 B1 Weigh House Street
100 C5 Welbeck Street
100 C6 Welbeck Way
103 F1 Wellesley Terrace
105 J1 Wellington Street
100 E6 Wells Street
102 E1 Wenlock Road
103 F1 Wenlock Street
103 K5 Wentworth Street
101 F1 Werrington Street
107 H4 Western Street
104 A6 West Halkin Street
103 F1 Westland Place
106 A5 Westminster Bridge Road
100 B5 Westmoreland Street
107 G6 Weston Street
107 H4 Weston Street
102 C5 West Poultry Avenue
102 D5 West Smithfield
106 C7 West Square
105 G1 West Street
103 K7 West Tenter Street
100 C5 Weymouth Street
102 E1 Wharf Road
102 A2 Wharton Street
100 B5 Wheatley Street
103 K4 Wheler Street
101 J6 Whetstone Park
101 H2 Whidborne Street
102 C2 Whiskin Street
103 K3 Whitby Street
105 G2 Whitcomb Street
107 H5 White's Grounds
103 K5 White's Row
103 K6 Whitechapel High Street
103 F3 Whitecross Street
102 C7 Whitefriars Street
105 H4 Whitehall
105 H4 Whitehall Court
105 H3 Whitehall Place
107 G4 White Hart Yard
104 C3 White Horse Street
103 J6 White Kennett Street
106 D2 White Lion Hill
100 E4 Whitfield Street
106 B4 Whittlesey Street
101 J1 Wicklow Street
103 J5 Widegate Street
100 C6 Wigmore Place
100 B6 Wigmore Street
107 H6 Wild's Rents
101 J6 Wild Street
104 E6 Wilfred Street
103 K5 Wilkes Street
105 H2 William IV Street
100 E2 William Road
103 H3 Willow Street
107 J7 Willow Walk
102 B2 Wilmington Square
102 B2 Wilmington Street
103 G5 Wilson Street
104 A5 Wilton Crescent
104 A5 Wilton Place
104 A5 Wilton Row
104 C6 Wilton Street
100 C5 Wimpole Mews
100 C5 Wimpole Street
101 F5 Windmill Street
102 E1 Windsor Terrace
105 F1 Winnett Street
100 E6 Winsley Street
101 G3 Woburn Place
101 G4 Woburn Square
102 C3 Woodbridge Street
107 J6 Woods Place
102 E6 Wood Street
106 B4 Wooton Street
103 H6 Wormwood Street
103 H4 Worship Street
101 K3 Wren Street
102 C2 Wyclif Street
102 C2 Wynyat Street
102 B2 Yardley Street
105 H2 York Boulevard
100 B3 York Bridge
100 B4 York Gate
105 K4 York Road
100 A5 York Street
100 B4 York Terrace East
100 A4 York Terrace West
101 H1 York Way
106 E3 Zoar Street

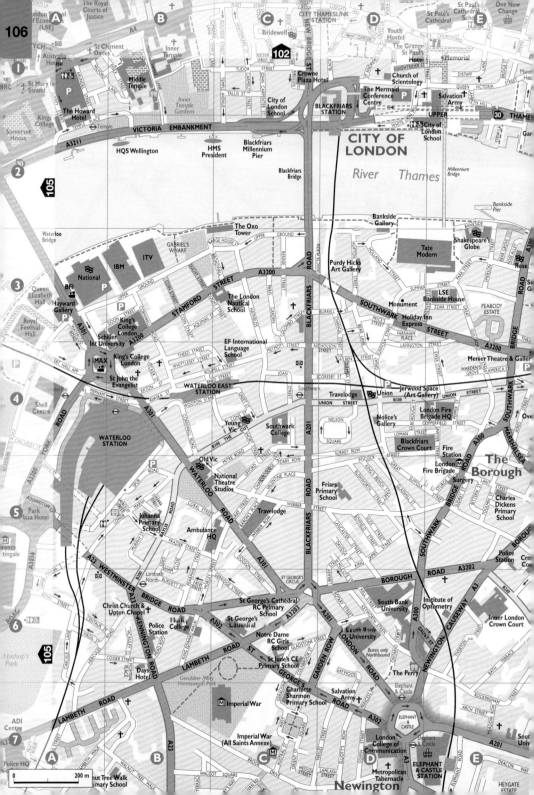

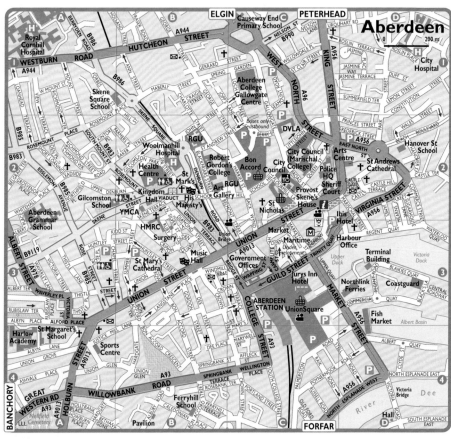

C4 Affleck Street
A3 Albert Place
D4 Albert Quay
A3 Albert Street
B4 Albury Road
A4 Albyn Lane
A3 Albyn Place
A3 Alford Place
B1 Ann Street
A4 Ashvale Place
C2 Back Wynd
B2 Baker Street
D2 Beach Boulevard
A1 Belgrave Terrace
C2 Belmont Street
C2 Berry Street
A1 Berryden Road
B2 Blackfriars Street
D3 Black's Lane
D3 Blaikies Quay
B4 Bon Accord Crescent
B3 Bon Accord Street
B3 Bon Accord Terrace
C3 Bridge Street
C2 Broad Street
B4 Caledonian Place
C3 Carmelite Street
D2 Castle Hill
D2 Castle Terrace
D2 Castlegate
D3 Central Roadway
A3 Chapel Street
B1 Charlotte Street
D4 Clyde Street
C3 College Street
D2 Commerce Street

D3 Commercial Quay
D1 Constitution Street
B1 Craigie Street
B3 Crimon Place
B3 Crown Street
C3 Crown Terrace
B4 Dee Place
B3 Dee Street
B2 Denburn Road
B3 Diamond Street
D1 Duff Street
D2 East North Street
A2 Eden Place
A2 Esslemont Avenue
B2 Farmers Place
B4 Ferryhill Terrace
C2 Flourmill Lane
A1 Forbes Street
B1 Fraser Road
D2 Frederick Street
C1 Gallowgate
B1 George Street
B1 Gerrard Street
B2 Gilcomston Park
B3 Golden Square
B3 Gordon Street
A4 Great Western Road
A2 Grosvenor Place
C3 Guild Street
D2 Hadden Street
D2 Hanover Street
A4 Hardgate
B4 Hardgate
C2 Harriet Street
B2 Hill Street
A4 Holburn Street

A1 Holland Street
A4 Hollybank Place
A4 Howburn Place
A3 Huntley Street
B1 Hutcheon Street
D2 James Street
D1 Jasmine Place
D1 Jasmine Terrace
D1 Jasmine Way
B2 John Street
B1 Jopp's Lane
A4 Justice Mill Lane
A3 Kidd Street
C1 King Street
A2 Kintore Place
B3 Langstane Place
A2 Leadside Road
D1 Lemon Street
C2 Littlejohn Street
A1 Loanhead Terrace
C1 Loch Street
B1 Maberly Street
D2 Marischal Street
C4 Marywell Street
D2 Mearns Street
A1 Mount Street
C1 Nelson Street
D4 North Esplanade East
D4 North Esplanade West
B2 North Silver Street
A2 Northfield Place
C4 Old Ford Road
C4 Palmerston Road
C4 Park Street
C4 Portland Street

C4 Poynernook Road
D2 Princes Street
C2 Queen Street
C4 Raik Road
D3 Regent Quay
D3 Regent Road
A2 Richmond Street
A1 Richmond Terrace
A2 Richmond Walk
A3 Rose Place
A3 Rose Street
B4 Rosebank Terrace
A3 Rosemount Place
A2 Rosemount Viaduct
D1 Roslin Place
B1 Roslin Terrace
A3 Rubislaw Place
A3 Rubislaw Terrace
B3 Ruby Lane
C4 Russell Road
B2 St Andrew Street
C1 St Clair Street
C4 St Mary's
C2 School Hill
C1 Seamount Road
C3 Shiprow
A2 Short Loanings
B2 Skene Square
A3 Skene Street
B3 Skene Terrace
C4 South College Street
D4 South Esplanade East
A3 South Mount Street
B2 Spa Street
B1 Spring Garden
B4 Springbank Street

B4 Springbank Terrace
C4 Stell Road
D2 Sugarhouse Lane
B3 Summer Street
D1 Summerfield Terrace
A3 Thistle Lane
A3 Thistle Place
A3 Thistle Street
C3 Trinity Quay
B3 Union Bridge
A4 Union Glen
A4 Union Grove
B3 Union Row
B3 Union Street
B2 Union Terrace
A2 Upper Denburn
C3 Upper Quay
D1 Urquhart Road
D4 Victoria Bridge
D4 Victoria Road
A3 Victoria Street
A1 View Terrace
D2 Virginia Street
D2 Wales Street
C3 Wapping Street
D3 Waterloo Quay
A3 Waverley Lane
A3 Waverley Place
C4 Wellington Place
A4 West Mount Street
C1 West North Street
A1 Westburn Road
A2 Whitehall Place
A4 Willowbank Road
C1 Willowdale Place
B3 Windmill Brae

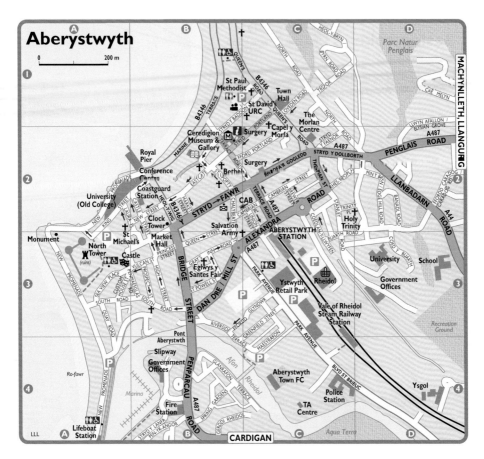

C3	Alexandra Road	B3	High Street	A3	South Road
D2	Banadl Road	A2	King Street	B4	Spring Gardens
C4	Boulevard St Brieuc	A2	Laura Place	C2	Stanley Road
C2	Brewer Street	D2	Llanbadarn Road	B2	Stryd Portland
B3	Bridge Street	D1	Llwyn Afallon	B2	Stryd Y Baddon
C3	Buarth Road	C1	Loveden Road	C2	Stryd Y Dollborth
C1	Byrn Road	C4	Maesyrafon	C2	Stryd Y Faenor
D1	Cae Melyn	B2	Marine Terrace	B4	Stryd Y Lanfa
B2	Cambrian Place	B2	Market Street	B2	St-Y-Popty
C2	Cambrian Street	B3	Mill Street	B2	Terrace Road
D2	Caradog Road	D2	Min Y Bryn	C2	Thespian Street
B2	Castle Street	A2	New Promenade	C1	Trefor Road
B2	Chalybeate Street	B2	New Street	C2	Trinity Place
C2	Coedlan-Y-Llwyfen	C1	North Road	C2	Union Street
D3	Coed Y Buarth	C3	Park Avenue	B3	Vulcan Street
A3	Custom House	D2	Penglais Road	B2	Y Stryd Fawr
	Street	A3	Penmaesglas Road		
B3	Dan Dre	B4	Penparcau Road		
B2	Eastgate	B4	Pen-Yr-Angor		
D2	Edge Hill Road	B3	Pont Aberystwth		
D1	Elysian Grove	B3	Princess Street		
D2	Ffordd Caradog	B3	Prospect Street		
B3	Ffordd Glyndwr	A3	Quay Road		
B2	Fford Portland	B1	Queen's Road		
B4	Gerddi Rheidol	B3	Queen Street		
B4	Glanrafon Terrace	C2	Rhes-Y-Poplys		
B3	Gray's Inn Road	C2	Rhodfa'r Gogledd		
C3	Greenfield Street	B3	Riverside Terrace		
C1	Heol-Y-Bryn	B3	St Powell Street		
B2	Heol-Y-Wig	A3	Sea View Place		

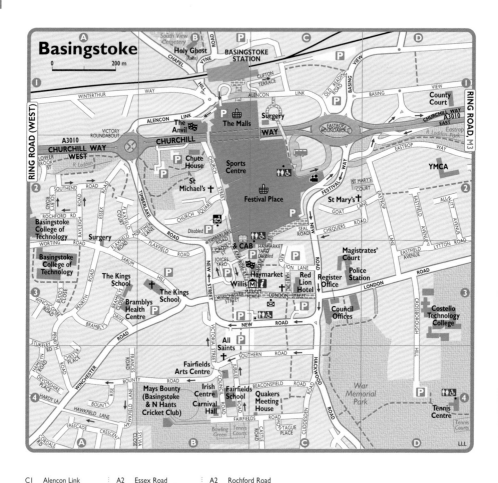

C1	Alencon Link	A2	Essex Road	A2	Rochford Road
D2	Allnutt Avenue	B4	Fairfields Road	C2	St Mary's Court
C1	Basing View	C2	Festival Way	A3	Sarum Hill
C4	Beaconsfield Road	A2	Flaxfield Court	C2	Seal Road
A4	Bounty Rise	A3	Flaxfield Road	A2	Solby's Road
A4	Bounty Road	A4	Frances Road	A2	Southend Road
A3	Bramblys Close	A4	Frescade Crescent	B4	Southern Road
A3	Bramblys Drive	C2	Goat Lane	A3	Stukeley Road
A3	Budd's Close	C4	Hackwood Road	B4	Sylvia Close
C4	Castle Road	A4	Hamelyn Road	B2	Timberlake Road
B1	Chapel Hill	A4	Hardy Lane	B3	Victoria Street
C2	Chequers Road	A4	Hawkfield Lane	A1	Victoria Roundabout
A4	Chester Place	C3	Haymarket Yard	B1	Vyne Road
B2	Churchill Way	B3	Joices Yard	A3	Winchcombe Road
D1	Churchill Way East	B4	Jubilee Road	A4	Winchester Road
A2	Churchill Way West	D3	London Road	B3	Winchester Street
B2	Church Square	C3	London Street	A1	Winterthur Way
B2	Church Street	A2	Lower Brook Street	A3	Worting Road
B3	Church Street	D3	Lytton Road	C3	Wote Street
C4	Cliddesden Road	B3	Market Place		
C1	Clifton Terrace	C3	May Place		
A4	Cordale Road	C4	Montague Place		
B4	Council Road	A2	Mortimer Lane		
D3	Crossborough Hill	B3	New Road		
B3	Cross Street	C2	New Road		
A4	Devonshire Place	B3	New Street		
D2	Eastfield Avenue	C1	Old Reading Road		
D2	Eastrop Lane	A3	Penrith Road		
C1	Eastrop Roundabout	A2	Rayleigh Road		
D2	Eastrop Way	C3	Red Lion Lane		

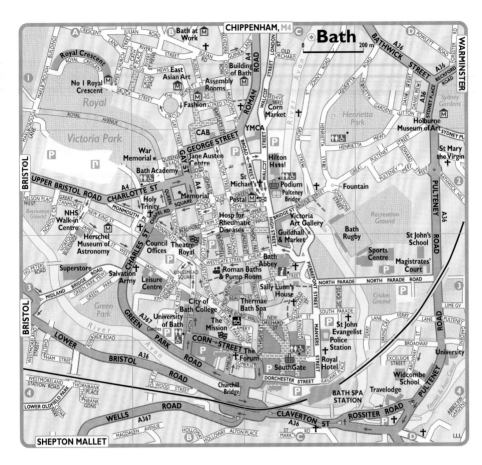

D4	Abbey View Gardens	DI	Daniel Mews	CI	London Street	B2	Queen Street	A4	Westmoreland Station Road
BI	Alfred Street	DI	Daniel Street	B3	Lower Borough Walls	C2	Quiet Street		
B4	Alton Place	C4	Dorchester Street	A3	Lower Bristol Road	C4	Railway Place	A4	Westmoreland Street
B4	Ambury	D2	Duke Street	A4	Lower Oldfield Park	A4	Riverside Road	B2	Wood Street
B3	Amery Lane	D2	Edward Street	C3	Manvers Street	BI	Rivers Street	B4	Wood Street
D4	Archway Street	D4	Excelsior Street	AI	Marlborough Buildings	BI	Rivers Street Mews	C3	York Street
C2	Argyle Street	D3	Ferry Lane	A2	Marlborough Lane	CI	Roman Road		
B3	Avon Street	DI	Forester Road	A3	Midland Bridge Road	C4	Rossiter Road		
BI	Bartlett Street	BI	Gay Street	B3	Milk Street	AI	Royal Avenue		
B2	Barton Street	C2	George Street	B2	Milsom Street	AI	Royal Crescent		
D2	Bathwick Hill	A2	Great Pulteney Street	A2	Monmouth Place	BI	Russel Street		
DI	Bathwick Street	A3	Great Stanhope Street	B2	Monmouth Street	B3	St James's Parade		
B2	Beauford Square	A3	Green Park	A2	Nelson Place West	B4	St John's Road		
B3	Beau Street	A3	Green Park Mews	B2	New Bond Street	C4	St Mark's Road		
DI	Beckford Road	A3	Green Park Road	C3	New King Street	C3	Saw Close		
CI	Beehive Yard	B2	Green Street	C3	New Orchard Street	D3	Somerset Street		
BI	Belvedere	C2	Grove Street	A3	Norfolk Buildings	C3	Southgate Street		
BI	Bennett Street	DI	Guinea Lane	A2	Norfolk Crescent	B3	South Parade		
B3	Bridewell Lane	DI	Henrietta Gardens	C3	North Parade	CI	Spring Crescent		
C2	Bridge Street	C2	Henrietta Mews	D3	North Parade Road	C4	Stall Street		
C2	Broad Street	CI	Henrietta Road	B4	Oak Street	DI	Sutton Street		
D4	Broadway	C2	Henrietta Street	B2	Old King Street	DI	Sydney Place		
AI	Brock Street	C3	Henry Street	CI	Old Orchard	D2	Sydney Place		
BI	Cath Place	C2	High Street	C3	Old Orchard Street	BI	The Circus		
A4	Cedar Way	B4	Holloway	BI	Oxford Row	A4	Thornbank Gardens		
B2	Chapel Road	B3	Hot Bath Street	B3	Parsonage Lane	A4	Thornbank Place		
A3	Charles Street	A3	Ivo Peters Road	C3	Pierrepont Street	B2	Trim Street		
A2	Charlotte Street	B3	James Street West	DI	Powlett Road	C2	Union Passage		
C3	Cheap Street	C2	Johnstone Street	B2	Princes Street	B2	Union Street		
A4	Cheltenham Street	B2	John Street	C2	Pulteney Bridge	C2	Upper Borough Walls		
B4	Churchill Bridge	AI	Julian Road	D3	Pulteney Gardens	A2	Upper Bristol Road		
BI	Circus Mews	B3	Kingsmead North	D2	Pulteney Mews	AI	Upper Church Street		
BI	Circus Place	B3	Kingsmead Square	D2	Pulteney Road	C2	Walcot Street		
C4	Claverton Street	C3	Kingston Road	B2	Queens Parade Place	A4	Wells Road		
B4	Corn Street	BI	Lansdown Road	B2	Queen Square	B3	Westgate Buildings		
AI	Crescent Lane	D3	Lime Grove	B2	Queen Street	B3	Westgate Street		

D3	Albert Street	D2	Dalton Street	B2	Lionel Street	C4	Queens Drive	A1	Vittoria Street
D4	Allison Street	D4	Dean Street	B1	Livery Street	A3	Queensway	B3	Waterloo Street
D1	Aston Street	D4	Digbeth	C3	Lower Temple	A3	Queensway Tunnel	B1	Water Street
C2	Barwick Street	C4	Dudley Street		Street	C1	St Chads	C1	Weaman Street
C1	Bath Street	B3	Eden Place	B1	Ludgate Hill		Queensway	C1	Whittall Street
B4	Beak Street	C4	Edgbaston Street	B2	Margaret Street	C4	St Jude's Pass		
C3	Bennetts Hill	B2	Edmund Street	C3	Martineau Way	D4	St Martin's Square		
A4	Berkley Street	B3	Ethel Street	B1	Mary Ann Street	C2	St Philip's Place		
B4	Blucher Street	A2	Fleet Street	D4	Moat Lane	A2	Saturday Bridge		
A3	Bridge Street	D3	Freeman Street	D3	Moor Street	B4	Severn Street		
A3	Brindley Drive	A4	Gas Street	D3	Moor Street	C1	Shadwell Street		
A3	Broad Street	A2	George Street		Queensway	C1	Smallbrook		
A1	Brook Street	D4	Gloucester Street	B4	Navigation Street		Queensway		
B3	Brunel Street	B4	Gough Street	C3	Needless Alley	C1	Snow Hill		
C2	Bull Street	A1	Graham Street	A1	Newhall Hill		Queensway		
A3	Cambridge Street	A4	Granville Street	B2	Newhall Street	C4	Station Street		
C3	Cannon Street	B2	Great Charles	D3	New Meeting Street	D2	Steelhouse Lane		
D3	Carrs Lane		Street Queensway	B3	New Street	C3	Stephenson Street		
B3	Chamberlain Square	D3	High Street	D2	Newton Street	B3	Suffolk Street		
A2	Charlotte Street	B3	Hill Street	B1	Old Snow Hill		Queensway		
C2	Cherry Street	C4	Hinckley Street	D2	Old Square	A2	Summer Row		
B2	Church Street	A2	Holland Street	A2	Paradise Circus	B3	Swallow Street		
C2	Colmore Circus	A4	Holliday Street	B3	Paradise Street	C2	Temple Row		
	Queensway	A1	James Street	D3	Park Street	C2	Temple Row West		
B3	Colmore Row	D1	James Watt	D4	Park Street	C3	Temple Street		
B4	Commercial Street		Queensway	C4	Pershore Street	D2	The Priory		
B2	Cornwall Street	B4	John Bright Street	B3	Pinfold Street		Queensway		
C3	Corporation Street	C4	Ladywell Walk	C1	Printing House	C3	Union Street		
B1	Cox Street	D4	Ladywell Walk		Street	D1	Vesey Street		
D2	Dale End	D1	Lancaster Circus			B3	Victoria Square		

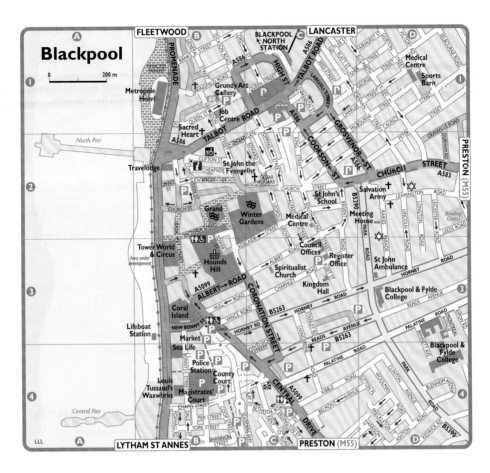

B1	Abingdon Street	B4	Dale Street	B3	New Bonny Street
B3	Adelaide Street	B2	Deansgate	C4	Palatine Road
B3	Albert Road	B1	Dickson Road	D2	Park Road
C2	Alfred Street	C2	Edward Street	D2	Peter Street
D4	Ashton Road	D1	Elizabeth Street	B4	Pier Street
B2	Bank Hey Street	C1	Fisher Street	B1	Princess Parade
B1	Banks Street	B4	Foxhall Road	B1	Promenade
C4	Belmont Avenue	D4	Freckleton Street	B1	Queen Street
D3	Bennett Avenue	B1	General Street	D2	Raikes Parade
C4	Bethesda Road	D1	George Street	C3	Reads Avenue
B2	Birley Street	D1	Gorton Street	C2	Regent Road
D4	Blenheim Avenue	D2	Granville Road	C4	Ribble Road
B4	Bonny Street	C1	Grosvenor Street	D3	Ripon Road
C1	Buchanan Street	D4	Harrison Road	B4	Seasiders Way
C1	Butler Street	C4	Havelock Street	C1	Seed Street
D1	Caunce Street	C1	High Street	D1	Selbourne Road
C2	Cedar Square	B3	Hornby Road	C2	South King Street
C4	Central Drive	B3	Hull Road	B1	Springfield Road
B4	Chapel Street	C4	Kay Street	C3	Stanley Road
C1	Charles Street	C4	Kent Road	C1	Swainson Street
C3	Charnley Road	C2	King Street	B2	Talbot Road
B2	Cheapside	C1	Larkhill Street	C2	Topping Street
B2	Church Street	D2	Leamington Road	B2	Tower Street
C2	Church Street	D2	Leicester Road	B3	Vance Road
B2	Clifton Street	C2	Leopold Grove	B2	Victoria Street
D4	Clinton Avenue	D2	Lincoln Road	D1	Victory Road
C2	Cookson Street	C3	Livingstone Road	B2	West Street
B4	Coop Street	B1	Lord Street	D4	Woolman Road
C3	Coronation Street	C4	Louise Street	B4	York Street
B2	Corporation Street	C1	Milbourne Street		

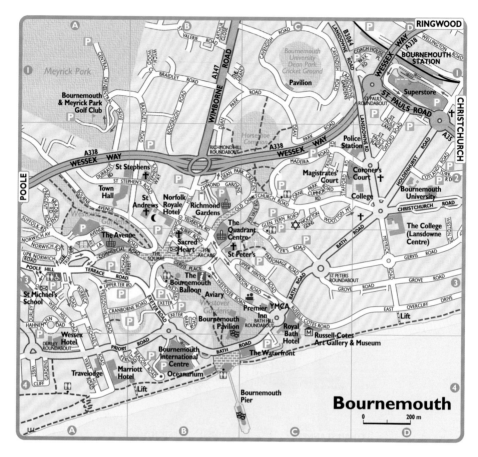

Bournemouth

0   200 m

B3	Albert Road	C2	Glen Fern Road	A2	St Stephen's Road
B1	Arthur Close	C3	Grove Road	B1	St Valerie Road
A3	Avenue Lane	A3	Hahnemann Road	C2	Stafford Road
A3	Avenue Road	B3	Hinton Road	B2	Stephen's Way
B4	Bath Road	D2	Holdenhurst Road	A2	Suffolk Road
B4	Beacon Road	A4	Kerley Road	A3	Terrace Road
B2	Bodorgon Road	C1	Lansdowne Gardens	B3	The Arcade
A2	Bourne Avenue	C1	Lansdowne Road	B1	The Deans
A2	Bradburne Road	C2	Lorne Park Road	B3	The Square
B1	Braidley Road	C2	Madeira Road	A3	The Triangle
C1	Cavendish Road	D3	Meyrick Road	A3	Tregonwell Road
A1	Central Drive	A3	Norwich Avenue	C2	Trinity Road
D2	Christchurch Road	A3	Norwich Road	C3	Upper Hinton Road
D1	Coach House Place	C2	Old Christchurch	A3	Upper Norwich
A3	Commercial Road		Road		Road
D2	Cotlands Road	A3	Orchard Street	A3	Upper Terrace Road
A3	Cranborne Road	D2	Oxford Road	D1	Wellington Road
A2	Crescent Road	D1	Park Road	A2	Wessex Way
C2	Cumnor Road	C3	Parsonage Road	A3	West Hill Road
B2	Dean Park Crescent	A3	Poole Hill	D2	Weston Drive
B2	Dean Park Road	A4	Priory Road	B3	Westover Road
A3	Durley Road	A3	Purbeck Road	B1	Wimborne Road
A2	Durrant Road	B2	Richmond Gardens	C2	Wootton Gardens
D3	East Overcliff Drive	B3	Richmond Hill	C2	Wootton Mount
B3	Exeter Crescent	C3	Russell Cotes Road	B1	Wychwood Close
B3	Exeter Park Road	A3	St Michael's Road	B2	Yelverton Road
B3	Exeter Road	D1	St Pauls Lane	D2	York Road
C2	Fir Vale Road	D2	St Paul's Place		
B3	Gervis Place	D1	St Pauls Road		
D3	Gervis Road	C3	St Peter's Road		

Bradford

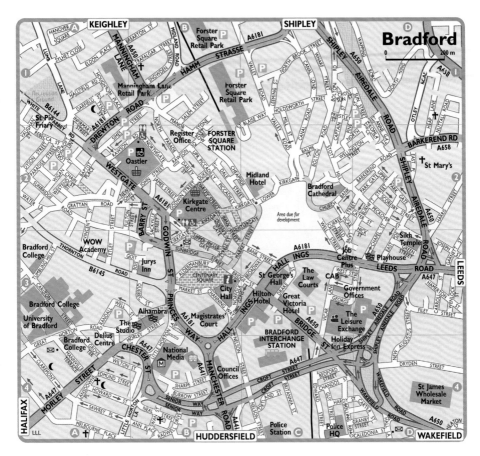

B3	Aldermanbury	B2	Dale Street	C1	Holdsworth Street	D2	Nuttall Road	B1	Trafalgar Street
D2	Anne Gate	A1	Darfield Street	A1	Houghton Place	D1	Otley Road	B3	Tyrell Street
B4	Ann Place	B2	Darley Street	A4	Howard Street	A2	Paradise Street	A1	Tyson Street
C2	Balme Street	C3	Drake Street	B3	Hustlergate	D2	Park Gate	B3	Upper Miller Gate
B2	Bank Street	A2	Drewton Road	A1	Infirmary Street	D2	Peckover Street	D2	Upper Park Gate
A2	Baptist Place	D4	Dryden Street	A1	James Street	B2	Piccadilly	B2	Upper Piccadilly
D2	Barkerend Road	B2	Duke Street	B2	John Street	C2	Pine Street	C1	Valley Road
B2	Barry Street	A2	Dyson Street	D3	Joseph Street	C4	Portland Street	A2	Vaughan Street
C4	Bedford Street	D3	East Parade	B3	Kirkgate	C1	Priestley Street	C3	Vicar Lane
C4	Bolling Road	D2	East Place	D2	Komla Close	B3	Princes Way	A3	Vincent Street
C2	Bolton Road	A4	Edmund Street	A4	Lansdowne Place	B2	Queen's Gate	D4	Wakefield Road
B1	Brearton Street	C4	Edward Street	D3	Leeds Road	B4	Radwell Drive	D1	Wapping Road
C3	Bridge Street	A1	Eldon Place	C1	Leeming Street	A3	Randall Well Street	A2	Water Lane
C4	Britannia Street	C2	Field Street	A4	Little Horton Lane	A2	Rawson Road	C2	Wellington Street
C3	Broadway	D3	Filey Street	A2	Longcroft Link	B2	Rawson Square	C2	Well Street
D2	Burnett Street	A2	Fulton Street	C2	Lower Kirkgate	A2	Rebecca Street	D3	Wenlock Street
B4	Burrow Street	D3	Garnett Street	A1	Lumb Lane	B3	Sackville Street	A2	Westend Street
D4	Caledonia Street	C3	George Street	B4	Manchester Road	C1	St Blaise Way	A2	Westgate
C1	Canal Road	B2	Godwin Street	A1	Manningham Lane	A2	Simes Street	C3	West Street
C2	Captain Street	B3	Goit Side	A4	Mannville Terrace	B1	Snowden Street	C1	Wharf Street
A3	Carlton Street	C4	Granby Street	B1	Manor Row	B2	Stone Street	A1	White Abbey Road
D3	Carroll Street	A2	Grattan Road	B3	Market Street	C2	Stott Hill	A2	Wigan Street
D4	Carter Street	A4	Great Horton Road	A4	Melbourne Place	A2	Sunbridge Road	A4	Wilton Street
D2	Cater Street	D3	Green Street	B1	Midland Road	B3	Sunbridge Road		
B3	Centenary Square	A4	Grove Terrace	C1	Mill Street	D1	Sun Street		
A2	Chain Street	C4	Guy Street	A4	Morley Street	B4	Swan Street		
C4	Chandos Street	A1	Hallfield Road	B4	Neal Street	A1	Sylhet Close		
B3	Channing Way	B4	Hall Ings	B1	Nelson Street	B2	Tetley Street		
D3	Chapel Street	D4	Hall Lane	D4	New Augustus Street	A3	Thornton Road		
B2	Cheapside	D3	Hamerton Street	A2	New John Street				
A4	Chester Street	B1	Hamm Strasse	B3	Norfolk Gardens				
C2	Church Bank	C4	Hardy Street	C1	North Brook Street				
A4	Claremont	D2	Harris Street	B2	Northgate				
C4	Croft Street	D2	Heap Lane	B1	North Parade				
C1	Cross Sun Street	D4	Heaton Street	C2	North Street				
C2	Currer Street	D2	Hick Street	D1	North Wing				

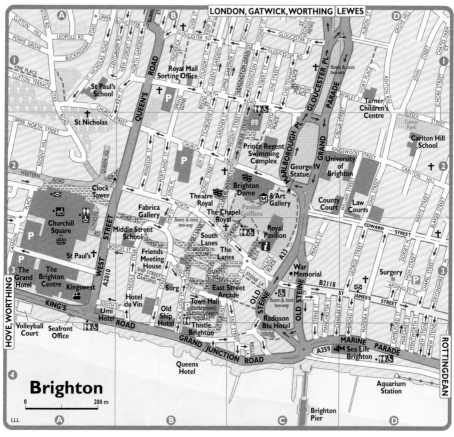

Brighton

0 ——— 200 m

A2	Air Street	D3	Dorset Place	A1	Leopold Road	A2	Queen Square	B2	Windsor Street
D1	Albion Street	B3	Dukes Lane	B4	Little East Street	B2	Queen's Road		
D3	Ardingley Street	B2	Duke Street	D4	Madeira Place	A2	Regency Road		
D1	Ashton Rise	A1	Dyke Road	C4	Manchester Street	A2	Regent Hill		
B3	Bartholomew	C3	East Street	D4	Margaret Street	C2	Regent Street		
	Square	C2	Edward Street	D4	Marine Parade	C1	Robert Street		
B3	Black Lion Street	D1	Elmore Street	B3	Market Street	C1	St George's Mews		
D3	Blaker Street	B1	Foundry Street	B3	Market Street	D3	St James's Street		
C1	Blenheim Place	B1	Frederick Street	C2	Marlborough Place	A1	St Nicholas Road		
B2	Bond Street	B2	Gardner Street	B3	Meeting House Lane	B3	Ship Street Gardens		
A3	Boyces Street	D3	George Street	B3	Middle Street	A3	South Street		
B1	Bread Street	C1	Gloucester Place	D1	Morley Street	B1	Spring Gardens		
B3	Brighton Place	B1	Gloucester Road	B1	New Dorset Street	C3	Steine Lane		
B3	Brighton Square	C1	Gloucester Street	B2	New Road	C4	Steine Street		
C4	Brills Lane	B4	Grand Junction	D4	New Steine	D2	Sussex Street		
D4	Broad Street		Road	B3	Nile Street	C1	Sydney Street		
A1	Buckingham Road	C2	Grand Parade	B1	North Gardens	B2	Tichborne Street		
D4	Camelford Street	D1	Grove Hill	C2	North Place	C1	Tidy Street		
A3	Cannon Place	D3	High Street	B1	North Road	B1	Upper Gardner		
D2	Carlton Hill	D1	Ivory Place	B2	North Street		Street		
A1	Centurion Road	B2	Jew Street	C3	Old Steine	A1	Upper Gloucester		
D3	Chapel Street	D2	John Street	B1	Over Street		Road		
C4	Charles Street	C2	Jubilee Street	C3	Palace Place	A2	Upper North Street		
D1	Chates Farm Court	B1	Kemp Street	C3	Pavilion Buildings	A1	Vine Place		
C1	Cheltenham Place	C1	Kensington Gardens	B2	Portland Street	C1	Vine Street		
A1	Church Street	C1	Kensington Street	A1	Powis Grove	D4	Wentworth Street		
C2	Circus Street	B1	Kew Street	B3	Prince Albert Street	A2	Western Road		
A1	Clifton Hill	B2	King Place	C3	Princes Place	A3	West Street		
A1	Clifton Terrace	A3	King's Road	C3	Prince's Street	D3	White Street		
D3	Devonshire Place	C2	Kingswood Street	B1	Queen's Gardens	D2	William Street		

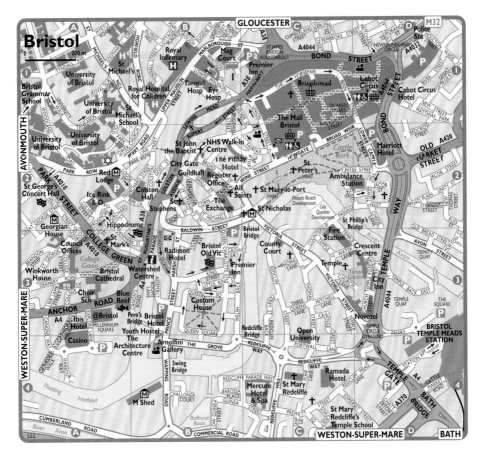

B1	Alfred Hill	B2	Corn Street	B1	Lower Maudlin Street	C4	Redcliffe Hill	C3	Temple Street
A3	Anchor Road	B1	Cottage Place	B2	Lower Park Row	B4	Redcliffe Parade West	D3	Temple Way
B3	Assembly Rooms Lane	C3	Counterslip	B4	Low Guinea Street	C4	Redcliffe Way	B1	Terrell Street
D3	Avon Street	B3	Crow Lane	B1	Marlborough Hill	C4	Redcliff Mead Lane	B4	The Grove
B2	Baldwin Street	A2	Culver Street	B1	Marlborough Street	C3	Redcliff Street	C1	The Horsefair
B4	Barossa Place	A4	Cumberland Road	B3	Marsh Street	D2	Redcross Street	C2	The Pithay
D4	Bath Bridge	C1	Cumberland Street	A3	Millennium Square	D1	River Street	D3	The Square
C1	Bond Street	A3	Deanery Road	C3	Mitchell Lane	A1	Royal Fort Road	C3	Thomas Lane
D2	Bond Street	A3	Denmark Street	B1	Montague Street	B2	Rupert Street	C3	Three Queens Lane
A3	Brandon Steep	B1	Dighton Street	A1	Myrtle Road	D2	Russ Street	D2	Tower Hill
B1	Bridewell Street	B1	Eugene Street	D1	New Street	B1	St Augustine's Parade	A2	Trenchard Street
C3	Bristol Bridge	A3	Explore Lane	D2	New Thomas Street	B2	St George's Road	D3	Trinity Quay
C1	Broadmead	C2	Fairfax Street	C2	Newgate	C4	St James Barton	A1	Tyndall Avenue
D2	Broad Plain	C3	Ferry Street	D2	Old Bread Street		Roundabout	C1	Union Street
B3	Broad Quay	D3	Friary	D2	Old Market Street	C4	St Matthias Park	D3	Unity Street
B2	Broad Street	A3	Frog Lane	A2	Old Park Hill	A1	St Michael's Hill	D2	Unity Street
C2	Broad Weir	A2	Frogmore Street	D1	Orange Street	B3	St Michaels Street	A1	University Walk
C1	Brunswick Square	A3	Great George Street	A2	Orchard Street	A3	St Phillip's Bridge	B1	Upper Maudlin Street
B3	Canon's Road	D1	Great George Street	A2	Park Street	C1	St Stephen's Street	D1	Victoria Street
A3	Canons Way	B4	Guinea Street	C2	Passage Street	D1	St Thomas Street	D1	Wade Street
C3	Canynge Street	A4	Harbour Way	C1	Pembroke Street	A1	Silver Street	B4	Wapping Road
C2	Castle Street	C1	Haymarket	C1	Penn Street	B2	Small Street	C3	Water Lane
A4	Cathedral Walk	A2	Hill Street	B3	Pero's Bridge	C2	Somerset Square	B3	Welsh Back
D4	Cattle Market Road	B1	Horfield Road	A2	Perry Road	B2	Somerset Street	B1	Whitson Street
B4	Challoner Court	D3	Horton Street	C2	Philadelphia Street	C3	Southwell Street	C2	Wine Street
D4	Chatterton Street	B2	Host Street	B2	Pipe Lane	D4	Station Approach	A1	Woodland Road
D2	Cheese Lane	D1	Houlton Street	C4	Portwall Lane	D2	Straight Street		
C3	Church Lane	D2	Jacob Street	C4	Prewett Street	B4	Swing Bridge		
D3	Church Street	B3	King Street	B3	Prince Street	A1	Tankards Close		
B2	Clare Street	B2	Leonard Lane	C4	Pump Lane	B3	Tel Avenue		
A3	College Green	B3	Lewins Mead	C1	Quakers Friars	C3	Temple Back		
A3	College Square	B3	Little King Street	B3	Queen Charlotte Street	D3	Temple Back East		
A3	College Street	A2	Lodge Street	B3	Queen Square	D3	Temple Circle Gyratory		
B2	Colston Avenue	D2	Lower Castle Street	C2	Queen Street	D4	Temple Gate		
B2	Colston Street	A2	Lower Church Lane	C3	Redcliff Back	D3	Temple Quay		
B4	Commercial Road	A3	Lower Lamb Street	C3	Redcliffe Bridge	D3	Temple Rose		

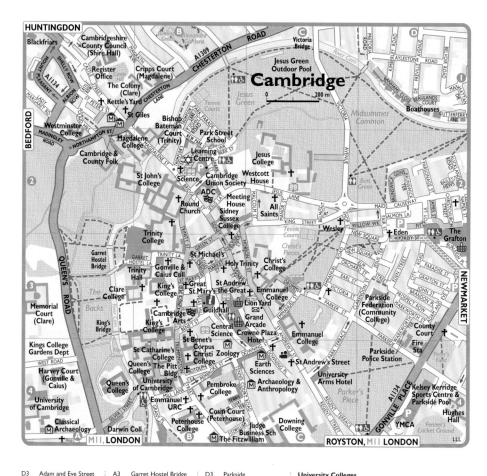

D3	Adam and Eve Street
A1	Albion Row
D2	Auckland Road
D1	Aylestone Road
D2	Bailey Mews
D1	Banhams Close
D1	Beaulands Court
C2	Belmont Place
D1	Belvoir Road
B3	Bene't Street
B4	Botolph Lane
D3	Brandon Place
B2	Bridge Street
D2	Brunswick Gardens
D2	Brunswick Terrace
B2	Burleigh Place
A1	Castle Row
A1	Castle Street
B1	Chesterton Lane
B1	Chesterton Road
D2	Christchurch Street
D3	City Road
C3	Clarendon Street
D1	Cutterferry Lane
D1	De Freville Avenue
C4	Downing Place
B4	Downing Street
C3	Drummer Street
C3	Earl Street
D3	Eden Street
D3	Elm Street
C3	Emmanuel Road
D2	Fair Street
D2	Fitzroy Lane
D3	Fitzroy Street
B4	Fitzwilliam Street

A3	Garret Hostel Bridge
A3	Garret Hostel Lane
D4	Gonville Place
D3	Grafton Street
B4	Grant Place
B3	Green Street
B3	Hobson Street
D2	James Street
B2	Jesus Lane
D3	Jesus Terrace
D3	John Street
D1	Kimberley Road
A3	King's Bridge
B3	King's Parade
C2	King Street
A1	Lady Margaret Road
B2	Lower Park Street
A2	Madingley Road
B2	Magdalene Street
A1	Magrath Avenue
D2	Maids Causeway
C2	Malcolm Street
D1	Manhattan Drive
C2	Manor Street
B3	Market Street
B4	Mill Lane
D4	Mortimer Road
A1	Mount Pleasant
A2	Napier Street
B2	New Park Street
C2	New Square
A2	Northampton Street
C3	Orchard Street
C3	Paradise Street
C3	Parker Street
B1	Park Parade

D3	Parkside
B2	Park Street
C4	Park Terrace
D2	Parsonage Street
B3	Peas Hill
B4	Pembroke Street
A1	Pound Hill
D1	Pretoria Road
D3	Prospect Row
A3	Queen's Road
C4	Regent Street
C4	Regent Terrace
B3	Rose Crescent
C5	St Andrew's Street
B2	St John's Road
B3	St Mary's Street
A1	St Peter's Street
D2	Salmon Lane
A1	Shelly Row
C2	Shop Street
B2	Sidney Street
A4	Silver Street
B3	Sussex Street
B4	Tennis Court Road
B4	Tennis Court Terrace
B2	Thompson's Lane
B3	Trinity Lane
B2	Trinity Street
B4	Trumpington Street
C1	Victoria Avenue
C1	Victoria Bridge
C3	Victoria Street
D3	Warkworth Street
D3	Warkworth Terrace
A4	West Road
C2	Willow Walk

University Colleges

C3	Christ's College
A3	Clare College
B4	Corpus Christi College
A4	Darwin College
C4	Downing College
C3	Emmanuel College
B3	Gonville & Caius College
D4	Hughes Hall
C2	Jesus College
B3	King's College
A2	Magdalene College
B4	Pembroke College
B4	Peterhouse College
A4	Queen's College
B4	St Catharine's College
B2	St John's College
C3	Sidney Sussex College
B3	Trinity College
B3	Trinity Hall

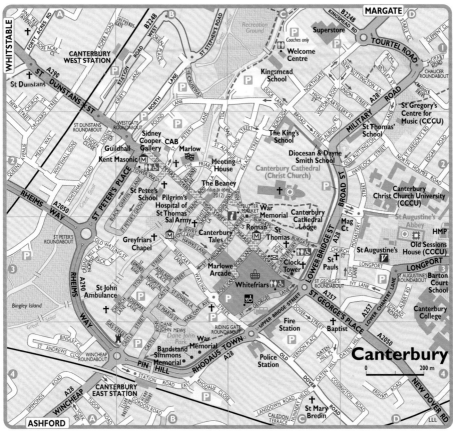

B3	Adelaide Place	B4	Elgar Bretts Court	D1	New Ruttington Lane	C3	St Georges Lane	A2	Whitehall Gardens
D3	Albert Road	D4	Ersham Road			C3	St George's Place	A2	Whitehall Road
C2	Albion Place	A4	Gas Street	B1	North Lane	C3	St George's Street	A4	Wincheap
B2	All Saints Lane	B4	Gordon Road	C1	Northgate	D2	St Gregory's Road	A4	York Road
D1	Alma Street	B2	Guildhall Street	D1	Notley Street	B3	St Johns Lane		
C1	Artillery Street	D2	Havelock Street	C4	Nunnery Fields	B3	St Margaret's Street		
A3	Back Lane	B3	Hawks Lane	C4	Oaten Hill	B3	St Marys Street		
B3	Beercart Lane	B4	Henry Court	C4	Oaten Hill Place	B3	St Peter's Grove		
B2	Best Lane	B2	High Street	C4	Old Dover Road	B2	St Peter's Lane		
A4	Bingley Court	B3	Hospital Lane	D2	Old Ruttington Lane	A3	St Peter's Place		
A3	Black Griffin Lane	C3	Ivy Lane	A3	Old Watling Street	B2	St Peters Street		
C2	Borough	B3	Jewry Lane	A2	Orchard Street	B1	Shepherdsgate		
D2	Broad Street	C2	King Street	B1	Orient Place	B4	Station Road East		
C3	Burgate	B1	Kirby's Lane	C2	Palace Street	A1	Station Road West		
C2	Butter Market	C4	Lansdown Road	C3	Parade	B3	Stour Street		
C4	Caledon Terrace	A2	Linden Close	B4	Pin Hill	D1	Sturry Road		
C3	Canterbury Lane	A2	Linden Grove	B2	Pound Lane	C2	Sun Street		
B4	Castle Row	C3	Link Lane	A2	Queens Avenue	B1	The Causeway		
B3	Castle Street	D3	Longport	A3	Rheims Way	B2	The Friars		
B3	Church Lane	D3	Love Lane	B4	Rhodaus Close	D1	Tourtel Road		
A1	Church Street	C3	Lower Bridge Street	B4	Rhodaus Town	B2	Tower Way		
C4	Cossington Road	D4	Lower Chantry Lane	A1	Rose Acre Close	A4	Tudor Road		
D1	Craddock Drive			B3	Rose Lane	D1	Union Street		
A3	Creine Mill Lane North	B3	Marlowe Avenue	B3	Rosemary Lane	C4	Upper Bridge Street		
		A2	Mead Way	B2	St Alphege Lane	C4	Vernon Place		
B4	Dane John Mews	C3	Mercery Lane	A4	St Andrews Close	C1	Victoria Row		
C3	Dover Street	D2	Military Road	A2	St Dunstans Roundabout	B3	Watling Street		
C1	Duck Lane	B1	Mill Lane			A2	Westgate Roundabout		
D2	Edgar Road	D3	Monastery Street	A1	St Dunstans Street				
D3	Edward Road	D4	New Dover Road	B3	St Edmunds Road	B3	White Horse Lane		

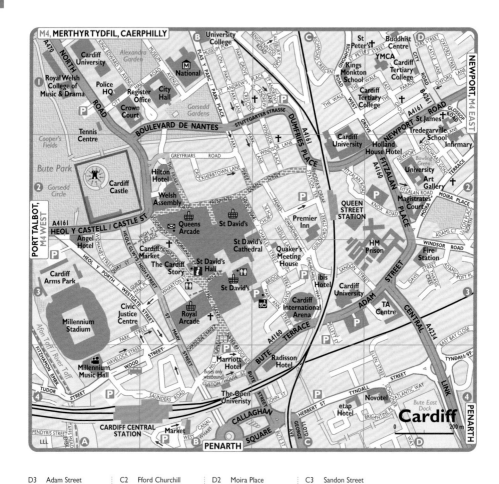

D3	Adam Street	C2	Fford Churchill	D2	Moira Place	C3	Sandon Street
D2	Adams Court	D2	Fitzalan Place	D2	Moira Terrace	B4	Saunders Road
D3	Adamscroft Place	D2	Fitzalan Road	B1	Museum Avenue	D4	Schooner Way
D4	Atlantic Way	A4	Fitzhamon	B1	Museum Place	C1	Senghennydd Road
B2	Boulevard De		Embankment	D2	Newport Road Lane	B1	Stuttgarter Strasse
	Nantes	D1	Glossop Road	A1	North Luton Place	A4	Taffs Mead
C3	Bridge Street	B2	Greyfriars Road	A1	North Road		Embankment
D4	Brigantine Place	C3	Guildford Street	D1	Oxford Lane	D3	Tharsis Crescent
C4	Bute Street	A3	Guildhall Place	D1	Oxford Street	B2	The Friary
C3	Bute Terrace	A4	Havelock Street	B1	Park Grove	B3	The Hayes
B4	Callaghan Square	B3	Hayes Bridge Road	B1	Park Lane	D1	The Parade
B3	Caroline Street	B2	Heol Siarl	B1	Park Place	C1	The Walk
D1	Castle Lane	A2	Heol Y Castell	A3	Park Street	B3	Trinity Street
A2	Castle Street	B2	Heol Y Frenhines	C3	Pellett Street	A4	Tudor Street
D3	Central Link	A3	Heol Y Porth	A4	Pendyris Street	D4	Tyndall Street
B2	Charles Street	B3	Heole Glwys	B1	Plas Y Parc	D1	Vere Street
C2	Church Place	C4	Herbert Street	A3	Quay Street	C2	Wesley Lane
C2	Churchill Way	B3	High Street	B2	Queen Street	B4	West Canal Wharf
A1	City Hall Road	B2	High Street Arcade	C2	Rhodfa'r Orsaf	C1	West Grove
D1	City Road	B3	Hills Street		Station Terrace	A3	Westgate Street
B2	Crockherbtown	D2	Howard Gardens	C1	Richmond Crescent	B3	Wharton Street
	Lane	C4	John Street	C1	Richmond Road	C2	Windsor Lane
B4	Custom House	A1	King Edward VII	B1	St Andrew's	C1	Windsor Place
	Street		Avenue		Crescent	D3	Windsor Road
C3	David Street	D2	Knox Road	C1	St Andrew's Lane	A3	Womanby Street
D3	Davis Street	C4	Lloyd George	B1	St Andrew's Place	A4	Wood Street
C2	Dumfries Place		Avenue	B2	St John Street	B3	Working Street
D3	East Bay Close	B1	Lon Y Parc	B3	St Mary Street		
D1	East Grove	C3	Mary Ann Street	C1	St Peter's Street		
D4	Ellen Street	B4	Mill Lane	C1	Salisbury Road		

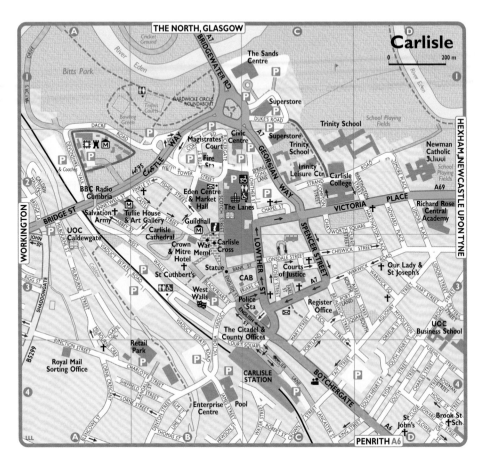

A2	Abbey Street	C3	Currie Street	A4	Lorne Crescent	A3	Viaduct Estate Road
D3	Aglionby Street	A1	Dacre Road	A4	Lorne Street	C2	Victoria Place
A2	Annetwell Street	B4	Denton Street	C2	Lowther Street	B4	Victoria Viaduct
B3	Bank Street	A2	Devonshire Walk	C3	Mary Street	D3	Warwick Road
B3	Blackfriars Street	C1	Duke's Road	A1	Mayor's Drive	D3	Warwick Square
A4	Blencowe Street	D4	Edward Street	A3	Milbourne Crescent	C4	Water Street
C4	Botchergate	B4	Elm Street	A3	Milbourne Street	B2	West Tower Street
D4	Bowman Street	B3	English Street	D3	Myddleton Street	B3	West Walls
A2	Bridge Lane	B2	Finkle Street	D3	North Alfred Street		
A2	Bridge Street	B2	Fisher Street	D3	Orfeur Street		
B1	Bridgewater Road	D4	Flower Street	D3	Petteril Street		
D3	Broad Street	C3	Friars Court	B2	Peter Street		
C3	Brunswick Street	D4	Fusehill Street	C4	Portland Place		
A2	Caldew Maltings	C2	Georgian Way	C3	Portland Square		
B2	Castle Street	D4	Grey Street	B4	Randall Street		
B2	Castle Way	D2	Hartington Place	B2	Rickergate		
C3	Cecil Street	D2	Hartington Street	A3	Rigg Street		
A3	Chapel Place	D3	Hart Street	C4	Robert Street		
C2	Chapel Street	B4	Hewson Street	D4	Rydal Street		
D4	Charles Street	D2	Howard Place	B2	Scotch Street		
A4	Charlotte Street	D4	Howe Street	A3	Shaddongate		
C2	Chatsworth Square	B4	James Street	A4	Sheffield Street		
C3	Chiswick Street	A3	John Street	D3	South Alfred Street		
D4	Close Street	A4	Junction Street	D4	South Henry Street		
C4	Collier Lane	C4	King Street	C2	Spencer Street		
C2	Compton Street	C4	Lancaster Street	C2	Spring Gardens Lane		
B2	Corp Road	B4	Lime Street				
B4	Court Square	D2	Lismore Place	C2	Strand Road		
C3	Crosby Street	D3	Lismore Street	C4	Tait Street		
C4	Crown Street	C3	Lonsdale Street	B4	Thomas Street		

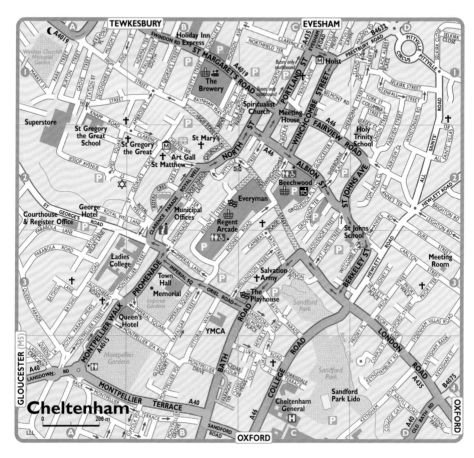

D1	Albert Place	D4	Corpus Street	D2	Leighton Road	C1	Prestbury Road	D3	Sidney Street
C2	Albion Place	B2	Crescent Place	D3	London Road	D3	Priory Parade	A1	Station Street
C2	Albion Street	B2	Crescent Terrace	D1	Malden Road	D4	Priory Place	B4	Suffolk Parade
D2	All Saints' Road	A1	Devonshire Street	A1	Market Street	D3	Priory Street	B1	Swindon Road
D2	All Saints' Villas Road	B1	Duke Street	A1	Milsom Street	D3	Priory Terrace	D3	Sydenham Villas Road
B1	Ambrose Street	B1	Dunalley Street	C4	Mitre Street	D3	Priory Walk	D2	Tom Price Close
D4	Argyll Road	C1	Evesham Road	B1	Monson Avenue	B3	Promenade	B4	Trafalgar Street
D4	Avenall Park	D2	Fairview Close	B4	Montpellier Drive	A4	Queens Lane	C1	Trinity Lane
A4	Back Montpellier	C2	Fairview Road	B4	Montpellier Grove	A3	Queens Parade	D2	Union Street
	Terrace	D2	Fairview Street	B4	Montpellier Parade	B2	Regent Street	C3	Vernon Place
C3	Bath Parade	A3	Fauconberg Road	B4	Montpellier Spa Road	B3	Rodney Road	B4	Vittoria Walk
B4	Bath Road	D1	Glenfall Street	A4	Montpellier Street	B1	Rose & Crown Passage	C3	Wellington Street
C2	Bath Street	B4	Glesanda Court	A4	Montpellier Terrace	B2	Royal Crescent	C2	Winchcombe Street
C4	Bathville Mews	C2	Gloucester Place	A4	Montpellier Walk	A4	Royal Parade Mews	D2	Winstonian Road
B1	Baynham Way	C2	Grosvenor Place South	A1	New Street	B1	Royal Well	C3	Witcombe Place
A3	Bayshill Lane	C3	Grosvenor Street	B1	Normal Terrace	A2	Royal Well Lane	D1	York Street
A3	Bayshill Road	C2	Grosvenor Terrace	C1	Northfield Terrace	B2	Royal Well Place		
A3	Bayshill Villas Lane	A1	Grove Street	C1	North Place	D2	St Anne's Road		
C1	Belmont Road	B1	Henrietta Street	B2	North Street	D2	St Anne's Terrace		
C3	Belmore Place	A1	Hereford Place	D4	Old Bath Road	B2	St George's Place		
B1	Bennington Street	D3	Hewlett Place	C4	Olio Lane	A2	St George's Road		
C3	Berkeley Street	D3	Hewlett Road	B3	Oriel Road	B1	St George's Street		
D1	Black Albert Place	A1	High Street	C4	Orrisdale Terrace	A2	St James' Square		
D2	Brighton Road	C2	High Street	D3	Oxford Street	C3	St James Street		
A1	Burton Street	B3	Imperial Lane	A3	Parabola Lane	C2	St Johns Avenue		
C3	Cambray Place	B3	Imperial Square	A3	Parabola Road	C4	St Luke's		
D3	Carlton Street	D1	Jersey Street	B4	Paragon Terrace	C3	St Luke's Place		
B4	Cedar Court	A2	Jessop Avenue	A1	Park Street	C4	St Luke's Road		
B2	Chester Walk	D4	Keynsham Bank	D1	Pittville	B1	St Margaret's Road		
B2	Church Street	D4	Keynshambury Road	B1	Pittville Circus	B1	St Paul's Street South		
B2	Clarence Parade	D4	Keynsham Road	C1	Pittville Lawn	B4	Sandford Road		
C1	Clarence Road	D4	Keynsham Street	C1	Pittville Mews	C3	Sandford Street		
B2	Clarence Street	A1	King Street	B2	Pittville Street	D1	Selkirk Close		
D4	College Gate	A1	Knapp Road	D1	Portland Square	D1	Selkirk Street		
C4	College Road	A4	Lansdown Crescent	C1	Portland Street	C2	Sherborne Place		
D1	Columbia Street	A4	Lansdown Road	B2	Post Office Lane	C2	Sherborne Street		

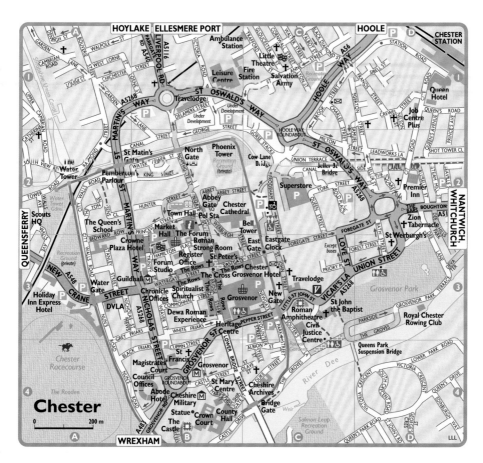

B2	Abbey Square	B1	Delamere Street	B1	Liverpool Road	D2	Russell Street	A2	Tower Road
B2	Abbey Street	A1	Denbigh Street	A1	Lorne Street	C1	St Anne Street	C1	Trafford Street
C4	Albion Street	D3	Deva Terrace	A1	Louise Street	D4	St John's Road	B3	Trinity Street
D2	Bath Street	C4	Duke Street	C3	Love Street	C3	St John Street	D3	Union Street
A3	Bedward Row	B3	Eastgate Street	B4	Lower Bridge Street	A2	St Martin's Way	C2	Union Terrace
C1	Black Diamond	D4	Edinburgh Way	D4	Lower Park Road	C4	St Olave Street	A1	Upper Cambrian
	Street	C1	Egerton Street	C1	Lyon Street	B1	St Oswald's Way		Road
A4	Black Friars	C2	Foregate Street	C2	Milton Street	B2	St Werburgh Street	C3	Vicar's Lane
C2	Bold Place	C3	Forest Street	D1	Nelson Street	C2	Samuel Street	D4	Victoria Crescent
D2	Boughton	D1	Francis Street	A3	New Crane Street	D2	Seaville Street	B1	Victoria Road
A1	Bouverie Street	C2	Frodsham Street	C3	Newgate Street	D2	Seller Street	C3	Volunteer Street
B3	Bridge Street	A1	Garden Lane	A3	Nicholas St Mews	C2	Seller Street Bridge	A2	Walls Avenue
C1	Brook Street	B2	George Street	B3	Nicholas Street	A2	Sens Close	A1	Walpole Street
A1	Cambrian Road	C2	Gloucester Street	B2	Northgate Street	B4	Shipgate Street	C1	Walter Street
C2	Canal Side	A4	Grey Friars	A3	Nun's Road	D2	Shot Tower Close	B3	Watergate Street
B2	Canal Street	D3	Grosvenor Park	B1	Parkgate Road	D1	Sibell Street	B2	Water Tower Street
B4	Castle Drive		Terrace	D3	Parkside	C3	Souter's Lane	B3	Weaver Street
B4	Castle Street	B4	Grosvenor Road	C3	Park Street	D4	South Crescent	A1	West Lorne Street
A2	Catherine Street	B4	Grosvenor	C3	Pepper Street		Road	B3	White Friars
C1	Charles Street		Roundabout	D2	Prince's Avenue	A2	South View Road	C2	York Street
A1	Chichester Street	B4	Grosvenor Street	B2	Princess Street	A3	Stanley Street		
D2	City Road	B3	Hamilton Place	C3	Priory Place	D1	Station Road		
A2	City Walls Road	C1	Hoole Way	D2	Queen's Avenue	D2	Steam Mill Street		
B3	Commonhall Street	C2	Hoole Way	D4	Queen's Drive	C4	Steele Street		
C1	Cornwall Street		Roundabout	C4	Queen's Park Road	C1	Talbot Street		
C2	Cow Lane Bridge	B2	Hunter Street	D4	Queens Park	D2	The Bars		
D1	Crewel Street	B2	King Street		Suspension Bridge	C4	The Groves		
B4	Cuppin Street	D2	Leadworks Lane	D1	Queen's Road	D2	The Square		
D2	Dee Hills Park	C3	Little St John Street	C2	Queen Street	A2	The Yonne		
D2	Dee Lane			A2	Raymond Street				

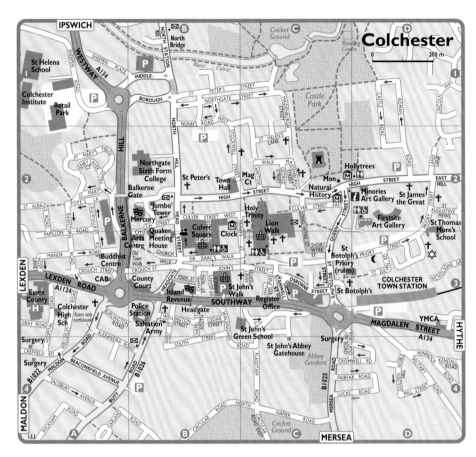

C3	Abbey Gates	A3	Gray Road	A2	Pope's Lane	A1	Westway
A3	Alexandra Road	B3	Headgate	C4	Portland Road	C3	Whitewell Road
A3	Balkerne Hill	B2	Head Street	D3	Priory Street	A4	Wickham Road
A4	Beaconsfield Avenue	A2	Henry Laver Court	C3	Queen Street	C2	William's Walk
A3	Burlington Road	B2	High Street	A2	Rawstorn Road	D4	Winnock Road
A4	Butt Road	A4	Hospital Road	D1	Roman Road		
D1	Castle Road	A3	Hospital Lane	A2	St Alban's Road		
B3	Cedar Street	D4	Kendall Road	D2	St Augustine Mews		
B3	Chapel Street North	D2	Land Lane	C3	St Botolph's Street		
		A3	Lexden Road	C2	St Helen's Lane		
B3	Chapel Street South	D1	Lincoln Way	B3	St John's Avenue		
B3	Church Street	C2	Long Wyre Street	B3	St John's Street		
B3	Church Walk	C4	Lucas Road	D3	St Julian Road		
C4	Circular Road East	D3	Magdalen Street	A2	St Mary's Fields		
B4	Circular Road North	C4	Maidenburgh Street	B1	St Peter's Street		
A4	Creffield Road	A4	Maldon Road	A4	Salisbury Avenue		
C4	Cromwell Road	A3	Manor Road	A1	Sheepen Place		
A3	Crouch Street	C4	Mersea Road	A1	Sheepen Road		
B3	Crouch Street	B1	Middleborough	C3	Short Wyre Street		
A2	Crowhurst Road	D4	Military Road	B3	Sir Isaac's Walk		
C2	Culver Street East	D4	Mill Street	B4	South Street		
B2	Culver Street West	C4	Napier Road	B3	Southway		
D2	East Hill	D3	Nicholsons Green	C3	Stanwell Street		
B3	Essex Street	B1	North Bridge	B2	Trinity Street		
C4	Fairfax Road	B1	Northgate Street	B3	Walsingham Road		
C4	Flagstaff Road	B1	North Hill	A4	Wellesley Road		
A4	Garland Road	B1	North Station Road	B3	Wellington Street		
C2	George Street	B1	Nunn's Road	B1	West Stockwell Street		
D4	Golden Noble Hill	C3	Osborne Street				
		A3	Papillon Road	B4	West Street		

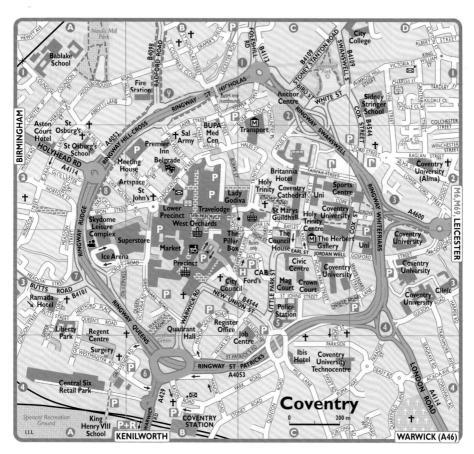

A1	Abbotts Lane	D4	Deasy Road	D1	King William Street	A3	Queen's Road	C4	Swift Road
D4	Acacia Avenue	B1	Draper's Field	B2	Lamb Street	B3	Queen Victoria	B2	The Precinct
D1	Albert Street	C3	Earl Street	B1	Leicester Row		Road	B1	Tower Street
D2	Alma Street	B4	Eaton Road	C3	Little Park Street	C4	Quinton Road	C2	Trinity Street
A2	Barras Lane	C2	Fairfax Street	D4	London Road	B1	Radford Road	B2	Upper Hill Street
C2	Bayley Lane	D3	Far Gosford Street	D2	Lower Ford Street	D2	Raglan Street	A4	Upper Wells Street
C1	Bird Street	C1	Foleshill Road	A2	Lower Holyhead	A4	Regent Street	A2	Upper York Street
B1	Bishop Street	D2	Ford Street		Road	A2	Ringway Hill Cross	D1	Victoria Street
B2	Bond Street	B4	Friars Road	B4	Manor House Road	A3	Ringway Queens	D1	Vine Street
B2	Broadgate	C4	Furlong Road	B4	Manor Road	A3	Ringway Rudge	D2	Vogue Close
B2	Burge Street	D1	Gazelle Close	A3	Meadow Street	B1	Ringway St Nicholas	B3	Warwick Road
A3	Butts Road	A2	Gloucester Street	A1	Meriden Street	B4	Ringway St Patricks	B4	Warwick Road
A3	Butts Street	A4	Gordon Street	A1	Middleborough	C1	Ringway Swanswell	B3	Warwick Row
D1	Canterbury Street	D3	Gosford Street		Road	D2	Ringway Whitefriars	A2	Watch Close
B2	Chapel Street	B3	Greyfriars Lane	C4	Mile Lane	D4	Rodyard Way	B2	Well Street
D1	Charles Street	B3	Greyfriars Road	A1	Mill Street	B1	St Columba's Close	A4	Westminster Road
C1	Chauntry Place	A4	Grosvenor Road	A2	Minster Road	C3	St Johns Street	C3	White Friars Lane
A2	Chester Street	D2	Grove Street	C3	Much Park Street	B1	St Nicholas Street	D3	White Friars Street
C3	Cheylesmore	D3	Gulson Road	B3	New Union Street	B4	St Patrick's Road	C1	White Street
D1	Clifton Street	C2	Hales Street	A2	Norfolk Street	C3	Salt Lane	D2	Winchester Street
D1	Colchester Street	D3	Harper Road	D4	Paradise Street	D4	Seagrave Road	A3	Windsor Street
C1	Cook Street	C3	Hay Lane	B4	Park Road	C4	Short Street	D1	Yardley Street
C2	Cope Street	A3	Hertford Place	C4	Parkside	C2	Silver Street	A3	York Street
D4	Cornwall Road	A1	Hewitt Avenue	C2	Pepper Lane	A2	Spon Street		
B2	Corporation Street	C3	High Street	A2	Percy Street	A3	Stanley Road		
A1	Coundon Road	B2	Hill Street	D1	Primrose Hill Street	B4	Stoney Road		
A1	Coundon Street	D2	Hodd Street	C2	Priory Row	C1	Stoney Stanton		
D1	Cox Street	A2	Holyhead Road	C2	Priory Street		Road		
D2	Cox Street	C3	Jordan Well	C4	Puma Way	D3	Strathmore Avenue		
A3	Croft Road	D1	Kildale Close	D4	Quarryfield Lane	C1	Swanswell Street		

Darlington

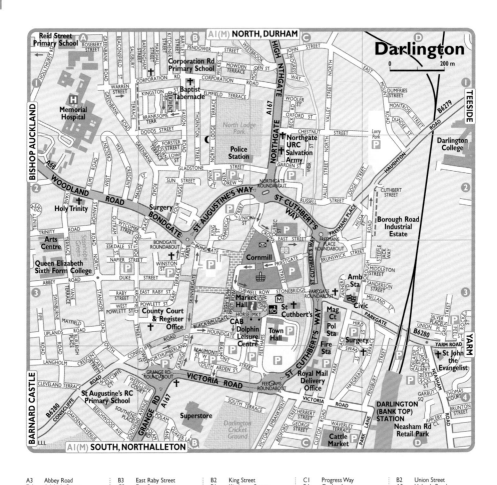

A3	Abbey Road	B3	East Raby Street	B2	King Street	C1	Progress Way	B2	Union Street
D4	Adelaide Street	C3	East Street	B1	Kitchener Street	B4	Quaker Lane	A3	Uplands Road
D4	Albert Street	B1	Elmfield Terrace	A4	Langholm Crescent	C2	Quebec Street	C2	Valley Street North
D4	Appleby Close	A2	Elms Road	A3	Larchfield Street	A3	Raby Street	A2	Vane Terrace
B1	Barningham Street	A3	Eskdale Street	C2	Lodge Street	B3	Raby Terrace	C4	Victoria Embankment
B1	Bartlett Street	C4	Feethams	B2	Lowe Street	D3	Rocket Street	B4	Victoria Road
A1	Beaconsfield Street	C4	Feethams Roundabout	B1	Marshall Street	C4	Rockingham Street	A1	Warren Street
B3	Beaumont Street	A3	Fife Road	A2	Maude Street	A1	Rosebery Street	C4	Waverley Terrace
B4	Beaumont Street West	B2	Forster Street	A3	Mayfield	C2	Russell Street	C2	Weir Street
C1	Beck Road	B2	Four Riggs	D3	Melland Street	B2	St Augustine's Way	C1	Westbrook Way
C4	Bedford Street	C2	Freemans Place	D3	Middleton Street	C2	St Cuthbert's Way	A4	Westcliffe Court
A4	Beechwood Avenue	C3	Freemans Place	D1	Montrose Street	D4	St James Place	A2	West Crescent
B3	Blackwellgate		Roundabout	C1	Mowden Street	A1	Salisbury Terrace	A3	West Powlett Street
D3	Bondgate	D4	Garbutt Square	B1	Mowden Terrace	B3	Salt Yard	B3	West Row
B3	Bondgate Roundabout	C2	Garden Street	A3	Napier Street	D3	Sanderson Street	B4	West Street
D3	Borough Road	C4	George Street	D4	Neasham Road	A1	Sanson Street	B1	Wilkes Street
B1	Branksome Terrace	B2	Gladstone Street	C2	Northgate	B2	Selbourne Terrace	B3	Winston Street
C3	Brunswick Street	B4	Grange Road	C2	Northgate Roundabout	D3	Silver Place	A2	Woodland Road
D4	Brunton Street	B4	Grange Road	B2	North Lodge Terrace	B3	Skinnergate	C1	Wooler Street
A3	Burleigh Place		Roundabout	B4	Northumberland Street	B4	South Arden Street	A2	Wycombe Street
C1	Chestnut Street	A1	Greenbank Road	A4	Oakdene Avenue	A4	Southend Avenue	D3	Yarm Road
C3	Church Row	D3	Green Street	A2	Outram Street	A4	Southend Place		
A4	Cleveland Terrace	C4	Hargreave Terrace	C1	Oxford Street	B4	South Terrace		
C4	Clifton Road	D2	Haughton Road	D3	Parkgate	A2	Stanhope Road North		
B2	Commercial Street	C4	Herbert Street	C3	Parkgate Roundabout	A3	Stanhope Road South		
A4	Coniscliffe Road	C1	High Northgate	D4	Park Lane	C3	Stonebridge		
B1	Corporation Road	B3	High Row	C4	Park Place	B2	Sun Street		
C2	Crown Street	C2	Hilda Street	D3	Peel Street	C4	Swan Street		
D2	Cuthbert Street	C3	Hird Street	B1	Pendower Street	A3	Swinburne Road		
B1	Derwent Street	A1	Hollyhurst Road	C2	Pensbury Street	C3	Tannery Yard		
B1	Dodds Street	B3	Horse Market	B4	Polam Lane	D4	Thomas Court		
A3	Duke Street	B3	Houndgate	B4	Polam Road	B1	Thornton Street		
D1	Dumfries Street	D3	Jack Way Steeple	A3	Portland Place	B3	Trinity Mews		
D1	Dundee Street	C1	John Street	B3	Powlett Street	A2	Trinity Road		
B1	Easson Road	B2	Kendrew Street	C3	Priestgate	B3	Tubwell Row		
D1	East Mount Road	B1	Kingston Street	D4	Princes Street	D3	Union Place		

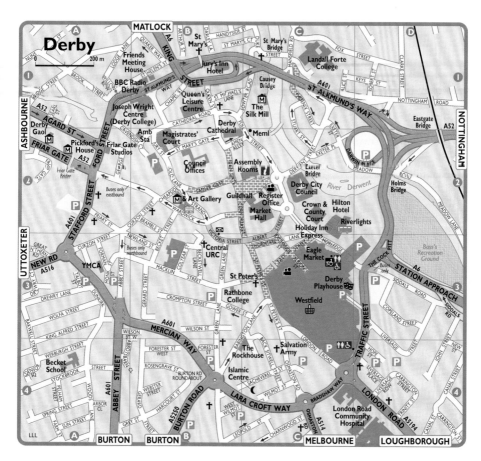

Grid	Street	Grid	Street	Grid	Street	Grid	Street	Grid	Street
A4	Abbey Street	D1	Clarke Street	A2	George Street	C3	Morledge	C1	Stuart Street
A4	Abbotsbarn Close	B3	Colyear Street	B3	Gerard Street	A3	Newland Street	A4	Sun Street
A1	Agard Street	D3	Copeland Street	B3	Gower Street	A3	New Road	A3	Talbot Street
C3	Albert Street	B2	Corn Market	A3	Great Northern	D4	New Street	D3	The Cock Pitt
C3	Albion Street	A2	Crompton Street		Road	D1	Nottingham Road	C3	Thorntree Lane
C1	Alice Street	C2	Curzon Street	B3	Green Lane	A1	Nuns Street	D4	Traffic Street
B2	Amen Alley	B1	Darley Lane	A4	Grey Street	C4	Osmaston Road	D4	Trinity Street
A4	Arbor Close	C2	Darwin Place	B1	Handyside Street	A4	Pelham Street	B2	Victoria Street
B1	Arthur Street	C2	Derwent Street	B4	Harcourt Street	C1	Phoenix Street	B2	Wardwick
B4	Babington Lane	A3	Drewry Court	D2	Holms Bridge	B1	Quaker Way	B4	Webster Street
C4	Back Sitwell Street	A3	Drewry Lane	D4	Hope Street	B1	Queen Street	A4	Werburgh Street
A3	Bakwell Street	C1	Duke Street	B2	Iron Gate	D1	Robert Street	B4	West Wilmot Street
B3	Becket Street	A3	Dunkirk	D4	John Street	B4	Rosengrave Street	A1	Willow Row
B3	Becketwell Lane	C3	East Street	B2	Jury Street	C4	Sacheverel Street	C4	Wilmot Street
B2	Bold Lane	D1	Eastgate Bridge	D1	Keys Street	B2	Sadler Gate	B3	Wilson Street
C4	Bradshaw Way	C2	Edensor Square	A4	King Alfred Street	C1	St Alkmund's Way	A3	Wilson Street West
B2	Bramble Street	C3	Exchange Street	B1	King Street	B1	St Helen's Street	A3	Wolfa Street
A1	Bridge Street	C2	Exeter Bridge	B4	Lara Croft Way	C1	St Mary's Bridge	A4	Woods Lane
A1	Brook Street	C2	Exeter Place	B4	Leopold Street	B1	St Mary's Court		
B4	Burton Road	C2	Exeter Street	D4	Liversage Place	B2	St Mary's Gate		
B4	Burton Road	A4	Farm Street	D4	Liversage Row	B1	St Michael's Lane		
	Roundabout	A2	Ford Street	D3	Liversage Street	C3	St Peter's Street		
D4	Canal Street	B4	Forester Street	A1	Lodge Lane	A1	Searl Street		
D4	Carrington Street		West	C3	London Road	D3	Siddals Road		
B1	Cathedral Road	B4	Forester Street	B3	Macklin Street	C1	Sowter Road		
C1	Causey Bridge	A3	Forman Street	C1	Mansfield Road	A4	Spring Street		
A2	Cavendish Court	C1	Fox Street	D2	Meadow Lane	A3	Stafford Street		
B1	Chapel Street	C1	Friar Gate	D2	Meadow Road	D3	Station Approach		
C4	Charnwood Street	A2	Friary Street	B3	Mercian Way	A4	Stockbrook Street		
B2	Cheapside	B1	Full Street	A3	Monk Street	B2	Strand		

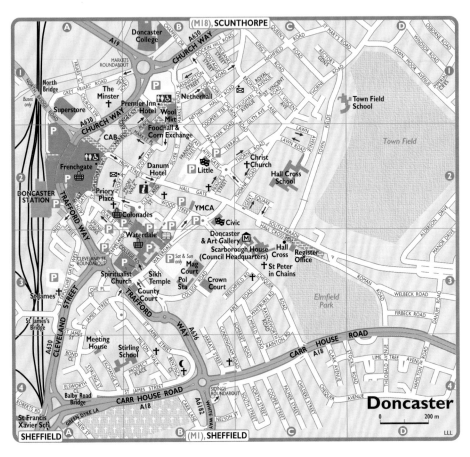

Doncaster

0   200 m

D3	Alderson Drive
B3	Apley Road
A4	Balby Road Bridge
B3	Beechfield Road
B4	Bentinck Close
A4	Bond Close
C1	Broxholme Lane
C4	Carr House Road
B4	Carr Lane
B1	Chappell Drive
C4	Chequer Avenue
C3	Childers Street
C4	Childers Street
B1	Christ Church Road
A1	Church Street
A1	Church View
B1	Church Way
C4	Clark Avenue
A4	Cleveland Street
A3	Cleveland Street Roundabout
B3	College Road
C4	Cooper Street
B2	Coopers Terrace
B1	Copley Road
B3	Cunningham Road
D3	Danum Road
B1	Dockin Hill Road
A2	Duke Street
B2	East Laith Gate

C3	Elmfield Road
A4	Elsworth Close
A4	Exchange Street
D3	Firbeck Road
B2	Frances Street
A1	Friars' Gate
B2	Georges Gate
C2	Glyn Avenue
A4	Green Dyke Lane
A1	Grey Friars' Road
A3	Grove Place
C1	Hall Cross Hill
B2	Hall Gate
D4	Hamilton Road
B1	Hannington Street
A2	High Street
C1	Highfield Road
D1	Imperial Crescent
B4	Jarratt Street
C1	King's Road
C2	Lawn Avenue
C2	Lawn Road
D4	Lime Tree Avenue
D3	Manor Drive
A2	Market Place
B1	Market Road
A1	Markets Roundabout
B1	Milbanke Street
B4	Milton Walk

B1	Montague Street
B4	Nelson Street
B1	Nether Hall Road
A4	New Street
A1	North Bridge
A1	North Bridge Road
C4	North Street
D1	Osborne Road
C4	Palmer Street
B2	Park Road
B2	Park Terrace
B2	Prince's Street
A2	Priory Place
B2	Priory Walk
B4	Prospect Place
C1	Queen's Road
C4	Rainton Road
C3	Ravensworth Road
C1	Rectory Gardens
C2	Regent Square
A4	Roberts Road
D3	Roman Road
C1	Royal Avenue
B4	St James Street
A3	St James's Bridge
C1	St Mary's Road
A2	St Sepulchre Gate
A3	St Sepulchre Gate West
C1	St Vincent Avenue

C1	St Vincent Road
B2	Scot Lane
B4	Sidings Roundabout
B2	Silver Street
B3	Somerset Road
C2	South Parade
C4	South Street
A2	Spring Gardens
A4	Stirling Street
C4	Stockil Road
D4	Theobald Avenue
C1	Thorne Road
C2	Thorne Road
C2	Town Fields
D1	Town Moor Avenue
A2	Trafford Way
C1	Vaughan Avenue
B3	Waterdale
D3	Welbeck Road
A2	West Laith Gate
A3	West Street
C3	Whitburn Road
B4	White Way
D1	Windsor Road
B2	Wood Street

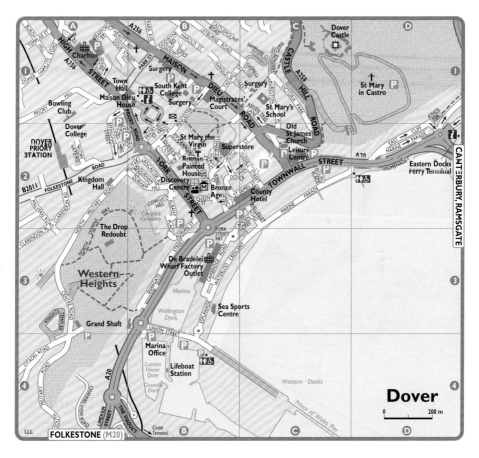

Dover

0   200 m

B3	Adrian Street	B1	Godwyne Road	B2	Queen's Gate
B2	Albany Place	B1	Harold Street	B2	Queen Street
C1	Ashen Tree Lane	C1	Heritage Gardens	B2	Russell Street
D1	Athol Terrace	A1	Hewitt Road	B2	St James Street
B2	Biggin Street	A1	High Street	C1	Samphire Close
A1	Burgh Hill	B2	King Street	A2	Saxon Street
B3	Cambridge Road	A3	Knights Templar	B3	Snargate Street
C2	Camden Crescent	B2	Lancaster Road	A4	South Military Road
B2	Cannon Street	C1	Laureston Place	B2	Stembrook
C1	Castle Hill Road	B1	Leyburne Road	C1	Taswell Close
B1	Castlemount Road	A4	Limekiln Street	B1	Taswell Street
B2	Castle Street	B1	Maison Dieu Road	A1	Templar Street
A3	Centre Road	A2	Malvern Road	A4	The Viaduct
A4	Channel View Road	C2	Marine Parade	A1	Tower Hamlets
B2	Church Street	D2	Marine Parade		Road
A4	Citadel Road	B2	Military Road	C2	Townwall Street
A3	Clarendon Place	B2	Mill Lane	B3	Union Street
A2	Clarendon Road	B2	New Street	C1	Victoria Park
B2	Cowgate Hill	A2	Norman Street	B3	Waterloo Crescent
A1	Crafford Street	A3	North Downs Way	C2	Wellesley Road
B2	Dolphin Lane	A3	North Military Road	A1	Wood Street
C2	Douro Place	B1	Park Avenue	B2	York Street
A1	Dour Street	B1	Park Street	B3	York Street
B2	Durham Close	B2	Pencester Road		Roundabout
B2	Durham Hill	A1	Peter Street		
D2	East Cliff	A2	Priory Gate Road		
A2	Effingham Street	A1	Priory Hill		
B3	Esplanade	A1	Priory Road		
A2	Folkestone Road	B2	Priory Street		
B1	Godwyne Close	D2	Promenade		

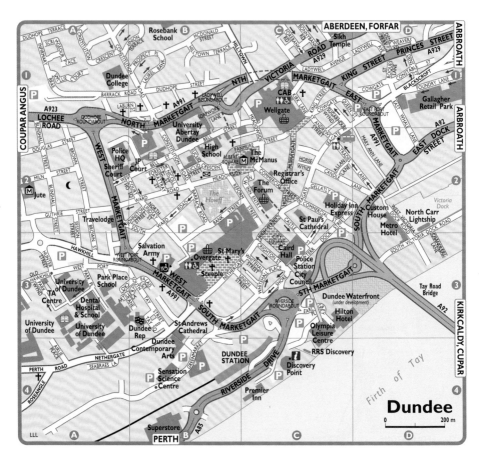

A4	Airlie Place	C3	Dock Street	C1	Ladywell Avenue	B2	Reform Street	A3	West Port
B2	Albert Square	A2	Douglas Street	D1	Ladywell	B4	Riverside Drive		Roundabout
C2	Allan Lane	A1	Dudhope		Roundabout	C3	Riverside	D2	West Victoria Dock
A3	Artillery Lane		Roundabout	B1	Laurel Bank		Roundabout		Road
B2	Bank Street	B1	Dudhope Street	A1	Lochee Road	A4	Roseangle	C3	Whitehall Place
A1	Barrack Road	A1	Dudhope Terrace	D1	Marketgait	C2	St Andrews Street	C3	Whitehall Street
B2	Barrack Road	C3	Earl Grey Place	C1	Marketgait East	D1	St Roques Lane		
B2	Bell Street	D2	East Dock Street	D2	Mary Ann Lane	A1	Scrimgeour Place		
D1	Blackscroft	D1	East Port	B1	McDonald Street	A4	Seabraes Lane		
A2	Blinshall Street		Roundabout	B2	Meadowside	C2	Seagate		
C1	Bonnybank Road	D1	East Whale Lane	A2	Miln Street	A2	Session Street		
A2	Brown Street	B2	Euclid Crescent	C2	Murraygate	C3	Shore Terrace		
C2	Candle Lane	B2	Euclid Street	A4	Nethergate	A1	Smillie Court		
C2	Castle Street	C1	Forebank Road	C2	New Inn Entry	B1	Soapwork Lane		
D3	Chandlers Lane	B2	Forester Street	B2	Nicoll Street	C3	South Marketgait		
C3	City Square	D1	Foundry Lane	B2	North Lindsay	B3	South Tay Street		
C2	Commercial Street	B4	Greenmarket		Street	C3	South Victoria		
D1	Constable Street	A2	Guthrie Street	A1	North Marketgait		Dock Road		
A1	Constitution	A3	Hawkhill	C1	North Victoria	B2	South Ward Road		
	Crescent	C3	High Street		Road	C1	Sugarhouse Wynd		
A1	Constitution Road	B1	Hilltown	A3	Old Hawkhill	D3	Tay Road Bridge		
B2	Constitution Road	B1	Hilltown Terrace	B3	Palais Court	B3	Tay Square		
A2	Court House	C2	Horse Wynd	B2	Panmure Street	C2	Trades Lane		
	Square	A3	Hunter Street	A3	Park Place	B3	Union Street		
C1	Cowgate	A1	Infirmary Brae	A3	Park Wynd	B1	Union Terrace		
D1	Cowgate	C1	Johnston Street	A4	Perth Road	B2	Ward Road		
C3	Crighton Street	C1	King Street	D1	Princes Street	D1	Weavers Yard		
A3	Cross Lane	C1	Kirk Lane	B1	Prospect Place	A2	West Bell Street		
D1	Dens Brae	A1	Laburn Street	C1	Queen Street	A2	West Marketgait		
D1	Dens Street			B2	Rattray Street	A3	West Port		

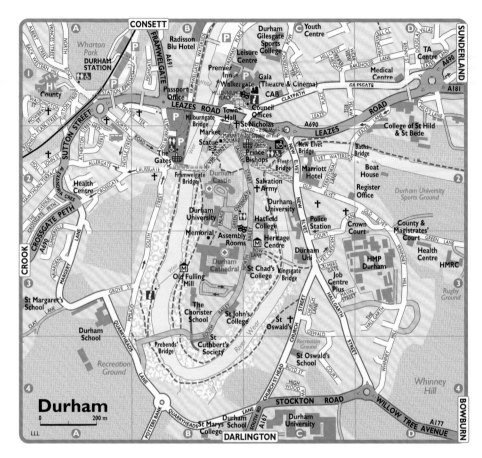

A1	Albert Street	D3	Green Lane	C2	Old Elvet	D3	Whinney Hill
A2	Alexandria Crescent	A3	Grove Street	C3	Oswald Court	D4	Willow Tree Avenue
A2	Allergate	C3	Hallgarth Street	B2	Owengate		
A2	Atherton Street	A2	Hawthorn Terrace	B2	Palace Green		
A1	Back Western Hill	B1	Highgate	C3	Palmers Gate		
C1	Bakehouse Lane	C4	High Road View	C1	Pelaw Rise		
C2	Baths Bridge	C2	High Street	A3	Pimlico		
C3	Bow Lane	C1	Hillcrest	B4	Potters Bank		
C4	Boyd Street	A2	Holly Street	B4	Prebends' Bridge		
A3	Briardene	A2	John Street	A1	Princes' Street		
C3	Church Lane	C1	Keiper Heights	C1	Providence Row		
C4	Church Street	C3	Kingsgate Bridge	A3	Quarryheads Lane		
C4	Church Street Head	D1	Leazes Lane	A2	Redhills Lane		
A3	Clay Lane	D2	Leazes Place	D1	Renny Street		
C1	Claypath	C1	Leazes Road	B2	Saddler Street		
C3	Court Lane	B1	Leazes Road	D1	St Hild's Lane		
A2	Crossgate	A3	Margery Lane	B2	Silver Street		
A3	Crossgate Peth	B2	Market Square	B3	South Bailey		
D1	Douglas Villas	C3	Mavin Street	C4	South Road		
C2	Elvet Bridge	D1	Mayorswell Close	B3	South Street		
C3	Elvet Crescent	B1	Milburngate Bridge	A1	Station Approach		
C2	Elvet Waterside	B2	Millburngate	C4	Stockton Road		
C1	Finney Terrace	B1	Millennium Place	A3	Summerville		
A2	Flass Street	A1	Mowbray Street	A2	Sutton Street		
B1	Framwelgate	A2	Neville Street	A1	Tenter Terrace		
B2	Framwelgate Bridge	C2	New Elvet	C2	Territorial Lane		
B1	Framwelgate Waterside	C2	New Elvet Bridge	A2	The Avenue		
B1	Freeman Place	A2	New Street	D3	The Hall Garth		
C1	Gilesgate	C3	North Bailey	A1	Waddington Street		
		A1	North Road	C1	Wear View		

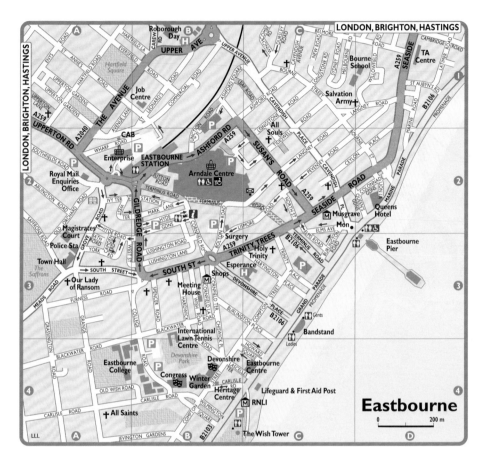

Eastbourne

0   200 m

A2	Arlington Road	A1	Enys Road	A3	Meads Road	A1	Upperton Gardens
B2	Ashford Road	A1	Eversfield Road	C1	Melbourne Road	A1	Upperton Lane
B1	Ashford Square	A3	Furness Road	C1	New Road	A1	Upperton Road
A1	Avenue Lane	B2	Gildredge Road	C2	North Street	A3	West Street
A3	Bath Road	C3	Grand Parade	A2	Old Orchard Road	A2	West Terrace
C1	Belmore Road	A3	Grange Road	A4	Old Wish Road	A2	Wharf Road
A4	Blackwater Road	A3	Grassington Road	C2	Pevensey Road	D1	Willowfield Road
B3	Bolton Road	A3	Grove Road	C3	Promenade	B4	Wilmington Square
C1	Bourne Street	B3	Hardwick Road	D2	Queen's Gardens	C1	Winchcombe Road
B3	Burlington Place	A1	Hartfield Lane	A2	Saffrons Road	B3	Wish Road
C3	Burlington Road	A1	Hartfield Road	A1	St Anne's Road	A3	York Road
D1	Cambridge Road	C1	Hartington Place	D1	St Aubyn's Road		
A3	Camden Road	C4	Howard Square	B1	St Leonard's Road		
B1	Carew Road	B2	Hyde Gardens	D1	Seaside		
A4	Carlisle Road	A2	Hyde Road	C2	Seaside Road		
C1	Cavendish Avenue	A2	Ivy Terrace	A2	Southfields Road		
C1	Cavendish Place	A4	Jevington Gardens	A3	South Road		
C2	Ceylon Place	B2	Junction Road	B3	South Street		
B3	Chiswick Place	C2	Langney Road	B3	Spencer Road		
B3	College Road	B4	Lascelles Terrace	B2	Station Street		
D2	Colonnade Gardens	D1	Latimer Road	C2	Susan's Road		
B1	Commercial Road	B1	Leaf Road	C1	Sydney Road		
B4	Compton Street	D2	Lion Lane	B2	Terminus Road		
B3	Cornfield Lane	B2	Lismore Road	C3	Terminus Road		
B2	Cornfield Road	C1	Longstone Road	A1	The Avenue		
B3	Cornfield Terrace	B3	Lushington Lane	C2	Tideswell Road		
B3	Devonshire Place	B3	Lushington Road	C3	Trinity Place		
C1	Dursley Road	D2	Marine Parade	B3	Trinity Trees		
C2	Elms Avenue	D1	Marine Road	B1	Upper Avenue		
C3	Elms Road	B2	Mark Lane				

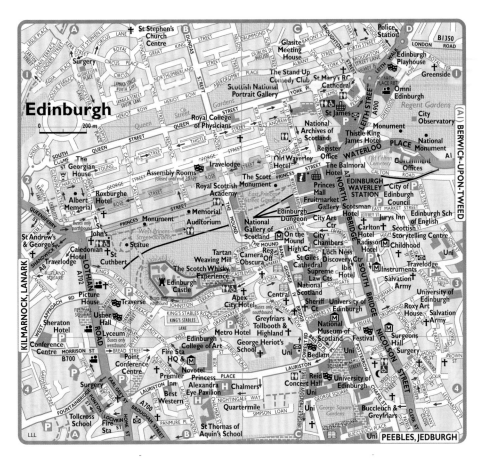

B1	Abercromby Place
D3	Adam Street East
D3	Adam Street West
A2	Ainslie Place
C1	Albany Street
A3	Alva Street
C3	Bank Street
C1	Barony Street
A4	Bread Street
D4	Briery Bauks
C4	Bristo Place
C4	Bristo Square
B4	Brougham Street
C1	Broughton Street
D1	Broughton Street Lane
D4	Brown Street
C4	Buccleuch Place
D2	Calton Road
A3	Cambridge Street
C3	Candlemaker Row
A1	Canning Street
B3	Carlton Street
B2	Castle Street
A3	Castle Terrace
B4	Chalmers Street
C3	Chambers Street
D4	Chapel Street
A2	Charlotte Lane
A2	Charlotte Square
A1	Circus Lane
A1	Circus Place
D4	Clerk Street
C3	Cockburn Street
A3	Cornwall Street
D4	Cowan's Close

C3	Cowgate
D4	Davie Street
A1	Dean Terrace
A1	Doune Terrace
C1	Drummond Place
D3	Drummond Street
C1	Dublin Meuse
C1	Dublin Street
A4	Dunbar Street
B1	Dundas Street
A4	Earl Grey Street
D2	East Market Street
C1	Elder Street
B3	Esplanade
C4	Forrest Road
C1	Forth Street
A4	Fountainbridge
B2	Frederick Street
A4	Gardener's Crescent
C3	George IV Bridge
C4	George Square
A2	George Street
D4	Gilmour Street
A2	Glenfinlas Street
B4	Glen Street
A1	Gloucester Lane
A1	Gloucester Place
B3	Grassmarket
B1	Great King Street
D1	Greenside Row
A3	Grindlay Street
C3	Guthrie Street
D4	Haddon's Court
B2	Hanover Street
C1	Hart Street

B3	Heriot Bridge
B4	Heriot Place
A1	Heriot Row
C3	High Street
B2	Hill Street
A4	Home Street
A2	Hope Street
D4	Howden Street
B1	Howe Street
A1	India Place
A1	India Street
D3	Infirmary Street
A1	Jamaica Street North Lane
A1	Jamaica Street South Lane
D2	Jeffrey Street
B3	Johnston Terrace
B4	Keir Street
A1	Kerr Street
B3	King's Stables Lane
A3	King's Stables Road
A2	Lady Lawson Street
B4	Lauriston Gardens
B4	Lauriston Place
B4	Lauriston Street
C3	Lawnmarket
D2	Leith Street
D1	Leith Walk
A1	Leslie Place
A4	Lochrin Street
D1	London Road
A3	Lothian Road
C2	Market Street
C4	Middle Meadow Walk
A4	Morrison Street

B3	Mound Place
B1	Nelson Street
D2	New Street
D4	Nicolson Square
D3	Nicolson Street
B4	Nightingale Way
C2	North Bridge
A2	North Castle Street
C1	North St Andrew Street
C1	North St David Street
B1	Northumberland Street
B4	Panmure Place
D1	Picardy Place
D1	Picardy Place Roundabout
D3	Pleasance
A4	Ponton Street
D4	Potterrow
A2	Princes Street
A2	Queensferry Street
A2	Queen Street
B3	Ramsay Lane
A2	Randolph Lane
D4	Richmond Lane
D3	Richmond Place
A2	Rose Street
A1	Royal Circus
D1	Royal Terrace
A3	Rutland Place
C2	St Andrew Square
C1	St James Place
D3	St John's Hill
D3	St John Street
D4	St Leonard's Street
D3	St Mary's Street
D4	St Patrick Street

A1	St Stephen Street
B1	St Vincent Street
A1	Saunders Street
A4	Semple Street
A3	Shandwick Place
C4	Simpson Loan
D3	South Bridge
A2	South Charlotte Street
D3	South College Street
A2	South St David Street
C2	South St Andrew Street
C2	South St David Street
B4	Spittal Street
B2	The Mound
B2	Thistle Street
D1	Union Street
C3	Victoria Street
C1	Waterloo Place
C2	Waverley Bridge
A2	Wemyss Place
A3	West Approach Road
D4	West Nicolson Street
B3	West Port
D4	West Richmond Street
C4	Windmill Street
C1	York Lane
C1	York Place
A2	Young Street

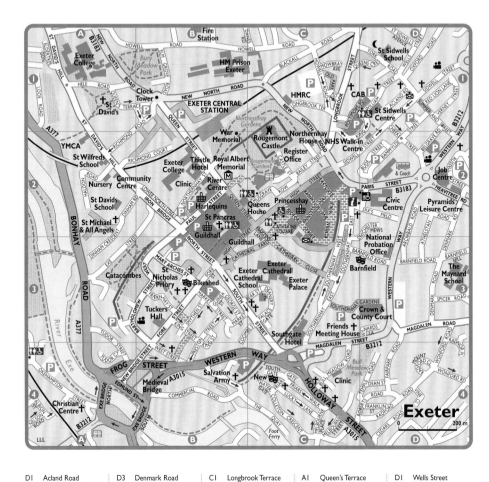

D1	Acland Road	D3	Denmark Road	C1	Longbrook Terrace	A1	Queen's Terrace	D1	Wells Street
D3	Archibald Road	A3	Dinham Crescent	A1	Looe Road	B1	Queen Street	B4	Western Way
D3	Athelstan Road	A2	Dinham Road	B2	Lower North Street	D4	Radford Road	B4	West Street
C2	Bailey Street	D2	Dix's Field	C4	Lucky Lane	D3	Radnor Place	D4	Wonford Road
C2	Bampfylde Lane	C2	Eastgate	D3	Magdalen Road	D1	Red Lion Lane	D3	Wynards Lane
D2	Bampfylde Street	A4	Edmund Street	C4	Magdalen Street	B2	Richmond Court	D1	York Road
D3	Barnfield Hill	A1	Eldertree Garden	B3	Market Street	A2	Richmond Road		
D3	Barnfield Road	B1	Elm Grove Road	C2	Martins Lane	C4	Roberts Road		
B3	Bartholomew Street	A4	Exe Bridge North	B3	Mary Arches Street	C2	Roman Walk		
	West	B4	Exe Bridge South	C4	Melbourne Place	D2	Russell Street		
C3	Bear Street	A3	Exe Street	C4	Melbourne Street	A1	St David's Hill		
C2	Bedford Street	D4	Fairpark Road	D4	Mount Radford	D1	St Sidwells Avenue		
D2	Belgrave Road	B3	Fore Street		Close	C2	Sidwell Street		
C1	Blackall Road	D4	Franklin Street	C1	Mowbray Avenue	D1	Sidwell Street		
A2	Bonhay Road	C4	Friars Gate	C2	Musgrave Row	B3	Smythen Street		
D2	Bude Street	C4	Friars' Walk	A4	Nelson Road	C3	Southernhay East		
C4	Bull Meadow Road	B3	Friern Hay Street	A4	New Bridge Street	C3	Southernhay		
C2	Castle Street	A4	Frog Street	A1	New North Road		Gardens		
C3	Cathedral Close	B3	George Street	B2	Northernhay Street	C3	Southernhay West		
B3	Cathedral Yard	B3	Guinea Street	B3	North Street	C4	Southgate		
C2	Catherine Square	A2	Haldon Road	A4	Okehampton Street	B3	South Street		
D4	Cedars Road	D2	Heavitree Road	C1	Old Park Road	D3	Spicer Road		
D1	Cheeke Street	A1	Hele Road	D1	Oxford Road	D1	Summerland Street		
C3	Chichester Mews	C2	High Street	C3	Palace Gate	D4	Temple Road		
C4	Colleton Crescent	C4	Holloway Street	D2	Paris Street	C4	The Quay		
B4	Commercial Road	B1	Howell Road	B2	Paul Street	A4	Tudor Court		
B3	Coombe Street	B2	Iron Bridge	B3	Poltimore Square	A3	Tudor Street		
B1	Danes Road	B3	King Street	B4	Preston Street	D1	Verney Street		
C3	Deanery Place	D1	King William Street	C2	Princesshay	D4	Vine Close		
D4	Dean Street	C1	Longbrook Street	C1	Queens Crescent	C4	Watergate		

D4	Albion Street	C1	Dobbie's Loan	D4	London Road	A4	Riverview Place	A2	West George Lane
B3	Argyle Arcade	A3	Douglas Street	B1	Maitland Street	A4	Robertson Street	A2	West George Street
A3	Argyle Street	B3	Drury Street	C2	Martha Street	A1	Rose Street	B2	West Nile Street
D1	Baird Street	C2	Dundas Street	C4	Mart Street	D2	Rottenrow	B2	West Regent Lane
A1	Bath Lane	C4	Dunlop Street	B4	Maxwell Street	B3	Royal Exchange Square	A2	West Regent Street
A1	Bath Street	D4	Dyer's Lane	A3	McAlpine Street	D4	St Andrew's Square	A4	West Street
D3	Bell Street	A1	Elmbank Street	B1	McPhater Street	D4	St Andrew's Street	C3	Wilson Street
A2	Bishop Lane	B4	Fox Street	C3	Miller Street	D2	St James Road	A3	York Street
D3	Blackfriars Street	D4	Gallowgate	B1	Milton Street	C2	St Mungo Avenue		
D1	Black Street	A1	Garnet Street	B3	Mitchell Street	A2	St Vincent Lane		
A2	Blythswood Square	C3	Garth Street	D4	Moir Street	B2	St Vincent Place		
A3	Blythswood Street	C2	George Square	D4	Molendinar Street	A2	St Vincent Street		
A3	Bothwell Lane	C2	George Street	D3	Montrose Street	C4	Saltmarket		
A2	Bothwell Street	B4	George V Bridge	A4	Morrison Street	A1	Sauchiehall Lane		
C4	Bridgegate	B4	Glasgow Bridge	C4	New Wynd	A1	Sauchiehall Street		
B4	Bridge Street	C3	Glassford Street	C2	North Frederick Street	A1	Scott Street		
A4	Broomielaw	B3	Gordon Street	C2	North Hanover Street	C4	Shipbank Lane		
A3	Brown Street	C2	Grafton Place	D2	North Portland Street	D3	Shuttle Street		
C3	Brunswick Street	C3	Hanover Street	D1	North Wallace Street	C3	South Frederick Street		
A1	Buccleuch Street	D4	High Street	A3	Oak Street	C1	Stafford Street		
B3	Buchanan Street	A1	Hill Street	C4	Osborne Street	D4	Steel Street		
A3	Cadogan Street	A2	Holland Street	B4	Oswald Street	C4	Stockwell Place		
C1	Calgary Street	A3	Holm Street	A4	Paisley Road	C4	Stockwell Street		
B1	Cambridge Street	B3	Hope Street	C4	Parnie Street	D2	Taylor Place		
D3	Candleriggs	B4	Howard Street	D3	Parsonage Square	D2	Taylor Street		
B4	Carlton Place	C3	Hutcheson Street	A2	Pitt Street	A4	Tradeston Bridge		
C2	Cathedral Street	C3	Ingram Street	B1	Port Dundas Road	C4	Trongate		
A4	Centre Street	B4	Jamaica Street	B4	Portland Street	D4	Turnbull Street		
A4	Clyde Place	A3	James Watt Street		Suspension Bridge	B3	Union Place		
B4	Clyde Street	C1	Kennedy Street	C3	Queen Street	B3	Union Street		
C3	Cochrane Street	C1	Killermont Street	B2	Renfield Lane	C3	Virginia Street		
B4	Commerce Street	A4	Kingston Street	B2	Renfield Street	D3	Walls Street		
D1	Couper Street	C4	King Street	B1	Renfrew Lane	A3	Waterloo Street		
B1	Cowcaddens Road	C1	Kyle Street	A1	Renfrew Street	A3	Wellington Lane		
A1	Dalhousie Lane	B1	Larbert Street	D2	Richmond Street	B3	Wellington Street		
B4	Dixon Street	D1	Lister Street	A4	Riverview Gardens	A3	West Campbell Street		

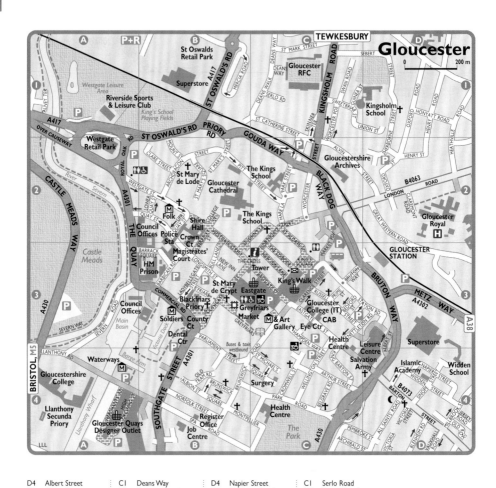

D4	Albert Street	C1	Deans Way	D4	Napier Street	C1	Serlo Road
B4	Albion Street	C3	Eastgate Street	C3	Nettleton Road	A3	Severn Road
D4	All Saints' Road	B1	Gouda Way	B3	New Inn Lane	A3	Severn Way
A1	Alney Terrace	D2	Great Western	C3	New Inn Lane	D2	Sherborne Street
C2	Alvin Street		Road	B4	Norfolk Street	D4	Sinope Street
B2	Archdeacon Street	B3	Greyfriars	C3	Northgate Street	C1	Skinner Terrace
C4	Archibald Street	C1	Guinea Street	D4	Old Row	B3	Southgate Street
C4	Arthur Street	C3	Hampden Way	B4	Old Tram Road	B4	Southgate Street
B3	Barbican Road	C2	Hare Lane	A1	Over Causeway	B4	Spa Road
B3	Barrack Square	D2	Heathville Road	D1	Oxford Road	C3	Station Road
D4	Barton Street	D1	Henry Road	D2	Oxford Street	C1	Swan Road
C3	Bedford Street	D2	Henry Street	C1	Park Road	G1	Sweetbriar Street
C4	Belgrave Road	A4	High Orchard Street	C2	Park Street	B3	The Cross
B3	Berkeley Street	D1	Honyatt Road	B3	Parliament Street	C3	The Oxbode
C2	Black Dog Way	D4	Jersey Road	C4	Pembroke Street	A2	The Quay
B3	Blackfriars	C4	King Barton Street	B2	Pitt Street	C1	Union Street
D4	Blenheim Road	C1	Kingsholm Road	C3	Prime Street	B2	Upper Quay Street
B4	Brunswick Road	C3	King's Square	B1	Priory Road	D4	Vauxhall Road
B4	Brunswick Square	B3	Ladybellegate Street	B2	Quay Street	D4	Victoria Street
C3	Bruton Way	A4	Llanthony Road	A2	Royal Oak Road	C4	Wellington Street
D3	Bruton Way	D2	London Road	C3	Russell Street	A2	Westgate Street
B3	Bull Lane	B3	Longsmith Street	C2	St Aldate Street	B2	Westgate Street
A2	Castle Meads Way	B2	Lower Quay Street	C1	St Catherine Street	D4	Widden Street
D2	Claremont Road	C3	Market Parade	B3	St John's Lane	C2	Worcester Parade
C3	Clarence Street	A4	Merchants' Road	C1	St Mark Street	C2	Worcester Street
B2	Clare Street	B1	Mercia Road	B2	St Mary's Square		
B2	College Street	D3	Metz Way	B2	St Mary's Street		
B3	Commercial Road	D4	Millbrook Street	C4	St Michael's Square		
C4	Cromwell Street	B4	Montpellier	B1	St Oswald's Road		
C1	Deans Walk	B2	Mount Street	C1	Sebert Street		

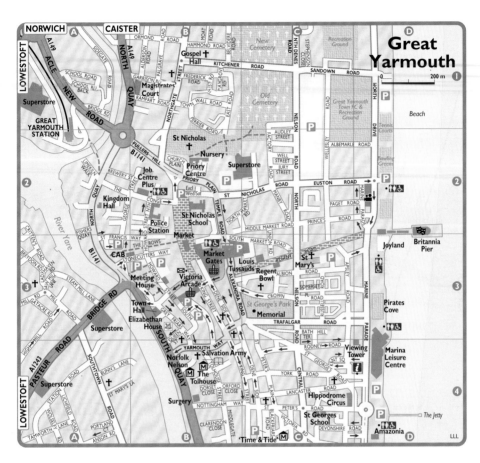

A1	Acle New Road	B1	Garrison Road	C2	North Market Road	B3	South Quay
C2	Albemarle Road	A3	Gatacre Road	A2	North Quay	A4	Southtown Road
C3	Albion Road	A2	George Street	B1	Northgate Street	A4	Station Road
B1	Alderson Road	B3	Grey Friars Way	B4	Nottingham Way	A3	Steam Mill Lane
B3	Alexandra Road	B1	Hammond Road	B4	Orford Close	C1	Stephenson Close
A4	Anson Road	A3	High Mill Road	B1	Ormond Road	B3	Stonecutters Way
C3	Apsley Road	B2	Howard Street	C2	Paget Road	A4	Tamworth Lane
C2	Audley Street		North	B1	Palgrave Road	B2	Temple Road
C3	Bath Hill Terrace	B3	Howard Street	A4	Pasteur Road	A2	The Conge
B1	Belvidere Road		South	A4	Portland Court	B3	The Rows
C4	Blackfriars Road	C2	Jury Street	C2	Prince's Road	B4	Tolhouse Street
A2	Brewery Street	C4	Kent Square	B2	Priory Plain	B1	Town Wall Road
A3	Breydon Road	B3	King Street	B4	Queen Street	C3	Trafalgar Road
A1	Bridge Road	B1	Kitchener Road	B1	Rampart Road	C3	Union Road
A3	Bridge Road	A3	Ladyhaven Road	C3	Regent Road	C4	Victoria Road
A4	Bunn's Lane	C4	Lancaster Road	C4	Rodney Road	C2	Well Street
B2	Church Plain	A4	Lichfield Road	C3	Russell Road	C2	Wellesley Road
B4	Clarendon Close	A2	Limekiln Walk	A3	St Francis Way	B1	West Road
A3	Critten's Road	C2	Manby Road	C4	St George's Road	A4	Wolseley Road
C3	Crown Road	D3	Marine Parade	A4	St Mary's Lane	B4	Yarmouth Way
B3	Dene Side	B1	Maygrove Road	B2	St Nicholas Road	C4	York Road
C4	Devonshire Road	C2	Middle Market Road	C4	St Peter's Plain		
B4	Dorset Close	B4	Middlegate	C4	St Peter's Road		
B1	East Road	A3	Mill Road	C1	Sandown Road		
C2	Euston Road	B1	Moat Road	A3	Saw Mill Lane		
C2	Factory Road	C3	Nelson Road	A1	School Road		
B1	Ferrier Road		Central	A1	School Road Back		
A2	Fishers Quay	C1	Nelson Road North	A1	Sidegate Road		
B1	Frederick Road	C1	North Denes Road	C3	Somerset Place		
B2	Fullers Hill	D1	North Drive	C3	South Market Road		

Guildford

C4	Abbot Road	D3	Harvey Road	C3	Pewley Hill	B1	Woodbridge Road
B3	Angel Gate	C2	Haydon Place	D3	Pewley Way	B1	York Road
B1	Artillery Road	D4	High Pewley	B3	Phoenix Court		
C1	Artillery Terrace	B3	High Street	B4	Porridge Pot Alley		
A2	Bedford Road	C2	Jeffries Passage	A4	Portsmouth Road		
A3	Bridge Street	D2	Jenner Road	D4	Poyle Road		
C3	Bright Hill	B2	Laundry Road	B3	Quarry Street		
D3	Brodie Road	B2	Leapale Lane	C2	Sandfield Terrace		
B4	Bury Fields	B2	Leapale Road	D3	Semaphore Road		
B4	Bury Street	B1	Leas Road	C3	South Hill		
C4	Castle Hill	D2	London Road	C1	Springfield Road		
C3	Castle Street	A4	Mareschal Road	D1	Station Approach		
B3	Chapel Street	C3	Market Street	C1	Stoke Fields		
C2	Chertsey Street	C2	Martyr Road	C1	Stoke Road		
D2	Cheselden Road	A1	Mary Road	B3	Swan Lane		
B1	Church Road	B3	Millbrook	C3	Sydenham Road		
B2	College Road	B3	Mill Lane	A3	Testard Road		
B2	Commercial Road	B3	Millmead	C2	The Bars		
D2	Dene Road	B4	Millmead Terrace	A4	The Mount		
D2	Denmark Road	A4	Mount Pleasant	B3	The Shambles		
B1	Drummond Road	D1	Nightingale Road	C3	Tunsgate		
C1	Eagle Road	B3	North Street	A3	Upperton Road		
D2	Epsom Road	C1	Onslow Road	D1	Victoria Road		
C1	Falcon Road	B3	Onslow Street	A1	Walnut Tree Close		
C4	Fort Road	C3	Oxford Road	C2	Ward Street		
D1	Foxenden Road	C2	Pannells Court	C4	Warwicks Bench		
A3	Friary Bridge	B3	Park Street	B1	Wharf Road		
B3	Friary Street	D3	Pewley Bank	A3	Wherwell Road		
B1	George Road	D4	Pewley Fort Inner	B1	William Road		
A2	Guildford Park Road		Court	A3	Wodeland Avenue		

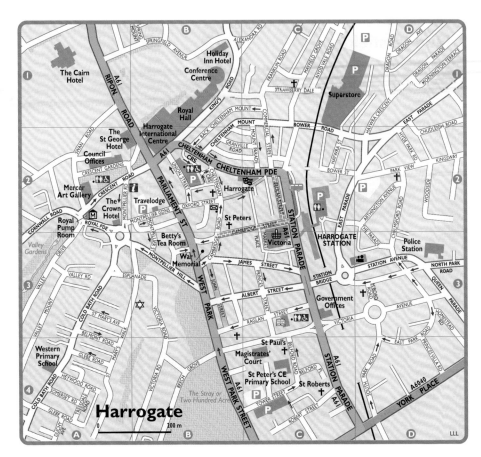

C3	Albert Street	D4	East Park Road	D3	Queen Parade
B1	Alexandra Road	A3	Esplanade	C3	Raglan Street
D2	Arthington Avenue	C1	Franklin Road	A1	Ripon Road
B2	Back Cheltenham Mount	A4	Glebe Road	C4	Robert Street
		B2	Granville Road	A2	Royal Parade
B4	Beech Grove	C2	Haywra Street	A3	St Mary's Avenue
C4	Belford Place	A4	Heywood Road	A4	St Mary's Walk
C4	Belford Road	D3	Homestead Road	A4	Somerset Road
A3	Belmont Road	D2	Hyde Park Road	D4	South Park Road
C2	Beulah Street	D2	Hywra Crescent	B1	Springfield Avenue
C1	Bower Road	B3	James Street	B1	Spring Mount
C2	Bower Street	B3	John Street	D3	Station Avenue
B3	Cambridge Road	B1	King's Road	C3	Station Bridge
C2	Cambridge Street	D2	Kingsway	C2	Station Parade
D3	Chelmsford Road	C3	Market Place	C1	Strawberry Dale
B2	Cheltenham Crescent	D3	Marlborough Road	A2	Swan Road
B2	Cheltenham Mount	C1	Mayfield Grove	D2	The Parade
B2	Cheltenham Parade	B2	Montpellier Gardens	A4	Treesdale Road
D2	Chudleigh Road	B3	Montpellier Hill	B2	Union Street
A3	Cold Bath Road	A2	Montpellier Road	A3	Valley Drive
C1	Commercial Street	B2	Montpellier Street	A3	Valley Mount
A2	Cornwall Road	D1	Mornington Terrace	A3	Valley Road
A2	Crescent Gardens	C2	Mount Parade	C3	Victoria Avenue
A2	Crescent Road	D3	North Park Road	B3	Victoria Road
D1	Dragon Avenue	C1	Nydd Vale Road	B3	West Park
D1	Dragon Parade	B2	Oxford Street	B4	West Park Street
D1	Dragon Road	D2	Park View	D2	Woodside
A4	Duchy Avenue	B2	Parliament Street	D4	York Place
C2	East Parade	C3	Princes Street		
		D4	Princes Villa Road		

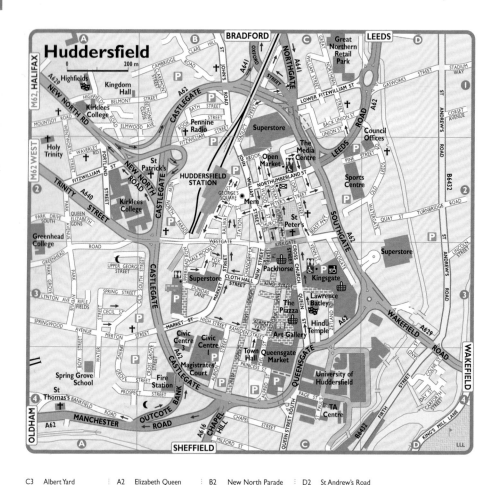

C3	Albert Yard	A2	Elizabeth Queen	B2	New North Parade	D2	St Andrew's Road
B4	Albion Street		Gardens	A1	New North Road	B2	St George's Square
C4	Alfred Street	A1	Elmwood Avenue	B4	New Street	B1	St John's Road
C1	Back Union Street	D4	Firth Street	C1	Northgate	C4	St Paul's Street
A4	Bankfield Road	A2	Fitzwilliam Street	C2	Northumberland	C2	St Peter's Street
B1	Bath Street	B2	Fitzwilliam Street		Street	D4	Sand Street
C2	Beast Market	B3	Fox Street	D2	Old Leeds Road	C2	Southgate
B1	Belmont Close	D1	Gasworks Street	B3	Old South Street	A4	Spring Grove Street
A1	Belmont Street	C1	Great Northern	C3	Oldgate	A3	Spring Street
A4	Bow Street		Street	B4	Outcote Bank	A3	Springwood Avenue
C2	Brook Street	A3	Greenhead Road	C1	Oxford Street	D1	Stadium Way
C2	Byram Street	B3	Half Moon Street	C4	Page Street	B2	Station Street
B1	Cambridge Road	B3	High Street	A2	Park Avenue	A2	Trinity Street
D4	Carforth Street	A1	Highfields Road	A2	Park Drive South	D2	Turnbridge Road
B1	Castlegate	B2	John William Street	A3	Park Grove	C1	Union Street
A3	Cecil Street	C3	King Street	C4	Peel Street	A3	Upper George
B3	Chancery Lane	D4	King's Mill Lane	C2	Pine Street		Street
B4	Chapel Hill	C3	Kirkgate	A2	Portland Street	B3	Upperhead Row
B4	Chapel Street	C2	Leeds Road	B4	Princess Street	C3	Venn Street
C2	Church Street	D3	Lincoln Street	A4	Prospect Street	B2	Viaduct Street
B1	Clare Hill	C2	Lord Street	D2	Quay Street	C3	Victoria Lane
B1	Claremont Street	C1	Lower Fitzwilliam	A2	Queen Elizabeth	D3	Wakefield Road
B3	Cloth Hall Street		Street		Gardens	A3	Water Street
D4	Colne Street	A3	Lynton Avenue	C3	Queen Street	D2	Watergate
D1	Croset Avenue	A4	Manchester Road	C4	Queen Street South	A2	Waverley Road
C3	Cross Church	C3	Market Place	C4	Queensgate	A2	Wentworth Street
	Street	B3	Market Street	B2	Railway Street	B3	Westgate
B4	Cross Grove Street	A3	Merton Street	B3	Ramsden Street	C1	William Street
D4	Day Street	B4	Milford Street	A3	Rifle Fields	C2	Wood Street
B3	Dundas Lane	A1	Mountjoy Road	B1	Rook Street	C3	Zetland Street

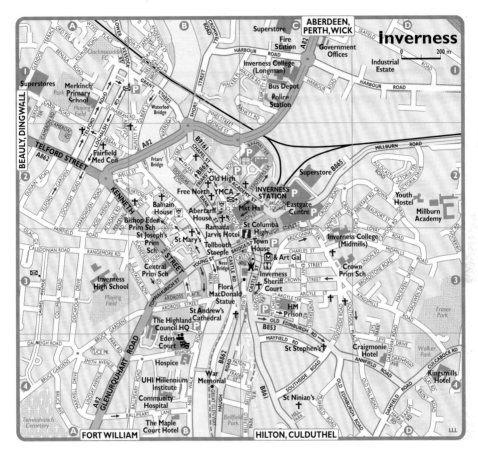

A2	Abban Street	B3	Castle Wynd	A4	Glenurquhart Road	C3	Mitchell's Lane	C3	View Place
A1	Abbey Court	D3	Cawdor Road	C3	Gordon Terrace	B3	Montague Row	B1	Walker Place
D2	Abertaff Road	B2	Celt Street	B1	Grant Street	C4	Muirfield Road	C1	Walker Road
B2	Academy Street	B2	Chapel Street	B4	Great Glen Way	A2	Muirtown Street	B1	Waterloo Bridge
B1	Anderson Street	C3	Charles Street	B2	Greig Street	B1	Nelson Street	A2	Wells Street
D4	Annfield Road	B2	Church Street	C1	Harbour Road	B3	Ness Bridge	A1	Wyvis Place
C3	Ardconnel Terrace	A3	Columba Road	D4	Harris Road	B3	Ness Walk	B3	Young Street
B3	Ardross Place	B1	Cromwell Road	A2	Harrowden Road	C3	Old Edinburgh Road		
B3	Ardross Street	C3	Crown Avenue	B4	Haugh Road	D4	Old Mill Road		
C3	Argyle Street	C2	Crown Circus	C3	High Street	A1	Ord Terrace		
C3	Argyle Terrace	D2	Crown Drive	C4	Hill Park	A4	Park Road		
A2	Attadale Road	C2	Crown Road	C3	Hill Street	B4	Paton Street		
D2	Auldcastle Road	C3	Crown Street	B2	Huntly Place	A2	Perceval Road		
A4	Balliefary Lane	D4	Culcabock Road	B2	Huntly Street	B3	Planefield Road		
B4	Balliefary Road	A4	Dalneigh Road	B1	India Street	C3	Porterfield Road		
B2	Bank Street	D4	Damfield Road	B1	Innes Street	B2	Queensgate		
D2	Beaufort Street	D4	Darnaway Avenue	D4	Islay Road	D4	Raasay Road		
C4	Bellfield Park	D4	Darnaway Road	B1	Jamaica Street	C2	Railway Terrace		
C4	Bellfield Terrace	C3	Denny Street	A2	Kenneth Street	A3	Rangemore Road		
A1	Benula Road	D3	Diriebught Road	A1	Kilmuir Road	B2	Riverside Street		
B1	Bernett Road	A3	Dochfour Drive	B3	King Street	B2	Rose Street		
A1	Birnie Terrace	B2	Douglas Row	D3	Kingsmills Road	A2	Ross Avenue		
B4	Bishops Road	A1	Dunabran Road	A3	Laurel Avenue	D1	Seafield Road		
B3	Bridge Street	A2	Dunain Road	D4	Leys Drive	B1	Shore Street		
D3	Broadstone Road	B3	Duncraig Street	D4	Leys Park	A4	Smith Avenue		
B1	Brown Street	D4	Erisky Road	A3	Lilac Grove	C3	Southside Place		
A4	Bruce Avenue	A3	Fairfield Road	A4	Lindsay Avenue	C4	Southside Road		
A4	Bruce Gardens	C2	Falcon Square	A2	Lochalsh Road	C2	Strothers Lane		
A4	Bruce Park	B4	Fraser Street	D3	Lovat Road	A2	Telford Gardens		
C1	Burnett Road	B2	Friars' Bridge	A1	Lower Kessock Street	A2	Telford Road		
A3	Caledonian Road	B2	Friars' Lane	D3	MacEwen Drive	A2	Telford Street		
A2	Cameron Road	B2	Friars' Street	B1	Madras Street	B3	Tomnahurich Street		
A2	Cameron Square	B2	George Street	A4	Maxwell Drive	D3	Union Road		
A1	Carse Road	B2	Gilbert Street	C4	Mayfield Road	C2	Union Street		
B3	Castle Road	B2	Glebe Street	D3	Midmills Road	D2	Victoria Drive		
C3	Castle Street	A1	Glendoe Terrace	D2	Millburn Road	D2	Victoria Terrace		

142 Ipswich

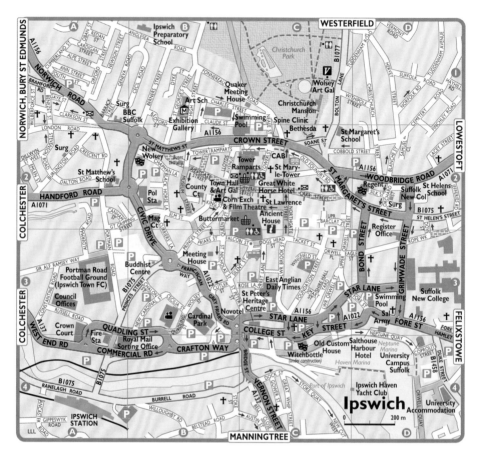

A3	Alderman Road	D1	Christchurch Street	D3	Fore Street	A1	Newson Street	B3	Silent Street
A1	Alpe Street	B2	Civic Drive	C3	Foundation Street	D1	Norfolk Road	D2	Silk Street
A4	Ancaster Road	A1	Clarkson Street	B3	Franciscan Way	C2	Northgate Street	A3	Sir Alf Ramsey Way
A1	Anglesea Road	B1	Claude Street	B3	Friars Street	A1	Norwich Road	C3	Smart Street
A1	Ann Street	C2	Cobbold Street	A1	Gaye Street	A1	Oban Street	C2	Soane Street
C4	Austin Street	C3	College Street	A1	Geneva Road	C2	Old Foundry Road	A1	South Street
A1	Barrack Street	A4	Commercial Road	A4	Gippeswyk Road	D2	Orchard Street	C3	Star Lane
B2	Bedford Street	A3	Constantine Road	C4	Gower Street	A1	Orford Street	A2	Stevenson Road
C4	Bell Close	D4	Coprolite Street	A2	Great Gripping Street	C3	Orwell Place	C4	Stoke Quay
B4	Belstead Road	B4	Crafton Way			D4	Orwell Quay	B4	Stoke Street
A1	Benezet Street	A2	Crescent Road	C4	Great Whip Street	A4	Portman Road	D1	Suffolk Road
B1	Berners Street	B2	Crown Street	B3	Grey Friars Road	A3	Princes Street	C3	Tacket Street
B2	Black Horse Lane	A1	Cumberland Street	D3	Grimwade Street	B3	Princes Street	B2	Tower Ramparts
D2	Blanche Street	B2	Curriers' Lane	A2	Handford Road	A2	Quadling Street	C2	Tower Street
C1	Bolton Lane	B3	Cutler Street	D1	Hayhill Road	B3	Quadling Street	D1	Tuddenham Avenue
D3	Bond Street	A2	Dalton Road	D1	Hervey Street	B3	Queen Street	C1	Tuddenham Road
A1	Bramford Road	A2	Dillwyn Street West	B1	High Street	A4	Ranelagh Road	C3	Turret Lane
C4	Bridge Street	C4	Dock Street	D2	Jefferies Street	A1	Redan Street	C2	Upper Barclay Street
A2	Burlington Road	C3	Dogs Head Street	C4	Key Street	D1	Road Vermont		
B4	Burrell Road	D2	Dove Street	B2	King Street	D3	Rope Walk	C3	Upper Orwell Street
A2	Canham Street	D4	Duke Street	D2	Lacey Street	C3	Rose Lane		
A1	Cardigan Street	B1	Dyke Street	B2	Lloyds Avenue	A3	Russell Road	C4	Vernon Street
C2	Carr Street	C3	Eagle Street	A2	London Road	B1	St George's Street	A3	West End Road
C2	Cavern Street	B2	Elm Street	C3	Lower Brook Street	D2	St Helen's Street	B2	Westgate Street
B3	Cecilia Street	A2	Emlen Street	C3	Lower Orwell Street	C2	St Margaret's Street	A1	Wilberforce Street
B1	Cecil Road	B3	Falcon Street	B2	Museum Street	B2	St Matthews Street	B4	Willoughby Road
D1	Cemetery Road	C4	Felaw Street	C1	Neale Street	B3	St Nicholas Street	C3	Wingfield Street
B3	Chalon Street	D2	Finchley Road	D3	Neptune Quay	B3	St Peter's Street	C1	Withipole Street
B2	Chapman Lane	B1	Fonnereau Road	B3	New Cardinal Street	D2	Samuel Close	B3	Wolsey Street
B1	Charles Street	D3	Fore Hamlet	C4	New Cut West	C3	Shire Hall Yard	D2	Woodbridge Road

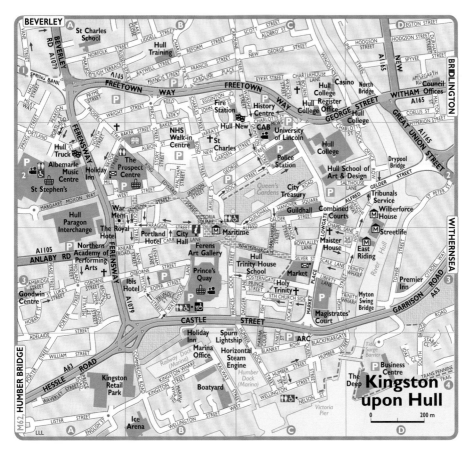

A4	Adelaide Street	A4	English Street	D1	Malton Street	C4	Queen Street	B4	Wellington Street West
B2	Albion Street	A2	Ferensway	C2	Manor Street	B4	Railway Street	A2	West Street
C1	Aldborough Street	C4	Finkle Street	A2	Margaret Moxon Way	B1	Raywell Street	C3	Whitefriargate
D3	Alfred Gelder Street	C3	Fish Street	C4	Marina Court	B1	Reed Street	A4	William Street
A3	Anlaby Road	B1	Francis Street	B4	Marine Wharf	B1	Reform Street	C1	Wincolmlee
D1	Applegarth Road	A1	Freetown Way	C3	Market Place	B3	Roper Street	D1	Witham
A2	Baker Street	D2	Gandhi Way	A1	Marlborough Terrace	A1	Russell Street	C1	Worship Street
A1	Beverley Road	D3	Garrison Road	A3	Melville Street	A3	St Luke's Street	A1	Wright Street
C4	Blackfriargate	B2	George Street	A3	Midland Street	D2	St Peter Street		
B1	Blake Close	C1	George Street	A1	Milky Way	C2	Salthouse Lane		
C4	Blanket Row	D1	Great Union Street	A2	Mill Street	B2	Saville Street		
B2	Bond Street	C2	Grimston Street	B3	Myton Street	C3	Scale Lane		
C1	Bourne Street	C2	Guildhall Road	D3	Myton Swing Bridge	C1	Scott Street		
C3	Bowlalley Lane	A1	Hall Street	C4	Nelson Street	C3	Silver Street		
A2	Brook Street	A3	Hanover Court	D1	New Cleveland Street	D4	South Bridge Road		
A3	Cambridge Street	C2	Hanover Square	B2	New Garden Street	C3	South Church Side		
B1	Caroline Place	A4	Hessle Road	C1	New George Street	B2	South Street		
B1	Caroline Street	C3	High Street	A1	Norfolk Street	A1	Spring Bank		
B3	Carr Lane	A3	Hobart Street	D1	North Bridge	A2	Spring Street		
B3	Castle Street	D1	Hodgson Street	A2	North Street	A4	Spruce Road		
C2	Chapel Lane	C3	Humber Dock Street	A3	Osborne Street	D1	Spyvee Street		
B1	Charles Street	C4	Humber Street	B2	Paragon Street	D4	Stabbs Close		
C2	Charlotte Street	D2	Hyperion Street	C3	Parliament Street	B2	Story Street		
C2	Charlotte Street	D4	Idas Close	A2	Pearson Street	C1	Sykes Street		
	Mews	B2	Jameson Street	A3	Pease Street	D3	Tower Street		
C1	Charterhouse Lane	B2	Jarratt Street	B1	Percy Street	D4	Trans Pennine Trail		
D3	Citadel Way	B1	John Street	C4	Pier Street	D3	Trinity Wharf		
D1	Coelus Street	B2	King Edward Street	A3	Porter Street	B3	Trundle Street		
B4	Commercial Road	B4	Kingston Street	A2	Portland Place	A3	Upper Union Street		
C3	Dagger Lane	B4	Kingston Wharf	A2	Portland Street	A1	Vane Street		
D2	Dock Office Row	B3	Lenham Lane	C3	Posterngate	C3	Vicar Lane		
B2	Dock Street	C3	Liberty Lane	C3	Prince Street	B2	Victoria Square		
D2	Drypool Bridge	B1	Liddell Street	B3	Princes Dock Street	B2	Waltham Street		
D1	Durham Street	D1	Lime Street	C1	Princess Street	B3	Waterhouse Lane		
B1	Egginton Street	A4	Lister Street	A1	Prospect Street	A4	Waverley Street		
D1	Egton Street	C3	Lowgate	A1	Pryme Street	C4	Wellington Street		

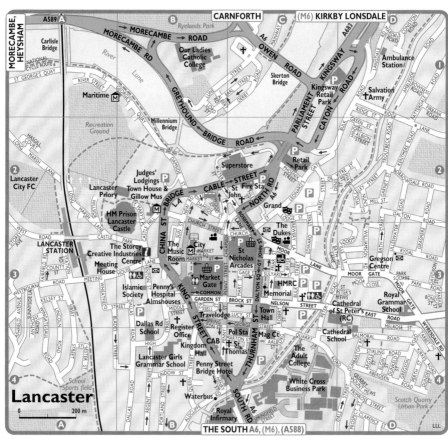

Lancaster

0   200 m

C4	Aalborg Street	B3	Dallas Road	D4	Kirkes Road	D4	Perth Street	D2	Troutbeck Road
D4	Aberdeen Road	D2	Dalton Road	D1	Langdale Road	C3	Peter's Street Mews	D3	Ulleswater Road
B1	Albert Road	C3	Dalton Square	A3	Lincoln Road	C2	Phoenix Street	B2	Water Street
D2	Albion Street	B2	Damside Street	B4	Lindow Street	B4	Portland Street	A3	Westbourne Road
B4	Aldcliffe Road	D3	Davidson Street	C2	Lodge Street	D4	Primrose Street	A3	West Road
C2	Alfred Street	C2	Denis Street	A2	Long Marsh Lane	D4	Prospect Street	A3	Wheatfield Street
D1	Ambleside Road	C1	Derby Road	B1	Lord Street	C4	Quarry Road	D3	Williamson Road
A4	Anthony Road	C2	De Vitre Street	C3	Lucy Street	B4	Quarry Mount Mews	A3	Wingate-Saul Road
D4	Argyle Street	D4	Dumbarton Road	B1	Lune Street	C4	Quarry Road	D2	Wolseley Street
A4	Ashfield Avenue	D4	Dundee Street	C1	Mainway	B4	Queen Street	B2	Wood Street
D4	Balmoral Road	D4	Dunkeld Street	D1	Mardale Road	B4	Regent Street	D3	Woodville Street
C3	Bath Mill Lane	B1	Earl Street	B3	Market Road	D1	Ridge Lane	D3	Wyresdale Road
D3	Bath Street	D3	East Road	B3	Market Square	D1	Ridge Street	A1	River Street
A3	Blades Street	C3	Edward Street	B3	Market Street	C3	Robert Street		
D3	Bond Street	D4	Elgin Street	B4	Marton Street	C2	Rosemary Lane		
D2	Borrowdale Road	A3	Fairfield Road	C3	Mary Street	B3	Russell Street		
D1	Bowness Road	B3	Fenton Street	A3	Meeting House Lane	D3	Rydal Road		
C2	Brewery Lane	D1	Firbank Road	D3	Melrose Street	A1	St George's Quay		
B2	Bridge Lane	C3	Friar Street	B3	Middle Street	C2	St Leonard's Gate		
C3	Brock Street	C3	Gage Street	B2	Millennium Bridge	B2	St Mary's Place		
C3	Bryer Street	D2	Garnet Street	D2	Mill Street	C4	St Peter's Road		
D2	Bulk Road	C3	George Street	D3	Moor Close	D2	Shaw Street		
C3	Bulk Street	D3	Grasmere Road	D3	Moor Gate	A3	Sibsey Street		
B2	Cable Street	D2	Green Street	C3	Moor Lane	C1	Skerton Bridge		
A1	Carlisle Bridge	D4	Gregson Road	A1	Morecambe Road	C4	South Road		
B3	Castle Hill	B1	Greyhound Bridge Road	C3	Nelson Street	C4	Springfield Street		
A3	Castle Park	A2	Hasgill Court	B2	New Road	B3	Spring Garden Street		
C2	Caton Road	B4	Henry Street	C2	Nile Street	A3	Station Road		
C3	Cheapside	B4	High Street	C2	North Road	D4	Stirling Road		
B3	China Street	A2	Hillside	D2	Nun's Street	A3	Storey Avenue		
B2	Church Street	D2	Hinde Street	D3	Owen Road	C3	Sulyard Street		
D4	Clarence Street	A3	Kelsey Road	D3	Parker Street	A3	Sunnyside Lane		
B3	Common Garden Street	D2	Kentmere Road	D3	Park Road	B3	Sun Street		
D1	Coniston Road	B3	King Street	D3	Park Square	A4	Sylvester Street		
A3	County Street	C1	Kingsway	C2	Parliament Street	D4	Tarbet Street		
D4	Dale Street			D2	Patterdale Road	C4	Thurnham Street		
				B4	Penny Street				

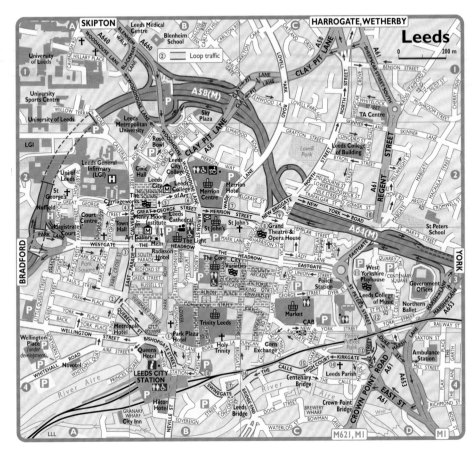

A4	Aire Street	D2	Cromwell Street	A2	Leighton Street	A3	Park Square North	C2	Trafalgar Street
B3	Albion Place	B3	Cross Arcade	A3	Leyland Road	A3	Park Square West	B3	Trinity Street
B2	Albion Street	D1	Cross Stamford Street	A3	Little Queen Street	A3	Park Street	C3	Union Street
D2	Argyle Road	C4	Crown Point Bridge	C1	Lovell Park Hill	D1	Pilot Street	B3	Upper Basinghall Street
A3	Back York Place	D4	Crown Point Road	C1	Lovell Park Road	B2	Portland Crescent	C3	Vicar Lane
B3	Bedford Street	C4	Crown Street	B3	Lower Basinghall Street	B2	Portland Way	C3	Victoria Quarter
B2	Belgrave Street	C4	Dock Street	C2	Lower Brunswick Street	A4	Princes Square	B2	Wade Lane
D1	Benson Street	C4	Duke Street	D2	Mabgate	D3	Quarry Hill	C4	Waterloo Street
B4	Bishopgate Street	C4	Duncan Street	D2	Macaulay Street	A3	Quebec Street	B1	Well Close Rise
A1	Blackman Lane	C3	Dyer Street	B3	Mark Lane	B2	Queen Square	A3	Wellington Street
A1	Blenheim Walk	A3	East Parade	D4	Marsh Lane	B2	Queen Square Court	A3	Westgate
B4	Boar Lane	D4	East Street	D4	Maude Street	A3	Queen Street	C4	Wharf Street
C4	Bowman Lane	C1	Elmwood Lane	C2	Melbourne Street	D3	Railway Street	A4	Whitehall Quay
D4	Bow Street	B2	Elmwood Road	B2	Merrion Street	D2	Regent Street	A4	Whitehall Road
C3	Bridge Street	D1	Firth Street	B2	Merrion Way	D4	Richmond Street	D1	Whitelock Street
B3	Briggate	D4	Flax Place	B2	Millennium Square	B3	Russell Street	A1	Willow Terrace Road
B3	Butts Court	C2	George Street	B4	Mill Hill	D3	St Cecilia Street	A1	Woodhouse Lane
C2	Byron Street	C2	Gower Street	D4	Mill Street	A3	St Mary's Street	D3	York Place
C4	Call Lane	A3	Grace Street	D2	Millwright Street	A3	St Paul's Street	D3	York Street
A2	Calverley Street	C2	Grafton Street	D1	Mushroom Street	D3	St Peter's Square		
B1	Carlton Carr	A2	Great George Street	B4	Neville Street	D3	St Peter's Street		
B1	Carlton Gate	B3	Greek Street	C3	New Briggate	D4	Saxton Street		
B1	Carlton Hill	C4	Harewood Street	B4	New Station Street	D1	Sheepscar Grove		
B1	Carlton Rise	C4	Harper Street	C2	New York Road	D1	Sheepscar Street South		
A1	Cavendish Road	C3	Harrison Street	C3	New York Street	D2	Skinner Lane		
C4	Centenary Bridge	C4	High Court	C2	Nile Street	A3	Somers Street		
D3	Centenary Square	A1	Hillary Place	A4	Northern Street	B3	South Parade		
C3	Central Road	D2	Hope Road	C2	North Street	B4	Sovereign Street		
D1	Cherry Row	B3	Infirmary Street	C1	Oatland Drive	B4	Swinegate		
B3	City Square	C3	King Edward Street	A3	Oxford Place	C3	Templar Place		
B2	Clay Pit Lane	A3	King Street	A3	Oxford Row	C3	Templar Street		
B3	Commercial Street	C3	Kirkgate	A3	Park Cross Street	C4	The Calls		
B4	Concordia Street	B3	Lady Lane	A3	Park Lane	D4	The Garth		
C2	Concord Street	A3	Lands Lane	A3	Park Place	B3	The Headrow		
C3	County Arcade	B4	Leeds Bridge	A3	Park Row	D4	The Lane		
				A3	Park Square East	A2	Thoresby Place		

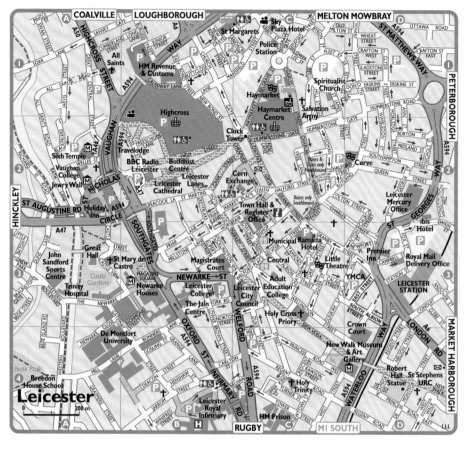

C1	Abbey Street	D3	Conduit Street	C2	Haymarket	B1	New Road	B3	Southgates
C3	Albion Street	D2	Constitution Hill	B4	Henshaw Street	C4	Newtown Street	C3	Stamford Street
A1	All Saints Road	D1	Crafton Street East	A1	Highcross Street	C3	New Walk	D3	Station Street
D3	Andover Street	D1	Crafton Street West	B2	Highcross Street	D2	Nichols Street	D3	Swain Street
D1	Ann Street	C4	Crescent Street	B2	High Street	D3	Northampton Street	A1	Swan Street
A2	Bath Lane	A1	Cumberland Street	C1	Hill Street	B3	Norton Street	A3	The Newarke
A4	Bede Island Road	B4	Deacon Street	B3	Horsefair Street	C1	Old Milton Street	C4	Tower Street
A3	Bede Street	D4	De Montfort Square	B2	Hotel Street	D1	Ottawa Road	C4	Turner Street
C1	Bedford Street	D4	De Montfort Street	C2	Humberstone Gate	B3	Oxford Street	C4	Upper King Street
C1	Belgrave Gate	C3	Dover Street	D1	Humberstone Road	B2	Peacock Lane	A2	Vaughan Way
C1	Belgrave Street	C3	Duke Street	B4	Infirmary Road	C4	Pelham Street	D2	Vestry Street
C3	Belvoir Street	C3	Dunkirk Street	B4	Jarrom Street	A1	Pingle Street	D4	Waterloo Way
C3	Bishop Street	A3	Duns Lane	A1	Jarvis Street	B3	Pocklington Walk	C3	Welford Road
A2	Blackfriars Street	D1	Earl Street	B1	Junior Street	D4	Princess Road East	A2	Welles Street
B4	Bonners Lane	B1	East Bond Street Lane	C3	King Street	C4	Princess Road West	C3	Wellington Street
C3	Bowling Green Street	D3	East Street	C1	Lee Street	D2	Queen Street	A3	Western Boulevard
A3	Braunstone Gate	C1	Eldon Street	A3	Little Holme Street	C4	Rawson Street	C4	West Street
B1	Burgess Street	D1	Erskine Street	D3	London Road	C4	Regent Road	D4	West Walk
D2	Burton Street	C1	Fleet Street	B1	Long Lane	D4	Regent Street	D1	Wharf Street South
B1	Buttclose Lane	C2	Fox Lane	B3	Lower Brown Street	A2	Richard III Road	D1	Wheat Street
C1	Byron Street	D3	Fox Street	C1	Lower Lee Street	B3	Richmond Street	D1	Wimbledon Street
C3	Calais Hill	C2	Free Lane	B3	Magazine Square	B3	Rupert Street	B4	Winifred Street
C3	Calais Street	B2	Freeschool Lane	B1	Mansfield Street	C2	Rutland Street	C2	Yeoman Street
D3	Campbell Street	B3	Friar Lane	B2	Market Place South	A2	St Augustine Road	B3	York Road
B2	Cank Street	C2	Gallowtree Gate	C3	Market Street	D2	St George Street	C3	York Street
B4	Carlton Street	A3	Gateway Street	D2	Midland Street	D2	St Georges Way		
A3	Castle Street	D1	Gladstone Street	C4	Mile Street	C1	St James Street		
A3	Castle View	D3	Glebe Street	A4	Mill Lane	B2	St Martins		
B1	Causeway Lane	B4	Gosling Street	B3	Millstone Lane	D1	St Matthews Way		
C1	Charles Street	C2	Granby Street	D1	Morledge Street	A2	St Nicholas Circle		
C3	Chatham Street	B4	Grange Lane	D4	Nelson Street	B1	Sandacre Street		
C2	Cheapside	A4	Grasmere Street	A4	Newarke Close	A1	Sanvey Gate		
B1	Church Gate	B1	Gravel Street	B3	Newarke Street	B1	Short Street		
D3	Church Street	A1	Great Central Street	B1	New Bond Street	A1	Soar Lane		
D1	Clyde Street	B2	Greyfriars	A3	New Park	D3	South Albion Street		
C2	Colton Street	C2	Halford Street	D3	Newport Place	D2	Southampton Street		

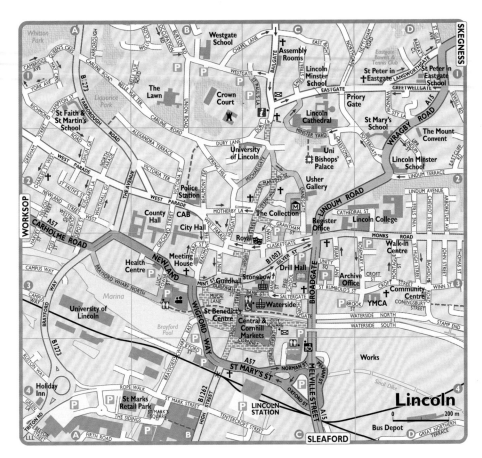

B2	Alexandra Terrace	B4	Cornhill	B3	Lucy Tower Street
D2	Arboretum Avenue	D3	Croft Street	A1	May Crescent
A2	Ashlin Green	C2	Danesgate	C4	Melville Street
D3	Bagholme Road	A3	Depot Street	C2	Michaelgate
C1	Bailgate	B2	Dury Lane	C2	Minster Yard
C3	Bank Street	C1	East Bight	B3	Mint Lane
D1	Barrat's Close	D2	Eastcliff Road	B3	Mint Street
B3	Beaumont Fee	C1	Eastgate	D3	Monks Road
B4	Bedford Street	A4	Firth Road	D3	Montague Street
A4	Beevor Street	A3	Foss Street	B2	Motherby Lane
B1	Belle Vue Road	C3	Free School Lane	B3	Much Lane
A1	Belle Vue Terrace	C3	Friars Lane	A2	Nelson Street
A3	Brayford Way	C2	Grantham Street	D1	Nettleham Road
B4	Brayford Wharf East	D4	Great Northern	B3	Newland
A3	Brayford Wharf		Terrace	A2	Newland Street
	North	A4	Green Lane		West
C3	Broadgate	C2	Greestone Place	C4	Norman Street
C3	Brook Street	D1	Greetwellgate	C1	Northgate
B1	Burton Road	A2	Gresham Street	A2	North Parade
A1	Cambridge Avenue	B3	Guildhall Street	B1	Occupation Road
A3	Campus Way	A1	Hampton Street	B3	Orchard Street
A2	Carholme Road	A3	Harvey Street	C4	Oxford Street
A1	Carline Road	B3	High Street	B3	Park Street
C2	Cathedral Street	B3	Hungate	C4	Pelham Street
B1	Chapel Lane	C1	James Street	D2	Pottergate
A2	Charles Street West	D3	John Street	A1	Queen's Crescent
D2	Cheviot Street	D1	Langworthgate	A1	Richmond Road
C3	City Square	D2	Lindum Avenue	A4	Rope Walk
C3	Clasketgate	C2	Lindum Road	D3	Rosemary Lane
D3	Coningsbury Street	D2	Lindum Terrace	A2	Rudgard Lane

A4	Ruston Way	D2	Vine Street
A2	St Faith's Street	C3	Waterside North
D1	St Giles Avenue	C3	Waterside South
D3	St Hugh Street	A2	Westbourne Grove
B4	St Mark's Square	B1	Westgate
B4	St Mark Street	A2	West Parade
C2	St Martin's Street	A2	Whitehall Grove
B4	St Mary's Street	B3	Wigford Way
C1	St Paul's Lane	B1	Willis Close
C3	St Rumbold's Street	D1	Winnow Sty Lane
C3	Saltergate	D2	Winn Street
D1	Sewell Road	D2	Wragby Road
C3	Silver Street	A1	Yarborough
C4	Sincil Street	A1	Yarborough Road
B2	Spring Hill	A1	York Avenue
D3	Stamp End		
C2	Steer Hill		
C3	Swan Street		
B4	Tentercroft Street		
A2	The Avenue		
A4	The Sidings		
D3	Thomas Street		
C3	Thorngate		
A4	Triton Road		
B1	Union Road		
C3	Unity Square		
D2	Upper Lindum		
	Street		
B2	Victoria Street		
B2	Victoria Terrace		

Liverpool

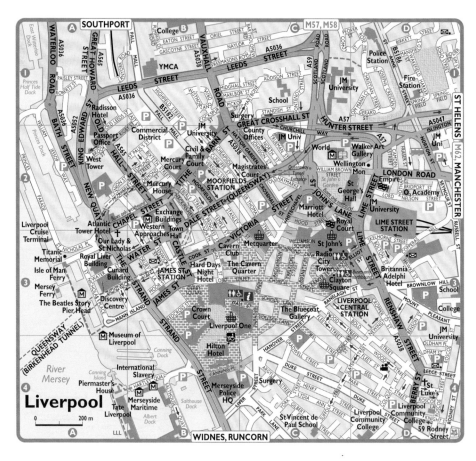

C1	Addison Street	B3	Drury Lane	D4	Leece Street	B1	Pickop Street	B2	Stanley Street
C4	Argyle Street	C4	Duke Street	A1	Leeds Street	A2	Princes Parade	B3	Strand Street
A1	Bath Street	B1	East Street	D2	Lime Street	B2	Princess Street	C4	Suffolk Street
D3	Benson Street	B1	Eaton Street	B4	Liver Street	B1	Pumpfields Road	C3	Tarleton Street
D4	Berry Street	B2	Eberle Street	D2	London Road	A4	Queensway	B2	Temple Street
D1	Bidder Street	B2	Edmund Street	D2	Lord Nelson Street		(Birkenhead Tunnel)	A3	The Strand
D1	Birkett Street	C3	Elliot Street	B3	Lord Street	C3	Ranelagh Street	B2	Tithe Barn Street
B2	Bixteth Street	A2	Fazakerley Street	C4	Lydia Ann Street	B3	Redcross Street	D1	Tom Mann Close
D3	Bold Street	B3	Fenwick Street	A3	Mann Island	D3	Renshaw Street	C2	Trueman Street
D3	Bolton Street	C3	Fleet Street	D1	Mansfield Street	C3	Richmond Lane	A2	Union Street
C3	Bosnett Street	C1	Fontenoy Street	B1	Marlborough Street	A2	Rigby Street	B1	Vauxhall Road
D2	Bridport Street	D2	Fraser Street	C1	Marybone	A1	Roberts Street	B2	Vernon Street
A2	Brook Street	B1	Freemasons Row	B1	Midghall Street	D4	Rodney Street	B3	Victoria Street
D3	Brownlow Hill	D1	Gascoyne Street	B2	Moorfields	D4	Roscoe Street	D1	Wakefield Street
A3	Brunswick Street	C4	Gilbert Street	B3	Moor Street	D1	Rose Hill	B3	Wall Street
D2	Camden Street	C4	Gradwell Street	D3	Mount Pleasant	D2	Russell Street	A1	Waterloo Road
B4	Canning Place	C1	Great Crosshall Street	A2	Newington	D2	St Anne Street	A3	Water Street
B3	Castle Street	A1	Great Howard Street	A2	New Quay	C2	St John's Lane	B1	Westmorland Drive
A2	Chapel Street	B2	Hackins Hey	B3	North John Street	D1	St Josephs Crescent	C2	Whitechapel
B2	Cheapside	C4	Hanover Street	C2	North Street	A3	St Nicholas Place	C2	William Brown Street
D1	Christian Street	D1	Harker Street	D2	Norton Street	B2	St Paul's Street	A1	William Jessop Way
C2	Churchill Way	B4	Hartley Quay	A1	Old Hall Street	B4	Salthouse Quay	C3	Williamson Square
C3	Church Street	B2	Hatton Garden	D4	Oldham Place	C3	School Lane	C3	Williamson Street
B1	Cockspur Street	D3	Hawke Street	D4	Oldham Street	C1	Scotland Road	C3	Wood Street
C3	College Lane	C4	Henry Street	C2	Old Haymarket	C3	Seel Street	C4	York Street
D4	Colquitt Street	B1	Highfield Street	A2	Old Leeds Street	D4	Seel Street		
C1	Comus Street	C2	Hood Street	B1	Oriel Street	D2	Seymour Street		
C4	Concert Street	D2	Hotham Street	B2	Ormond Street	D1	Sim Street		
B3	Cook Street	C1	Hunter Street	A1	Paisley Street	C2	Sir Thomas Street		
D3	Copperas Hill	D2	Islington	B1	Pall Mall	D3	Skelhorne Street		
D3	Cropper Street	B3	James Street	C3	Paradise Street	C4	Slater Street		
C2	Crosshall Street	C2	Johnson Street	C3	Parker Street	D1	Soho Street		
B2	Cunliffe Street	A2	King Edward Street	C4	Park Lane	D1	Springfield		
B2	Dale Street	D4	Knight Street	D4	Park Street	D1	Stafford Street		
	(Queensway)	A1	Lanyork Road	C1	Peover Street	C1	Standish Street		
B3	Derby Square								

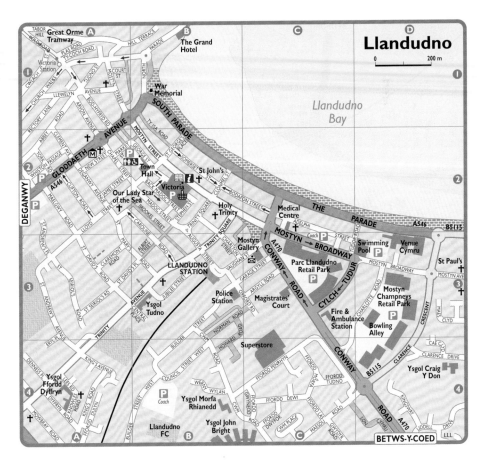

Llandudno

0   200 m

Llandudno Bay

BETWS-Y-COED

A2	Abbey Road	B3	Cwm Road	D4	Lon Cymru	B2	Trinity Square
C2	Adelphi Street	C3	Cylch Tudur	B2	Madoc Street	A1	Tudno Street
B3	Albert Street	A2	Deganwy Avenue	A2	Maelgwy Road	C3	Tudor Road
C3	Argyll Road	A4	Denness Place	D3	Maes Clyd	A1	Ty-Coch Road
A1	Arvon Avenue	A4	Dyffryn Road	C4	Maesdu Road	B1	Ty Isa Road
B3	Augusta Street	A4	Eryl Place	A2	Market Street	B3	Vaughan Street
B2	Back Madoc Street	C4	Ffordd Dewi	D3	Mostyn Avenue	B4	Werny Wylan
B2	Bodafon Street	A4	Ffordd Dulyn	C3	Mostyn Broadway	A2	Whiston Passage
A1	Bod-Hyfryd Road	C4	Ffordd Dwyfor	A1	Mostyn Street	A2	York Road
B2	Brookes Street	C4	Ffordd Gwynedd	A4	Mowbray Road		
B4	Builder Street	C4	Ffordd Las	A2	New Street		
A4	Builder Street West	C4	Ffordd Morfa	B3	Norman Road		
D4	Cae Clyd	C4	Ffordd Penrhyn	B1	North Parade		
B2	Caroline Road	C4	Ffordd Tudno	A1	Old Road		
B3	Central Place	B3	Garage Street	B3	Oxford Road		
A2	Chapel Street	A2	George Street	A1	Plas Road		
D3	Charlotte Road	A2	Gloddaeth Avenue	A2	Rectory Lane		
B3	Charlton Street	C4	Gwydyr Road	A3	St Andrew's Avenue		
A1	Church Walks	A1	Hill Terrace	A2	St Andrew's Place		
A3	Claremont Road	B4	Howard Road	A3	St David's Place		
D4	Clarence Crescent	A2	James Street	A3	St David's Road		
D4	Clarence Drive	B3	Jubilee Street	B2	St George's Place		
A2	Clement Avenue	A4	King's Avenue	A2	St Mary's Road		
A2	Clifton Road	A4	King's Road	A3	St Seiriol's Road		
B2	Clonmel Street	D4	Kingsway	B2	Somerset Street		
C3	Conway Road	A4	Knowles Road	B2	South Parade		
B4	Council Street West	A4	Lees Road	B1	Stephen Street		
A1	Court Street	D4	Liddell Drive	A1	Tabor Hill		
A1	Cwlach Street	A1	Llewelyn Avenue	C2	The Parade		
C4	Cwm Place	A2	Lloyd Street	A3	Trinity Avenue		

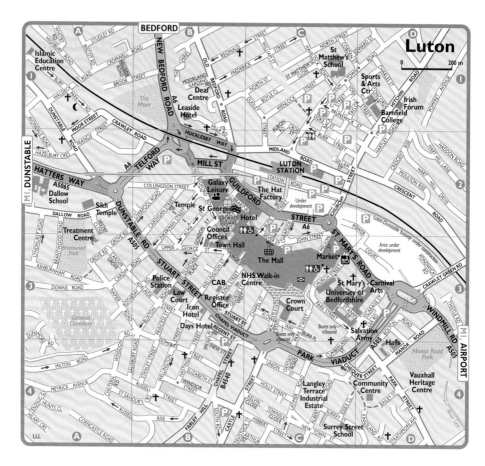

B3	Adelaide Street	B2	Collingdon Street	D2	Hartley Road	C1	North Street	C4	Townsley Close
C4	Albert Road	D1	Concorde Street	B4	Hastings Street	B1	Old Bedford Road	C4	Union Street
C1	Albion Road	D3	Crawley Green	A2	Hatters Way	C4	Oxford Road	B3	Upper George
B2	Alma Street		Road	C1	Havelock Road	C3	Park Street		Street
C4	Arthur Street	A1	Crawley Road	A2	Hazelbury Crescent	D4	Park Street	D3	Vicarage Street
A3	Ashburnham Road	D2	Crescent Rise	C4	Hibbert Street	C3	Park Street West	A1	Waldeck Road
C1	Back Street	D2	Crescent Road	A1	Highbury Road	C4	Park Viaduct	B4	Wellington Street
D4	Bailey Street	A1	Cromwell Road	C1	High Town Road	D1	Pomfret Avenue	C1	Wenlock Street
A1	Biscot Road	C1	Cross Street	D1	Hitchin Road	D3	Pondwicks Road	C1	William Street
D3	Bolton Road	C4	Cumberland Street	C4	Holly Street	D2	Power Court	D3	Windmill Road
C1	Boyle Close	A2	Dallow Road	B2	Hucklesby Way	B3	Princess Street	B4	Windsor Street
A3	Brantwood Road	C1	Dudley Street	B3	Inkerman Street	B3	Regent Street	A4	Winsdon Road
C1	Brunswick Street	C1	Duke Street	C3	John Street	B1	Reginald Street	C1	York Street
C3	Burr Place	B4	Dumfries Street	C4	Kelvin Close	A3	Rothesay Road		
C2	Burr Street	A1	Dunstable Road	D4	Kingsland Road	A4	Russell Rise		
A1	Bury Park Road	A2	Dunstable Road	B3	King Street	B4	Russell Street		
C2	Bute Street	D1	Edward Street	C4	Latimer Road	C3	St Ann's Street		
B3	Buxton Road	C4	Essex Close	D3	Lea Road	C3	St Mary's Road		
A3	Cardiff Road	B4	Farley Hill	B2	Liverpool Road	C1	St Matthew's Close		
B2	Cardigan Street	A1	Frederick Street	D4	Manor Road	A4	Salisbury Road		
B4	Castle Street	B3	George Street	C3	Melson Street	C3	Silver Street		
B4	Chapel Street	B3	George Street West	A4	Meyrick Avenue	B4	Stanley Street		
B3	Chapel Viaduct	C2	Gillam Street	C2	Midland Road	C2	Station Road		
D1	Charles Street	B3	Gordon Street	B2	Mill Street	D4	Strathmore Avenue		
C3	Cheapside	A3	Grove Road	A4	Milton Road	B3	Stuart Street		
C4	Chequer Street	B2	Guildford Street	A1	Moor Street	C4	Surrey Street		
A4	Chiltern Road	D2	Haddon Road	D2	Moulton Rise	B4	Tavistock Street		
C2	Church Road	D2	Hart Hill Drive	A3	Napier Road	C1	Taylor Street		
C3	Church Street	D2	Hart Hill Lane	B1	New Bedford Road	B2	Telford Way		
C1	Cobden Street	D2	Hartley Road	C4	New Town Street	D3	Thistle Road		

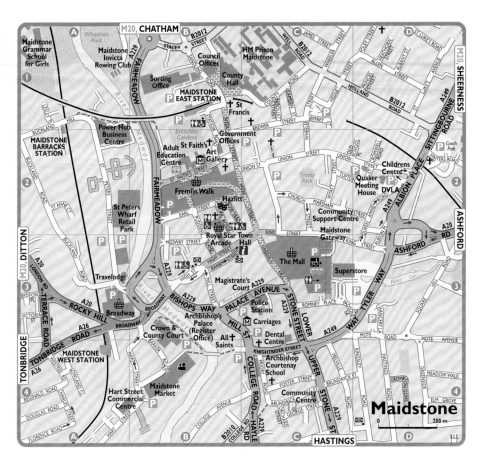

D1	Albany Street	C4	George Street	C4	Priory Road	C1	Woollett Street
D2	Albion Place	D4	Greenside	B2	Pudding Lane	C2	Wyatt Street
D1	Allen Street	A4	Hart Street	D2	Queen Anne Road		
D3	Ashford Road	D4	Hastings Road	A4	Reginald Road		
B3	Bank Street	C4	Hayle Road	A3	Rocky Hill		
B4	Barker Road	D1	Heathorn Street	C3	Romney Place		
A3	Bedford Place	C1	Hedley Street	B2	Rose Yard		
B3	Bishops Way	B3	High Street	A4	Rowland Close		
C2	Brewer Street	D1	Holland Road	A2	St Anne Court		
B3	Broadway	C1	James Street	B2	St Faith's Street		
C4	Brunswick Street	C1	Jeffrey Street	D1	St Luke's Avenue		
A2	Buckland Hill	C3	King Street	D1	St Luke's Road		
A2	Buckland Road	D4	Kingsley Road	A2	St Peters Street		
C1	Camden Street	C4	Knightrider Street	B1	Sandling Road		
D3	Chancery Lane	A1	Lesley Place	D2	Sittingbourne Road		
A4	Charles Street	A3	London Road	D3	Square Hill Road		
C2	Church Street	C3	Lower Stone Street	B1	Stacey Street		
B4	College Avenue	B2	Market Buildings	B1	Station Road		
C4	College Road	C2	Marsham Street	A3	Terrace Road		
C1	County Road	D4	Meadow Walk	A4	Tonbridge Road		
D4	Crompton Gardens	B3	Medway Street	C2	Tufton Street		
D2	Cromwell Road	B3	Melville Road	C2	Union Street		
A4	Douglas Road	B3	Mill Street	C4	Upper Stone Street		
B2	Earl Street	D3	Mote Avenue	A3	Victoria Street		
D4	Elm Grove	D3	Mote Road	D2	Vinters Road		
B1	Fairmeadow	D2	Old School Place	C3	Wat Tyler Way		
A4	Florence Road	C4	Orchard Street	B1	Week Street		
D1	Foley Street	C3	Padsole Lane	C1	Well Road		
C4	Foster Street	B3	Palace Avenue	A4	Westree Road		
C3	Gabriel's Hill	D1	Princes Street	C1	Wheeler Street		

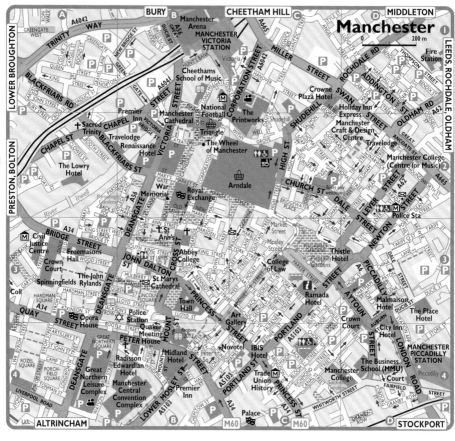

C4	Abingdon Street	B3	Cheapside	D3	Hilton Street	B4	Mount Street	B3	St Ann Street
D1	Addington Street	D3	China Lane	B3	Hope Street	B3	Mulberry Street	B3	St James Square
C1	Angel Street	C4	Chorlton Street	D2	Houndsworth Street	B4	Museum Street	B4	St James Street
A4	Artillery Street	C2	Church Street	B1	Hunt's Bank	B1	New Bridge Street	B2	St Mary's Gate
A3	Atkinson Street	D4	Cobourg Street	A3	Jackson's Row	B2	New Cathedral Street	A3	St Mary's Parsonage
D4	Auburn Street	B2	College Land	B3	John Dalton	C1	New George Street	B2	St Mary Street
D3	Aytoun Street	A1	Collier Street	A1	John Street	B2	New Market	B4	St Peter's Square
A3	Back Bridge Street	B3	Concert Lane	C2	John Street	D3	Newton Street	C2	Salmon Street
C3	Back George Street	C2	Copperas Street	C2	Joiner Street	C3	New York Street	C2	Shudehill
C2	Back Piccadilly	B2	Corporation Street	B3	Kennedy Street	A1	Nicholas Street	B3	Soap Street
A2	Back South Parade	D1	Crosskeys Street	A1	King Street	A1	Norton Street	B3	South King Street
D1	Bendix Street	B3	Cross Street	B3	King Street	C2	Oak Street	D2	Spear Street
A1	Blackfriars Road	B3	Dale Street	A3	King Street West	B2	Old Bank Street	C3	Spring Gardens
A2	Blackfriars Street	C2	Dantzic Street	D3	Lena Street	D2	Oldham Road	D3	Station Approach
C4	Bloom Street	A4	Deansgate	D2	Lever Street	D2	Oldham Street	C1	Swan Street
A1	Boond Street	D2	Dean Street	B3	Lincoln Square	B3	Pall Mall	D3	Tariff Street
A2	Booth Street	B4	Dickinson Street	A4	Little John Street	C3	Parker Street	C2	Thomas Street
B3	Booth Street	A3	Dolefield	D3	Little Lever Street	B4	Peter Street	D1	Thompson Street
A4	Bootle Street	D3	Ducie Street	A4	Liverpool Road	D3	Piccadilly	B3	Tib Lane
B3	Bow Lane	C2	Edge Street	B3	Lloyd Street	C3	Piccadilly Gardens	C2	Tib Street
B3	Brazenose Street	C4	Fairfield Street	D4	London Road	C3	Pine Street	B1	Todd Street
D3	Brewer Street	D2	Faraday Street	B1	Long Millgate	B3	Police Street	A4	Tonman Street
A3	Bridge Street	C4	Faulkner Street	A4	Longworth Street	A4	Porchfield Square	A1	Trinity Way
C2	Bridgewater Place	B1	Fennel Street	D2	Loom Street	C4	Portland Street	C2	Turner Street
B3	Brown Street	B3	Fountain Street	A4	Lower Byrom Street	D3	Port Street	A1	Viaduct Street
A1	Bury Street	A3	Gartside Street	B4	Lower Mosley Street	B3	Princess Street	B2	Victoria Bridge Street
A4	Byrom Street	B4	George Street	D1	Ludgate Street	A2	Quay Street	B2	Victoria Street
A1	Cable Street	A1	Gravel Lane	C4	Major Street	A3	Quay Street	D2	Warwick Street
C4	Canal Street	D2	Great Ancoats Street	C3	Marble Street	A1	Queen Street	A4	Watson Street
B2	Cateaton Street	B1	Great Ducie Street	B2	Market Street	A3	Queen Street	C2	Well Street
B2	Cathedral Street	A4	Great Northern Square	B3	Marsden Street	C4	Reyner Street	C3	West Mosley Street
D1	Chadderton Street	A1	Greengate	D1	Marshall Street	C4	Richmond Street	C4	Whitworth Street
C3	Chain Street	C1	Hanover Street	D1	Mason Street	D3	Roby Street	B4	Windmill Street
A2	Chapel Street	A3	Hardman Square	C1	Miller Street	D1	Rochdale Road	C3	Withy Grove
C3	Charlotte Street	A3	Hardman Street	C3	Minshull Street	A3	Sackville Street	A3	Wood Street
D3	Chatham Street	C2	High Street	C3	Mosley Street	B2	St Anns Square	C3	York Street

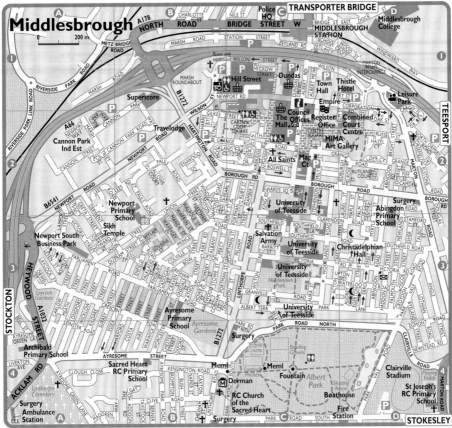

D3	Abingdon Road	A3	Carlow Street	D1	Fry Street	B3	Manor Street	C2 St Aidans Drive
A4	Acklam Road	B4	Caxton Street	B2	Garnet Street	D3	Maple Street	B2 St Pauls Road
C3	Acton Street	C2	Centre Square	B2	Gilkes Street	A1	Marsh Road	C2 Smith Street
B4	Addison Road	B4	Chester Street	B3	Glebe Road	B1	Marsh Road	D2 Somerset Street
B4	Aire Street	D4	Clairville Road	D2	Grange Road	A2	Marsh Street	C3 Southfield Lane
B3	Albany Street	C3	Clarendon Road	D2	Grange Road	D2	Marton Road	C3 Southfield Road
C1	Albert Mews	B3	Clifton Street	C3	Granville Road	A3	Meath Street	C2 Stamford Street
C2	Albert Road	B4	Clive Road	B3	Gresham Road	D2	Melrose Street	C1 Station Street
C3	Albert Terrace	A4	Clough Close	A2	Greta Street	A1	Metz Bridge Road	C2 Stephenson Street
C2	Amber Street	B3	Colville Street	D3	Haddon Street	B2	Monkland Close	B3 Stowe Street
D3	Angle Street	D1	Corporation Road	B3	Harewood Street	D3	Myrtle Street	A4 Surrey Street
B3	Aske Road	B4	Costa Street	B4	Harford Street	B4	Napier Street	D3 Talbot Street
B3	Athol Street	B3	Craven Street	B3	Harris Street	D3	Newlands Road	B4 Tavistock Street
D3	Audrey Street	A3	Crescent Road	B2	Hartington Road	A2	Newport Road	B3 Tennyson Street
B4	Ayresome Park Road	D3	Croydon Road	C2	Head Street	D4	Newstead Road	C3 Ulla Street
A4	Ayresome Street	A2	Derwent Street	A3	Heywood Street	D2	North Ormsby Road	A3 Union Street
C3	Barritt Street	B3	Diamond Road	D2	Horsefield	A3	Outram Street	C2 University Boulevard
B4	Berner Street	D1	Dock Street	A3	Howard Street	B4	Oxford Street	C3 Upton Street
C1	Bolckow Street	C1	Dundas Mews	D2	Jedburgh Street	D3	Palm Street	C3 Victoria Road
C2	Borough Road	D3	Egerton Street	B4	Kensington Road	C3	Park Lane	A3 Victoria Street
C2	Boswell Street	D4	Egmont Road	A4	Kildare Street	C4	Park Road South	B2 Walpole Street
B3	Bow Street	D2	Elder Court	C2	King Edwards Square	D4	Park Vale Road	B2 Warren Street
B2	Bretnall Street	D2	Elm Street	B2	Kingston Street	A3	Parliament Road	B4 Warwick Street
C1	Bridge Street East	D2	Elstone Road	A3	Lamport Street	C2	Pearl Street	D3 Waterloo Road
C1	Bridge Street West	C2	Emily Street	C3	Laura Street	B2	Peel Street	B3 Waverley Street
D2	Bright Street	B3	Enfield Street	D3	Laurel Street	C3	Pelham Street	A3 Wembley Street
B4	Brompton Street	D3	Errol Street	A3	Laycock Street	B3	Percy Street	A4 Wicklow Street
A2	Bulmer Way	D3	Esher Street	A2	Lees Road	B3	Portman Street	B2 Wilson Street
B4	Bush Street	B2	Eshwood Square	A4	Leinster Road	B3	Princes Road	C3 Wilton Street
D3	Byelands Street	A4	Essex Street	A3	Leven Street	A2	Riverside Park Link Road	B2 Windsor Street
B3	Cadogan Street	C2	Fairbridge Street	B4	Linthorpe Road	A1	Riverside Park Road	D1 Windsor Way
A2	Cannon Park Road	D3	Falkland Street	A4	Longford Street	B3	Romney Street	C3 Woodlands Road
A2	Cannon Park Way	D3	Falmouth Street	B3	Lonsdale Street	D3	Roscoe Street	B4 Worcester Street
A2	Cannon Street	B3	Fern Street	A3	Lorne Street	C2	Ruby Street	B3 Wylam Street
C2	Captain Cook Square	B3	Finsbury Street	D3	Lothian Road	D2	Russel Street	C1 Zetland Place
D2	Cargo Fleet Road	B2	Fleetham Street	B3	Lovaine Street	D2	Rutland Court	C1 Zetland Road

Milton Keynes

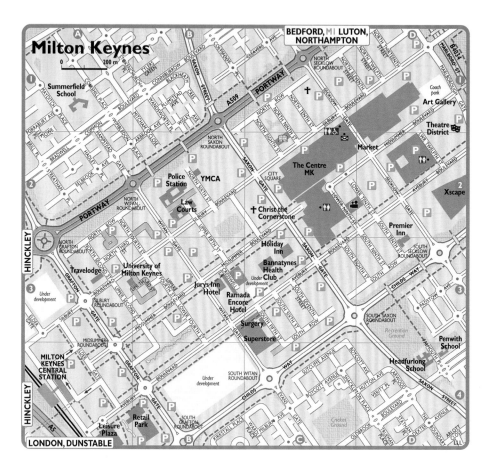

B2	Arbrook Avenue	B3	Lower Fourth Street	A3	North Third Street	D2	South Tenth Street
D4	Arlott Close	C2	Lower Ninth Street	D1	North Thirteenth	C4	South Witan
A4	Avebury Boulevard	C2	Lower Tenth Street	D1	North Twelfth		Roundabout
B1	Blackheath Crescent	D2	Lower Twelfth		Street	D4	Statham Place
C4	Boycott Avenue		Street	A2	North Witan	A1	Stokenchurch Place
A2	Bradwell Common	D1	Marlborough Gate		Roundabout	A2	Streatham Place
	Boulevard	D1	Marlborough Street	C4	Oldbrook Boulevard	C4	Sutcliffe Avenue
A2	Brill Place	A1	Maydiitch Place	D3	Padstow Avenue	D4	The Boundary
B4	Childs Way	B3	Midsummer	B1	Plumstead Avenue	D4	Trueman Place
C2	City Square		Boulevard	A2	Portway	B1	Tylers Green
C1	Cleavers Avenue	A4	Midsummer	B2	Saxon Gate	B2	Upper Fifth Street
A1	Coleshill Place		Roundabout	B1	Saxon Street	B3	Upper Fourth Street
B1	Coltsfoot Place	C4	Milburn Avenue	D4	Saxon Street	A3	Upper Second
B1	Conniburrow	B1	Mitcham Close	C1	Secklow Gate		Street
	Boulevard	C1	North Eighth Street	C4	Shackleton Place	B3	Upper Third Street
B3	Cresswell Lane	C1	North Eleventh	A3	Silbury Boulevard	D4	Verity Place
D4	Dexter Avenue	A2	North Fourth Street	A3	Silbury Roundabout	B1	Wandsworth Place
A2	Eelbrook Avenue	A3	North Grafton	C3	South Eighth Street	C4	Wardle Place
A3	Elder Gate		Roundabout	C3	South Fifth Street	A1	Wimbledon Place
A4	Elder Gate	C1	North Ninth Street	B4	South Grafton	B1	Wisley Avenue
C4	Evans Gate	A3	North Row		Roundabout	B2	Witan Gate
D3	Falmouth Place	C1	North Row	D2	South Ninth Street		
A1	Forrabury Avenue	B2	North Saxon	C3	South Row		
A3	Grafton Gate		Roundabout	D3	South Row		
A2	Hadley Place	C1	North Secklow	D3	South Saxon		
A2	Hampstead Gate		Roundabout		Roundabout		
D4	Hutton Avenue	A3	North Second	D3	South Secklow		
B4	Kirkstall Place		Street		Roundabout		
D4	Larwood Place	B2	North Sixth Street	C3	South Seventh		
A2	Leasowe Place	C1	North Tenth Street	C3	South Sixth Street		

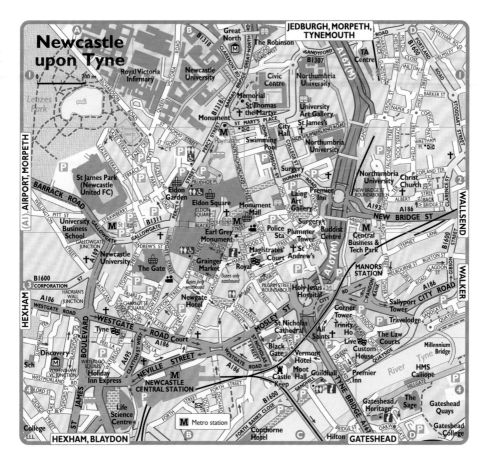

Newcastle upon Tyne

JEDBURGH, MORPETH, TYNEMOUTH

AIRPORT, MORPETH (A1)

HEXHAM

WALLSEND

WALKER

HEXHAM, BLAYDON

GATESHEAD

M Metro station

D2	Albert Street	C3	Dean Street	D3	Jubilee Road	D3	Pandon
D2	Argyle Street	A4	Duke Street	C4	King Street	D3	Pandon Bank
D2	Back New Bridge Street	C2	Durant Road	B2	Leazes Crescent	A4	Peel Lane
D1	Barker Street	B2	Eldon Square	B2	Leazes Lane	B2	Percy Street
A2	Barrack Road	B3	Falconar's Court	B2	Leazes Park Road	C2	Pilgrim Street
B1	Barras Bridge	D2	Falconer Street	A2	Leazes Terrace	C3	Pilgrim Street Roundabout
A3	Bath Lane	B3	Fenkle Street	C4	Lombard Street		
B2	Blackett Street	B4	Forth Banks Close	A4	Lord Street	B4	Pink Lane
D3	Blagdon Street	B4	Forth Street	B3	Loth Market	A2	Pitt Street
A4	Blandford Square	A3	Friars Street	B3	Low Friar Street	D1	Portland Road
A4	Blandford Street	A2	Gallowgate	B3	Market Street	B2	Prudhoe Place
C4	Bridge Street	A3	Gallowgate Junction	D3	Melbourne Street	D3	Quayside
C3	Broad Church	A4	George Street	D1	Milton Close	D4	Quayside
D3	Buxton Street	D3	Gibson Street	D1	Milton Place	C4	Queen Street
D1	Byron Street	D1	Gladstone Terrace	C3	Mosley Street	B1	Queen Victoria Road
D2	Camden Street	B3	Grainger Street	D1	Naper Street		
C3	Caruol Square	C1	Great North Road	B3	Nelson Street	A1	Richardson Road
A3	Charlotte Square	C3	Grey Street	B4	Neville Street	D2	Rock Terrace
D1	Chester Street	B3	Groat Market	D2	New Bridge Street	A2	St Andrew's Street
C3	City Road	A3	Hadrian's Wall Junction	C2	New Bridge Street Roundabout	D3	St Ann's Street
B1	Claremont Road					A4	St James Boulevard
D2	Clarence Street	D1	Harrison Place	B3	Newgate Street	B1	St Mary's Road
B3	Clayton Street	D1	Helmsley Road	C2	Northumberland Road	C4	St Nicholas Street
A4	Clayton Street West	C1	Henry Square			B2	St Thomas' Court
C2	College Street	C3	High Bridge	B2	Northumberland Street	B1	St Thomas' Street
D2	Copland Terrace	C3	Hillgate			D3	Sandgate
D1	Coppice Way	C3	Hood Street	B3	Nun Street	C4	Sandhill
A3	Corporation Street	C1	Jesmond Road West	D4	Oakwellgate	C1	Sandyford Road
B3	Cross Street	C2	John Dobson Street	B4	Orchard Street	D2	Shield Street
				C2	Oxford Street	D2	Simpson Terrace
B4	South Street						
D3	Stepney Lane						
D1	Stoddart Street						
A3	Stowell Street						
A2	Strawberry Place						
A4	Summerhill Terrace						
A2	Terrace Place						
D3	Tower Street						
C4	Tyne Bridge						
A4	Wakenshaw VC Junction						
A4	Waterloo Square						
A4	Waterloo Street						
A2	Wellington Street						
A3	Westgate Road						
A4	Westmorland Road						
A3	West Walls						
D2	Wretham Place						

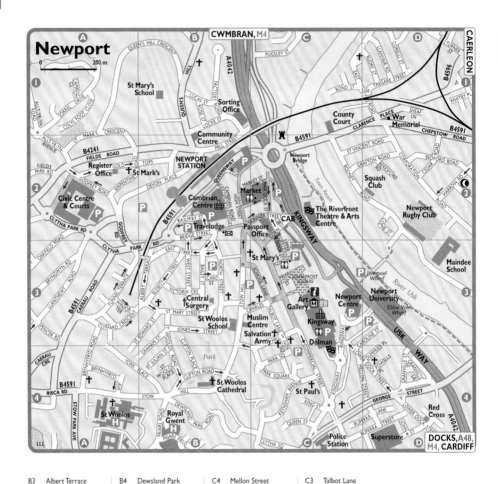

B3	Albert Terrace	B4	Dewsland Park	C4	Mellon Street	C3	Talbot Lane
A2	Allt-Yr-Yn Avenue		Road	B2	Mill Street	D1	Tregare Street
B3	Bailey Street	D4	Dumfries Place	B3	North Street	A3	Tunnel Terrace
D2	Bedford Road	B3	East Street	A3	Oakfield Road	C2	Upper Dock Street
B3	Blewitt Street	C1	East Usk Road	C4	Park Square	C3	Upper Dock Street
C1	Bond Street	B1	Factory Road	C1	Pugsley Street	D3	Usk Way
B2	Bridge Street	A2	Fields Road	B1	Queen's Hill	B3	Victoria Crescent
A3	Bryngwyn Road	B4	Friars Field	A1	Queen's Hill	B3	West Street
A4	Brynhyfryd Avenue	B4	Friars Road		Crescent	A4	York Place
A4	Brynhyfryd Road	C3	Friar Street	C4	Queen Street		
A4	Caerau Crescent	D4	George Street	B2	Queensway		
A3	Caerau Road	A2	Godfrey Road	A4	Risca Road		
B2	Cambrian Road	A2	Gold Tops	C2	Rodney Road		
D3	Caroline Street	C2	Grafton Road	D1	Rudry Street		
D2	Cedar Road	D4	Granville Lane	C4	Ruperra Lane		
C3	Charles Street	D4	Granville Street	D4	Ruperra Street		
D1	Chepstow Road	B2	High Street	B3	St Edward Street		
B4	Clifton Place	C3	Hill Street	B4	St Julian Street		
B4	Clifton Road	C3	John Frost Square	A2	St Mark's Crescent		
A3	Clyffard Crescent	D4	John Street	B3	St Mary Street		
A2	Clytha Park Road	B3	Jones Street	C2	St Vincent Road		
C4	Clytha Square	C4	Keynsham Avenue	B3	St Woolos Road		
A1	Colts Foot Close	C4	King Street	C3	School Lane		
C4	Commercial	C2	Kingsway	A2	Serpentine Road		
	Street	C4	Kingsway	C2	Skinner Street		
D1	Corelli Street	A3	Llanthewy Road	A1	Sorrel Drive		
C2	Corn Street	B1	Locke Street	A3	Spencer Road		
D2	Corporation Road	B1	Lucas Street	B3	Stow Hill		
B2	Devon Place	B2	Market Street	B4	Stow Hill		
				A4	Stow Park Avenue		

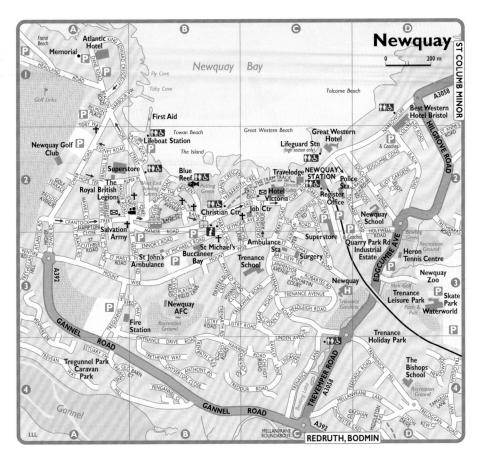

C3	Agar Road	D2	Eliot Gardens	B3	Listry Road	B3	St Michael's Road	D2	Tretherras Road
D2	Albany Road	B3	Ennor's Road	D4	Luxon Drive	A2	St Piran's Road	B4	Trethewey Way
A2	Alma Place	A4	Estuary View	A2	Manor Road	C3	St Thomas' Road	A4	Trevean Way
B4	Anthony Road	C3	Fairview Terrace	B2	Marcus Hill	B2	Seymour Avenue	C4	Trevemper Road
A3	Atlantic Road	A2	Fernhill Road	B3	Mayfield Crescent	B2	South Quay Hill	A2	Trevose Avenue
B2	Bank Street	A2	Fore Street	B3	Mayfield Road	C2	Springfield Road	D2	Ualia Road
C3	Bay View Terrace	A3	Gannel Road	D4	Meadowside	A2	Sydney Road	B3	Vivian Close
B2	Beachfield Avenue	A2	Golf Terrace	C4	Mellanvrane Lane	D4	Tamarish Lane		
B2	Beach Road	B2	Gover Lane	C4	Mellanvrane	B2	The Crescent		
A1	Beacon Road	C4	Gresham Close		Roundabout	C2	The Tram Track		
A1	Belmont Place	C3	Grosvenor Avenue	C2	Michel Lane	A1	Toby Way		
C2	Berry Road	A2	Hampton Close	D4	Middleton Crescent	C2	Tolcarne Road		
C2	Bridge Road	A1	Harbour View	A3	Mount Wise	C2	Tor Road		
A2	Chapel Hill	A2	Hawke Close	D2	Narrowcliff	A2	Tower Road		
B4	Cheviot Road	B4	Hawkins Road	C2	Oakleigh Terrace	B2	Trebarwith Crescent		
C4	Cheviot Road	A1	Headland Road	A4	Old Barn Court	B4	Tredour Road		
C4	Chichester Crescent	A3	Headleigh Road	C2	Pargolla Road	C4	Treforda Road		
B4	Chynance Drive	A3	Highertower Road	B4	Penannel Close	D2	Tregoss Road		
	Road	D1	Hilgrove Road	C3	Penmartin Court	A3	Tregunnel Hill		
B4	Chyverton Close	D3	Holywell Road	A3	Penmere Drive	A4	Tregunnel Hill		
B3	Clevedon Road	A2	Hope Terrace	A3	Pentire Drive	B3	Trelawney Road		
C3	Clifden Close	B2	Island Crescent	B3	Playing Field Lane	D4	Treloggan Lane		
C2	Cliff Road	A2	Jubilee Street	C4	Rawley Lane	D4	Treloggan Road		
D2	Colvreath Road	D4	Kew Close	A3	Reeds Way	B4	Trembath Crescent		
A2	Crantock Street	A1	King Edward	C3	Robartes Road	C3	Trenance Avenue		
A1	Dane Road		Crescent	D2	St Anne's Road	C4	Trenance Lane		
C2	East Street	B2	King Street	A3	St Cuthbert's Road	C3	Trenance Road		
D3	Edgcumbe Avenue	C3	Lanhenvor Avenue	B3	St George's Road	B3	Trenarth Road		
D2	Edgcumbe Gardens	C4	Linden Avenue	A3	St John's Road	D4	Treninnick Hill		
D2	Eliot Court	C4	Linden Crescent	A3	St Mary's Road	A3	Trethellan Hill		

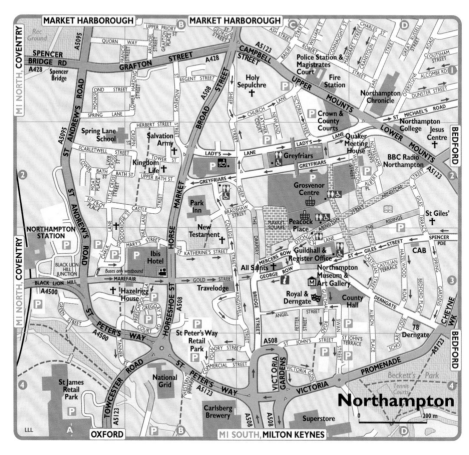

C2	Abington Street	B2	Crispin Street	B1	Lower Harding Street	C2	Sheep Street
D2	Albert Place	D3	Derngate			D2	Lower Mounts	A1	Spencer Bridge
D3	Albion Place	A3	Doddridge Street	A3	Marefair	A1	Spencer Bridge Road
D1	Alcombe Road	D1	Dunster Street	C1	Margaret Street	D3	Spencer Parade
C3	Angel Street	C3	Dychurch Lane	C2	Market Square	D3	Spring Gardens
B1	Arundel Street	D1	Earl Street	C3	Mercers Row	A1	Spring Lane
C1	Ash Street	C3	Fetter Street	A2	Moat Place	C3	Swan Street
C1	Bailiff Street	A2	Fitzroy Place	A1	Monkspond Street	A4	Tanner Street
A2	Bath Street	B4	Foundry Street	C1	Newland	C2	The Drapery
D3	Bedford Place	A1	Francis Street	D2	Notredame Mews	D2	The Ridings
A3	Black Lion Hill	B3	Freeschool Lane	D1	Overstone Road	A4	Towcester Road
A3	Black Lion Hill Junction	C3	Gold Street	B3	Pike Lane	B2	Tower Street
B2	Bradshaw Street	B3	Gold Street	A1	Quorn Way	B2	Upper Bath Street
C3	Bridge Street	B1	Grafton Place	B1	Regent Street	C1	Upper Mounts
B1	Broad Street	A1	Grafton Street	C1	Robert Street	B1	Upper Priory Street
C1	Campbell Street	D1	Great Russell Street	A2	St Andrew's Road	C4	Victoria Gardens
D3	Castilian Street	A3	Green Street	B1	St Andrew's Street	C4	Victoria Promenade
D3	Castilian Terrace	B3	Gregory Street	B1	St George's Street	C1	Victoria Street
B2	Castle Street	B2	Greyfriars	D3	St Giles Street	D2	Wellington Street
A3	Chalk Lane	C3	Guildhall Road	D2	St Giles' Terrace	B4	Western Wharf
D1	Charles Street	D3	Hazelwood Road	C4	St John's Street	C1	William Street
D3	Cheyne Walk	B2	Herbert Street	C4	St John's Terrace		
C1	Church Lane	B3	Horse Market	B3	St Katherine's Street		
D1	Cloutsham Street	B3	Horseshoe Street	A3	St Mary's Street		
B2	College Street	C3	Kingswell Street	D1	St Michael's Road		
B4	Commercial Street	B2	Lady's Lane	B4	St Peter's Way		
C1	Connaught Street	C1	Latymer Court	A2	Scarletwell Street		
B3	Court Road	A2	Little Cross Street	A2	Scholars Close		
D1	Cranstoun Street	A2	Lower Bath Street	D4	Sheep Street		
		A2	Lower Cross Street	B1	Sheep Street		

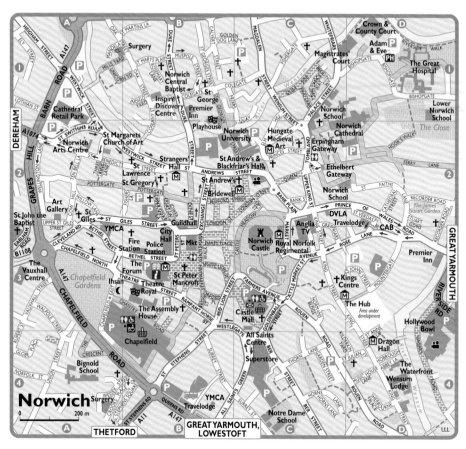

D4	Abbey Lane	B2	Exchange Street	D4	Music House Lane	B1	St Georges Street	C1	Wensum Street
B4	All Saints Green	C3	Farmers Avenue	B1	Muspole Street	A2	St Giles Street	A4	Wessex Street
C2	Bank Plain	D2	Ferry Lane	A4	Norfolk Street	D3	St Johns Street	B3	Westlegate
C2	Bank Street	C1	Fishergate	C3	Normans Buildings	C4	St Julian Street	A1	Westwick Street
A1	Barn Road	B2	Fishers Lane	A1	Oak Street	B1	St Martins Lane	D4	Wherry Road
C1	Bedding Lane	B1	Friars Quay	C2	Opie Street	B1	St Marys Plain	C1	Whitefriars
B2	Bedford Street	C4	Garden Street	B3	Orford Place	B3	St Peters Street	B3	White Lion Street
C4	Ber Street	B3	Gentlemans Walk	C1	Palace Street	B4	St Stephens Road	A2	Willow Lane
A3	Bethel Street	A4	Globe Place	C1	Pigg Lane	A4	St Stephens Square		
D1	Bishopgate	C3	Goldenball Street	A2	Pottergate	B4	St Stephens Street		
B3	Brigg Street	B1	Golden Dog Lane	C2	Prince of Wales	A2	St Swithins Road		
B1	Calvert Street	A2	Grapes Hill		Road	D2	St Verdast Street		
C3	Castle Meadow	C3	Greyfriars	C2	Princes Street	D4	Sherbourne Place		
D2	Cathedral Street	B3	Haymarket	C1	Quay Side	D2	Stuart Gardens		
C3	Cattle Market Street	A1	Heigham Street	B4	Queens Road	B4	Surrey Street		
B3	Chantry Road	D4	Hobrough	C2	Queen Street	A2	Ten Bell Lane		
A3	Chapelfield East	D2	Hook's Walk	B3	Rampant Horse	B3	Theatre Street		
A3	Chapelfield North	C4	Horns Lane		Street	A4	The Crescent		
A3	Chapelfield Road	B1	Indigo Yard	D2	Recorder Road	C4	Thorn Lane		
A3	Cleveland Road	C1	Joseph Lancs Way	B3	Red Lion Street	A2	Three King Lane		
B1	Colegate	C4	Kilderkin Yard	D3	Riverside Road	C2	Tombland		
B2	Coslany Street	C2	King Street	D1	Riverside Walk	A1	Unicorn Yard		
A2	Cow Hill	B2	London Street	C3	Rose Lane	A4	Union Street		
A4	Crooks Place	A1	Lothian Street	B1	Rosemary Lane	B2	Upper Goat Lane		
B3	Davey Place	B2	Lower Goat Lane	C3	Rouen Road	C2	Upper King Street		
B2	Dove Street	C1	Magdalen Street	A4	Rupert Street	A2	Upper St Giles		
B1	Duke Street	A1	Mandela Close	B2	St Andrews Street		Street		
A3	Earlham Road	C3	Market Avenue	D4	St Anne Lane	A3	Vauxhall Street		
C2	Elm Hill	A1	Mills Yard	A2	St Benedicts Street	A3	Walpole Street		
A1	Ely Street	D3	Mountergate	D2	St Faiths Lane	A2	Wellington Lane		

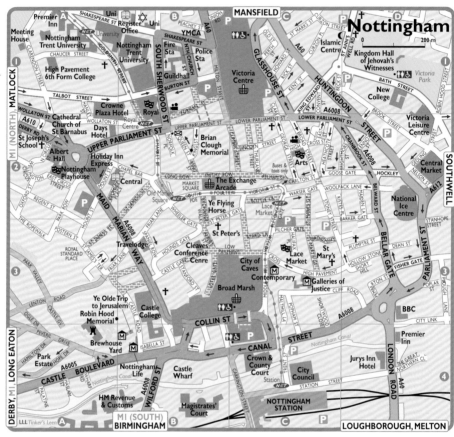

B3	Albert Street	C2	East Street	B3	Low Pavement	C2	Ristes Place	B4	Wilford Street
D2	Barker Gate	B2	Exchange Walk	D2	Maiden Lane	D1	Robin Hood Street	A1	Wollaton Street
D1	Bath Street	D3	Fisher Gate	A2	Maid Marian Way	A3	Royal Standard Place	C2	Woolpack Lane
C1	Beck Street	C3	Fletcher Gate	C3	Maltmill Lane	D1	St Ann's Well Road		
D3	Bellar Gate	B1	Forman Street	B2	Market Square	A3	St James's Street		
D2	Belward Street	A3	Friar Lane	B2	Market Street	B2	St James's Street		
C2	Bottle Lane	B3	Friar Lane	C3	Middle Hill	A3	St James's Terrace		
D2	Brightmore Street	D2	Gedling Street	B1	Milton Street	C3	St Marks Gate		
C2	Broad Street	C2	George Street	A2	Mount Street	C1	St Marks Street		
C3	Broadway	C1	Glasshouse Street	A3	Mount Street	C3	St Mary's Gate		
A2	Bromley Place	A1	Goldsmith Street	D2	Nelson Street	B3	St Peter's Gate		
D1	Brook Street	C2	Goose Gate	B2	Norfolk Place	A1	Shakespeare Street		
B1	Burton Street	C3	Halifax Place	B1	North Church Street	D3	Short Hill		
C3	Byard Lane	A4	Hamilton Drive	A2	North Circus Street	C3	Shortwood Close		
C4	Canal Street	A1	Hanley Street	A3	Ogle Drive	B2	Smithy Row		
C2	Carlton Street	A4	Haslam Street	C1	Old Street	B2	South Parade		
C4	Carrington Street	C2	Heathcote Street	A2	Oxford Street	B1	South Sherwood Street		
A4	Castle Boulevard	C2	High Cross Street	A4	Palatine Street	B3	Spaniel Row		
B3	Castle Gate	C3	High Pavement	A3	Park Row	B3	Stanford Street		
A3	Castle Grove	D2	Hockley	A3	Park Valley	D3	Stanhope Street		
B3	Castle Road	D3	Hollow Stone	D3	Parliament Street	C4	Station Street		
B2	Chapel Bar	A4	Hope Drive	B1	Peachey Street	C2	Stoney Street		
A1	Chaucer Street	B3	Hounds Gate	C2	Pelham Street	A1	Talbot Street		
D3	City Link	C1	Howard Street	D3	Pemberton Street	D4	The Great Northern		
A1	Clarendon Street	C1	Huntingdon Street	C1	Perth Street		Close		
C1	Clare Street	B4	Isabella Street	A4	Peveril Drive	A3	The Ropewalk		
C3	Cliff Road	C1	Kent Street	C3	Pilcher Gate	C2	Thurland Street		
B4	Collin Street	B2	King Edward Street	D3	Plough Lane	C4	Trent Street		
C1	Convent Street	B2	King Street	D3	Plumptre Street	B1	Union Road		
D2	Cranbrook Street	C2	Lennox Street	C3	Popham Street	A2	Upper Parliament Street		
C2	Cumber Street	A3	Lenton Road	D3	Poplar Street	C2	Victoria Street		
C1	Curzon Place	A2	Lincoln Street	A3	Postern Street	C2	Warser Gate		
C1	Curzon Street	B3	Lister Gate	B2	Poultry	C3	Weekday Cross		
D3	Dean Street	D4	London Road	B2	Queen Street	D3	Wellington Circus		
A2	Derby Road	B2	Long Row	A2	Regent Street	A4	Wharf Road		
A2	East Circus Street	C2	Lower Parliament Street	C1	Rick Street	B2	Wheeler Gate		

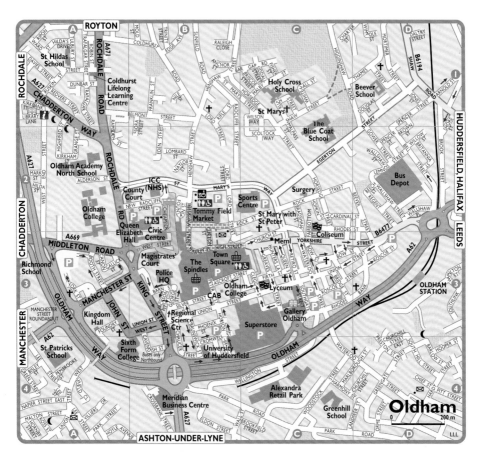

A2	Alderson Street	B4	Crossbank Street	C1	Horsedge Street	B3	Peter Street	B1	Sunfield Road
B1	Anchor Street	B2	Curzon Street	A4	Hoyle Avenue	B3	Phoenix Street	D1	Thames Street
D1	Arnold Street	D1	Daltry Street	C3	Hunters Lane	D4	Pitt Street	A1	Trafalgar Street
B3	Ascroft Street	A1	Davies Street	B3	Jackson Pit	D4	Preston Street	B1	Trinity Street
B1	Bar Gap Road	D1	Douglas Street	A3	John Street	C3	Queen Street	A1	Tulbury Street
D4	Barlow Street	A1	Dunbar Street	D1	Jones Street	B1	Radcliffe Street	B3	Union Street
B3	Barn Street	B2	Eden Street	B3	King Street	B1	Raleigh Close	A4	Union Street West
D2	Beech Street	B1	Edge Avenue	A1	Kirkbank Street	A1	Ramsden Street	B3	Union Street West
D2	Beever Street	C2	Egerton Street	A2	Kirkham Street	A1	Redvers Street	A4	Villiers Drive
D2	Bell Street	B4	Eldon Street	C4	Landseer Street	D2	Regent Street	D2	Wallshaw Place
B1	Belmont Street	C3	Fairbottom Street	A4	Lee Street	C3	Retiro Street	D2	Wallshaw Street
A4	Bisley Street	C3	Firth Street	D2	Lemnos Street	C3	Rhodes Bank	B4	Wall Street
A3	Booth Street	C1	Fisher Street	A1	Library Lane	C2	Rhodes Street	A1	Ward Street
C3	Bow Street	B2	Flora Street	B2	Lombard Street	B1	Rifle Street	C3	Waterloo Street
C2	Bradshaw Street	A3	Foundry Street	B1	Lord Street	A1	Ripon Street	B4	Wellington Street
C3	Bridge Street	B2	Fountain Street	C1	Malby Street	A1	Robin Street	A2	West End Street
C1	Briscoe Street	B1	Franklin Street	C1	Malpass Street	A1	Rochdale Road	B3	West Street
D2	Britannia Street	A3	Gallick Street	A4	Malton Street	B2	Rock Street	C1	Whitehall Street
C4	Brookfield Street	B3	George Street	A3	Manchester Street	C3	Roscoe Street	D2	Willow Street
D2	Brook Street	D2	Gower Street	A3	Manchester Street	A4	Ross Street	C1	Wilson Way
D2	Brown Street	A2	Grange Street		Roundabout	A1	Ruskin Street	D1	Wimpole Street
B3	Brunswick Street	C3	Greaves Street	B3	Market Place	C1	Ruth Street	C4	Woodstock Street
A3	Canon Street	D4	Greengate Street	A2	Mark Street	A1	St Hilda's Drive	C3	Yorkshire Street
C2	Cardinal Street	A4	Green Street	C4	Marlborough Street	B1	St Marys Street	A3	York Street
B3	Cavendish Street	D3	Hamilton Street	A3	Middleton Road	B2	St Mary's Way		
A1	Chadderton Way	D4	Hardy Street	B1	Mold Street	C2	Scoltock Way		
C1	Charter Street	C4	Harmony Street	D1	Mortimer Street	D1	Shaw Road		
B3	Chaucer Street	B2	Henshaw Street	A4	Napier Street East	C1	Shaw Street		
B2	Cheapside	C1	Higginshaw Road	B2	Naylor Street	A4	Shield Close		
D4	Chief Street	A2	Highfield Street	A2	New Radcliffe Street	D2	Shore Street		
D4	Churchill Street	B3	High Street	B1	Nile Street	C1	Siddall Street		
D4	Churchill Street East	A2	Hilda Street	A3	Oldham Way	B3	Silver Street		
C3	Church Street	B3	Hobson Street	D4	Orme Street	C3	Southgate Street		
C3	Clegg Street	D4	Hooper Street	B4	Park Road	D4	South Hill Street		
B1	Coldhurst Road	C2	Hopkin Street	A4	Park Street	D3	Southlink		
B4	Cromwell Street	A4	Hornby Street	A4	Pembrooke Street	D2	Spencer Street		

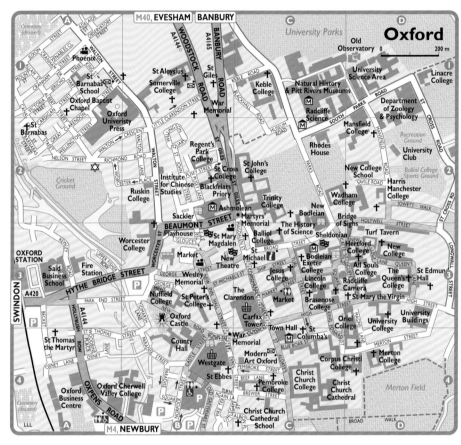

Oxford

A1	Adelaide Street	D2	Holywell Street	B4	Paradise Street	B2	Walton Lane	D3	New College
A1	Albert Street	A3	Hythe Bridge Street	A3	Park End Street	A1	Walton Street	B3	Nuffield College
C4	Albion Place	A1	Jericho Street	C1	Parks Road	B2	Wellington Square	D3	Oriel College
A1	Allam Street	D2	Jowett Walk	C4	Pembroke Street	A2	Wellington Street	C4	Pembroke College
B1	Banbury Road	A1	Juxon Street	B4	Pike Terrace	A4	Woodbine Place	B2	Regent's Park
B3	Beaumont Street	C1	Keble Road	B2	Pusey Lane	B1	Woodstock Road		College
A3	Becket Street	C3	King Edward Street	B2	Pusey Street	A2	Worcester Place	B2	Ruskin College
C4	Beef Lane	A1	King Street	D3	Queen's Lane	B3	Worcester Street	B2	St Cross College
C1	Blackhall Road	B2	Little Clarendon	C4	Queen Street			C2	St John's College
C4	Blue Boar Street		Street	C3	Radcliffe Square		**University Colleges**	B3	St Peter's College
B4	Bonn Square	B4	Littlegate Street	A3	Rewley Road			B1	Somerville College
C4	Brewer Street	D3	Longwall Street	A2	Richmond Road	D3	All Souls College	D3	The Queen's
C3	Broad Street	C2	Magdalen Street	C4	St Aldate's	C3	Balliol College		College
D4	Broad Walk	D3	Magpie Lane	A2	St Barnabas Street	C3	Brasenose College	C2	Trinity College
A1	Canal Street	D2	Mansfield Road	D1	St Cross Road	A4	Cherwell Valley	D3	University College
A2	Cardigan Street	C3	Market Street	B4	St Ebbes Street		College	D2	Wadham College
B4	Castle Street	D4	Merton Street	B2	St Giles	C4	Christ Church	B3	Worcester College
C3	Catte Street	A1	Mount Street	B2	St John Street		College		
C3	Cornmarket Street	C2	Museum Road	B3	St Michael's Street	D4	Corpus Christi		
A1	Cranham Street	A2	Nelson Street	A4	St Thomas' Street		College		
A1	Cranham Terrace	D3	New College Lane	D2	Savile Road	C3	Exeter College		
B3	George Street	B3	New Inn Hall Street	C3	Ship Street	D2	Harris Manchester		
B3	George Street	B3	New Road	C2	South Parks Road		College		
	Mews	B4	Norfolk Street	B3	Tidmarsh Lane	D3	Hertford College		
B3	Gloucester Street	A1	Observatory Street	C3	Turl Street	C3	Jesus College		
A2	Great Clarendon	B4	Old Greyfriars	B4	Turn Again Lane	C1	Keble College		
	Street		Street	A3	Upper Fisher Row	D1	Linacre College		
A1	Hart Street	A4	Osney Lane	A1	Venables Close	C3	Lincoln College		
C3	High Street	A4	Oxpens Road	A1	Victoria Street	D2	Mansfield College		
A3	Hollybush Row	B4	Paradise Square	A2	Walton Crescent	D4	Merton College		

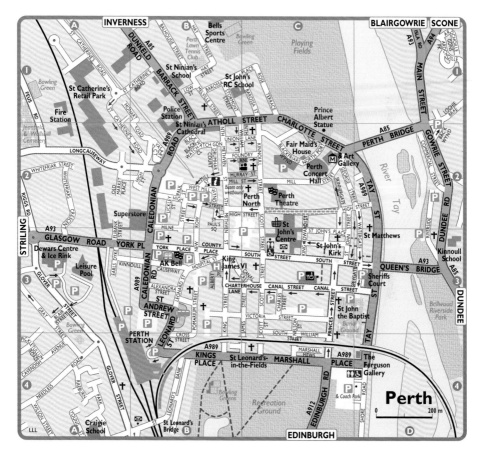

B3	Albert Place	D2	Gowrie Street	B2	North William	B2	Vasart Court
B3	Alexandra Street	A3	Gray Street		Street	C3	Victoria Street
D1	Ardchoille Gardens	B1	Hay Street	A2	Old Market Place	D2	Watergate
D1	Ardchoille Park	B2	High Street	B2	Paul Street	B2	West Mill Wynd
B1	Atholl Street	B3	Hospital Street	D2	Perth Bridge	A2	Whitefriars
D2	Back Wynd	D1	Isla Road	A4	Pickletullum Road		Crescent
B1	Balhousie Street	C3	James Street	B3	Pomarium Street	A2	Whitefriar Street
B1	Barossa Place	C3	King Edward Street	C3	Princes Street	A4	Wilson Street
B1	Barrack Street	B4	Kings Place	D3	Queen's Bridge	A3	York Place
C2	Blackfriars Wynd	B3	King Street	A4	Raeburn Park	A4	Young Street
B2	Black Watch Garden	A3	Kinnoull Causeway	A2	Riggs Road		
B3	Caledonian Road	C2	Kinnoull Street	D3	Riverside		
C3	Canal Street	B3	Leonard Street	C1	Rose Terrace		
A4	Cavendish Avenue	D1	Lochie Brae	B3	St Andrew Street		
C3	Charles Street	A2	Longcauseway	A1	St Catherine's Road		
C2	Charlotte Street	B1	Low Street	C3	St John's Place		
B3	Charterhouse Lane	D1	Main Street	C3	St John Street		
D2	Commercial Street	C4	Marshall Mews	B4	St Leonard's Bank		
B3	County Place	C4	Marshall Place	B2	St Paul's Square		
B4	Cross Street	B1	Melville Street	C2	Scott Street		
D3	Dundee Road	B2	Mill Street	D4	Shore Road		
B1	Dunkeld Road	B2	Milne Street	C2	Skinnergate		
A3	Earls Dyke	A1	Monart Road	B2	South Methven		
C4	Edinburgh Road	B2	Murray Street		Street		
A3	Elibank Street	A4	Needless Road	C3	South Street		
A1	Feus Road	C3	Nelson Street	C4	South William Street		
B2	Foundry Lane	B3	New Row	D3	Speygate		
C2	George Street	B2	North Methven	B1	Stormont Street		
A3	Glasgow Road		Street	D2	Tay Street		
A3	Glover Street	C2	North Port	B2	Union Lane		

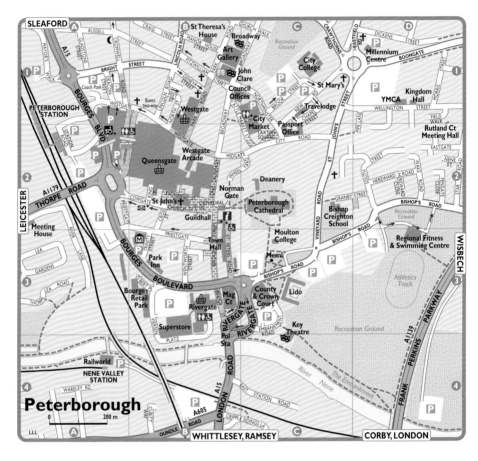

B3	Albert Place
C3	Bishop's Road
D1	Boongate
A1	Bourges Boulevard
B3	Bridge Street
A1	Bright Street
B2	Broadway
C1	Brook Street
B2	Cathedral Square
B1	Cattle Market Street
C1	Chapel Street
B2	Church Street
C1	Church Walk
C2	City Road
B2	Cowgate
B1	Craig Street
C1	Crawthorne Road
B4	Cripple Sidings Lane
A1	Cromwell Road
B2	Cross Street
B4	Cubitt Way
A1	Deacon Street
D1	Dickens Street
D1	Eastfield Road
D2	Eastgate
C4	East Station Road
C3	Embankment Road
B2	Exchange Street
D2	Fengate Close
D1	Field Walk

B1	Fitzwilliam Street
D4	Frank Perkins Parkway
B1	Geneva Street
A1	Gladstone Street
C2	Granby Street
D2	Hereward Close
D2	Hereward Road
B2	King Street
C2	Laxton Square
A3	Lea Gardens
B1	Lincoln Road
B4	London Road
B2	Long Causeway
B1	Manor House Street
A1	Mayor's Walk
B2	Midgate
D1	Morris Street
D2	Nene Street
C1	New Road
C1	Northminster
B1	North Street
B4	Oundle Road
B1	Park Road
B1	Peet Street
D2	Pipe Lane
A2	Priestgate
B3	Rivergate
A2	River Lane
A1	Russell Street

C2	St John's Street
B3	St Peters Road
D2	South Street
D2	Star Road
A2	Station Road
A3	Thorpe Lea Road
A2	Thorpe Road
B3	Trinity Street
B3	Viersen Platz
C3	Vineyard Road
D2	Wake Road
A4	Wareley Road
D1	Wellington Street
B3	Wentworth Street
A1	Westgate

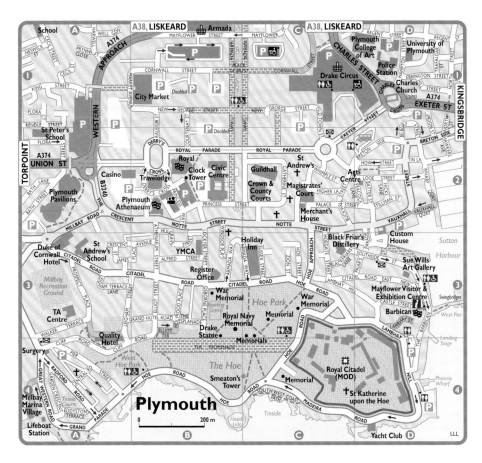

B3	Alfred Street	A2	Flora Street	B1	Mayflower Street	D4	The Barbican
B1	Armada Way	D3	Friar's Parade	A2	Millbay Road	A2	The Crescent
B3	Armada Way	A4	Garden Crescent	D1	Moon Street	B3	The Esplanade
B2	Athenaeum Street	B3	Grand Hotel Road	B3	Mulgrave Street	B4	The Promenade
A2	Bath Lane	A4	Grand Parade	A1	Neswick Street	D2	Tin Lane
A2	Bath Street	A4	Great Western	B1	New George Street	D1	Trafalgar Street
D2	Batter Street		Road	D3	New Street	A2	Union Street
D2	Bilbury Street	D1	Hampton Street	D1	North Street	D2	Vauxhall Quay
C3	Blackfriars Lane	A1	Harwell Street	B2	Notte Street	D2	Vauxhall Street
D2	Breton Side	D2	Hawkers Avenue	C1	Old Town Street	A3	Walker Terrace
C2	Buckwell Street	D2	Hicks Lane	B3	Osborne Place	A1	Well Garden
C2	Catherine Street	C2	Higher Lane	C2	Palace Street	A2	Western Approach
A1	Cecil Street	D1	Hill Street	C2	Peacock Lane	D2	Wharf Quay
A4	Central Road	C3	Hoe Approach	A4	Pier Street	C2	Whimple Street
D1	Charles Cross	C3	Hoegate Street	B1	Place de Brest	B2	Windsor Place
C1	Charles Street	B4	Hoe Road	B2	Princess Street	C3	Zion Street
A3	Citadel Road	C3	Hoe Street	B2	Princess Way		
C3	Citadel Road East	B3	Holyrood Place	A3	Prospect Place		
A4	Cliff Road	D2	How Street	A1	Prynne Close		
B1	Cornwall Street	A1	King Street	A4	Radford Road		
B2	Courtenay Street	C3	Lambhay Hill	B2	Raleigh Street		
A3	Crescent Avenue	D3	Lambhay Hill	D1	Regent Street		
B2	Derry's Cross	D3	Lambhay Street	A1	Rendle Street		
D1	Ebrington Street	A3	Leigham Street	B2	Royal Parade		
A4	Eddystone Terrace	A3	Leigham Terrace	A3	St James Place		
B3	Elliot Street		Lane	D3	Southside Street		
B3	Elliot Terrace	B3	Lockyer Street	C4	South West		
C2	Exeter Street	D2	Looe Street		Coast Path		
A1	Flora Court	C4	Madeira Road	D2	Stillman Street		
		A1	Market Avenue	C3	Sussex Street		

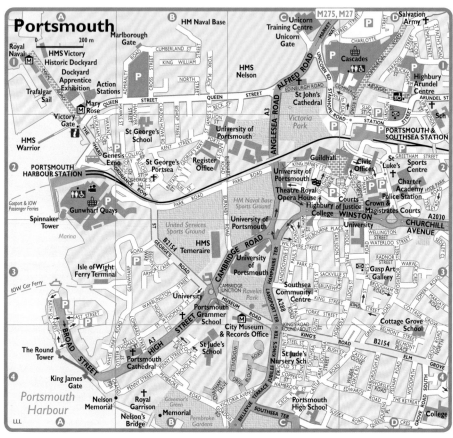

B1	Admiralty Road	B1	Cross Street	B1	King William Street	B2	St James's Street	D2	Winston Churchill
D2	Alec Rose Lane	B1	Cumberland Street	C3	Landport Terrace	B4	St Nicholas Street		Avenue
C1	Alfred Road	B1	Curzon Howe Road	C3	Landsdowne Street	C3	St Paul's Road	D4	Woodpath
C1	Alfred Street	C3	Earlsdon Street	B2	Lion Street	B4	St Thomas's Street	C4	Woodville Drive
C2	Anglesea Road	A3	East Street	C4	Little Southsea Street	D3	Sedsley Close	D4	Worsley Road
B3	Armory Lane	C1	Edinburgh Road	B3	Lombard Street	D2	Slindon Street	D4	Yarborough Road
D1	Arundel Street	D3	Eldon Street	A1	Main Road	D3	Somers Road	C3	Yorke Street
C3	Astley Street	D4	Elm Grove	D3	Margate Road	C4	Southsea Terrace	B1	York Place
A3	Bath Square	C4	Flint Street	C1	Market Way	C4	South Street		
B1	Beck Street	C4	Gold Street	D2	Mary Rose Street	C1	Stanhope Road		
B3	Beehive Way	B4	Gordon Road	C3	Melbourne Place	D2	Station Street		
C4	Bellevue Terrace	A4	Grand Parade	D3	Middle Street	C4	Steel Street		
D4	Belmont Place	C4	Great Southsea Street	B3	Museum Road	C4	Stone Street		
D4	Belmont Street	D4	Green Road	C4	Norfolk Street	B2	Sun Street		
B1	Bishop Street	D2	Greetham Street	B1	North Street	D1	Surrey Street		
C4	Blount Road	D3	Grosvenor Street	B2	Ordnance Row	C4	Sussex Road		
B2	Britain Street	D4	Grove Road North	B4	Oyster Street	D1	Temple Street		
A4	Broad Street	D4	Grove Road South	D1	Paradise Street	A2	The Hard		
D3	Brougham Road	C2	Guildhall Walk	B2	Park Road	D4	The Retreat		
C3	Brunswick Street	B3	Gunwharf Road	B2	Park Street	D2	Tyseley Road		
D1	Buckingham Street	C4	Hambrook Street	B4	Peacock Lane	C1	Unicorn Road		
B2	Burnaby Road	C3	Hampshire Terrace	B4	Pelham Road	D1	Upper Arundel		
C4	Bush Street East	B1	Hanover Street	B4	Pembroke Road		Street		
B2	Butcher Street	A2	Havant Street	B4	Penny Street	B4	Victoria Avenue		
B3	Cambridge Junction	B1	Hawke Street	B2	Portland Street	B2	Victory Road		
B3	Cambridge Road	B3	Highbury Street	D4	Queens Crescent	C3	Waltham Street		
D4	Castle Close	B4	High Street	D4	Queens Place	B3	Warblington Street		
C4	Castle Road	D2	Hyde Park Road	A1	Queen Street	D3	Warwick Crescent		
C4	Cecil Place	D1	Jacob's Street	D3	Radnor Street	D3	Waterloo Street		
D1	Charlotte Street	C4	Jubilee Terrace	C4	Sackville Street	A3	West Street		
B4	Chatham Drive	B2	Kent Street	C4	St Edwards Road	A4	White Hart Road		
A2	Clock Street	C2	King Henry I Street	D1	St Faith's Road	A2	Wickham Street		
B2	College Street	C4	King's Road	B3	St George's Road	D4	Wilberforce Road		
D1	Commercial Road	C4	King's Road Roundabout	B2	St George's Square	C1	Willis Road		
C4	Copper Street	C4	King's Terrace	D3	St George's Way	C3	Wiltshire Street		
D3	Cottage Grove	C3	King Street	D3	St James's Road				

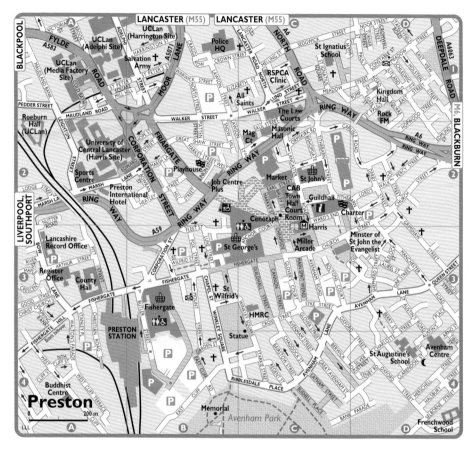

A1	Adelphi Street	D1	Cromwell Street	D2	Hopwood Street	A3	Pitt Street	A1	Victoria Street
C3	Anchor Court	C3	Cross Street	D1	Jutland Street	D2	Pole Street	B1	Walker Street
D4	Arno Street	B1	Crown Street	C2	Lancaster Road	D3	Princess Street	A3	Walton's Parade
A3	Arthur Street	D1	Deepdale Road	C1	Lancaster Road North	D1	Pump Street	C2	Ward's End
C4	Avenham Lane	D2	Derby Street	C4	Latham Street	D3	Queen Street	B1	Warwick Street
C3	Avenham Road	C2	Earl Street	D3	Laurel Street	C4	Regent Street	A4	West Cliff
C3	Avenham Street	B4	East Cliff	B1	Lawson Street	B4	Ribblesdale Place	A4	West Cliff Terrace
C4	Bairstow Street	B4	East Cliff Road	A2	Leighton Street	B2	Ring Way	B3	Winkley Square
C4	Bank Parade	D1	East Street	A2	Lodge Street	A3	River Street		
D3	Berry Street	D1	East View	D2	Lord's Walk	D3	Rose Street		
C4	Berwick Road	D2	Edmund Street	C1	Lund Street	D4	St Austin's Place		
C2	Birley Street	A2	Edward Street	B3	Lune Street	D3	St Austin's Road		
C2	Bishopgate	D1	Egan Street	C3	Main Sprit Weind	C1	St Ignatius Square		
D3	Blelock Street	B1	Elizabeth Street	D3	Manchester Road	D1	St Paul's Road		
C3	Boltons Court	A3	Fishergate	A3	Maple Crescent	D1	St Paul's Square		
A3	Bow Lane	A4	Fishergate Hill	C2	Market Street	A1	St Peter's Square		
B2	Bowran Street	C1	Fish Street	B2	Market Street West	B1	St Peter's Street		
A1	Brook Street	B3	Fleet Street	A2	Marsh Lane	B3	St Wilfrid Street		
C4	Bushell Place	B3	Fox Street	A1	Maudland Bank	C2	Saul Street		
B3	Butler Street	B2	Friargate	A1	Maudland Road	D1	Schleswig Street		
C3	Cannon Street	A1	Fylde Road	C1	Meadow Street	C1	Sedgwick Street		
C2	Carlisle Road	B4	Garden Street	C1	Melling Street	D4	Selborne Street		
C4	Chaddock Street	C3	Glover's Court	A1	Mill Hill	D1	Shaw Street		
B3	Chapel Street	C3	Glover Street	B1	Moor Lane	D3	Shepherd Street		
D4	Charlotte Street	A3	Good Street	B3	Mount Street	D4	Silver Street		
C3	Cheapside	C4	Great Avenham Street	D1	Noor Street	B2	Snow Hill		
A3	Christ Church Street	B2	Great Shaw Street	A4	North Cliff Street	A3	Spring Bank		
A3	Christian Road	D2	Grimshaw Street	C1	North Road	D1	Stanleyfield Road		
C3	Church Street	C3	Guildhall Street	B1	North Street	A3	Stanley Place		
D4	Clarendon Street	D4	Halsbury Street	A2	Nutter Road	C4	Starkie Street		
A4	Cliff Street	B1	Harrington Street	D3	Oak Street	C3	Syke Street		
A1	Cold Bath Street	B2	Heatley Street	C2	Ormskirk Road	D4	Tenby Road		
D1	Constable Street	D4	Herschell Street	C3	Oxford Street	D4	Tiber Street		
B2	Corporation Street	B2	Hill Street	B2	Patten Street	C2	Tithebarn Street		
B3	Corporation Street	D1	Holstein Street	A1	Pedder Street	D1	Turner Street		
B1	Craggs Row	B2	Hope Street	D2	Percy Street	B2	Union Street		

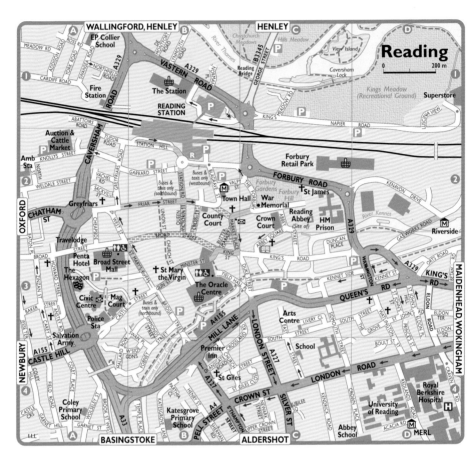

A1	Abattoirs Road	C4	Crown Place	C3	Kennet Side	D4	Redlands Road	A2	Weldale Street
C3	Abbey Square	C4	Crown Street	D3	Kennet Street	A1	Ross Road	A2	West Street
C2	Abbey Street	B4	Deansgate Road	C1	King's Meadow	A2	Sackville Street	A4	Wolseley Street
D4	Acacia Road	B1	De Montfort Road		Road	B4	St Giles Close	B3	Yield Hall Place
A1	Addison Road	C3	Duke Street	D3	King's Road	D3	St John's Hill	A1	York Road
A3	Anstey Road	C3	Duncan Place	B3	King Street	D3	St John's Road	A3	Zinzan Street
A3	Baker Street	C3	East Street	A2	Knollys Street	D3	St John's Street		
B4	Barthia Close	A3	Eaton Place	C3	Livery Close	B3	St Mary's Butts		
D3	Betam Road	D3	Eldon Place	C4	London Road	B4	Sherman Road		
B2	Blagrave Street	D3	Eldon Road	C3	London Street	C3	Sidmouth Street		
D4	Boult Street	D3	Eldon Square	D1	Luscinia View	C4	Silver Street		
B3	Bridge Street	D3	Eldon Terrace	B1	Lynmouth Road	B3	Simmonds Street		
A3	Broad Street	A4	Field Road	A4	Mallard Row	B4	Southampton Street		
A4	Brook Street West	B4	Fobney Street	B2	Market Place	C3	South Street		
B3	Buttermarket	C2	Forbury Road	A1	Meadow Road	B2	Station Hill		
A1	Cardiff Road	B2	Friar Street	B4	Mill Lane	B2	Station Road		
A3	Carey Street	A4	Garnet Hill	B3	Minster Street	B3	Swan Place		
A4	Castle Crescent	A4	Garnet Street	C1	Napier Road	A1	Swansea Road		
A4	Castle Hill	B2	Garrard Street	C4	Newark Street	B4	Temple Place		
A3	Castle Street	D3	Gas Works Road	B1	Norman Place	C2	The Forbury		
A2	Caversham Road	C1	George Street	A1	Northfield Road	D3	The Grove		
A2	Chatham Street	A2	Greyfriars Road	A2	North Street	A2	Tudor Road		
A2	Cheapside	B3	Gun Street	D3	Orts Road	B2	Union Street		
B3	Church Street	B4	Henry Street	B4	Parthia Close	C4	Upper Crown		
B4	Church Street	A3	Howard Street	B4	Pell Street		Street		
A4	Coley Hill	A3	Jesse Terrace	D3	Prince's Street	A2	Vachel Road		
A4	Coley Place	C4	Jubilee Square	C3	Queen's Road	B2	Valpy Street		
D4	Craven Road	B4	Katesgrove Lane	B2	Queen Victoria	B1	Vastern Road		
B4	Crossland Road	D2	Kenavon Drive		Street	B4	Waterside Gardens		
B2	Cross Street	C4	Kendrick Road	B1	Reading Bridge	D3	Watlington Street		

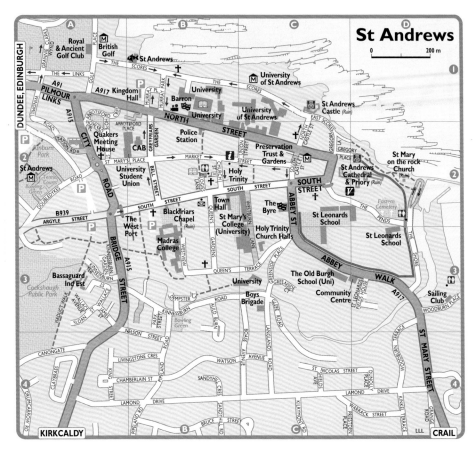

St Andrews

0   200 m

C2	Abbey Street	B2	Greyfriars Garden	D3	St Mary Street
C3	Abbey Walk	A2	Hope Street	C4	St Nicolas Street
A1	Abbotsford Crescent	A2	Howard Place	B4	Sandyhill Crescent
		A3	James Street	B4	Sandyhill Road
A2	Abbotsford Place	C4	Kilrymont Road	C4	Shields Avenue
A2	Argyle Street	A4	King Street	A3	Sloan Street
B3	Auld Burn	D4	Kinkel Terrace	C2	South Castle Street
B2	Bell Street	A3	Kinnessburn Garden	B2	South Street
C3	Boase Avenue	B3	Kinnessburn Road	A2	Station Road
A3	Bridge Street	A3	Kinnessburn Terrace	A1	The Links
B4	Bruce Street	A4	Lamond Drive	D2	The Pends
A4	Canongate	C3	Langlands Road	A1	The Scores
A4	Chamberlain Street	A4	Livingstone Crescent	D3	The Shore
B2	Church Street			C2	Union Street
A2	City Road	B2	Logies Lane	A3	Viaduct Walk
A4	Claybraes	B2	Market Street	A3	Wallace Avenue
B3	Dempster Court	B1	Murray Park	A3	Wallace Street
A2	Doubledykes Road	B1	Murray Place	C4	Warrack Street
A4	Drumcarrow Road	A3	Nelson Street	B4	Watson Avenue
D4	Dunolly Place	C2	North Castle Street	C2	Westburn Lane
C1	East Scores	B1	North Street	B3	Westview
C3	Glebe Road	B3	Park Street	A1	Windmill Road
A1	Golf Place	A1	Pilmour Links	D3	Woodburn Place
D4	Grange Road	B4	Pipeland Road	D4	Woodburn Terrace
A1	Grannie Clarks Wynd	C4	Priestden Place		
C3	Greenside Court	B2	Queen's Gardens		
C3	Greenside Place	B3	Queen's Terrace		
C2	Gregory Lane	D3	St Leonards Field House		
C2	Gregory Place	A2	St Mary's Place		

Salisbury

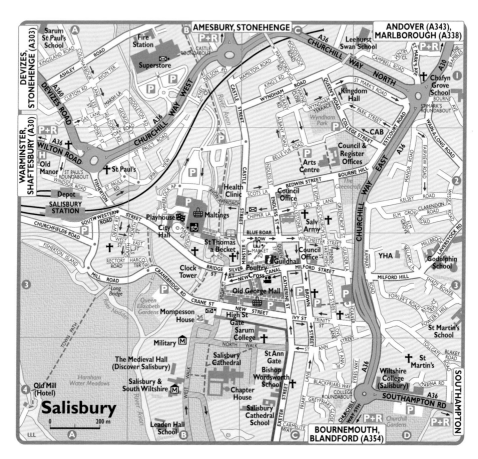

C1 Albany Road	A1 Coldharbour Lane	B1 Hulse Road	C1 Queen's Road	D4 Tollgate Road
A1 Ashley Road	D4 College Roundabout	C3 Ivy Street	C3 Queen Street	C3 Trinity Street
B2 Avon Approach	C1 College Street	D2 Kelsey Road	D3 Rampart Road	D1 Ventry Close
A1 Avon Terrace	B3 Cranebridge Road	A1 Kingsland Road	A3 Rectory Road	D1 Wain-A-Long Road
C2 Bedwin Street	B3 Crane Street	C1 King's Road	C2 Rollestone Street	D2 Wessex Road
D3 Bellamy Lane	C3 Culver Street	B1 Kivel Court	C4 St Ann Place	A3 West Street
C2 Belle Vue Road	A1 Devizes Road	D3 Laverstock Road	C4 St Ann Street	B4 West Walk
C4 Blackfriars Way	A3 Dew's Road	A1 Less Street	C2 St Edmund's Church	A2 Wilton Road
D4 Blakey Road	B3 East Street	A3 Long Bridge	Street	C3 Winchester Street
C3 Blue Boar Row	D2 Elm Grove Road	C3 Love Lane	D1 St Mark's Avenue	A2 Windsor Road
D1 Bourne Avenue	C2 Endless Street	B3 Malthouse Lane	D1 St Mark's Road	C1 Woodstock Road
C2 Bourne Hill	D2 Estcourt Road	D2 Manor Road	D1 St Mark's	C1 Wyndham Road
D1 Brambles The	C4 Exeter Street	D4 Marina Road	Roundabout	C1 Wyndham Terrace
B3 Bridge Street	D4 Eyres Way	C3 Market Square	A2 St Pauls Road	A2 York Road
C3 Brown Street	D2 Fairview Road	C1 Marlborough Road	B2 St Paul's Road	
D3 Byways Close	A3 Fisherton Island	A1 Marsh Lane	A2 St Paul's	
D1 Campbell Road	A2 Fisherton Street	A1 Meadow Road	Roundabout	
C4 Carmelite Way	D3 Fowler's Hill	A1 Middleton Road	C2 Salt Lane	
B1 Castle Roundabout	D3 Fowler's Road	D3 Milford Hill	C2 Scots Lane	
B1 Castle Street	C4 Friary Lane	C3 Milford Street	D3 Shady Bower	
C3 Catherine Street	A1 Gas Lane	D3 Millbrook	A1 Sidney Street	
C2 Chipper Lane	A1 George Street	A3 Mill Road	B3 Silver Street	
A2 Churchfields Road	C3 Gigant Street	C3 Minster Street	D4 Southampton Road	
D3 Churchill Way East	C2 Greencroft Street	B1 Nelson Road	A3 South Street	
C1 Churchill Way	C4 Greyfriars Close	B3 New Canal	A2 South Western	
North	D2 Grove Elm	B3 New Street	Road	
C4 Churchill Way South	C3 Guilder Lane	B3 North Street	B2 Spire View	
B2 Churchill Way West	B1 Hamilton Road	B4 North Walk	B2 Summerlock	
D2 Clarendon Road	B3 Harcourt Terrace	D1 Park Street	Approach	
A1 Clifton Road	B3 High Street	C3 Pennyfarthing Street	C1 Swayne's Close	

Scarborough

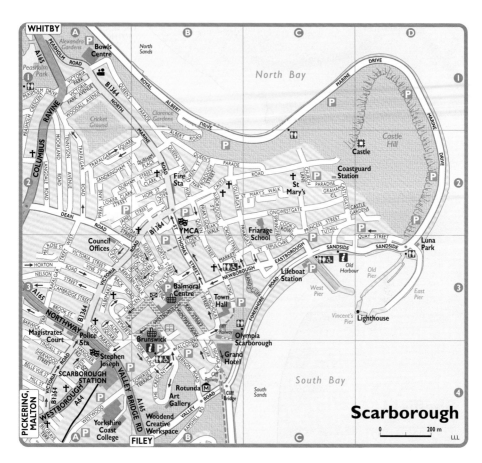

B3	Aberdeen Street	A2	Durham Street	A2	Oxford Street
B3	Aberdeen Terrace	C3	Eastborough	C2	Paradise
A3	Aberdeen Walk	B3	Elder's Street	A2	Peasholm Crescent
A3	Albemarle Back Road	B4	Falconers Road	A1	Peasholm Drive
		C3	Foreshore Road	A1	Peasholm Road
A3	Albemarle Crescent	B2	Friargate	C2	Princess Street
B2	Albert Road	B2	Friar's Garden	D3	Quay Street
A3	Alma Parade	B2	Friar's Walk	A1	Queen's Parade
A3	Alma Square	C2	Graham Close	B2	Queen's Terrace
B2	Auborough Street	A4	Hanover Road	B2	Queen Street
B3	Bar Street	B2	Hope Street	B4	Ramshill Road
A3	Barwick Terrace	A3	Hoxton Road	B2	Regent Street
B3	Bedford Street	B3	Huntress Row	B1	Royal Albert Drive
A4	Belgrave Terrace	A2	James Street	C2	St Mary's Walk
A4	Belle Vue Street	B3	King Street	B4	St Nicholas Cliff
C3	Bland's Cliff	A2	Langdale Road	B3	St Nicholas Street
A3	Brook Street	C2	Longwestgate	C3	St Sepulchre Street
A3	Cambridge Street	A2	Lower Clark Street	B2	St Thomas Street
C2	Castle Gardens	C1	Marine Drive	A2	Sandringham Street
C2	Castlegate	B3	Market Street	C3	Sandside
B2	Castle Road	B2	Marlborough Street	A4	Sherwood Street
C2	Church Lane	A3	Melrose Street	B4	Somerset Terrace
B2	Clark Street	A4	Mill Street	C2	Springfield
B4	Cliff Bridge	A2	Moorland Road	B3	Sussex Street
A3	Clifton Street	A3	Nelson Street	B3	Swan Hill Road
A2	Columbus Ravine	B3	Newborough	A2	Tennyson Avenue
C2	Cook's Row	B2	New Queen Street	B4	The Crescent
B2	Cross Street	A1	North Marine Road	A4	Tindall Street
A2	Dean Road	B3	North Street	B2	Tollergate
B2	Durham Place	A3	Northway	A2	Trafalgar Road

A2	Trafalgar Square
A3	Trafalgar Street West
C2	Tuthill
B3	Union Street
A4	Valley Bridge Road
B4	Valley Road
B4	Vernon Road
A1	Victoria Park
A1	Victoria Park Avenue
A4	Victoria Road
A3	Victoria Street
A3	Vine Street
A4	Westborough
A4	West Square
A4	Westwood
A1	Woodall Avenue
A2	Wrea Lane
B4	York Place

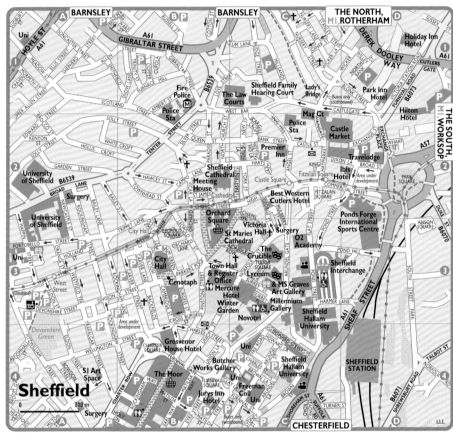

A1	Allen Street	B1	Copper Street	C2	Harts Head	B2	North Church Street	D1	Sussex Street
C2	Angel Street	B1	Cotton Street	B2	Hawley Street	C1	Nursery Lane	C4	Sydney Street
D3	Anson Square	A1	Craven Street	C2	Haymarket	C1	Nursery Street	D4	Talbot Street
C3	Arundel Gate	B3	Cross Burgess Street	A4	Headford Street	A3	Orange Street	B2	Tenter Street
C4	Arundel Lane	B1	Cupola	C2	High Street	B3	Orchard Lane	B2	Townhead Street
C4	Arundel Street	D1	Cutlers Gate	A3	Holland Street	B3	Orchard Street	A4	Trafalgar Street
B3	Backfields	D1	Derek Dooley Way	A2	Hollis Croft	B2	Paradise Street	B1	Trinity Street
A2	Bailey Lane	A3	Devonshire Street	B3	Holly Street	D2	Park Square	B3	Trippet Lane
A2	Bailey Street	A3	Division Street	A4	Holy Green	B3	Pinstone Street	C3	Tudor Square
B3	Balm Green	C2	Dixon Lane	C4	Howard Lane	C1	Plum Lane	C4	Turner Street
C2	Bank Street	A1	Doncaster Street	C4	Howard Street	C3	Pond Hill	B4	Union Lane
B3	Barkers Pool	D2	Duke Street	A1	Hoyle Street	C3	Pond Street	B4	Union Street
D1	Blonk Street	B4	Earl Way	C1	Joiner Street	A3	Portobello Street	A1	Upper Allen Street
A4	Bowdon Street	C2	East Parade	A2	Kenyon Street	B2	Queen Street	B2	Vicar Lane
C1	Bridge Street	A1	Ebenezer Street	C2	King Street	A3	Rockingham Lane	D1	Victoria Station Road
A2	Broad Lane	A2	Edward Street	C1	Lady's Bridge	A2	Rockingham Street	C2	Waingate
D2	Broad Street	A3	Eldon Street	B1	Lambert Street	B4	Rockingham Way	B1	Ward Street
A2	Brocco Street	A1	Ellis Street	C4	Leadmill Road	B1	Russell Street	A4	Wellington Street
A4	Broom Grove	D2	Exchange Place	B3	Leopold Square	B2	St James Street	B2	West Bar
A4	Broomhall Street	D2	Exchange Street	B3	Leopold Street	C2	Scargill Croft	A3	Westfield Terrace
C4	Brown Lane	B4	Eyre Lane	B1	Love Street	A1	Scotland Street	A3	West Street
C4	Brown Street	B4	Eyre Road	A3	Mappin Street	D4	Sheaf Street	D2	Wharf Street
B3	Burgess Street	C4	Eyre Street	B4	Matilda Lane	A1	Shepherd Street	A2	White Croft
B3	Cambridge Street	C2	Fig Tree Lane	B4	Matilda Street	C4	Shoreham Street	D1	Wicker
B2	Campo Lane	C2	Fitzalan Square	B4	Matilda Way	D4	Shrewsbury Road	C1	Wicker Lane
B3	Carver Lane	A4	Fitzwilliam Street	A1	Meadow Street	B2	Silver Street	D1	Willey Street
B3	Carver Street	C3	Flat Street	C2	Meetinghouse Lane	A1	Smithfield Street	C2	York Street
C1	Castlegate	B1	Furnace Hill	C1	Millsands	B1	Snig Hill		
C2	Castle Street	B4	Furnival Gate	A4	Milton Street	B1	Snow Lane		
C2	Chapel Walk	B4	Furnival Road	A1	Morpeth Street	A2	Solly Street		
B4	Charles Street	C4	Furnival Square	C2	Mulberry Street	D3	South Street Park		
A4	Charter Row	A2	Garden Street	C2	Newcastle Street	C1	Stanley Street		
B4	Charter Square	C2	George Street	C2	New Street	A1	Sudbury Street		
B2	Church Street	B1	Gibraltar Street	D4	Norfolk Road	C4	Suffolk Road		
B4	Clay Lane	C3	Harmer Lane	B3	Norfolk Row	C3	Surrey Place		
C2	Commercial Street			C3	Norfolk Street	C3	Surrey Street		
				D1	North Bank				

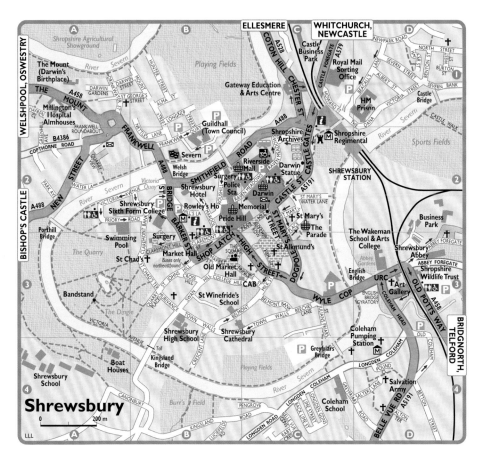

D3	Abbey Foregate	C1	Coton Hill	B4	Luciefelde Road	C2	St Mary's Street
D1	Albert Street	B4	Crescent Lane	B2	Mardol	C2	St Mary's Water
B1	Alma Street	B3	Cross Hill	B3	Market Street		Lane
D4	Alton Terrace	A1	Darwin Gardens	C3	Milk Street	D4	Salters Lane
C4	Back Lime Street	A1	Darwin Street	D4	Moreton Crescent	D1	Severn Bank
B2	Barker Street	C3	Dogpole	B1	Mount Street	D1	Severn Street
D1	Beacall's Lane	A1	Drinkwater Street	B3	Murivance	B3	Shop Latch
C3	Beeches Lane	C3	English Bridge	B1	Nettles Lane	B2	Smithfield Road
C4	Belle Vue Gardens	D3	English Bridge	D1	Newpark Road	B3	Swan Hill
D4	Belle Vue Road		Gyratory	A2	New Street	D1	The Dana
B3	Belmont	C3	Fish Street	D1	North Street	A1	The Mount
C3	Belmont Bank	A2	Frankwell	D3	Old Coleham	B3	The Square
D1	Benyon Street	B2	Frankwell Quay	D3	Old Potts Way	B3	Town Walls
D4	Betton Street	A2	Frankwell	A2	Park Avenue	A2	Victoria Avenue
B2	Bridge Street		Roundabout	C4	Pengrove	D1	Victoria Street
D1	Burton Street	A2	Greenhill Avenue	A3	Porthill Bridge	A2	Water Lane
C2	Butcher Row	C4	Greyfriars Bridge	D4	Pound Close	D1	Water Street
A4	Canonbury	C4	Greyfriars Road	C2	Pride Hill	B2	Welsh Bridge
D1	Castle Bridge	A1	Hafren Close	B3	Princess Street	D1	West Street
C1	Castle Foregate	C3	High Street	A2	Priory Road	C3	Wyle Cop
C2	Castle Gates	B2	Hill's Lane	B3	Quarry Place		
C2	Castle Street	C1	Howard Street	A2	Quarry View		
D1	Castle Walk	B1	Hunter Street	C4	Raby Crescent		
C1	Chester Street	B4	Kingsland Bridge	B2	Raven Meadows		
B3	Claremont Bank	B4	Kingsland Road	B2	Roushill		
B3	Claremont Hill	C4	Lime Street	B3	St Chad's Terrace		
B3	Claremont Street	C4	Longden Coleham	A1	St George's Street		
D3	Coleham Head	C4	Longden Gardens	B3	St Johns Hill		
B3	College Hill	C4	Longden Road	C3	St Julians Friars		
A2	Copthorne Road	B1	Longner Street	C2	St Mary's Place		

B1	Above Bar Street	B3	Forest View	B2	Ogle Road	B3	Upper Bugle Street
C3	Back of the Walls	B4	French Street	C3	Orchard Lane	C2	Vincent's Walk
B2	Bargate Street	D3	Glebe Road	C4	Orchard Place	A1	Western Esplanade
C3	Bell Street	D1	Golden Grove	C4	Oxford Street	B3	Western Esplanade
C3	Bernard Street	B3	Hamtun Street	C1	Palmerston Road	B1	West Marlands
A1	Blechynden Terrace	B2	Hanover Buildings	B1	Park Walk		Road
C4	Briton Street	A2	Harbour Parade	A2	Pirelli Street	A2	West Quay Road
C1	Broad Green	B1	Havelock Road	C4	Platform Road	B3	West Street
C3	Brunswick Square	A3	Herbert Walker	B4	Porter's Lane	D3	White Star Place
B4	Bugle Street		Avenue	B2	Portland Street	B4	Winkle Street
C3	Canal Walk	B4	High Street	B1	Portland Terrace	C1	Winton Street
D4	Canute Road	C2	Houndwell Place	B2	Pound Tree Road		
D3	Captains Place	D2	James Street	C4	Queens Terrace		
D3	Carpathia Drive	C1	Johnson Street	C4	Queen's Way		
B2	Castle Way	D4	John Street	D3	Richmond Street		
D3	Central Bridge	C3	King Street	D4	Royal Crescent		
C4	Central Road	C1	Kingsway		Road		
C3	Challis Court	C4	Latimer Street	C3	Russell Street		
D2	Chapel Road	C3	Lime Street	D2	St Mary's Place		
B1	Civic Centre Road	C4	Lower Canal Walk	D1	St Mary Street		
D2	Coleman Street	D3	Marsh Lane	B3	St Michael Street		
D3	College Street	D2	Maryfield	A3	Solent Road		
D2	Cook Street	B4	Mayflower	A1	Southbrook Road		
C1	Cossack Green		Roundabout	C2	South Front		
D1	Craven Street	D3	Nelson Street	C2	Strand		
D3	Duke Street	D4	Neptune Way	C1	Sussex Road		
C3	Eastgate Street	C1	New Road	D4	Terminus Terrace		
C1	East Park Terrace	D1	Northam Road	D2	The Compass		
C3	East Street	C1	North Front	D3	Threefield Lane		
C2	Evans Street	D4	Ocean Way	B4	Town Quay		

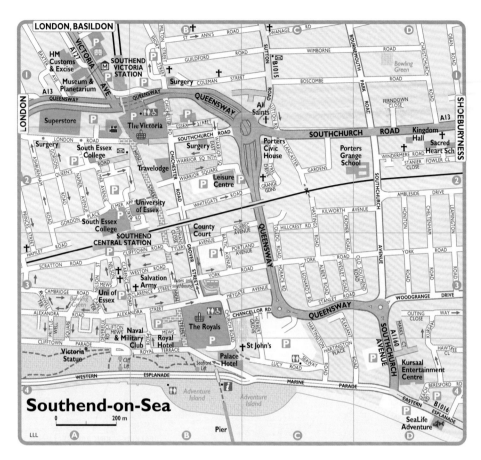

Southend-on-Sea

0   200 m

Pier

C3	Albert Road	B1	Essex Street	A3	Nelson Mews	A1	Victoria Avenue
A3	Alexandra Road	D1	Ferndown Close	A3	Nelson Street	B2	Warrior Square East
A3	Alexandra Street	D2	Fowler Close	D1	Oban Road	B2	Warrior Square
D2	Ambleside Drive	A2	Gordon Place	D3	Old Southend Road		North
A2	Ashburnham Road	A2	Gordon Road	D3	Outing Close	B2	Warrior Square
B3	Baltic Avenue	C2	Grange Gardens	B2	Pitmans Close	C3	Wesley Road
A1	Baxter Avenue	B3	Grover Street	C3	Pleasant Road	A4	Western Esplanade
D4	Beach Road	B1	Guildford Road	B3	Portland Avenue	B3	Weston Road
D4	Beresford Road	A3	Hamlet Road	A2	Princes Street	B2	Whitegate Road
C1	Boscombe Road	C4	Hartington Place	A3	Prittlewell Square	C1	Wimborne Road
D1	Bournemouth Park	C3	Hartington Road	B2	Quebec Avenue	D2	Windermere Road
	Road	C2	Hastings Road	A2	Queen's Road	D3	Woodgrange Drive
A3	Cambridge Road	D4	Hawtree Close	A1	Queensway	B3	York Road
A3	Capel Terrace	C3	Herbert Grove	B4	Royal Mews		
B3	Chancellor Road	B3	Heygate Avenue	B4	Royal Terrace		
D2	Cheltenham Road	B2	High Street	A3	Runwell Terrace		
B1	Chichester Road	C2	Hillcrest Road	B1	St Ann's Road		
D1	Christchurch Road	D2	Honiton Road	C3	St Leonard's Road		
B3	Church Road	C3	Horace Road	A3	Scratton Road		
A3	Clarence Road	C2	Kilworth Avenue	C4	Seaway		
B3	Clarence Street	D4	Kursaal Way	B1	Short Street		
A4	Clifftown Parade	C2	Lancaster Gardens	D2	Southchurch Avenue		
B3	Clifftown Road	D2	Leamington Road	B2	Southchurch Road		
A3	Clifton Mews	A2	London Road	D2	Stanier Close		
B1	Coleman Street	C4	Lucy Road	C3	Stanley Road		
C2	Cromer Road	A2	Luker Road	C1	Sutton Road		
A4	Devereux Road	C4	Marine Parade	C1	Swanage Road		
D4	Eastern Esplanade	D3	Marks Court	C2	Toledo Road		
A2	Elmer Approach	B1	Milton Street	B3	Tylers Avenue		
A2	Elmer Avenue	A2	Napier Avenue	C2	Tyrel Drive		

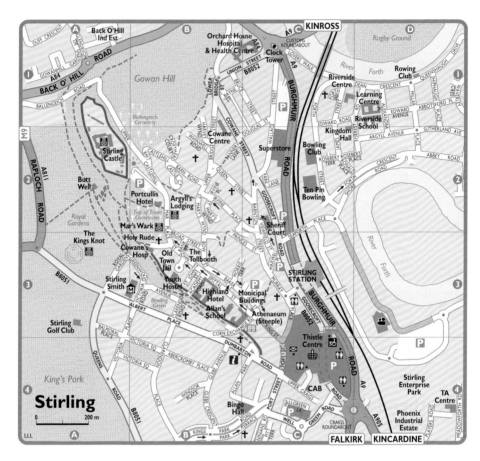

D2	Abbey Road	D1	Dean Crescent	C4	Ninians Road	C2	Viewfield Street
D1	Abbotsford Place	C2	Douglas Street	C2	Park Lane	C2	Wallace Street
B4	Abercromby Place	A1	Duff Crescent	B4	Park Terrace	D1	Waverley Crescent
B3	Academy Road	B4	Dumbarton Road	C4	Pitt Terrace	C4	Wellgreen Lane
A3	Albert Place	D1	Edward Avenue	D4	Players Road	C4	Wellgreen Road
D1	Alexandra Place	C1	Edward Road	C4	Port Street	B2	Whinwell Road
B4	Allan Park	D2	Forrest Road	B3	Princes Street	B4	Windsor Place
D2	Argyll Avenue	C2	Forth Crescent	D1	Queenshaugh Drive		
A1	Back O' Hill Road	C1	Forth Street	A4	Queens Road		
B3	Baker Street	C1	Forth View	B2	Queen Street		
A1	Ballengeich Road	B4	Glebe Avenue	A2	Raploch Road		
A3	Balmoral Place	B4	Glebe Crescent	C2	Ronald Place		
B3	Bank Street	A1	Glendevon Drive	C2	Rosebery Place		
B2	Barn Road	C2	Goosecroft Road	C2	Rosebery Terrace		
C2	Barnton Street	A1	Gowanhill Gardens	A3	Royal Gardens		
B1	Bayne Street	A3	Greenwood Avenue	B3	St John Street		
B3	Bow Street	B1	Harvey Wynd	B2	St Mary's Wynd		
B3	Broad Street	B2	Irvine Place	C3	Seaforth Place		
B1	Bruce Street	C2	James Street	D1	Shiphaugh Place		
C1	Burghmuir Road	B4	Kings Park Road	C2	Shore Road		
B2	Castle Court	C3	King Street	B3	Spittal Street		
B4	Clarendon Place	C1	Lovers Walk	D2	Sutherland Avenue		
B3	Clarendon Road	B1	Lower Bridge Street	B2	Tannery Lane		
B3	Corn Exchange	B2	Lower Castlehill	B1	Union Street		
	Road	B2	Mar Place	B2	Upper Bridge Street		
B1	Cowane Street	C3	Maxwell Place	A2	Upper Castlehill		
C4	Craigs Roundabout	D4	Meadowforth Road	C4	Upper Craigs		
B2	Crofthead Court	D1	Millar Place	A4	Victoria Place		
C1	Customs	B3	Morris Terrace	B3	Victoria Road		
	Roundabout	C3	Murray Place	A4	Victoria Square		

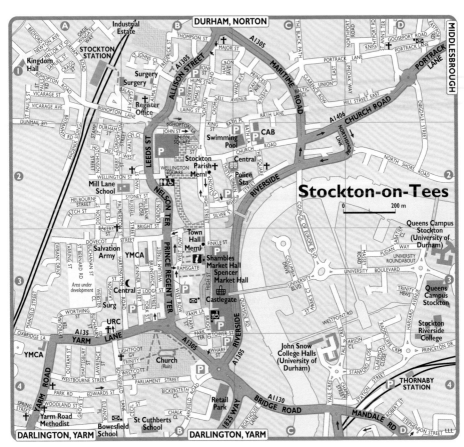

Stockton-on-Tees

0   200 m

B4	1825 Way	A2	Dixon Street	B1	Major Street	B2	Russell Street	A3	Webster Close
B1	Allison Street	A3	Dovecot Street	D4	Mandale Road	C1	Ryan Avenue	B2	Wellington Square
B1	Alma Street	D1	Dugdale Street	A3	Manfield Street	D3	Sabatier Close	A2	Wellington Street
A3	Bakery Street	A1	Dunmail Road	C1	Maritime Road	D1	St Ann's Terrace	A4	Westbourne Street
B1	Balaclava Street	A1	Durham Road	D3	Massey Road	A3	St Bernard Road	B4	Westcott Street
C1	Baltic Close	A2	Durham Street	A2	Melbourne Street	C3	St Mark's Court	C3	Westpoint Road
C1	Bath Lane	D1	Eastport Road	A1	Mellor Street	A1	St Pauls Road	B3	West Row
B2	Bath Place	A4	Edwards Street	B2	Middle Street	A1	St Paul's Street	B4	Wharf Street
A1	Bedford Street	A4	Eleanor Place	B2	Millbank Close	A1	Samuel Street	B3	William Street
B4	Bickersteth Close	A3	Ewbank Drive	A2	Mill Street West	A4	Shaftesbury Street	A4	Woodland Street
B2	Bishop Street	B1	Farrer Street	B2	Nelson Terrace	B2	Silver Street	A3	Worthing Street
A1	Bishopton Lane	B3	Finkle Street	A1	Newton Avenue	B3	Skinner Street	C4	Yale Crescent
A1	Bishopton Road	B1	Frederick Street	D1	Northport Road	A4	Spring Street	A4	Yarm Lane
C4	Boathouse Lane	D3	Fudan Way	C2	Northshore Link	A2	Stamp Street	A4	Yarm Road
B1	Bone Street	D1	Gooseport Road	D2	North Shore Road	D4	Stanford Close	B3	Yarm Street
A4	Bowesfield Lane	A4	Grove Street	B1	Norton Road	D4	Station Street	B3	York Street
B3	Bridge Road	B1	Haffron Avenue	A1	Orde Wingate Way	D4	Stephenson Street		
C4	Bridge Road	A3	Hartington Road	A4	Outram Street	B1	St Johns Close		
B2	Bright Street	D3	Harvard Avenue	A4	Oxbridge Lane	B2	Sydney Street		
A1	Britannia Road	B2	High Street	A2	Palmerston Street	A3	Tarring Street		
B3	Brunswick Street	D1	Hill Street East	B4	Parkfield Road	C1	The Black Path		
A3	Buchanan Street	B1	Hume Street	A4	Park Road	C2	The Square		
A2	Bute Street	A2	Hutchinson Street	B4	Park Terrace	B2	Thistle Green		
B2	Carlton Close	B2	John Street	B4	Parliament Street	B1	Thomas Street		
B4	Cecil Street	B2	King Street	C4	Pearson Close	B1	Thompson Street		
B4	Chalk Close	D1	Knightport Road	A2	Petch Street	B4	Tower Street		
C4	Chapel Street	B2	Knowles Street	A2	Phoenix Sidings	D3	Trinity Mews		
D1	Church Road	B1	Laing Street	D1	Portrack Lane	B4	Trinity Street		
D4	Claremont Close	A4	Lawrence Street	B3	Prince Regent Terrace	B2	Union Square		
C1	Clarence Row	A3	Lawson Street	A4	Princess Avenue	C1	Union Street East		
A2	Columbia Drive	B2	Leeds Street	D4	Princeton Drive	C3	University Boulevard		
C3	Corportion Street	A3	Leybourne Terrace	C3	Quayside Road	D3	University Roundabout		
A2	Council Of Europe Blvd	B4	Lightfoot Grove	D3	Raddcliffe Crescent	B2	Vane Street		
A1	Cragg Street	D1	Limeoak Way	B3	Ramsgate	A1	Vicarage Avenue		
B1	Cromwell Avenue	B2	Lobdon Street	C2	Riverside	A1	Vicarage Street		
A2	Derby Street	B3	Lodge Street	D4	Robert Street	C1	Wade Avenue		

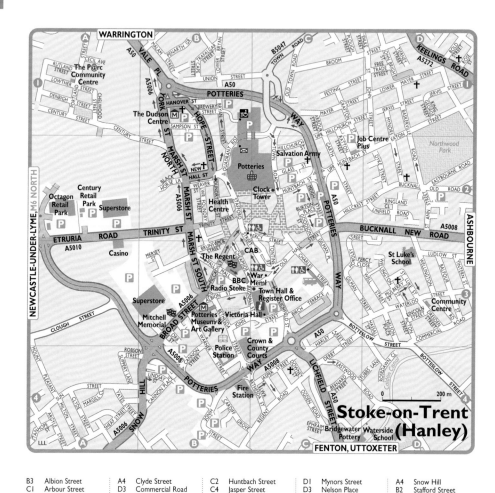

B3	Albion Street	A4	Clyde Street	C2	Huntbach Street	D1	Mynors Street	A4	Snow Hill
C1	Arbour Street	D3	Commercial Road	C4	Jasper Street	D3	Nelson Place	B2	Stafford Street
A4	Argyle Street	A1	Denbigh Street	D1	Jervis Street	B2	New Hall Street	A4	Stanhope Street
B3	Bagnall Street	C4	Derby Street	D1	John Bright Street	C4	Ogden Road	D4	Stubbs Lane
D3	Balfour Street	C1	Dilke Street	B3	John Street	C3	Old Hall Street	A4	Sun Street
D1	Baskerville Road	C4	Downey Street	D1	Keelings Road	C1	Old Town Road	D1	Tierney Street
C4	Bernard Street	D3	Dresden Street	D1	King George Street	B3	Orb Street	C3	Tontine Street
B3	Bethesda Street	D2	Dyke Street	C3	Lichfield Street	B3	Pall Mall	C2	Town Road
C3	Birch Terrace	D2	Eastbourne Road	D3	Lincoln Street	B1	Penarth Grove	B1	Trafalgar Street
B2	Black Horse Lane	C4	Eastwood Road	B4	Lindsay Street	C3	Percy Close	B2	Trinity Street
D1	Bold Street	D2	Eaton Street	D2	Linfield Road	C2	Percy Street	B1	Union Street
C3	Botteslow Street	C4	Ephraim Street	C4	Lower Bethesda	B3	Piccadilly	C2	Upper Hillchurch
B1	Brewery Street	A2	Etruria Road		Street	D3	Picton Street		Street
B3	Broad Street	C1	Festing Street	B1	Lower Bryan Street	C1	Plough Street	C2	Upper Huntbach
C1	Broom Street	B2	Foundry Street	B2	Lower Foundry	A1	Portland Street		Street
B3	Brunswick Street	D1	Free Trade Street		Street	B1	Potteries Way	A1	Vale Place
B1	Bryan Street	C2	Garth Street	D1	Lower Mayer Street	B2	Quadrant Road	B3	Warner Street
C2	Bucknall New Road	C2	Gilman Place	A1	Lowther Street	C2	Ratton Street	D3	Waterloo Street
D2	Bucknall Old Road	C3	Gilman Street	D3	Ludlow Street	C4	Regent Road	B2	Weaver Street
C2	Burton Place	C2	Glass Street	B1	Malam Street	D2	Ringland Close	D3	Well Street
B4	Cannon Place	C2	Goodson Street	A4	Margill Close	A4	Robson Street	D3	Wellington Road
B4	Cannon Street	C1	Grafton Street	B2	Marsh Street North	D1	Rose Street	D3	Wellington Street
B1	Cape Street	B1	Hanover Street	B2	Marsh Street	D4	Rosedawn Close	A4	Yates Street
B4	Cardiff Grove	C4	Harley Street	B3	Marsh Street South	A1	Rutland Street	B1	York Street
A1	Cecil Avenue	D3	Hassall Street	C1	Mayer Street	D2	St Ann Street		
A1	Century Street	C2	Hillchurch	C2	Meigh Street	D1	St John Street		
C3	Charles Street	C2	Hillcrest Street	B3	Mersey Street	D3	St Luke Street		
B3	Cheapside	B4	Hinde Street	A4	Milton Street	B1	Sampson Street		
A1	Chelwood Street	B1	Hope Street	A4	Mount Pleasant	A4	Sheaf Street		
A3	Clough Street	C3	Hordley Street	D3	Mulberry Street	A4	Slippery Lane		

A3	Albany Road	B2	Greenhill Street	B4	Sanctus Drive	A2	Willows Drive
A2	Alcester Road	B3	Grove Road	A4	Sanctus Road		North
B2	Arden Street	C2	Guild Street	B4	Sanctus Street	B2	Windsor Street
C1	Avenue Road	B2	Henley Street	A4	Sandfield Road	B2	Wood Street
C2	Bancroft Place	C3	High Street	B3	Scholars Lane		
B1	Birmingham Road	B4	Holtom Street	A4	Seven Meadows		
B1	Brewery Street	C2	John Street		Road		
D2	Bridge Foot	B1	Kendall Avenue	B1	Shakespeare Street		
C2	Bridge Street	C2	Lock Close	C3	Sheep Street		
D2	Bridgeway	C1	Maidenhead Road	D4	Shipston Road		
B4	Broad Street	B2	Mansell Street	A3	Shottery Road		
A4	Brookvale Road	C1	Mayfield Avenue	C3	Shrieves Walk		
B4	Bull Street	B2	Meer Street	C3	Southern Lane		
D1	Cedar Close	C4	Mill Lane	A2	Station Road		
C3	Chapel Lane	C1	Mulberry Street	D3	Swan's Nest		
C3	Chapel Street	B4	Narrow Lane	A3	The Willows		
A4	Cherry Orchard	B4	New Broad Street	D3	Tiddington Road		
B4	Cherry Street	B4	New Street	B2	Town Square		
B3	Chestnut Walk	C2	Old Red Hen Court	D3	Tramway Bridge		
B3	Church Street	C4	Old Town	C2	Tyler Street		
B1	Clopton Road	A4	Orchard Way	C2	Union Street		
B4	College Lane	C2	Payton Street	C1	Warwick Court		
B4	College Mews	C1	Percy Street	D1	Warwick Crescent		
B4	College Street	B3	Rother Street	C2	Warwick Road		
B3	Ely Gardens	D1	Rowley Crescent	C3	Waterside		
B3	Ely Street	B4	Ryland Street	D1	Welcombe Road		
B3	Evesham Place	A3	St Andrew's	B2	Wellesbourne		
A4	Evesham Road		Crescent		Grove		
A4	Garrick Way	C1	St Gregory's Road	B1	Western Road		
C1	Great William Street	A3	St Martin's Close	B4	West Street		

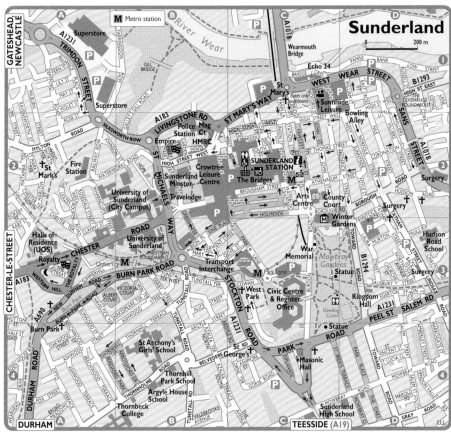

B4	Abbotsford Grove
A3	Albert Court
B3	Albion Place
B3	Alice Street
A1	Alliance Place
D4	Amberley Street
B3	Argyle Square
B4	Argyle Street
C4	Ashmore Street
A4	Ashwood Street
A4	Ashwood Terrace
C2	Athenaeum Street
B4	Azalea Terrace North
B4	Azalea Terrace South
C1	Bedford Street
A3	Beechwood Street
A4	Beechwood Terrace
B4	Belvedere Road
A4	Beresford Park
C2	Borough Road
C1	Bridge Crescent
C1	Bridge Street
A4	Broad Meadows
C2	Brougham Street
C3	Burdon Road
A3	Burn Park Road
D3	Chaytor Grove
A3	Chester Road
A2	Chester Terrace
A2	Chester Terrace North
D3	Churchill Street
A3	Clanny Street
D1	Cork Street
D2	Coronation Street
C3	Cowan Terrace
D3	Coxon Street

A1	Deptford Road
B3	Derby Street
B3	Derwent Street
A4	Durham Road
D1	East Cross Street
A4	Eden House Road
D3	Egerton Street
A3	Elmwood Street
B3	Elwin Terrace
C4	Esplanade
B1	Farringdon Row
C2	Fawcett Street
A1	Fern Street
A4	Fox Street
D2	Foyle Street
C2	Frederick Street
B2	Galley's Gill Road
B2	Garden Place
B1	Gill Bridge
C4	Gorse Road
D4	Gray Road
B2	Green Terrace
A2	Harlow Street
D4	Harold Square
D4	Harrogate Street
D4	Havelock Terrace
D4	Hendon Valley Road
D1	High Street East
B2	High Street West
C2	High Street West
C2	Holmeside
B2	Hope Street
D2	Hudson Road
A3	Hutton Street
A2	Hylton Road
A2	Johnson Street

C2	John Street
D3	Laura Street
A1	Lily Street
A1	Lime Street
D3	Lindsay Road
D2	Little Villiers Street
B2	Livingstone Road
C4	Lorne Terrace
D1	Low Street
B3	Mary Street
A2	Matamba Terrace
D1	Mauds Lane
A1	May Street
C2	Middle Street
A1	Milburn Street
D4	Mowbray Close
C4	Mowbray Road
D3	Murton Street
A3	New Durham Road
D2	Nile Street
D2	Norfolk Street
D3	Northcote Avenue
A4	Oakwood Street
B3	Olive Street
A4	Otto Terrace
B2	Paley Street
C1	Pann Lane
D1	Panns Bank
C3	Park Lane
D4	Park Place
C4	Park Road
D3	Pauls Road
D3	Peel Street
B3	Priestman Roundabout
A3	Raby Street
A2	Railway Row

A1	Ravensworth Street
A2	Rokeby Street
A2	Rosedale Street
A2	Rose Street
D1	Russell Street
C4	St Bede's Terrace
D4	St Lucia Close
A2	St Mark's Terrace
C2	St Mary's Way
B2	St Michaels Way
C2	St Thomas' Street
D4	St Vincent Street
D3	Salem Road
D4	Salem Street
D3	Salem Street South
D3	Salisbury Street
D2	Sans Street
B3	Shakespeare Terrace
A2	Silksworth Row
C2	South Street
C2	Station Street
B3	Stockton Road
A3	Summerhill
D2	Tatham Street
D2	Tatham Street Back
D3	Tavistock Place
C4	The Avenue
D1	The Exchange Roundabout
A2	The Leazes
D4	The Oaks
A3	The Retreat
A4	The Royalty
B4	Thornhill Terrace
B4	Thornholme Road
D3	Toward Road

A1	Trimdon Street
B3	Tunstall Road
B3	Tunstall Terrace
B3	Tunstall Terrace West
C2	Union Street
B4	Valebrooke Avenue
A4	Vale Street East
B3	Victoria Court
D2	Villiers Street
B3	Vine Place
A1	Violet Street
C2	Waterloo Place
A2	Waterworks Road
A4	Wearhead Drive
C1	Wearmouth Bridge
A2	Wentworth Terrace
A2	Westbourne Road
A3	Western Hill
B2	West Street
D2	West Sunnyside
C1	West Wear Street
A2	Wharncliffe Street
D1	William Street
C2	York Street

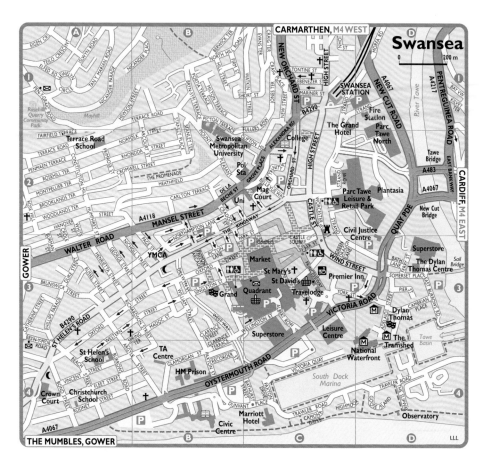

D3	Adelaide Street	C1	Craig Terrace	C2	High Street	B3	Park Street	C1	Strand
C3	Albert Row	A2	Crole Street	B1	Hill Street	C4	Paxton Drive	C2	Strand Row
C2	Alexandra Road	A2	Cromwell Street	A2	Humphrey Street	B4	Paxton Street	A1	Tan Y Marian Road
A4	Argyle Street	B2	De La Beche Street	A1	Islwyn Road	A2	Penmaen Terrace	D2	Tawe Bridge
D3	Bath Lane	B3	Dillwyn Street	C1	John Street	D1	Pentreguinea Road	A1	Teilo Crescent
C4	Bathurst Street	A3	Duke Street	C1	Jones Terrace	A1	Pen-Y-Graig Road	B1	Terrace Road
D1	Bay View	B4	Dunvant Place	D1	Kilvey Terrace	A3	Phillips Parade	A2	Terrace Road
A4	Beach Street	D2	East Bank Way	A1	Llewelyn Circle	B3	Picton Arcade	B2	The Kingsway
C2	Belle Vue Way	D3	East Burrows Road	B3	Madoc Street	B3	Picton Lane	B2	The Promenade
B1	Berwick Terrace	C1	Ebenezer Street	B2	Mansel Street	B1	Picton Terrace	D4	The Slipway
A4	Bond Street	A1	Eigen Crescent	C1	Mariner Street	D3	Pier Street	C1	Tontine Street
A2	Brooklands Terrace	C1	Elfed Road	B1	Milton Terrace	B1	Portia Terrace	C4	Trawler Street
A3	Brunswick Street	C1	Evans Terrace	A2	Montpellier Terrace	A2	Primrose Street	C2	Trinity Place
B1	Bryn-Syfi Terrace	A2	Fairfield Terrace	D1	Morfa Road	C3	Princess Way	C4	Victoria Quay
A3	Bryn-Y-Mor Road	D3	Ferry Street	B2	Mount Pleasant	D2	Quay Parade	C3	Victoria Road
A2	Burman Street	B1	Firm Street	D2	New Cut Bridge	B4	Recorder Street	A4	Vincent Street
A4	Burrows Road	A4	Fleet Street	D1	New Cut Road	A2	Rhondda Street	A3	Walter Road
C3	Caer Street	C1	Fullers Row	C1	New Orchard	A3	Richardson Street	C1	Watkin Street
D3	Cambrian Place	A3	George Street		Street	A4	Rodney Street	C3	Wellington Street
C4	Camona Drive	B4	Glamorgan Street	C1	New Street	A2	Rose Hill	A4	Western Street
B2	Carlton Terrace	D4	Goose Island	A1	Nicander Parade	A2	Rosehill Terrace	B3	West Way
C3	Castle Square	C3	Green Lane Dragon	B1	Nicander Place	A3	Russel Street	A2	White Street
C2	Castle Street	C2	Grove Place	A3	Nicholl Street	D3	Sail Bridge	B3	William Street
A3	Catherine Street	A2	Hanover Street	A2	Norfolk Street	A3	St Helen's Road	C3	Wind Street
B3	Clarence Street	B2	Harcourt Street	B2	Northampton Lane	B1	Short Street	A2	Woodlands Terrace
B4	Clarence Terrace	B2	Heathfield	B1	North Hill Road	B3	Singleton Street	C2	Worcester Place
C2	Clifton Hill	A3	Henrietta Street	C2	Orchard Street	D3	Somerset Place	C3	York Street
A2	Constituion Hill	A1	Hewson Street	A3	Oxford Street	B3	Spring Terrace		
B2	Cradock Street	C4	Highmoor	B4	Oystermouth Road	B1	Stanley Place		
C1	Craig Place	C1	High Street	B3	Page Street	B1	Stanley Terrace		

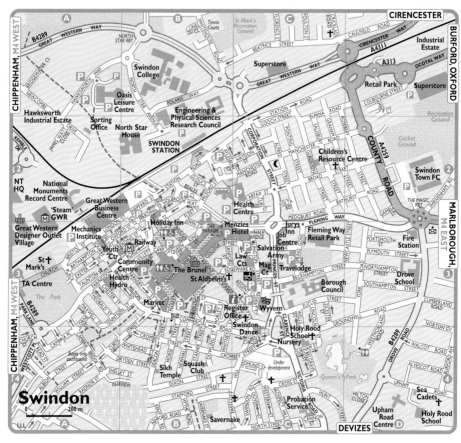

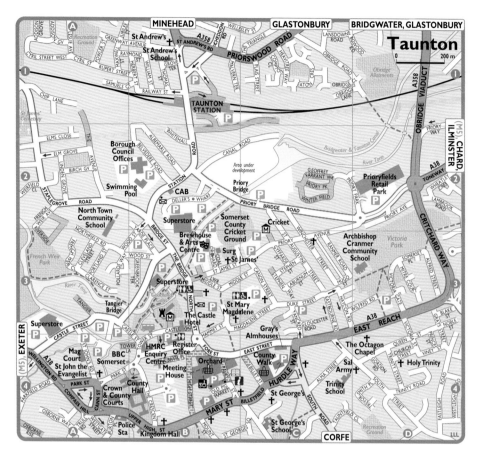

A1	Addison Grove	C3	Duke Street	D2	Lambrook Road	C3	Priory Avenue	B4	The Crescent
B2	Albemarle Road	C3	Eastbourne Road	C1	Lansdowne Road	B2	Priory Bridge	C1	The Triangle
D3	Alfred Street	D4	Eastleigh Road	A1	Leslie Avenue	C2	Priory Bridge Road	B1	Thomas Street
C4	Alma Street	D3	East Reach	A2	Linden Grove	C2	Priory Park	D2	Toneway
B4	Bath Place	C4	East Street	B3	Lower Middle Street	D2	Priory Way	A4	Tower Lane
B2	Belvedere Road	C1	Eaton Crescent	B3	Magdalene Street	D4	Queen Street	B4	Tower Street
C4	Billetfield	A2	Elm Grove	B1	Malvern Terrace	B1	Railway Street	D4	Trevor Smith Place
C4	Billet Street	A2	Elms Close	B4	Mary Street	C3	Ranmer Road	D4	Trinity Road
A2	Birch Grove	B4	Fore Street	A1	Maxwell Street	A1	Raymond Street	D4	Trinity Street
D3	Blake Street	A1	Fowler Street	B3	Middle Street	A3	Riverside	A4	Trull Road
C1	Bowood Road	A2	French Weir Avenue	D3	Mitre Court	A1	Rupert Street	B4	Upper High Street
B2	Bridge Street	A3	French Weir Close	B4	Mount Street	B1	St Andrew's Road	D3	Victoria Gate
A4	Burton Place	C2	Geoffrey Farrant	D3	Noble Street	C3	St Augustine Street	D3	Victoria Street
B2	Canal Road		Walk	A3	Northfield Road	B4	St Georges Square	D4	Viney Street
A4	Cann Street	C3	Gloucester Road	B3	North Street	B3	St James Street	A2	Weirfield Close
C3	Canon Street	D4	Gordon Road	C1	Obridge Close	A4	St John's Road	B1	Wellesley Street
B3	Castle Green	D3	Grays Street	C1	Obridge Lane	A1	Samuels Court	A4	Wellington Road
A4	Castle Street	B3	Greenbrook Terrace	C1	Obridge Road	D3	Somerset Place	A4	Westgate Street
B1	Cheddon Road	A1	Greenway Avenue	D2	Obridge Viaduct	C4	South Road	D4	Westleigh Road
A1	Chip Lane	B1	Grove Terrace	B4	Old Pig Market	D4	South Street	D2	Wheatley Crescent
D4	Church Street	C3	Gyffarde Street	A4	Osborne Rise	A2	Staplegrove Road	B2	Whitehall
A3	Clarence Street	B4	Hammet Street	A4	Osborne Way	B2	Station Road	C3	Wilfred Road
A3	Cleveland Street	C3	Haydon Road	A4	Parkfield Road	C3	Stephen Street	B1	William Street
B3	Coal Orchard	C1	Heavitree Way	A4	Park Street	C3	Stephen Way	C2	Winchester Street
A4	Compass Hill	B1	Herbert Street	B4	Paul Street	C3	Tancred Street	C2	Winter Field
C1	Compton Close	B4	High Street	C1	Plais Street	A3	Tangier	B3	Wood Street
D2	Critchard Way	C3	Hugo Street	A3	Pollards Way	A3	Tangier Bridge	B2	Yarde Place
A1	Cyril Street	C4	Hurdle Way	A3	Portland Street	C4	Tauntfield Close		
A1	Cyril Street West	A1	Jubilee Street	D3	Princes Street	A2	The Avenue		
B2	Deller's Wharf	C3	Laburnum Street	B1	Priorswood Road	B3	The Bridge		

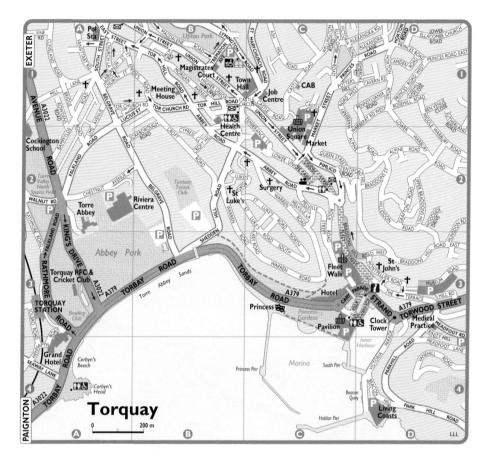

Torquay

0   200 m

B1	Abbey Road	A1	East Street	B1	Morgan Avenue	A1	South Street
D1	Alexandra Lane	C1	Ellacombe Road	D3	Museum Road	C2	Stentiford Hill Road
C1	Alexandra Road	A2	Falkland Road	C3	Palk Street	D3	Strand
C2	Alpine Road	C3	Fleet Street	B1	Palm Road	D1	Sutherland Road
C1	Ash Hill Road	D2	Grafton Road	D4	Parkhill Road	C2	Temperance Street
A1	Avenue Road	A4	Hennapyn Road	C1	Pembroke Road	D3	The Terrace
A2	Bampfylde Road	B1	Higher Union Lane	D1	Pennsylvania Road	A4	Torbay Road
D4	Beacon Hill	D2	Hillesdon Road	C2	Pimlico	A1	Tor Church Road
A1	Belgrave Road	D1	Hoxton Road	C1	Potters Hill	B1	Tor Hill Road
D1	Ben Venue Close	D3	Hunsdon Road	C1	Princes Road	D3	Torwood Street
D3	Braddons Hill Road	A3	King's Drive	D1	Princes Road East	B1	Trematon Ave
	East	A1	Laburnum Street	D1	Princes Road West	D3	Trinity Hill
C2	Braddons Hill Road	A2	Lime Avenue	C2	Queen Street	B1	Union Street
	West	D1	Lower Ellacombe	A2	Rathmore Road	D2	Upper Braddons Hill
D2	Braddons Street		Church Road	C2	Rock Road	D4	Vanehill Road
A1	Bridge Road	C2	Lower Union Lane	D1	Rosehill Close	A1	Vansittart Road
D1	Camden Road	D2	Lower Warbury	D1	Rosehill Road	C3	Vaughan Parade
C3	Cary Parade		Road	A1	Rowdens Road	D4	Victoria Parade
C3	Cary Road	A1	Lucius Street	A1	St Efride's Road	C1	Victoria Road
B1	Castle Circus	B1	Lymington Road	B2	St Luke's Road	A1	Vine Road
C1	Castle Lane	B1	Magdalene Road	C2	St Luke's Road	A2	Walnut Road
C1	Castle Road	C2	Market Street		North	C1	Warberry Road
D1	Cavern Road	D4	Meadfoot Lane	C2	St Luke's Road		West
A2	Chestnut Avenue	D3	Meadfoot Road		South	B2	Warren Road
A1	Church Lane	C2	Melville Lane	C1	St Marychurch Road	C1	Wellington Road
A1	Church Street	C2	Melville Street	B2	Scarborough Road	D2	Woodside Drive
A1	Cleveland Road	D1	Middle Warbury	A4	Seaway Lane		
B2	Croft Hill		Road	B3	Shedden Hill Road		
B2	Croft Road	A1	Mill Lane	A3	Solbro Road		
B2	Cypress Close	D3	Montpellier Road	D3	South Hill Road		

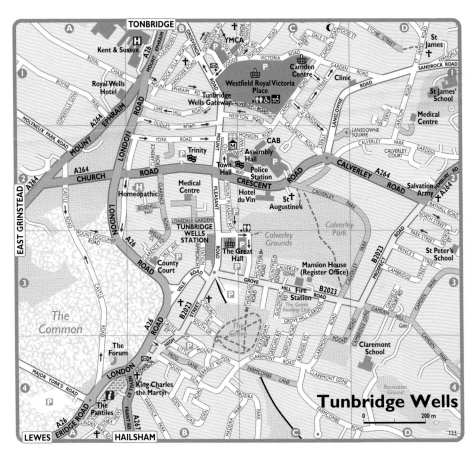

Tunbridge Wells

0   200 m

C1	Albert Street	B2	Clarence Row	B4	Madeira Park	B1	Rock Villa Road
C4	Arundel Road	B2	Crescent Road	A4	Major York's Road	B2	Rosehill Way
D2	Bayhall Road	B1	Culverden Street	B1	Meadow Road	A1	Royal Chase
C1	Belgrave Road	C1	Dale Street	A1	Molyneux Park	D1	St James' Road
B4	Berkeley Road	B1	Dudley Road		Road	D1	Sandrock Road
A1	Boyne Park	B4	Eden Road	C2	Monson Road	A1	Somerville Gardens
C4	Buckingham Road	A4	Eridge Road	B2	Monson Way	B3	South Green
D2	Calverley Court	C4	Farmcombe Lane	A3	Mount Edgcumbe	B3	Station Approach
C3	Calverley Gardens	C4	Farmcombe Road		Road	D1	Stone Street
C2	Calverley Park	D1	Ferndale	A2	Mount Ephraim	A4	Sussex Mews
D2	Calverley Park	A4	Frant Road	B1	Mount Ephraim	C3	Sutherland Road
	Gardens	B4	Frog Lane		Road	D1	The Ferns
C2	Calverley Road	C1	Garden Road	C3	Mountfield Gardens	C1	Tunnel Road
C1	Calverley Street	C1	Garden Street	C3	Mountfield Road	B1	Upper Grosvenor
D4	Cambridge Gardens	D3	George Street	B2	Mount Pleasant		Road
D3	Cambridge Street	B1	Goods Station Road		Avenue	B3	Vale Avenue
D3	Camden Hill	C4	Grecian Road	B2	Mount Pleasant	B3	Vale Road
D3	Camden Park	B1	Grosvenor Road		Road	C1	Victoria Road
C1	Camden Road	C3	Grove Hill Gardens	B4	Mount Sion	B4	Warwick Park
D2	Carlton Road	C3	Grove Hill Road	B4	Nevill Street	B3	Wells Close
A2	Castle Road	C3	Guildford Road	B1	Newton Road	C1	Wood Street
B3	Castle Street	B1	Hanover Road	C4	Norfolk Road	B2	York Road
B4	Chapel Place	B4	High Street	D2	North Street		
B3	Christchurch	C2	Lansdowne Road	D3	Oakfield Court		
	Avenue	D2	Lansdowne Square		Road		
A2	Church Road	B1	Lime Hill Road	D3	Park Street		
B2	Civic Way	A4	Linden Park Road	D2	Pembury Road		
C4	Claremont Gardens	B4	Little Mount Sion	C4	Poona Road		
C4	Claremont Road	A2	London Road	D3	Prince's Street		
B2	Clarence Road	B2	Lonsdale Gardens	D3	Prospect Road		

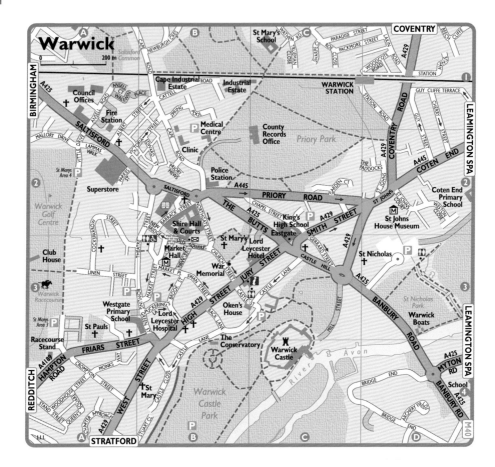

A2	Albert Street	D1	Guy Cliffe Terrace	C1	Sharpe Close
A1	Ansell Court	D1	Guy Street	C2	Smith Street
A1	Ansell Road	A4	Hampton Road	B1	Spring Pool
D4	Archery Fields	B3	High Street	A4	Stand Street
B3	Back Lane	B3	Jury Street	D1	Station Avenue
D3	Banbury Road	D1	Lakin Road	D1	Station Road
B2	Barrack Street	A2	Lammas Walk	B4	Stuart Close
D1	Beech Cliffe	A3	Linen Street	B3	Swan Street
B3	Bowling Green	A2	Mallory Drive	B3	Theatre Street
	Street	B3	Market Place	B2	The Butts
D4	Bridge End	B3	Market Street	D2	The Paddocks
B3	Brook Street	C3	Mill Street	C1	Trueman Close
B1	Cape Road	A4	Monks Way	A2	Victoria Street
B4	Castle Close	D4	Myton Road	A2	Vittle Drive
C3	Castle Hill	B2	New Bridge	A1	Wallin Place
B4	Castle Lane	B1	Newburgh Crescent	C1	Wathen Road
B3	Castle Street	B3	New Street	D2	Weston Close
B1	Cattell Road	B2	Northgate Street	A4	West Street
C2	Chapel Street	B3	Old Square	D1	Woodcote Road
A4	Charter Approach	C1	Packmore Street	A4	Woodhouse Street
D1	Cherry Street	C1	Paradise Street		
B3	Church Street	A2	Parkes Street		
A3	Cocksparrow Street	B2	Priory Mews		
D2	Coten End	C2	Priory Road		
D2	Coventry Road	B3	Puckering's Lane		
A4	Crompton Street	A4	Queen's Square		
B2	Edward Street	C1	Roe Close		
A4	Friars Street	D2	St Johns		
C2	Garden Court	D2	St Johns Court		
C3	Gerrard Street	A1	Saltisford		

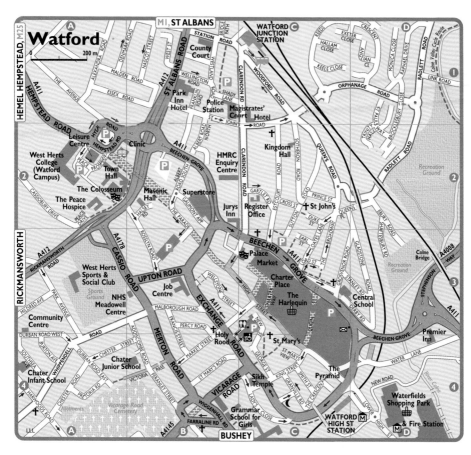

B3	Addiscombe Road	B2	Gaumont Approach	A4	Pretoria Road	B1	Wellington Road
B2	Albert Road North	C4	George Street	C2	Prince Street	B3	Wellstone Street
B2	Albert Road South	D3	Gladstone Road	C2	Queen's Road	B1	Westland Road
A1	Alexandra Road	C4	Granville Road	C3	Queen Street	B1	West Street
D1	Anglian Close	C3	Grosvenor Road	D2	Radlett Road	A4	Whippendell Road
C3	Beechen Grove	B2	Halsey Road	D1	Raphael Drive	B4	Wiggenhall Road
D2	Brocklesbury Close	A4	Harwoods Road	C1	Reeds Crescent	C1	Woodford Road
A4	Burton Avenue	A1	Hempstead Road	A3	Rickmansworth		
A2	Cassiobury Drive	C3	High Street		Road		
A3	Cassio Road	A2	Hyde Road	B3	Rosslyn Road		
C3	Charter Way	C1	Keele Close	B1	St Albans Road		
A4	Chester Road	C4	King Street	B1	St John's Road		
A4	Chester Street	C4	Lady's Close	B4	St Mary's Road		
C1	Clarendon Road	D1	Link Road	D1	St Pauls Way		
C2	Cross Street	C3	Loates Lane	B1	Shady Lane		
A1	Denmark Road	C3	Lord Street	D2	Shaftesbury Road		
C3	Derby Road	D4	Lower High Street	C4	Smith Street		
C2	Duke Street	B3	Malborough Road	C2	Sotheron Road		
A4	Durban Road East	A1	Malden Road	A4	Southsea Avenue		
A4	Durban Road West	B4	Market Street	C3	Stanley Road		
C3	Earl Street	B3	Merton Road	B1	Station Road		
D2	Ebury Road	A3	Mildred Avenue	D3	Stephenson Way		
A1	Essex Road	D1	Monica Close	C2	Sutton Road		
C2	Estcourt Road	B1	Nascot Street	A1	The Avenue		
B3	Exchange Road	D4	New Road	C3	The Broadway		
B4	Farraline Road	C3	New Street	C4	The Crescent		
B4	Feranley Street	C1	Orphanage Road	B2	The Parade		
B3	Francis Street	A3	Park Avenue	B3	Upton Road		
B1	Franklin Road	A2	Peace Prospect	B4	Vicarage Road		
C2	Gartlet Road	B3	Percy Road	D4	Water Lane		

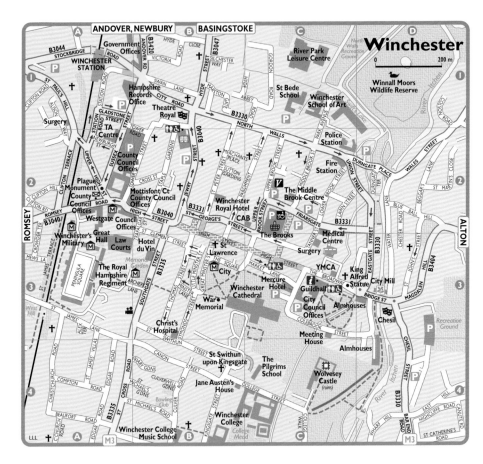

A3	Alex Terrace	D4	East Hill	A2	Romsey Road	B3	Trafalgar Street
A1	Alison Way	A4	Edgar Road	D4	St Catherine's Road	C2	Union Street
B1	Andover Road	C2	Friarsgate	B2	St Clement Street	C2	Upper Brook Street
A3	Archery Lane	B4	Friary Gardens	A4	St Cross Road	A2	Upper High Street
D4	Bar End Road	A1	Gladstone Street	B2	St George's Street	B1	Victoria Road
A4	Beaufort Road	C1	Gordon Road	A3	St James' Lane	D2	Wales Street
D2	Beggar's Lane	B3	Great Minster	A3	St James Terrace	D3	Water Lane
D2	Blue Ball Hill		Street	A4	St James' Villas	D4	Wharf Hill
D3	Bridge Street	D4	Highcliffe Road	D3	St John's Street		
B4	Canon Street	B2	High Street	D2	St Martin's Close		
D4	Canute Road	B1	Hyde Abbey Road	B4	St Michael's Gardens		
D3	Chesil Street	B1	Hyde Close	B4	St Michael's Road		
D2	Chester Road	B1	Hyde Street	A1	St Paul's Hill		
A4	Christchurch Road	B2	Jewry Street	B2	St Peter Street		
B1	City Road	B4	Kingsgate Street	B3	St Swithun Street		
A2	Clifton Hill	C2	Lawn Street	B3	St Thomas Street		
A1	Clifton Road	B3	Little Minster Street	B1	Silchester Way		
A2	Clifton Terrace	C2	Lower Brook Street	B3	Southgate Street		
C3	Colebrook Street	D3	Magdalen Hill	B2	Staple Gardens		
B4	College Street	C3	Market Lane	A1	Station Road		
C4	College Walk	B1	Marston Gate	A1	Stockbridge Road		
D1	Colson Road	B2	Merchants Place	A2	Sussex Street		
A4	Compton Road	A3	Mews Lane	B2	Sutton Gardens		
B2	Cross Street	C2	Middle Brook Street	B1	Swan Lane		
A3	Crowder Terrace	B3	Minster Lane	B3	Symonds Street		
B4	Culver Road	A2	Newburgh Street	C3	Tanner Street		
B4	Culverwell Gardens	B1	North Walls	C3	The Broadway		
D2	Durngate Place	B2	Parchment Street	B3	The Square		
D2	Durngate Terrace	C2	Park Avenue	A1	Tower Road		
D3	Eastgate Street	A3	Peninsula Square	A2	Tower Street		

Wolverhampton

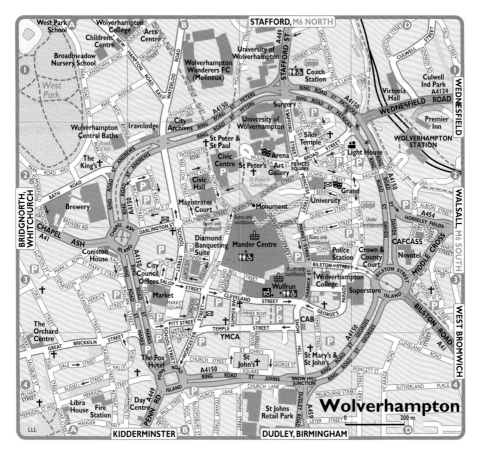

Ref	Name	Ref	Name	Ref	Name	Ref	Name	Ref	Name
D2	Albion Street	B3	Darlington Street	B3	London Place	B3	Pitt Street	C3	Snow Hill
A3	Alexander Street	B1	Drummond Street	C2	Long Street	D4	Powlett Street	C4	Snow Hill Junction
A1	Bath Avenue	C4	Dudley Road	A3	Lord Street	C2	Princes Square	C1	Stafford Street
A2	Bath Road	C2	Dudley Street	A4	Mander Street	C2	Princess Street	A3	Stephenson Street
B3	Bell Street	A1	Dunkley Street	B3	Market Square	B2	Queen Square	B4	Stewart Street
C2	Berry Street	D1	Field Street	C2	Market Street	C2	Queen Street	A2	Summerfield Road
D3	Bilston Road	B3	Fold Street	A2	Meadow Street	D4	Raby Street	B3	Summer Row
C3	Bilston Street	C2	Fryer Street	C4	Melbourne Street	A3	Raglan Street	D4	Sutherland Place
D3	Bilston Street Island	C3	Garrick Street	A4	Merridale Street	D2	Railway Drive	C3	Tempest Street
B2	Birch Street	C3	George's Parade	A4	Merridale Street	B2	Red Lion Street	B3	Temple Street
B4	Bloomsbury Street	C4	George Street		West	A4	Retreat Street	B4	Thomas Street
C4	Bond Street	D3	Gough Street	D3	Middle Cross	A2	Ring Road	C1	Thornley Street
A2	Brewery Road	A4	Graiseley Street	B2	Mitre Fold		St Andrews	C3	Tower Street
C2	Broad Street	A4	Great Brickkiln	B1	Molineux Alley	D2	Ring Road St Davids	D3	Union Street
C1	Camp Street		Street	B1	Molineux Street	C4	Ring Road	A4	Upper Zoar Street
C3	Castle Street	C1	Great Western	A1	New Hampton		St Georges	D4	Vicarage Road
A3	Chapel Ash		Street		Road East	B4	Ring Road St Johns	B3	Victoria Fold
A3	Chapel Ash Island	D1	Grimstone Street	B2	North Street	A3	Ring Road St Marks	B3	Victoria Street
A4	Cherry Street	A4	Hallet Drive	D3	Oxford Street	C1	Ring Road	D3	Walsall Street
B4	Church Lane	C1	Herbert Street	A1	Park Avenue		St Patricks	D3	Ward Street
B4	Church Street	A3	Herrick Street	A2	Park Crescent	B2	Ring Road St Peters	D3	Warwick Street
B2	Clarence Road	D2	Horseley Fields	A1	Park Road East	A4	Russell Street	B1	Waterloo Road
B2	Clarence Street	D4	Hospital Street	A2	Park Road West	B4	St John's Square	D1	Wednesfield Road
B3	Cleveland Passage	D1	Kennedy Road	B2	Paternoster Row	A3	St Mark's Road	C2	Westbury Street
D4	Cleveland Road	A1	Lansdown Road	B4	Paul Street	A3	St Mark's Street	B1	Whitemore Hill
B3	Cleveland Street	C4	Lever Street	B3	Peel Street	A4	Salisbury Street	C2	Whitmore Street
A3	Clifton Street	C2	Lichfield Street	A4	Pelham Street	B3	Salop Street	A4	Williamson Street
D2	Corn Hill	C1	Little's Lane	B4	Penn Road	B3	School Street	B4	Worcester Street
D1	Culwell Street	B4	Little St Brickkiln	B4	Penn Road Island	C2	Short Street	C2	Wulfruna Street
A4	Dale Street	D1	Lock Street	D2	Piper's Row	B3	Skinner Street	A4	Zoar Street

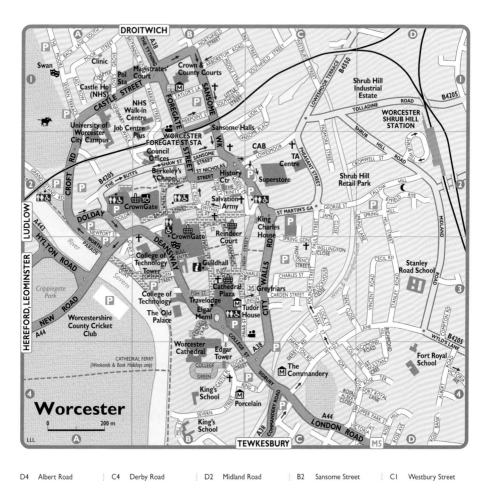

Worcester

0   200 m

D4	Albert Road	C4	Derby Road	D2	Midland Road	B2	Sansome Street	C1	Westbury Street
B2	Angel Place	A2	Dolday	B4	Mill Street	B1	Sansome Walk	C4	Wyld's Lane
B2	Angel Street	B1	East Street	A1	Moor Street	B4	Severn Street		
B1	Arboretum Road	A1	Easy Row	A2	Newport Street	A1	Severn Terrace		
A1	Back Lane South	B4	Edgar Street	A3	New Road	B2	Shaw Street		
C3	Blockhouse Close	B1	Farrier Street	C3	New Street	D2	Shrub Hill		
A1	Britannia Road	B3	Fish Street	B1	Northfield Street	C1	Shrub Hill Road		
B2	Broad Street	B1	Foregate Street	A3	North Parade	C4	Sidbury		
B3	Bull Entry	C4	Fort Royal Hill	C1	Padmore Street	C1	Southfield Street		
D2	Byfield Rise	D4	Fort Royal Lane	C3	Park Street	A3	South Quay		
C3	Carden Street	C3	Foundry Street	C2	Pheasant Street	C3	Spring Gardens		
B4	Castle Place	C3	Friar Street	B1	Pierpoint Street	D2	Spring Hill		
A1	Castle Street	C2	George Street	C3	Providence Street	D2	Spring Lane		
A4	Cathedral Ferry	A2	Grandstand Road	B3	Pump Street	D3	Stanley Road		
D3	Cecil Road	C3	Hamilton Road	A3	Quay Street	D2	Tallow Hill		
B3	Charles Street	B3	High Street	B2	Queen Street	B1	Taylor's Lane		
A1	Charter Place	D2	Hill Street	D3	Richmond Hill	A2	The Butts		
B2	Church Street	A3	Hylton Road	D4	Richmond Road	B2	The Cross		
C3	City Walls Road	A1	Infirmary Walk	D4	Rose Avenue	A1	The Moors		
C4	Cole Hill	C2	James Close	D4	Rose Bank	B2	The Shambles		
B4	College Green	B4	King Street	D4	Rose Hill	B2	The Trinity		
B3	College Street	C1	Lion Court	D4	Rose Terrace	B1	The Tything		
B3	College Yard	B1	Little Southfield	C4	Royal Albert Close	C1	Tolladine Road		
C4	Commandery Road		Street	C2	St Martin's Gate	B2	Trinity Street		
D3	Compton Road	C3	Lock Street	B2	St Nicholas Street	C3	Union Street		
B3	Copenhagen Street	C4	London Road	C3	St Paul's Street	D4	Upper Park Street		
A2	Croft Road	A1	Love's Grove	B2	St Swithin Street	D4	Victoria Avenue		
C2	Cromwell Street	C2	Lowesmoor	D4	St Wulstan's	C4	Victoria Place		
B3	Deansway	C1	Lowesmoor Terrace		Crescent	D3	Vincent Road		
C3	Dent Close	B1	Middle Street	B2	Sansome Place	C3	Wellington Close		

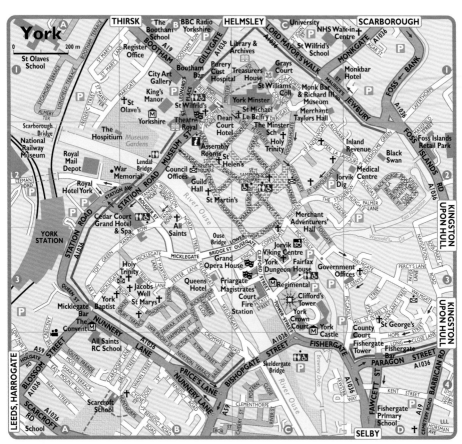

D1	Agar Street	B4	Ebor Street	C1	Lord Mayor's Walk	C4	Postern Close
C2	Aldwark	B3	Fairfax Street	C3	Lower Ousegate	B4	Price's Lane
A1	Almery Terrace	D4	Fawcett Street	B3	Lower Priory Street	C3	Priory Street
B4	Baile Hill Terrace	C2	Feasegate	C2	Low Petergate	A3	Queen Street
D4	Barbican Road	B3	Fetter Lane	A3	Lowther Terrace	C4	River Street
A3	Bar Lane	C4	Fewster Way	D2	Mansfield	D3	Rosemary Court
B4	Bishopgate Street	C2	Finkle Street	D3	Margaret Street	B2	Rougier Street
B3	Bishophill Junior	C4	Fishergate	C2	Market Street	C2	St Andrewgate
B3	Bishophill Senior	D1	Foss Bank	B1	Marygate	B4	St Benedict Road
D2	Black Horse Lane	C3	Fossgate	A3	Micklegate	D3	St Denys' Road
B2	Blake Street	D2	Foss Islands Road	D3	Mill Street	B2	St Helen's Square
A4	Blossom Street	D2	Foss View	B1	Minster Yard	C1	St John Street
B1	Bootham	A1	Frederic Street	C1	Monkgate	B1	St Leonard's Place
B1	Bootham Row	C2	Garden Place	A4	Moss Street	B3	St Martins Lane
A1	Bootham Terrace	D3	George Street	B2	Museum Street	A1	St Mary's
B3	Bridge Street	B1	Gillygate	D3	Navigation Road	A1	St Mary's Lane
B3	Buckingham Street	C2	Goodramgate	B2	New Street	A1	St Marys Terrace
D4	Cemetery Road	B4	Hampden Street	B4	Newton Terrace	C1	St Maurice's Road
C4	Cherry Street	C3	High Ousegate	B2	North Street	C2	St Sampson's Square
C2	Church Street	B1	High Petergate	A3	Nunnery Lane	C2	St Saviourgate
C4	Clementhorpe	A4	Holgate Road	B4	Nunthorpe Road	C2	St Saviours Place
C3	Clifford Street	D4	Hope Street	C1	Ogleforth	A2	Scarborough Bridge
C1	College Street	D4	Horsman Avenue	B3	Ouse Bridge	A4	Scarcroft Lane
C2	Colliergate	D2	Hungate	D2	Palmer Lane	A4	Scarcroft Road
B2	Coney Street	D1	Jewbury	D2	Palmer Street	C2	Shambles
C3	Coppergate	D4	Kent Street	D2	Paragon Street	A4	Shaw's Terrace
B4	Cromwell Road	D2	Kings Pool Walk	A4	Park Street	B3	Skeldergate
B4	Cygnet Street	C3	King Street	C2	Parliament Street	C4	Skeldergate Bridge
B4	Dale Street	B4	Kyme Street	C2	Pavement	A4	South Parade
B2	Davygate	B3	Lambert Street	D3	Paver Lane	C2	Spen Lane
C1	Deangate	D1	Layerthorpe	D2	Peasholme Green	B2	Spurriergate
B3	Dewsbury Terrace	A2	Leeman Road	C3	Peckitt Street	A2	Station Avenue
B4	Dove Street	B2	Lendal	D3	Peel Street	A3	Station Road
B2	Duncombe Place	B2	Lendal Bridge	D3	Percy's Lane	B2	Stonegate
D2	Dundas Street	D4	Long Close Lane	C3	Piccadilly	B4	Swann Street
A4	East Mount Road	A1	Longfield Terrace	D2	Ponds Garth	C2	Swinegate
						A1	Sycamore Terrace
						B3	Tanner Row
						B2	Tanners Moat
						A4	The Crescent
						C2	The Stonebow
						A3	Toft Green
						C3	Tower Street
						B3	Trinity Lane
						B4	Victor Street
						D3	Walmgate
						B2	Wellington Road
						D4	Willis Street

Major airports

London Heathrow Airport

16 miles west of London

Telephone: 0844 335 1801 or visit *heathrowairport.com*
Parking: short-stay, long-stay and business parking is available.
For booking and charges tel: 0844 335 1000
Public Transport: coach, bus, rail and London Underground.
There are several 4-star and 3-star hotels within easy reach of the airport.
Car hire facilities are available.

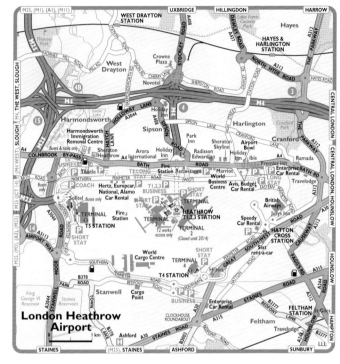

London Gatwick Airport

35 miles south of London

Telephone: 0844 335 1802 or visit *gatwickairport.com*
Parking: short and long-stay parking is available at both the North and South terminals.
For booking and charges tel: 0844 811 8311 or visit *parking.gatwickairport.com*
Public Transport: coach, bus and rail.
There are several 4-star and 3-star hotels within easy reach of the airport.
Car hire facilities are available.

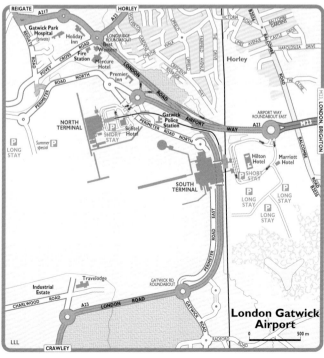

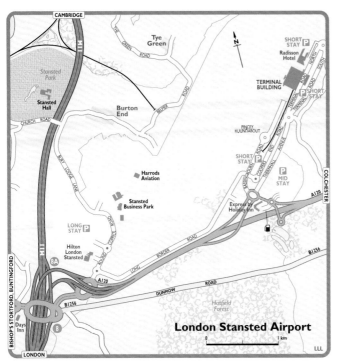

London Stansted Airport

36 miles north east of London

Telephone: 0844 335 1803 or visit *stanstedairport.com*
Parking: short, mid and long-stay open-air parking is available.
For booking and charges tel: 0844 335 1000
Public Transport: coach, bus and direct rail link to London on the Stansted Express.
There are several hotels within easy reach of the airport.
Car hire facilities are available.

London Luton Airport

33 miles north of London

Telephone: 01582 405100 or visit *london-luton.co.uk*
Parking: short-term, mid-term and long-stay parking is available.
For booking and charges tel: 01582 405 100
Public Transport: coach, bus and rail.
There are several hotels within easy reach of the airport.
Car hire facilities are available.

Major airports

London City Airport

7 miles east of London

Telephone: 020 7646 0088 or visit *londoncityairport.com*
Parking: short and long-stay open-air parking is available. For booking and charges tel: 0871 360 1390
Public Transport: easy access to the rail network, Docklands Light Railway and the London Underground.
There are 5-star, 4-star and 3-star hotels within easy reach of the airport.
Car hire facilities are available.

Birmingham International Airport

8 miles east of Birmingham

Telephone: 0844 576 6000 or visit *birminghamairport.co.uk*
Parking: short, mid-term and long-stay parking is available. For booking and charges tel: 0844 576 6000
Public Transport: Air-Rail Link service operates every 2 minutes to and from Birmingham International Railway Station & Interchange.
There is one 3-star hotel adjacent to the airport and several 4 and 3-star hotels within easy reach of the airport.
Car hire facilities are available.

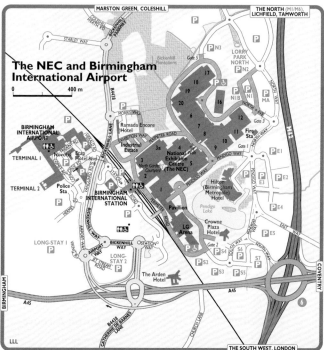

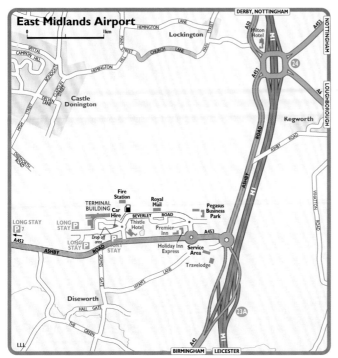

East Midlands Airport

15 miles south west of Nottingham, next to the M1 at junctions 23A and 24

Telephone: 0871 919 9000 or visit *eastmidlandsairport.com*
Parking: short and long stay parking is available.
For booking and charges tel: 0871 310 3300
Public Transport: bus and coach services to major towns and cities in the East Midlands. Call 0870 608 2608 for information.
There are several 3-star hotels within easy reach of the airport. Car hire facilities are available.

Manchester Airport

10 miles south of Manchester

Telephone: 0871 271 0711 or visit *manchesterairport.co.uk*
Parking: short and long-stay parking is available.
For booking and charges tel: 0871 310 2200
Public Transport: bus, coach and rail.
There are several 4-star and 3-star hotels within easy reach of the airport.
Car hire facilities are available.

Leeds Bradford International Airport

7 miles north east of Bradford and 9 miles north west of Leeds

Telephone: 0113 250 9696 or visit *leedsbradfordairport.co.uk*
Parking: short, mid-term and long-stay parking is available. For booking and charges tel: 0113 250 9696
Public Transport: bus service operates every 30 minutes from Bradford, Leeds and Otley. There are several 4-star and 3-star hotels within easy reach of the airport.
Car hire facilities are available.

Aberdeen Airport

7 miles north west of Aberdeen

Telephone: 0844 481 6666 or visit *aberdeenairport.com*
Parking: short and long-stay parking is available. For booking and charges tel: 0844 335 1000
Public Transport: regular bus service to central Aberdeen. There are several 4-star and 3-star hotels within easy reach of the airport.
Car hire facilities are available.

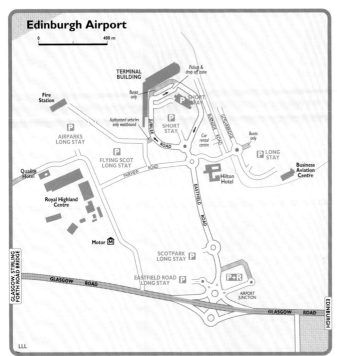

Edinburgh Airport
7 miles west of
Edinburgh

Telephone: 0844 481 8989 or
visit *edinburghairport.com*
Parking: short and long-stay
parking is available.
For booking and charges
tel: 0844 335 1000
Public Transport: regular bus
services to central Edinburgh.
There are several 4-star and
3-star hotels within easy reach
of the airport.
Car hire facilities are available.

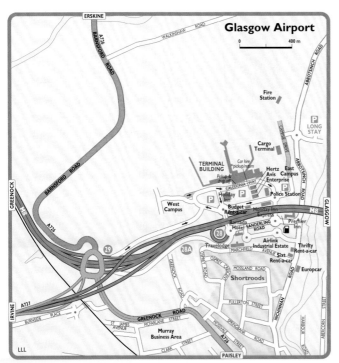

Glasgow Airport
8 miles west of Glasgow

Telephone: 0844 481 5555 or
visit *glasgowairport.com*
Parking: short and long-stay
parking is available.
For booking and charges
tel: 0844 335 1000
Public Transport: regular coach
services operate direct to central
Glasgow and Edinburgh.
There are several 3-star hotels
within easy reach of the airport.
Car hire facilities are available.

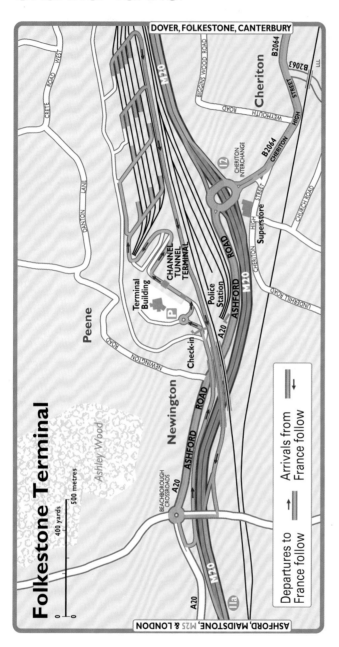

Folkestone Terminal

DOVER, FOLKESTONE, CANTERBURY

ASHFORD, MAIDSTONE, M25 & LONDON

Cheriton

B2064

B2063

BIGGINS WOOD ROAD

WEYMOUTH ROAD

HIGH STREET

CHERITON INTERCHANGE

12

B2064

CHERITON

HIGH STREET

Superstore

CHURCH ROAD

UNDERHILL ROAD

CRETE ROAD WEST

DANTON LANE

Peene

NEWINGTON ROAD

Terminal Building

P

CHANNEL TUNNEL TERMINAL

Police Station

Check-in

ASHFORD ROAD

M20

A20

Newington

ASHFORD ROAD

A20

Ashley Wood

BEACHBOROUGH CROSSROADS

M20

A20

11a

400 yards

500 metres

Departures to France follow

Arrivals from France follow